Prejudice, Politics,
and the American Dilemma

PREJUDICE, POLITICS, AND THE AMERICAN DILEMMA

EDITED BY

Paul M. Sniderman, Philip E. Tetlock,
and Edward G. Carmines

STANFORD UNIVERSITY PRESS
STANFORD, CALIFORNIA

Stanford University Press
Stanford, California
© 1993 by the Board of Trustees of the
Leland Stanford Junior University
Printed in the United States of America

CIP data appear at the end of the book

Original printing 1993
Last figure below indicates year of this printing:
03 02 01 00 99 98 97 96 95 94

Stanford University Press publications are distributed
exclusively by Stanford University Press within the
United States, Canada, and Mexico; they are
distributed exclusively by Cambridge University
Press throughout the rest of the world.

By way of friendship

to
William S. Berland
Reverend Al Carmines
Barbara Mellers

Acknowledgments

Some subjects are risky to discuss at universities nowadays, and race is surely among them. An awareness of the volatility of issues of race makes us all the more appreciative of the support and assistance extended to us, initially in funding the conference from which this book proceeded, and subsequently in facilitating the preparation of the manuscript itself.

The conference itself was sponsored by three research units of the University of California at Berkeley—the Survey Research Center (Percy Tannenbaum, director), the Institute of Personality and Social Research (Philip Tetlock, director), and the Institute of Human Development (Joseph Campos, director). In addition, the Graduate Division (Joseph Cerny, provost for research) generously assisted in preparation of the manuscript.

Our institutional debts to one side, our personal ones are sixfold. Lynn Geske-Morgan has been indispensable, at every step, from arrangements for the initial conference through preparation of the manuscript: we are immensely indebted to her acuity, thoroughness, and executive abilities. Lani Kask has played an essential supervisory role, the more crucial since the three editors are distributed over three universities. James Tedder has been of invaluable aid in supervising both the copy-editing and the correction of the galley proofs. Gordon R. Lawrence had the unfairly burdensome—and apart from this mention, entirely thankless—task of preparing the Bibliography. In getting the manuscript on paper, Maria del Carmen Torralba was a delight to work with: smart, speedy, and buoyant. Finally, Randall S. Peterson has proven to be a specially valuable colleague: quite apart from the exceptional role he played in preparing Chapter 9, of which he is a co-author, he has been of invaluable assistance in preparing all the other chapters, for which he should be recognized as at least an honorary co-author.

P.M.S., P.E.T., E.G.C.

Contents

Prejudice, Politics, and the American Dilemma

Prejudice and Politics: An Introduction

Paul M. Sniderman, Philip E. Tetlock, and Edward G. Carmines

There was a moment, perhaps in the summer of 1963 when Martin Luther King, Jr., spoke in Washington, D.C., when it seemed as if the American dilemma might be resolved. Not immediately, certainly not totally, but substantially resolved and within the lifetime of the children of the men and women, black and white, who had peacefully paraded up Pennsylvania Avenue and formed a sea of hundreds of thousands to listen to King tell of a dream.

The optimism born of the civil rights movement of the 1960's has long since died. Looking back, our perspective foreshortened by three decades, we may think the death followed almost immediately upon the birth. The mid 1960's witnessed landmark civil rights legislation, passed through Congress by confident majorities and signed into law by a committed president; the late 1960's saw riots in Watts, tanks rumbling down the streets of Detroit, cries of black power and separatist politics.

Or perhaps the death of optimism was later, not in the 1960's but in the 1970's, with the emergence of affirmative action signaling the eclipse of hope. Notice that in speaking this way, we do not have in mind the arguments now familiarly deployed against affirmative action, but rather those advanced in its favor. In a favored analogy of the day, President Lyndon Johnson likened blacks to a sprinter who had had his chains miraculously removed, after having been hobbled all his life, and who was then told, "Run, you are free to compete." The handicap was too great. The race had already started. Too much ground had to be made up. In short, the argument on behalf of affirmative action amounts to a confession: if American society and economy are left to their natural mode of operation, the American dilemma will never be resolved.

Gunnar Myrdal's *An American Dilemma* (1944) has shaped the thinking

of thoughtful observers about the issue of race for nearly half a century;
or, more accurately, since the work itself is multifaceted and complex, a
certain reading of it has become part of the intellectual furniture of informed citizens. That reading finds its purest expression in a deservedly
famous passage from Myrdal's introduction. He writes:

*The American Negro problem is a problem in the heart of the American. . . . The "American
Dilemma," referred to in the title of this book, is the ever-raging conflict between, on the one
hand, the valuations preserved on the general plane which we shall call the "American Creed,"
where the American thinks, talks, and acts under the influence of high national and Christian
precepts, and, on the other hand, the valuations on specific planes of individual and group
living, where personal and local interests; economic, social, and sexual jealousies; considerations
of community prestige and conformity; group prejudice against particular persons or types of
people; and all sorts of miscellaneous wants, impulses, and habits dominate his outlook.* (xlvii;
italics in original)

This formulation of the American dilemma has become ritualized; so
much so, we are persuaded, that it now obscures as much as summarizes
the contemporary politics of race: the very belief that we understand what
is before us has become an obstacle to our understanding.

If you wish to see how Myrdal's formulation has become an intellectual
icon, obstructing rather than assisting an understanding of the politics of
race, it is necessary only to stop and consider what a dilemma actually is. A
dilemma consists in the unavoidability of choosing either between a good
and a good, or between an evil and an evil. Dilemmas are morally excruci-
ating precisely because they require either the acceptance of a wrong or the
sacrifice of a good. But what does Myrdal's dilemma require a choice between? On the one side, "liberty, equality, justice and fair opportunity for
everybody"; on the other, prejudice, economic advantage, and the force
of custom. This may be a political conflict; it is hardly a moral dilemma.

And the cleavage between the politics of race a half century ago, when
Myrdal wrote, and now is precisely that race has become a dilemma—a
genuine dilemma, an achingly difficult dilemma. The choice is no longer
between right and wrong, between the values of the American creed and a
ragbag of irrational and self-serving beliefs: the choice now must be made
among competing values—including compassion, the freedom to achieve,
tolerance, the right to be judged on one's individual merits, the reach of
the state, and the autonomy of the family—in a word, among the very
values that have made up the American creed. This is not at all to suggest that prejudice and self-interest have disappeared: they remain potent
forces. But issues of race no longer turn on the normatively one-sided
axis that Myrdal memorialized. There is now a complexity of causality—
hence an ambiguity of responsibility—that has become the signature of
the contemporary politics of race.

No less fundamentally, Myrdal supposed that issues of race at the deepest level pivoted on a conflict in the minds of Americans—that is, in the minds of white Americans. From his point of view, what therefore required understanding was what white Americans believe and how they behave toward blacks, not what blacks themselves believe and do.

In contrast, we want to suggest that there has been a doubling of the American dilemma. Issues of race now are two-sided, and neither their difficulty nor their poignancy can rightly be gauged unless they are viewed not only from the perspectives of whites but also from those of blacks. We recognize, we should say at once, that our formulation of the American dilemma as two-sided is itself an oversimplification. For it implies that participants can be sorted into white and black only. In fact, there is a crucial need to appreciate and respect the diversity of racial politics in contemporary American society, and in particular, the tensions, as well as affinities, among the variety of minorities. Nor, in insisting on the need for at least a duality of perspectives, are we suggesting that the black understanding of issues of race has nothing to do with the white, or vice versa. All the same, we are suggesting—and about this we feel strongly— that race is no longer just a white man's problem, as Myrdal maintained. It is as necessary to take into account the experiences, attitudes, fears, hopes, difficulties, and prejudices of blacks as of whites.

It has been a half century since Myrdal wrote, a quarter century since the landmark civil rights acts of 1964 and 1965. An effort must be made to understand issues of race as they are now, not as they were a generation or more ago.

But how, concretely, is this to be done? The studies we have gathered together contribute, we believe, to a fresh understanding of prejudice, politics, and the American dilemma. They do not represent the last word in the answers that can be developed, but they do present fresh lines of questions and, what is more, deliberately interleaf two perspectives—the first taking up issues of race focusing on whites, the second on blacks.[1] But viewed from either perspective, our objective is to see anew the American dilemma.

Organization of the Book

The studies brought together in this book cover much territory—the use of group stereotypes by college students, the behavioral assessment of tolerance, cohort trends in stereotypes of blacks, the use by blacks of

[1] The two are by no means equally developed, not because we do not believe they are equally important, but because the reservoir of data and expertise available for an account of race focusing on whites is deeper than for blacks.

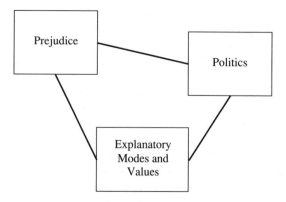

Fig. 1.1. Schematic outline.

stereotypes, explanations of inequality, the constraints on the reactions of blacks to middle-class American values, the politics of election campaigns, the bases of American thinking about racial policies—to give only a selective listing of the topics covered. Moreover, judged in terms, not of what is written about, but rather of who is doing the writing, this book represents a congregation of social sciences with more than the usual number of pews occupied by at least one representative,[2] including psychometricians, social and personality psychologists, sociologists, population demographers, and political scientists of several persuasions. This range of both substantive focus and disciplinary perspective seems to us valuable—indeed essential—if the complexity of issues of race is to be appreciated and respected. But of course this is obvious, and raises at once a companion question: given the range and diversity of the studies in this volume, what ties them together? And it is this question—of organization and coherence—that we want to concentrate on here.

Ironically, notwithstanding the diversity of the studies in this book, we want to emphasize that they are tailored, with one exception, to fit a specific analytic framework, set out in Figure 1.1.

Prejudice

Our point of departure is prejudice itself. For getting a fresh understanding of issues of race must begin, we are persuaded, by considering what, exactly, prejudice is.

This may sound like an odd question: surely everyone knows what

---

[2] The largest exception is economics and race, which we set aside because of the appearance of Schulman and Darity 1989, which is devoted exclusively to it.

prejudice is. Prejudice is, for instance, judging a black man to be lazy, not because you know anything about his personal qualities, but simply on the grounds of his skin color; equivalently but more generally, prejudice is reacting negatively to a person, not in response to individual qualities, but in reaction to his or her group membership. If anything at all is clear, nearly half a century having passed since publication of the two landmark studies of prejudice in America, Gunnar Myrdal's *The American Dilemma* and Theodore Adorno and his colleagues' *The Authoritarian Personality*, you would suppose it to be the meaning of *prejudice*. Surely that, at least, we know.

And the meaning of *prejudice* does seem obvious. What is in need of understanding is why some people accept ideas about others that are patently absurd: the anti-Semite, wild generalizations about Jews; the racial bigot, slanderous attributions to blacks. Prejudice thus centers on the acceptance of negative stereotypes about groups, and the companion question of how to combat prejudice accordingly centers on how to impeach beliefs that are simultaneously overgeneralized and oversimplified.

Prejudice, so construed, presents itself as a form of archaic thinking. But there has been a revolution in the psychology of social cognition, which has turned this view of prejudice, if not upside down, then inside out. The implications of this revolution are laid out in detail in Chapter 2 by Myron Rothbart and Oliver John, but the broader argument deserves to be set out here.

The revolutionary fulcrum is Henri Tajfel's work with "minimal groups" (1970). The experiment runs as follows. Dots are projected onto a screen for brief periods of time. Each subject is asked to estimate the number of dots for each slide; subsequently, the subjects are told, on an entirely random basis, that they have either underestimated or overestimated the number of dots. When they were then asked to allocate rewards to two other people, about whom the subjects knew only that one had counted the dots the way they had and the other had counted them differently, it was found that subjects systematically favored the person supposedly like them at the expense of the person ostensibly unlike them.

Here are "minimal groups" indeed. The subject shares no physical features with the other person; no cultural values; no similarities in belief, background, or prior experience—nothing to bind; equally, nothing to divide. Yet the heart of the problem of prejudice—double standards toward ingroup and outgroup—is nonetheless reproduced. It is possible to induce people systematically to favor one group over another given only a flimsy (and fictitious) basis for identification with one rather than the other. Tajfel's minimal-group experiment thus demonstrates vividly that the threshold of prejudice is low indeed.

There is a second, and no less discouraging, lesson taught by the psychology of social cognition. Employment of stereotypes was once supposed (e.g., in Lippmann 1922) to be, on the face of it, proof of simplemindedness. But stereotypes are not necessarily irrational. On the contrary, making use of them often assists inference, and stereotypes are, in any event, in the words of Roger W. Brown, "natural categories, an intrinsic essential and primitive aspect of cognition, and anyone who attempts to 'jawbone' natural categories out of existence has chosen not just an ineffective means but also an end whose realization would be disastrous" (1986: 587–88).

But where exactly does that leave the study of prejudice? Surely it does not follow that the indiscriminate stereotyping of blacks is to be passed off as an incidental, if regrettable, by-product of a natural and rational tendency to take advantage of all the information given? How, in any case, are natural and rational forms of categorization to be distinguished from "unnatural" and "irrational" ones?

From our perspective, the contribution of Rothbart and John in Chapter 2 is precisely to drive home how radical the questions that need to be asked about stereotypes and prejudice are. And the place to begin, which they modestly decline to stress, is their pioneering development of an instrument for the study of the incidence and stability of racial stereotypes.

It is only natural to assume, a quarter of a century after the civil rights movement reorganized the U.S. political party system itself (Carmines and Stimson 1989), that there must be libraries chock-full of studies documenting the frequency with which negative stereotypes of blacks are endorsed. There are, after all, series of opinion surveys of the country as a whole, conducted regularly on an annual and a biannual basis over the past thirty years or more, charting popular support for the principles of racial equality and policies designed to realize it. But however rich the harvest of information on other points these surveys yield, in terms of mapping the incidence and stability of racial stereotypes, their contribution is meager.

It is hard to credit this—certainly, we found it so—but not the least merit of Rothbart and John's Chapter 2 is that it convincingly shows just how flimsy the theoretical and empirical foundations of the study of racial stereotypes are. It must—or at any rate should—come as a shock to discover that the paradigmatic study of racial stereotypes is a study done in the 1950's, and that changes in the frequency and salience of such stereotypes over the past quarter century have been measured against a baseline of Princeton undergraduates.

Without minimizing the originality or value of the original study by D. Katz and K. W. Braly (1933), Rothbart and John deftly delineate the limitations of the Katz measurement procedure. Nor is theirs a merely negative project. For in addition to supplying a critique of previous measures of group stereotypes, they present an instrument of their own, offering illustrations of its value by drawing on their own uniquely designed study of the dynamics of stereotypes through an undergraduate experience. The procedure Rothbart and John have devised deserves to be publicized, we are persuaded, because it makes possible the resolution of key questions about the connections between prejudice and politics in the contemporary United States.

A still more radical cut at conceptualizing prejudice is offered, in Chapter 3, by Harrison Gough and Pamela Bradley. Their approach deserves to be set out with care, since if their initial results are to be credited, they have not only hit upon a different way to measure prejudice but have also made progress on a quite different way to account for it. Measures of prejudice, they observe, have been of one logical type—self-report. The most famous is the F scale. A set of statements is presented to people. Agreement with a statement is a sign of prejudice: the more statements a person agrees with, the more prejudiced he or she is. The F scale has classically included statements such as:

> No weakness or difficulty can hold us back if we have enough will-power.
>
> Sex crimes, such as rapes and attacks on children, deserve more than mere imprisonment; such criminals ought to be publicly whipped, or worse.
>
> People can be divided into two distinct classes—the weak and the strong.
>
> Much of our lives is controlled by plots hatched in secret places.
>
> Reading the stars can tell us a great deal about the future.

Such statements are marked by harsh and intemperate language; superstitious thinking; a tendency to reduce experience to dichotomies rather than recognize its complexity; and the expression of extreme sentiments, particularly of hostility and aggression. It takes little imagination to anticipate that some people will decline to agree with these statements. They may reject them because of reluctance to agree with assertions that are overly broad, whatever their content; or because they believe agreement would present an unflattering image of themselves. But in either case a subset of people who are in fact intolerant will decline to agree with expressions of intolerance, creating, in Gough and Bradley's terms, a problem of "false negatives."

The problem of false negatives has long bedeviled researchers of tolerance. Incontrovertibly, some people who are intolerant will refrain from responding to expressions of intolerance. But it has proven quite impossible to get agreement on either the proportion of false negatives or the risk of giving a false account of prejudice as a result of failing to classify false negatives correctly.

The difficulties appear intractable so long as the measure of prejudice relies on self-report: for however subtle the questions, and however complex the statistical analysis, the strategy relies on self-disclosure: to be classified as such, people must voluntarily confess themselves to be prejudiced. And it is against the limits of self-incriminatory measures that the originality of Gough and Bradley's proposal deserves to be measured.

Briefly, they propose that a person's degree of tolerance should be assessed, not in terms of what he or she is willing to report about himself to a stranger (namely, an interviewer), but rather on the basis of how tolerant he or she is judged to be by a well-acquainted third party.

In assessing Gough and Bradley's approach, we think it useful to distinguish between the larger strategy they propose and the specific tactics they have deployed to implement it. Methods are not useful or useless in themselves, only useful in varying degrees in illuminating how things work in reality. Judged by this standard, the results that Gough and Bradley report are potentially the key to a new understanding of the etiology of prejudice.

Of the manifold of relations that Gough and Bradley explore, a crucial subset concerns intellectual efficiency. Intellectual efficiency is assessed by a scale, specifically tailored for the job, included in the California Psychological Inventory (Gough 1987). Consider the pattern of differential correlations between the intellectual efficiency (Ie) scale and intolerance measured by self-report on the one hand and behaviorally on the other. The correlation between the Ie scale and the F scale is $-.42$; between the Ie scale and observer-judged intolerance, $-.16$. Parallel results, moreover, were observed for 82 of the spouses who took the College Vocabulary Test: the correlation between the Vocabulary Test and observer-judged intolerance is .02, between the Vocabulary Test and self-report intolerance, .22.

Why are these findings so important? Because they potentially cut the ground from under one of the leading explanations of prejudice. This explanation, advanced by many,[3] but most cogently and systematically by Gertrude Selznick and Stephen Steinberg (1969), holds that formal education is a primary social institution for reducing prejudice. The argument

---

[3] We should declare an interest: two of us have been proponents of the Selznick-Steinberg position (see, e.g., Sniderman, Tetlock, Glaser, Green, and Hout 1989); if a more generalized version of the Gough-Bradley argument holds up, we shall have to acknowledge that a major theme in our analysis of democratic politics—that education tends to foster principled support for democratic values—is mistaken.

runs as follows. The fewer years of formal education people have, the more impoverished the fund of broad information they have to draw on, and the more imperfectly developed their cognitive skills for analyzing the information at hand. In turn, the less information they have to draw on, and the less their capacity to analyze it, the less likely they are to recognize that intolerant ideas and sentiments, albeit popular, conflict with the official values of U.S. culture; and the less aware they are of such conflict, the less reluctant they will be to accept intolerant ideas and sentiments. Insofar as Selznick and Steinberg are correct, then, it follows that education genuinely combats a susceptibility to prejudice.

Gough and Bradley do not themselves discuss the role of education,[4] but one implication of their analysis reinforces a more skeptical account of the impact of schooling. As Mary Jackman in particular has argued (1978, 1981), education may only give the appearance of combatting prejudice. As she maintains, the better-educated chiefly have the advantage of having learned what it is appropriate to say—and what not to say. Jackman's critique thus draws support from the Gough-Bradley analysis at two levels. First, the Gough-Bradley critique of self-report measures of tolerance provides a proper psychometric rationale for skepticism, as against mere suspicion of insincerity. Second, the Gough-Bradley finding of divergent patterns of correlation between self-reported and behaviorally assessed intolerance and intellectual efficiency contributes a new piece of evidence substantially increasing the plausibility of Jackman's broader speculations.

For the record, we want to declare an interest in this issue. In some of our own work (e.g., Sniderman, Brody, and Kuklinski 1984; Sniderman, Tetlock, Glaser, Green, and Hout 1989; Sniderman, Brody, and Tetlock 1991), we have argued for the Selznick-Steinberg position. Although in assembling this volume our objective was to identify fresh lines of questioning, we had not anticipated that it would be our own work, along with others, that would be seen to need reexamination. For our part, the correct judgment to make now is not that Jackman's position has been shown to be correct—a complete linkage between the Gough-Bradley findings and her position is far from having been established—but rather that it has received a new lease on life and deserves to be considered a scientifically plausible possibility. However this may be, thanks to Gough and Bradley's contribution to this volume in Chapter 3, we are ourselves the beneficiaries of a stimulus to fresh thinking, albeit not quite in the way we had anticipated.

---

[4] It is worth reiterating that it is we, not Gough and Bradley, who are drawing a connection between their findings and the role of education in fostering tolerance.

The Gough-Bradley chapter makes a second fundamental contribution. Because of the admirable economy of their presentation, the weight of this contribution may not be obvious except to psychologists, and so we want to take a moment to underline its importance.

This second contribution of theirs strikes us as particularly worth commenting on because it represents the first enlargement of the circle of analysis connecting the assessment of prejudice to the causes of prejudice (Fig. 1.1). For the latter half of their chapter presents new evidence—in our judgment compelling evidence—that one of the primary causes of intolerance is personality. As Gough and Bradley put it: "Intolerance is therefore not a free-standing, isolated personal disposition, but rather an integral part of the way individuals express their feelings of incompleteness and inefficacy" (p. 80 below).

The claim that prejudice may be rooted in personality is, of course, a familiar one and a central idea in *The Authoritarian Personality* (1950), T. W. Adorno et al.'s classic study of the psychology of anti-Semitism. But the claim has always been hotly disputed, losing much of its persuasive force in consequence of compelling methodological critiques of the F scale (e.g., Christie and Jahoda 1954). The Gough-Bradley account breathes new life into the personological hypothesis, and for at least two reasons. The first we have already remarked: by adopting a behavioral assessment of intolerance, it sidesteps the methodological uncertainties of self-report. The second is no less consequential: by introducing a framework of personality that simultaneously takes account of both types and levels, the Gough-Bradley approach introduces a new level of complexity and sophistication in the analysis of the personological sources of prejudice. The analysis of personality and politics had been imprisoned, not only by the measurement indeterminacies of the F scale and its successors, but also by the cramped conceptions of personality in which analyses of prejudice have been entombed. Following the lead of *The Authoritarian Personality*, in spirit if not in detail, quantitative studies of personality and tolerance have tended to focus on a single dimension of variation—on self-esteem, for example (e.g., Sniderman 1975)—giving the impression that there is only one form of personality development that is pro-social and represents proper functioning. In contrast, a key contribution of the Gough-Bradley chapter in this volume is to sketch an analytic framework that recognizes a multiplicity of ways in which personality can be successfully organized, and to demonstrate that in terms of fostering tolerance, what is decisive is not personality type but rather level of psychological integration. The Gough-Bradley chapter thus makes a double contribution—first, specifying how intolerance is to be construed, then connecting the behavioral manifestation of intolerance to individuals' personalities, and in particular to their level of psychological integration.

It is important to cast the causal net more broadly, and in particular to consider not merely personological but social structural sources. In this connection, Chapter 4, by Sue Dowden and John Robinson, makes a contribution that deserves the most careful attention, in the process demonstrating that it can be as instructive to learn what is not, or is no longer, a source of tolerance as to learn what is. Dowden and Robinson pull together a massive data set summarizing trends in the country over the past twenty years, drawing on the General Social Survey, a national survey conducted by the National Opinion Research Center every year since 1972; the *Monitoring the Future* series, a series of surveys of high school seniors conducted by the University of Michigan since 1975; the National Election Studies, conducted every two years since 1952 by the Center for Political Studies at the Institute for Social Research at the University of Michigan; and finally, two surveys of Maryland, one in 1982 and the other in 1986, both conducted by the University of Maryland Survey Research Center. And not only do Dowden and Robinson amass the principal series of relevant trend data, they take a wide-angle view of the pertinent dimensions, encompassing legal/institutional (e.g., attitudes toward interracial marriage and open housing), social/interactional (e.g., having black friends or having interracial contact), and stereotypes (e.g., perceived causes of racial inequality and general "warmth" or "coolness" toward blacks).

Dowden and Robinson thus cover much ground, so in commenting on their analysis, we want to focus on only one of the questions they consider, albeit the major one—whether or not the trend toward increasing tolerance, apparent in the 1950's and 1960's and apparently built into the dynamics of American society, continues in the 1970's and 1980's?

By way of introduction, it is useful to put the Dowden-Robinson analysis in context, and in particular to see its lineage in the classic studies not of racial but of political tolerance. In his seminal study *Communism, Conformity and Civil Liberties* (1955), Samuel Stouffer painted an arresting portrait of the American public mind, detailing the frighteningly superficial commitment of ordinary citizens—indeed, very often their massive hostility—to the basic civil liberties and civil rights of controversial groups. Stouffer's principal theme was the imminent risk to essential rights owing to high levels of anxiety and intolerance, if not among leaders of American communities then certainly among the general public. But in crucial counterpoint, Stouffer advanced a second and more optimistic theme. He detected a concordant set of social trends at work favoring tolerance, among them increasing levels of education, the growth of mass media and the wider diffusion of knowledge, the rise of child-rearing practices that encouraged open-mindedness and discouraged authoritarianism, and geographical mobility that expanded people's range of experience and helped break down fear and aversion to others simply because of differences in background and appearance. So against a background of ignorance and intolerance, Stouffer saw the prospect of a new and more tolerant climate of opinion. As he summed up: "Great social, economic, and technological forces are operating slowly and imperceptibly on the side of spreading tolerance" (1955: 236).

Stouffer's prophecy gained credibility as longitudinal studies of tolerance, not only in the area of politics but also encompassing various aspects of prejudice, were mounted (cf. Quinley and Glock 1979). These surveys, by assessing the general public's levels of prejudice in various domains—racial, religious, and political—at successive points in time, revealed a trend of rising tolerance in American society, just as Stouffer had prophesied. No less important, this trend of rising tolerance gave every evidence of being built into the dynamics of U.S. society. On the one hand, an expansion of educational opportunities was under way, a fundamental dynamic, since more education went hand in hand with more tolerance; on the other, the climate of opinion reinforced itself as emerging cohorts showed themselves to be progressively more tolerant, not only because they tended to be educated, but because they were themselves shaped by the climate of opinion in the larger society in their younger, more impressionable years (cf. Davis 1975).

Notice that the critical aspect of Stouffer's prophecy has come to be age—understood in terms of birth cohorts. People who are younger turn out to be more tolerant on average, not primarily because people tend to grow less tolerant as they grow older, but because they enjoy at least a double advantage by virtue of being younger: having grown up when opportunities for education were expanding and when the overall climate of opinion was becoming progressively more tolerant. Moreover, the prophecy reformulated in terms of age can be expressed in two quite different ways. On the one hand, one may mean only that—at any given moment in time—people who are younger tend to be more tolerant than those who are older. On the other, having in mind at least two different points in time, one may mean to assert that people who are younger tend to be more tolerant at the later point in time than at the earlier.

In seeing precisely the change Dowden and Robinson detect in the dynamics of tolerance, and appreciating just why it seems to them ominous, it is important to keep in mind the difference between the two formulations. A final caveat: in commenting on what we take to be the most striking of the Dowden-Robinson results, certainly the finding that most dramatically underlines the need for attempting to see anew American thinking about issues of race, we shall focus specifically on age-relevant trends in the usage of racial stereotypes.

To summarize their principal result, Dowden and Robinson's findings suggest that the built-in dynamism Stouffer and others had remarked, capitalizing on the socialization of the young and contributing to a progressively more tolerant U.S. society, may have come to a stop. At a minimum, it is no longer the case in the 1970's and 1980's, as it was the case in the 1950's and 1960's, that the emergence of each new generation adds to U.S. society a cohort still more tolerant than its predecessor.

It is essential to see just what it does—and does not—mean to say this. Most crucially, it does not mean a backlash has begun. People socialized in the 1970's are not more negative in their images of blacks than those socialized in the 1960's. Nor is there a tendency nowadays for the relatively young—say, those between 18 and 25—to be more negative in their images of blacks than those who are older; and in certain specific respects—in, say, attributing either a lack of native ability or of motivation to succeed to blacks—the relatively young are significantly more likely to have a positive image than those who are relatively old. But however welcome it is to learn that a backlash of significant proportions is not under way, it is all the same disturbing to see that one of the engines that propelled U.S. society in a progressively more tolerant direction has come to a virtual stop. The rate of increase in tolerance among younger cohorts now approximates zero. Partly, this is a natural consequence of the very progress that has been made toward tolerance: where a consensus on some aspects of tolerance has been established—for example, in opposition to laws against interracial marriages—it emerged first among the youngest cohorts. Once the overwhelming proportion of the young have taken a stand in favor of tolerance, it necessarily follows that room for improvement is correspondingly diminished. But as Dowden and Robinson show, "ceiling effects"—to use the technical term—cannot be invoked as a general principle; and the most serious consideration should therefore be given to the suggestion of Dowden and Robinson that the built-in motor, fueled by generational replacement and propelling U.S. society in a progressively more tolerant direction, essentially came to a stop in the 1970's and 1980's.

There is, however, quite a different reason why racial politics since the civil rights bills of the 1960's has become problematic. For there is increasing concern that the problem of prejudice is possibly two-sided: not only are blacks the targets of the prejudice of others, but others may be the targets of their prejudice.

It is essential to stress, not simply that we know little about the issue of black prejudice, but that we almost certainly know far less than we think we know. For what chiefly impinge on the informed citizen are not the sentiments of blacks in general, but the attitudes and actions of the more politically active and ideologically committed among them. That there is a problem of prejudice among some of the most politically visible African Americans is plain enough, but it is quite a different matter to attempt a characterization of blacks in general.

To turn the issue of stereotyping around—to examine the stereotypes held by, rather than about, blacks—is the special contribution of Lee Sigelman, James Shockey, and Carol Sigelman in Chapter 5. As they point out, the answer to the question of black prejudice is both less certain and more complex than it may seem. The answer is less certain because the results of previous studies conflict, some finding blacks to be more prejudiced than whites, others finding blacks to be neither more nor less prejudiced than whites. More instructively, the question is more complex, partly because of the number of plausible arguments *ex ante* that yield conflicting expectations, five of which Sigelman, Shockey, and Sigelman specify explicitly: *cultural sharing*, or the notion that black-white differences in prejudice should be minimal, given that blacks and whites share a common, larger culture; *minority solidarity*, or the notion that blacks should be less given to prejudice against other groups, since they share with them a common bond as fellow victims of prejudice and discrimination; *racial conflict*, or the notion that blacks should be more prone than whites to prejudice against ethnic outgroups, since at least some whites are likely to categorize members of these outgroups as fellow whites; *vertical conflict*, or the notion that, as compared to whites, blacks should be more prone to prejudice against outgroups better off than they, but less prone to prejudice against outgroups as poorly off as they; and, finally, *horizontal conflict*, or the notion that the patterns of prejudice should be just the other way round, since relations with groups that are similar in status are most likely to be antagonistic.

It is to be emphasized, as Sigelman and his colleagues do, that the project of comparing prejudice between blacks and whites is more slippery than it may seem. Obviously, it would be misleading to conclude, having observed the reactions of both to an outgroup, that blacks are more prejudiced than whites, if it turned out that responding negatively to the outgroup was primarily a function of a person's level of education, and that blacks—precisely because they have themselves been the victims of prejudice and discrimination—tend to have had fewer years of education than whites. Differently put, it is necessary to discriminate between exogenous and endogenous factors, and this is just what Sigelman, Shockey, and Sigelman strive to do, first setting aside the impact of religious affiliation, age, education, and gender before comparing levels of prejudice between blacks and whites.

Still less obviously, there is the quite fundamental—and quite neglected—question of whether the notion of prejudice should be construed in the same way for blacks as for whites. The common practice is to proceed as though a measure of anti-Semitism, for example, is appropriate for blacks simply because it is appropriate for whites. But as Sigelman and his colleagues rightly point out, it is an empirical question—and a crucial one—whether attitudes toward outgroups are cognitively structured in the same way among blacks as whites. They accordingly present an in-depth analysis, drawing on confirmatory factor analysis and demonstrating that the same structure of latent factors obtains for blacks as for whites.

Beyond this, the substantive results of Sigelman and his colleagues underscore the complexities of prejudice now. For on the one hand, they demonstrate that, eliminating the impact of exogenous factors, blacks are not more likely than whites to hold negative stereotypes of Hispanics, but on the other hand, they also find that blacks are more likely than whites to endorse negative stereotypes of Jews.

The finding of greater anti-Semitism on the part of blacks is disconcerting, the more so inasmuch as Sigelman and his colleagues show that it gives the appearance of operating across the board and is not simply a function of a greater willingness on the part of blacks to endorse economically oriented stereotypes of Jews—a tendency Harold Quinley and Charles Glock had identified earlier and cautioned could give rise to misleading impressions of a dislike of Jews per se (1979: 56–57). Plainly, more must be learned, focusing less on the comparison of blacks and whites and more on the causes and consequences of anti-Semitism among blacks. But as a first approximation, the research of Sigelman, Shockey, and Sigelman calls attention to the risk that, in ways not anticipated and possibly not intended, there may be a deepening of the American dilemma under way.

The deepening of the dilemma is evident from a quite different perspective, and so we want to move now from a consideration of prejudice and stereotypes to our second theme—explanatory modes and values.

Explanatory Modes and Values

How Americans feel about blacks—the stereotypes they hold and the emotions they experience—is one strand of our concerns. A second set of concerns is the beliefs—the opinions, values, and working assumptions—that Americans bring to bear on the problem of racial inequality.

So expressed, our set of concerns seems a portmanteau, and an ominously bulky one at that. But we have aimed to give this book a specific focus; for what we want to examine are the terms in which Americans themselves understand the American dilemma now—to explore, that is, how they explain, if only to themselves—the position of blacks in U.S. society.

Approximately a decade ago, research on racial attitudes was given a new direction by the work of Charles Glock and his colleagues (Apostle et al. 1983). The core idea behind their research program was to shift the focus of analysis from prejudice to something they called "explanatory modes." The mere fact of holding a negative stereotype of blacks, they argued, is not necessarily a valid indicator either of how a person feels about blacks or of the position he or she is likely to take on racial policies. Consider the stereotype "Blacks are more likely to be in trouble with the police than whites." What does it mean to agree with this? One possibility is that a person dislikes blacks and is therefore ready to endorse a negative characterization of them. A quite different possibility is that a person may agree that blacks are more likely than whites to have an arrest record as a matter of fact, but interpret this as a direct consequence—regrettable but inevitable—of generations of immiseration and exploitation that blacks have suffered, in which case, so far from disliking blacks, he or she may actually sympathize with them.

Still more fundamentally, Glock and his colleagues argue that explanatory modes—the explanations that people give to account for the fact that blacks are less well-off than whites—operate as the vital link between perceptions of blacks on the one hand and prescriptions as to what should or should not be done for them on the other. This is potentially a radical claim, for it is tantamount to suggesting that the crucial feature in the architecture of people's thinking about racial policy issues is not prejudice per se but rather the explanations they favor of racial inequality.

The full implications of the Glock position have yet to be developed, but Chapter 6 by James Kluegel and Lawrence Bobo calls attention to one of the most subtle and potentially far-reaching aspects of it. From the outset of this line of research, it has been plain that two of the ways in which people may account for racial inequality dominate the others. These two are, to borrow Kluegel and Bobo's terminology, *individualist* and *structuralist*. Roughly, the difference between them is this. An individualist explanation posits that blacks are less well off than whites by virtue of a characteristic or attribute of blacks over which they have, or should be expected to have, control: the paradigm of an individualist explanation of racial inequality is thus that blacks could be as well off as whites if only they were to work hard. In contrast, a structuralist explanation attributes racial inequality to aspects of the situation in which blacks find themselves and over which they clearly could not have exercised control; thus, paradigmatic structuralist explanations are that blacks are worse off in consequence of previous discrimination or continuing exploitation.

The contrast between individualist and structuralist perspectives has come to dominate the analysis of explanatory modes. The two seem to operate as natural antipodes, the one hinging on "individual-blame," the other on "system-blame" (see, e.g., Jones 1986). And it cannot come as a surprise that people take markedly different views about what should or should not be done to assist blacks depending on whether they account for racial inequality in individualist or structuralist terms (e.g., Sniderman and Hagen 1985).

It is the signal merit of the Kluegel and Bobo chapter that it throws a new light, from a quite unexpected direction, on the contrast between individualist and structuralist perspectives. They point out that explanatory perspectives can appear in strong and weak forms. This applies to both antipodes, but—and this is a quite original suggestion by Kluegel and Bobo—it cuts more deeply at the structuralist than at the individualist pole.

What does it mean to say that it cuts more deeply? The prevalence of people subscribing to a genetic explanation of racial inequality—that is, an account postulating that blacks are less well off than whites because they are by nature less able—has diminished over the past two decades. But this qualification aside, individualist explanations focusing on blacks' putative unwillingness to work hard evidently maintain as strong a hold on the thinking of Americans. What is less obvious, and what Kluegel and Bobo call attention to, is whether the rival structuralist perspective has similarly maintained its coherence and impact.

The Kluegel and Bobo chapter is a nuanced one. But it seems to us quite impossible that, having read it, one can subscribe to Edward Jones's initial formulation that the natural alternatives divide between "system-blame" or "individual-blame" (1986). For on closer examination the notion of system-blame is systematically ambiguous, and, as Kluegel and Bobo give reason to believe, these ambiguities have infiltrated into the public understanding of issues of race.

Kluegel and Bobo's argument runs as follows. It is misleading to suggest that individualism and structuralism are natural antipodes. They do not necessarily represent the opposite poles of the same underlying factor. It is, rather, preferable to think of them as independent of each other, where the notion of independence minimally entails that either one of them can lose strength without the other in consequence dominating the thinking of ordinary Americans.

Still more specifically, Kluegel and Bobo suggest that the very notion of a "structuralist" or "system-blame" account of racial inequality has begun to unravel. Roughly, the logic of such an account ran like this: blacks suffer problems because of the legacy of generations of discrimination and exploitation; these problems, far from being of their own making, are the work of others; so blacks surely have a call on the assistance of others. But this account has begun to disentangle, Kluegel and Bobo suggest, in part because of the passage of time. Increasingly, memories of segregation and overt discrimination are fading, and as they do so, the meaning of the American dilemma is being altered, subtly but significantly. Many who appreciate that blacks suffered a heavy burden of prejudice in the past see prejudice as itself part of the past. So although they are prepared to acknowledge that what originally made blacks less well off was prejudice, they increasingly find it implausible to argue that prejudice is the reason blacks have continued to be less well off; and insofar as they view prejudice as an increasingly irrelevant explanation of current (as opposed to past) black problems, they will presumably be less willing to back government assistance to blacks.

Even putting to one side the unraveling of the notion that external circumstances are responsible for racial inequality, Kluegel and Bobo make an initial case for the complexity of contemporary American attitudes toward questions of race.

By *complexity* we mean that there are a number of separable basic orientations that underlie Americans' thinking about questions of race. Specifically, Kluegel and Bobo's thesis consists of two key assertions. The first is that structuralism and individualism represent, not opposite poles of the same factor, but rather two independent factors. The second is that, in addition to the two factors of structuralism and individualism, there is at least a third factor—prejudice—and possibly a fourth.

To suggest that there are a number of basic orientations, or building blocks, underlying Americans' thinking about race is to invite a fresh understanding of what the American dilemma consists of. For supposing the Kluegel-Bobo thesis is even approximately correct, then it is quite wrong to suggest that contemporary arguments over race can be reduced simply to a struggle over prejudice. Prejudice *is* a part, but the struggle is more vexed, partly because it is more complex, still more fundamentally because arguments over race, rather than reducing to conflicts simply between bigotry and self-interest on the one side and the dominant values of the American creed on the other, now also hinge on competing modes of explanation, such as structuralism and individualism, each of which is legitimate.

The awareness that issues of race are now morally complex, even morally problematic, in a way they never were before is gradually sinking in. The Kluegel-Bobo chapter highlights some of this complexity, focusing on the explanations of whites for blacks being worse off than whites. Chapter 7, by Jennifer Hochschild, throws an even harsher light on the moral complexities of race in the contemporary United States, focusing on the explanations blacks give for the success of blacks.

Without minimizing the economic strains and vulnerabilities that continue to plague many of the new black middle class, Hochschild underlines the quandaries of belief in which blacks who succeed in the United States find themselves by virtue of their very success. How ought middle-class blacks to account for their own "success," and, by implication, for the "failure" of fellow blacks? Is their success a proof that they have sold out? And whether or not they perceive their achievement as being a result of their having compromised themselves, do other blacks perceive it this way? What matters about these questions, we would suggest, is less the answers that particular individuals may give to them than the fact that they have become questions. Viewing issues of race through Myrdal's representation of the American dilemma, it would never have occurred to anyone to suspect that blacks would fall under an obligation to interrogate themselves when they succeeded. And that the fact of success has become problematic is itself an ironic index of the extent to which the American dilemma has become a genuine dilemma for blacks as well as for whites.

Hochschild's mode of analysis is primarily qualitative and phenomenological. But we suspect that even those with quite different methodological tempers will find her representation of some of the quandaries that confront middle-class blacks convincing. Middle-class blacks surely are subject to special professional strains, and the most self-lacerating of these revolves around the explanations that they—and others—give for their success. U.S. institutions, both public and private, have gone to lengths to better the opportunities of blacks that no one in Myrdal's America would have even dreamt of, and not the least irony of the new American dilemma is that this very effort to help blacks launch themselves may have helped undermine, not only the respect whites feel for blacks, but the respect blacks accord themselves.

It would indeed be a dilemma if a program like affirmative action, which takes as its object the advancement of blacks and minorities, has as its consequence the crippling of their self-esteem. Hochschild notes, rightly in our view, the absence of decisive evidence, but argues, surely persuasively, that the opinions of black writers on the issue of black self-respect must be given weight.

For our part, we think it useful to distinguish between two levels at which programs like affirmative action are wounding blacks. One is personal. Surely some blacks who have achieved success believe that their success stems, not from their merits or effort, but from affirmative action; and there is a risk that they in consequence think less of themselves. Notwithstanding that it is fashionable now to claim that the self-esteem of many blacks has been wounded in this way, we ourselves believe skepticism is called for: if weight should be given to the opinions of black writers, at least as much should be accorded to systematic comparisons of whites and blacks in the general population that have repeatedly demonstrated an absence of explicitly racial differences in self-esteem (Rosenberg and Simmons 1972; Simmons et al. 1978; Taylor and Walsh 1979).

Whatever the verdict with respect to individuals, though, the issue of self-esteem has taken on life with respect to politics and public life: that is, it has shaped the language of public discourse, and thereby shaped the contemporary politics of race.

Subtly but tellingly, Hochschild traces the problematic interplay of the discourse of victimization and the idea of equality, drawing on Orlando Patterson, who wrote:

There can be no moral equality where there is a dependency relationship among men; there will always be a dependency relationship where the victim strives for equality by vainly seeking the assistance of his victimizer. No oppressor can ever respect such a victim, whatever he may do for him, including the provision of complete economic equality. In situations like these we can expect sympathy, even magnanimity from men, but never—and it is unfair to expect otherwise—the genuine respect which one equal feels for another. (Patterson 1973: 52)

Whatever the political moral drawn from this—and it may range from radical to reactionary—it drives home the deep sense in which affirmative action has become a quandary, not only for whites, but also and laceratingly for blacks.

Public discussion of the tensions over equality has itself become stereotyped. The very triumph of the language of Myrdal, which initially sensitized thoughtful Americans to the pathologies of prejudice, has frozen patterns of speech and thought, making it harder to see the moral vicissitudes of equality in our time. And it is these unanticipated vicissitudes— the strains that the pursuit of equality for black males imposes on black females, for example, or the bitter rivalry of universalism and separatism as values for blacks—that Hochschild documents.

It would be wrong to reduce the strains of contemporary racial issues simply to the conflict of alternative explanatory modes. But it would also be a mistake to underestimate the strain over the explanation of black "failure" centered among whites and the strain over the explanation of black "success" centered among blacks. Differences over explanations matter partly because they carry with them judgments of esteem and merit;

still more fundamentally, they matter because giving an account of why a problem arose is halfway to recommending a policy of how it should be dealt with.

The link between explanation and prescription—between the reasons given for a social problem and the public policies devised to address it—is a fundamental one for politics. And it is to the politics of racial issues that we want now to turn.

Politics

How should one view post-civil-rights politics, not in this or that detail, but in terms of its overall nature and dynamics? What are the choices in broad analytic perspectives?

One alternative, social-dominance theory, is offered by Jim Sidanius and Felicia Pratto in Chapter 8. But before reviewing their argument, we should declare an interest: in Chapter 9, we set out our own point of view, one at odds with theirs. We are accordingly still more in their debt than we should ordinarily be, for they have formulated a rival perspective of uncommon generality and force, which has helped us appreciate the limitations of our own project.

And it is the generality of the Sidanius-Pratto perspective that is its most striking characteristic. Most research on race and the American experience—and our own is no exception—begins with the presupposition that the American dilemma needs to be understood in its own terms: an emphasis on comparison, although not entirely absent (see, e.g., Frederickson 1981), is conspicuously rare. In contrast, Sidanius and Pratto take the position that the fundamental dynamics of the American conflict over race cannot be understood except in a transnational context. For it is the nature of politics in general—and not of American politics in particular—that shape the conflict over race.

All polities, Sidanius and Pratto posit, are organized around the issue of dominance: but dominance specified in terms not of individuals but of groups. One or more groups—Sidanius and Pratto leave this unspecified[5]—are superordinate; the remainder, subordinate.

It is the political psychology of subordination that concerns Sidanius and Pratto. Their perspective folds together not one but two arguments,

[5] It will be instructive, as Sidanius and his colleagues develop their framework, to see the position they take on the number of superordinate groups. For it will help drive home the precise point they intend to make. As matters stand, it is not entirely clear in what sense exactly a superordinate group is a group. And supposing there can be more than one, then the crucial question becomes that of lines of conflict and accommodation, less between superordinate and subordinate—as Sidanius and Pratto suggest—than among the superordinate.

and the strength of their contribution consists in striking a balance between them. On the one hand, and this is the argument their chapter concentrates on, conflict within a society tends to be organized in terms of the cleavage between superordinate and subordinate. Consistent with this, Sidanius and Pratto present evidence, for example, that social groups are differentially (and consensually) ranked in terms of social status; that self-esteem and social status are positively (if weakly) correlated; that social status and caste maintenance (in the form of opposition to interracial dating and interracial marriage) are positively related.

On the other hand, Sidanius and Pratto take care to call attention to a crucial asymmetry: it is not hard to understand why superordinate groups should support the established political order, but why should subordinate groups? Most broadly, the answer is "legitimizing myths"—that is, "the entire class of attitudes, values, beliefs, or ideologies that serve to provide intellectual and moral justification for, and thus social legitimacy to, the unequal distribution of value in social systems" (see p. 177 below). But it is the specific twist they give the broad answer that makes their argument analytically provocative. A superordinate (or hegemonic) group can satisfy its desire for status by comparison with subordinate groups; however, subordinate groups according to social-dominance theory, so far from rejecting established standards, embrace them—even at their own expense:

All social systems will converge toward the establishment of stable, group-based hierarchies [italics in original]. Given this assumption, it would then seem perfectly reasonable and even necessary for members of high-status groups to discriminate against members of low-status groups, while members of low-status groups will tend not to discriminate against, but rather to discriminate in favor of and defer to, members of high-status groups [italics ours]. (p. 180 below)

The double-barreled quality of Sidanius and Pratto's argument—positing both cleavage and consensus—is reminiscent of Louis Hartz's (1955) analysis of ideology in the United States. What gave Hartz's argument subtlety and power was his insistence on the interdependence of conflict and consensus: far from denying the reality of conflict in U.S. politics, he emphasized that the terms of conflict were themselves embedded within the Lockean liberalism dominant in the United States; and so overt conflict, even when it claimed officeholders as casualties, further cemented the normative principles that give their offices power.

It is by no means clear that Sidanius and Pratto want to give to the principle of consensus—in the form of the "legitimizing myths" they discuss—the prominence that Hartz did. Indeed, their intention may be just the opposite, given the way they underline the curvilinearity of the relation between status and social dominance, calling attention to the potential for challenge to the dominant ideology not only from the ranks of the least well off but from those who are best off. Still, the curvilinearity hypothesis is asserted rather than empirically demonstrated, and there is necessarily some uncertainty over the exact form social-dominance theory will take until it is fully developed.

But even at its present stage of development, Sidanius and Pratto's social-dominance theory clearly represents an analytic framework sharply contrasting with our own. We want to set out our own view now, not in an effort to criticize their work, but rather with an eye to putting before the reader genuinely different alternatives.

Part of the difference lies in judgments about the "facts of the matter"; a still more fundamental part consists in differences in analytic objective. Sidanius and Pratto are striving for a truly general theory: an account of prejudice and inequality that holds everywhere and at all times. We part company with them at the outset, not so much over the issue of generalizing over place (though our empirical focus is strictly American), but more crucially over the objective of generalizing over time. For we believe that the key to seeing the politics of race now—not as one may either fear or wish that politics to be but as it actually is—is precisely to see that it has changed.

Myrdal's *The American Dilemma* has dominated the understanding of race as an issue in U.S. politics since its publication nearly fifty years ago. So far from being restricted to the social sciences, it has become part of the intellectual furniture of educated Americans, supplying the fundamental assumptions of successive cohorts who may themselves never have read, or possibly even heard of, Myrdal and his work. But for all the book's merits, and it is a monumental work, we have become persuaded that Myrdal's America is not a picture of the present-day United States: the politics of race has been transformed.

But supposing we are right, what is the nature of the transformation? The argument from change—the thesis that the racial politics of America has been transformed—is customarily an argument of optimism: a generation ago, when Myrdal wrote, a majority of Americans believed that blacks ought not to be able to order a meal in a restaurant and sit where a white might sit, or rent a room in a hotel and sleep where a white might sleep, or drink from a water fountain that a white might drink from; now, support for these positions has virtually vanished (Schuman, Steeh, and Bobo 1985).

There has been a transformation in American racial attitudes, and we do not mean to minimize its size or significance. But the language, the habits of thought, the assumptions of a generation ago are still in control;

and what is necessary is to see the politics of race, not as it was then, but as it is now.

Our theme is issue pluralism. It is a mistake, we shall demonstrate, to speak of *the* issue of race. There are instead multiple issues, and it is crucial to recognize this for two related reasons. First and negatively, it means that the reactions of Americans to the full array of racial issues are not dictated by racism; for if racism were dominant, they would necessarily tend to respond consistently to racial policies across the board, and, as we shall show, the most striking aspect of contemporary thinking about issues of race is precisely the modest consistency in racial policy preferences among white Americans. Second and positively, to say that there is not one but a plurality of racial issues is to say that the politics of race differs across them: the lineup of players—who favors and who opposes—changes, depending both on the domain from which a policy is drawn and the way in which it is framed. We shall only be able to illustrate the variability of the politics of race, but these illustrations should carry special weight since they exploit a new technology—computer-assisted interviewing— that marries the external validity advantages of survey research with the internal validity strengths of experimental design. Taking advantage of this new technology, we can show, for example, that the connection between ideology and racial policy preferences, far from being consistent, hinges on the framing of racial issues.

The specific findings we report to one side; the larger conclusion we draw concerns the character of post–civil rights politics in the United States. Many thoughtful people who once found issues of race cut-and-dried now find them troubling: while seeing themselves as committed to racial equality, they cannot give unqualified support to every public policy intended to assist blacks; and the fact that they cannot do so raises a question mark, in the eyes of others and sometimes in their own, about the sincerity of their commitment to racial equality.

Without suggesting that everyone who professes to believe in racial equality is sincere, we have become persuaded that questioning a person's commitment because of his or her unwillingness to support every racial policy intended to help blacks is itself suspect. It is suspect because the very nature of racial politics has changed. In Myrdal's America, the meaning of racial equality was agreed on: it consisted in the elimination of segregation. What distinguishes the contemporary politics of race is that it is only partly a battle between proponents and opponents of racial equality. For it is also, and perhaps more fundamentally, a battle between proponents and opponents of competing conceptions of racial equality.

In Chapter 9, we briefly characterize three agendas of race in contemporary American politics: the "race conscious," "social welfare," and "race

neutral." Without detailing the three agendas here, we do want to emphasize that they represent politically quite different ways of understanding
what it means to favor racial equality; politically quite different in that
conflict over them turns on quite different lines of cleavage and hence
involves quite different lineups of proponents and opponents.

Our chapter sets out the details of the argument of issue pluralism; here
we want simply to note a broad theme. Our concern is with the politics of
racial equality, the key word being *politics*. There is a paradox. On the one
hand, it is perfectly clear that the politics of race is driven by a number of
factors, among them prejudice and the clash of economic self-interest; but
on the other, what has not been as clear to commentators on U.S. politics
is that the conflict over race is in part driven by politics itself. The paradox
is thus that the politics of race is both a consequence and a cause of social
and economic cleavage over race.

What does it mean to say that politics is itself a cause of contemporary
cleavages over race? Most obviously, candidates competing for popular
support strive to turn the issues of the day to their advantage, and issues
of race are obviously no exception, whether invoked indirectly, as in
the Willie Horton ads of the Bush campaign, or directly, as in the anti–
affirmative action ads of the Jesse Helms campaign. But our own interest
has been in a less obvious way in which politics reinforces racial cleavages.

Consider affirmative action. It is surely obvious that a person who very
much dislikes blacks will oppose affirmative action. But can it work the
other way around: is it possible that some people may now come to dislike blacks because they so very much dislike affirmative action? Previous
studies could tell only that dislike of blacks and dislike of affirmative action
tend to be correlated—not which is cause and which effect. But we can
demonstrate, thanks to a new methodology uniting experimental design
and survey research, that the mere mention of affirmative action increases
dislike of blacks.

An emphasis on the shaping role of politics should by no means be
construed as a denial of the role of social, economic, and psychological
factors. But restricting attention to social and economic factors is a mistake, obscuring in particular the dynamics of contemporary conflict over
race. For the politics of race is now marked by a deep irony. The very policies most strenuously insisted upon to alleviate the burdens blacks labor
under inflame hostility and resentment against them.

The irony points to the transformation of race as an issue in U.S. politics. The racial politics of Myrdal's America were defined by a fundamental
conflict: between the dominant values of the American creed on the one
side and prejudice and self-interest on the other. The racial politics of the
contemporary United States are defined by a quite different conflict: be-

tween the policies implemented to help blacks on the one hand and some of the central values of the American creed on the other. We do not mean at all to suggest that prejudice has disappeared. But we do want to insist that the politics of race now has a moral bite to it that it previously lacked; for it is no longer simply a matter of rejecting prejudice in favor of the creed but of rejecting key elements of the creed itself.

What distinguishes our perspective is the idea that politics itself drives contemporary racial cleavages. This idea is given independent development in Chapter 10 by Edward Carmines and Richard Merriman, and it is important to survey at least the broad outline of their argument here.

As a starting point, they take advantage of a perfectly straightforward observation. Different racial policies—busing, employment assistance, equal rights to public accommodations, and fair housing, for example— enjoy very different levels of support among whites. But each of these policies is patently intended to help blacks. Therefore, whites' reactions to them cannot be primarily determined by their feelings toward blacks: for if their reactions were primarily determined by their feelings toward blacks, they would treat them alike, and indisputably they respond to them differently. Different race policies raise different issues.

But what does it mean to say this? What does the variation across racial issues tell us about the nature of contemporary American thinking about issues of race? It exposes, Carmines and Merriman suggest, a shift in the nature of the conflict over race. Broadly, they see the shift as we do: issues of race used to involve a conflict *between* the American creed and prejudice; now they hinge more directly on a conflict *over* the creed.

Carmines and Merriman observe that the conflict over the creed can take two different forms. One form of the conflict concerns Americans' attitudes to the power of government. Fear of government intrusiveness, of government coercion, is an honorable theme of U.S. politics, particularly focused around government at the federal level. The fear of government power runs through American political thought, beginning with the *Federalist* itself; and has featured as a more or less conspicuous theme in public commentary and opposition to government policies, particularly on the federal level, to assist blacks. A second form that the conflict over the creed takes in contemporary politics, according to Carmines and Merriman, turns on "classical liberalism." Classical liberalism captures a strain of American thinking, among its themes being the priority of the individual over the state; the right of individuals to pursue their own interests, including the right to acquire property; the responsibility of every individual to make as much of him- or herself as possible; and the role of self-reliance, not only as a spur to individual self-realization, but also as an instrument for societal progress. There is, Carmines and Merriman argue, a built-in antinomy between classical liberalism and support for public policies to assist blacks.

It has no doubt been remarked before that conflict over racial policy may take either or both of these forms. The special contribution of the Carmines and Merriman chapter is to demonstrate that one of these conflicts is deep, the other only superficial.

The superficial conflict concerns arguments over the proper role of government, or, more exactly, of fears of excessive government power. It is not, it should be emphasized, that Carmines and Merriman claim that these fears are insincere. Their thesis is skeptical rather than cynical: they argue that these fears and apprehensions of government power, sincere or not, are not the motivating force behind opposition to racial policies to assist blacks.

Analytically, Carmines and Merriman suggest a typology of racial issues. In their terminology, there are, first, issues of "prospective equal opportunity." The hallmark of such issues is the determination that blacks are to be treated fairly—which is to say, the same as whites—"from now on," a classic example being the outlawing of deliberate segregation in public schools and public accommodations. Quite apart from prospective equal opportunity issues are compensation issues, both retrospective and prospective. Compensation issues presuppose that the prevailing distribution of resources and opportunities is tainted, and that fairness requires their redistribution.

Harold Stanley's analysis of the presidential candidacies of Jesse Jackson in Chapter 11, the final chapter on race and politics, offers a reversal of perspective; indeed, a double reversal.

The first reversal could not be more obvious. Stanley analyzes whites' attitudes and acts—but in reaction to black attitudes and acts, in the figure of Jesse Jackson. We say "obvious," but that is in retrospect: one of the most seductive, and misleading, legacies of Myrdal's argument is the tacit assumption that the problem of race is at bottom, as he put, "the white man's problem,"[6] the presumption being that whites represent not only the obstacle to black equality but the means of realizing it. It is an assumption that profoundly underidentifies the politics of race; or what comes to the same thing, the profundity of the cleavage between the contemporary United States and Myrdal's America is arguably this: blacks are now actors, not just subjects, in the struggle over race.

Stanley centers his chapter on a close comparison of the Jackson candidacies of 1988 and 1984, focusing on the level of support Jackson secured, the mobilization of voters he managed, and the strategic sources of oppo-

[6] See, for example, Myrdal 1944.

sition he encountered. It is worth emphasizing that instead of relying on standard and readily accessible data sets like the National Election Studies and the General Social Survey, Stanley has taken the pains to base his analysis on network exit polls. These exit polls have two powerful advantages, one technical and the other conceptual. The technical advantage is this: by confining themselves to those leaving the voting booth, exit polls overcome a major problem plaguing standard surveys—the tendency of people to claim that they have voted when in fact they have not. The conceptual advantage of exit polls as a vehicle for the study of presidential primaries is still more fundamental; and since it underpins Stanley's distinctive analytic contribution, we want to say a few words about it.

To appreciate Stanley's second reversal of perspective, it is important to pause and try to make explicit the conventions that typically inform an analysis of race and U.S. politics. Typically, analysts focus on a relatively small set of personal characteristics of adult Americans—their incomes, party affiliations, outlooks on politics, levels of education, ethnicity, and the like, most, though not all, of them being relatively enduring characteristics of individuals. The object of analysis is, then, to establish the lines of cleavage for racial politics—that is, to demonstrate the extent to which individual Americans' positions on specific issues of race tend to correspond to their more or less fixed characteristics.

Much is to be gained from the customary analysis, but it invites—psychologically, if not logically—a static view of the politics of race, and calling attention to the political dynamics of race is the principal contribution of Stanley's chapter. Voters' racial reactions, he elegantly demonstrates, are not a constant: support for Jackson rose and fell, not only between the two presidential campaigns but within them, and still more crucially, the waxing and waning of Jackson's popular support was conditioned by the structure of the primaries as political institutions.

Stanley's larger argument is for a political theory of race. By *political theory*, we understand an account fashioned with two explanatory requirements in mind. The first requirement is sensitivity to the dynamics of preferences—to the patterns of change even over relatively short periods of time. The second requirement is sensitivity to the impact of procedures for making choices: how choices are made politically has something to do with the political choices that are made.

In a field of analysis preoccupied with deep-seated and enduring cleavages and dominated by concern with the impact of long-term factors, Stanley's contribution is to focus attention on the dynamics of racial politics, and to do so in the context of an explicitly political account. He thus emphasizes that a constitutive feature of presidential primaries as mechanisms of public choice is their distribution over time: the sequencing of primaries structures the rise and fall of candidates, not excluding Jackson. Beyond this, the logic of political competition enters—including the number of competitors; the breadth of their appeal, particularly to blacks (the "Mondale factor"); and the hitching of Republican primaries to Democratic primaries in 1988, but not in 1984.

There is thus a fluidity—or, better, a potential for variability—in American reactions to issues of race. Stanley recognizes, of course, that there are nontrivial constraints on the variability of popular reactions to Jackson, but his more telling point is precisely the range of levels of white favorability to Jackson between 1984 and 1988. We thus see Stanley as making a double-edged contribution to a specifically political theory of race, on the one side emphasizing the extent to which reactions to racial figures (and by extension, to racial issues) are fluid and variable, on the other side demonstrating the extent to which political reactions to racial figures are shaped by political institutions themselves, presidential primaries being his illustrative text.

There remains Chapter 12, Robert Hauser's searching examination of trends in college entry among African Americans. It could be argued that this chapter fits the template we have laid out, but the truth of the matter is that we should have included it whatever specific scheme of organization we had adopted. For it addresses a question that deserves the attention of Americans, black or white.

Notwithstanding the complexities, it is surely not dogmatic to believe that the future circumstances of life of African Americans hinge significantly on their encounter with higher education. But it is exceedingly difficult, even for a conscientious citizen, to put his or her hands on the facts of the matter: merely to be conscientious—itself no small undertaking—will not do. Partly the difficulty arises because of the thinness of our national statistical system in monitoring the transition from youth to adulthood. Partly, the problem is bred by the paradoxical politics of race.

The paradox briefly is this. Fairly clearly, people unsympathetic to blacks may wish to broadcast stories of black failure; less obviously, people sympathetic to blacks politically may have a still stronger incentive to do so. For they calculate that it is necessary to stress how bad the lot of blacks is in order to galvanize public support for government efforts to assist them. And so the best of intentions can give currency to the worst of racial stereotypes.

Among the most egregious of these stereotypes is the recent, and well-publicized, assertion that there are as many black men of college age in prison as attending college. This assertion was made by a black judge, not for the purpose of slandering young black men, but rather with an eye to dramatizing their plight. But it has achieved a wide circulation, in the process giving currency to the stereotype of the young black male as criminal. A companion statistic—that more young black men are under the control of the criminal system than are in college—has also been heavily publicized, also at the initiative of a person whose policy objectives, far from being hostile to blacks, were altogether sympathetic. Both assertions tarnish still further the image of blacks, and not the least reason for studying Hauser's chapter with care is to understand exactly, and not merely approximately, why both should be rejected.

Hauser divides his task in two, focusing first on the historical background of racial differences since 1940, paying particular attention to all levels of the educational system since 1960. Everything *is* in the details, and Hauser, in a simple but stunning display, demonstrates just how misleading simple summary statistics can be. As he observes, the overall gap between blacks and whites in median years of schooling had dwindled to less than half a year (12.6 for blacks and 13.0 for whites). It would be understandable if one were to conclude from this that the disparity in educational chances between blacks and whites had largely been overcome; understandable but quite wrong. Looking at the share of the population with a particular educational level rather than the average educational level of a population group, Hauser concludes: "As recently as 1970, the share of college graduates among African Americans was similar to that among whites in 1940. The chances of a white youth completing college remain about twice those of an African American youth" (p. 279 below).

Having summarized the longer-run trends, Hauser turns to his principal task of considering whether a decline in African American college entry has occurred and, given that the preponderance of the evidence suggests that it has, weighing the array of contending explanations for this decline. This may seem a straightforward question—has there been a slump in the chances of blacks for higher education?—and it surely is a public policy question of the first order. But the answer to it is exceedingly difficult to come by, and the difficulty in pinning it down supplies the text of the sermon Hauser quietly but compellingly preaches. There is, he demonstrates, a statistical void: once young people leave high school, from the point of view of the national statistical system, it is "almost as if they had dropped off the face of the earth" (p. 275 below).

Difficult or not, Hauser convincingly demonstrates that a decline has taken place in the rates of African American high school graduates entering college from the mid 1970's to the mid 1980's. Beyond this, he weighs the plausibility of a number of explanations. From our vantage point, we find his arguments ruling out putative declines in black academic performance particularly worth stressing. In the fog of ignorance and semi-information that so often envelopes discussion of issues of race, given that some aspects of blacks' circumstances are manifestly deteriorating, it is all too easy to fall into acquiescence of factually specious premises. It is exigent, therefore, to get the facts right, and as Hauser drives home, so far from the academic performance of black high school students deteriorating, it has improved steadily over the past two decades.

Beyond this, Hauser also shows that the balance of the evidence runs against an array of candidate explanations for the decline in black college chances, including a "return" to more appropriate levels after a temporary and artificial surge, a change in black family income, a turning away on the part of blacks from four-year degree programs, and competition from the military. But the object of the analysis is not merely negative. Having ruled out the explanations that manifestly conflict with the evidence on hand, Hauser calls attention to the most likely culprit: the chances of blacks for higher education dropped off from the mid 1970's through the 1980's, most likely because of decreasingly attractive terms of college support, both financial and social. Given the overheated rhetoric that so often obscures discussions of race, it should not count against Hauser's analysis that the policy remedy he locates is within our means to effect.

However that may be, the work that follows contributes to a fresher appreciation of the politics of race—to an understanding, that is, not of *the* dilemma of the 1940's and 1950's but of the skein of dilemmas of post–civil rights racial politics.

2

Intergroup Relations and Stereotype Change: A Social-Cognitive Analysis and Some Longitudinal Findings

Myron Rothbart and Oliver P. John

Can social psychology help us understand intergroup perception and conflict, particularly as applied to race? It is appropriate that a book such as this be interdisciplinary, since an understanding of race in America requires the collective wisdom of all students of social behavior. Many academic disciplines have approached the study of social problems with a mixture of chauvinism and hubris, and psychology has been no exception. The goal of this chapter, not without its own hubris, is to outline what psychology has to offer in understanding intergroup bias and, equally important, to place this contribution in a context that does not ignore the extraordinary power of social and economic forces to structure the reality of contemporary race relations in the United States. We first consider several social-psychological theories of intergroup bias, then examine the role of stereotypes in intergroup perception and, finally, discuss the special character of racial bias, considering prospects for its amelioration. Toward the end of this chapter, we describe some initial findings from our recent longitudinal study of stereotyping as these data relate to some of the ideas discussed earlier in this paper.

The first author was supported in part by National Institutes of Mental Health Grant MH40662 and the second author by Grant MH49255. Mary Rothbart, whose editorial acumen improved the style, organization, and substance of this paper, is acknowledged with gratitude.

A Short History of Social-Psychological Accounts
of Intergroup Conflict

What are the causes of intergroup bias and conflict? Let us first consider cases of *in vivo* conflict, that is, real-life conflict between naturally exist-ing groups where the conflict has, typically, a lengthy history. There is no dearth of examples. They include the conflict between (a) Protestants and Catholics in Northern Ireland, (b) Jews and Arabs in the Middle East, (c) whites and blacks in South Africa, (d) political factions within Cam-bodia, and (e) ethnic and religious divisions within India. In analyzing any one of these conflicts, there is a strong bias toward "particularism"—a tendency to view the conflict as inevitable given the inherent power of the specific factors unique to that conflict. In Northern Ireland, these factors include the relationship between the Protestants of Northern Ireland and the people of England, and the long history of conflict in Europe between Catholics and Protestants. In the Middle East, the conflict has its roots in antiquity and currently involves competition over territory, religious and cultural differences, and the twentieth-century history of the Jews as Nazi victims attempting to set up a Jewish state.

Even a cursory analysis of these real-world conflicts allows us to com-pile a lengthy list of factors potentially responsible for intensifying inter-group hostility. In the cases cited above, there is a strong element of real-istic conflict—that is, competition between groups for some important limited resource, such as economic, political, or social power.

However, there are a number of other factors present in addition to the realistic conflict. Traditionally, intergroup perception has been viewed as a process of "autistic hostility" (cf. Newcomb 1947), that is, a self-amplifying cycle of antagonism, separation, and unrealistically negative attributions. Hostility between the groups leads to avoidance, which in turn allows for even more unrealistic, negative perceptions, since these perceptions cannot easily be tested against reality. However, specifying the negative perceptions that are and those that are not "warranted by reality" is difficult in real-life settings. That portion of the stereotype that is not "warranted by reality" is usually what is meant by the term *prejudice*, and is considered to be "irrational" in character.

Historically, one of the dominant explanations for the irrational char-acter of intergroup bias has been the scapegoat theory (see, e.g., Dollard et al. 1939; Bettelheim and Janowitz 1949; Zawadski 1948). The scapegoat theory states that frustration, often impersonal and arbitrary, arouses ag-gression, which is then displaced onto a minority group (usually one that is powerless and historically despised). To the extent that feelings about the group are determined by aggressive impulses, this irrational hostility is then rationalized by attributing "plausible" negative characteristics to the group. To put this slightly differently, the origin of the perceptions of the group reside in the hostility of the observer, not in the actual characteristics of the group itself. Research on the authoritarian personality, much of which was done at Berkeley, was based on a variant of the displaced aggression model, where aggression aroused by parents was denied and displaced onto outgroups.

The scapegoat model was based on the principle of displaced aggression described in Freud's first theory of aggression and popularized in Dollard et al.'s *Frustration and Aggression* (1939). This book explicitly attempted to account for race hatred, citing what were to become classic data on the relation between a measure of economic prosperity (yield of cotton per acre in a southern county) and a measure of racial violence (lynching of blacks). Dollard et al. found strong support for the model, but subsequent analyses suggest their data analysis and interpretations are problematic. After the publication of *Frustration and Aggression*, the apotheosis of anti-Semitism under the Nazis was taken as further historical support for the power of scapegoating.

In addition to realistic conflict and unrealistic perceptions of the conflicting groups, there are differences in cultural values and beliefs, and often differences in language and in physical appearance. Dislike of groups that have dissimilar attitudes, values, and beliefs from our own is another explanation for intergroup hostility (Rokeach 1973). The issue of physical dissimilarity is clearly relevant to the issue of race and is one we try to deal with more extensively at the end of this chapter.

It is extremely difficult, in our view, to dissect the basic causes of intergroup hostility by examining naturally occurring, historically based conflict: in almost every conflict setting one can imagine, all of the plausible ingredients of conflict are intertwined. There are real differences between groups; there usually is social, economic, or political inequality among the groups; there is competition over limited resources; and there are unrealistically extreme (and negative) perceptions of the outgroup.

Recent research in social psychology may be able to offer some new insights into the nature of intergroup conflict and bias. First, it is apparent that despite the diversity of the groups involved in conflict, intergroup bias itself appears to be ubiquitous. Although the characters in the drama change, the drama itself appears to follow the same story line. Second, given the complexity of real-world conflict, research on intergroup bias that takes advantage of the benefits of laboratory research may be of value. Not surprisingly, however, insights about intergroup conflict arrived long before modern social psychology.

The Views of Swift, Freud, Sherif, and Tajfel

In 1726, Jonathan Swift (1667–1745) published *Gulliver's Travels*, in which he introduces two warring nations, the Little-Endians and the Big-Endians, whose long history of violent conflict results from the former preferring to break their eggs at the small end and the latter preferring to break them at the large end. This example offers a profound insight into the nature of intergroup conflict. Swift is satirizing the centuries of war between the Protestants and the Catholics as being fought over distinctions tantamount to the difference between breaking one's egg at the big or small end. In effect, Swift says that differences regarded as profound and intractable may, with a change in perspective, be thought of as trivial.

In 1922, Freud published *Group Psychology and the Analysis of the Ego*, in which he introduced the concept of the narcissism of small differences. In an eloquent passage he notes:

Every time two families become connected by a marriage, each of them thinks itself superior to or of better birth than the other. Of two neighboring towns each is the other's most jealous rival; every little canton looks down upon the others with contempt. Closely related races keep one another at arm's length; the South German cannot endure the North German, the Englishman casts every kind of aspersion upon the Scot, the Spaniard despises the Portuguese. We are no longer astonished that greater differences should lead to an almost insuperable repugnance, such as the Gallic people feel for the German, the Aryan for the Semite, and the white races for the colored. (Freud 1959b: 33)

In other words, trivial differences can be made the basis for invidious comparison, for viewing oneself as superior to another.

In the 1950's and 1960's, Muzafer Sherif, a well-known social psychologist, examined extant theories of intergroup conflict and argued that most of the views elaborated earlier were inadequate (see Sherif et al. 1988). According to Sherif, the best way to think about intergroup conflict is in terms of the functional relations between the groups, which can be competitive or cooperative in character. Sherif's view is more complex than traditionally believed. In particular, he argued that he could take a normal sample of young boys, more or less randomly assign them to different groups, define the functional relations between the groups as competitive or cooperative, and, with these manipulations, affect both the within-group attitudes of members toward one another and the hostile or friendly relations between the groups. This research is in the spirit of Swift and Freud, suggesting that a long history of conflict about values or beliefs is not necessary to establish hostility between two groups. Nor are any "real" differences, such as cultural, language, or physical differences, necessary to establish conflict. In Sherif's view, what is necessary is competition. What makes Sherif's view complex is that the competition need not be in vital areas necessary for survival, but can be competition in setting up tents, cleaning one's cabin, or on the baseball field.

A still more radical position was taken by an English social psychologist at the University of Bristol, Henri Tajfel, who took Swift's and Freud's ideas to their extreme, metaphorically speaking, and did the following set of experiments (Tajfel 1970). Public school boys in Bristol participated in a laboratory experiment in which large numbers of dots were projected onto a screen for a brief duration. Each subject was asked to estimate the number of dots for each slide. Afterward, the subjects were told they would be placed into two categories: those who had underestimated and those who had overestimated the number of dots. Each subject was then told whether he was an under- or overestimator; in reality, the feedback was random and there was no relation between the subjects' actual estimates and their categorization by the experimenter. Subjects were then given a complex series of decision matrices in which they could allocate rewards to two other anonymous students, where the two students were either both ingroup members, both outgroup members, or one was an ingroup and one an outgroup member. When both students were in the same category—that is, either in- or outgroup members—the subjects divided the resources equally. When it was an ingroup versus an outgroup member, the allocation was made to favor the ingroup member.

There is some controversy involving the interpretation of these matrices, but a number of replications have shown that subjects will favor ingroup over outgroup members (Billig and Tajfel 1973; Brewer and Silver 1978). Consider what has occurred in the Tajfel experiment. The two groups were not competing for a limited resource. There was no functional relation of competition or cooperation between the two groups. There was no historical enmity. There was no aroused frustration in the subjects. There was no objectively determined difference between the two groups; the groups did not differ in terms of language, culture, or physiognomy. They did differ on the putative dimension of under- and overestimation of dots. But there was mere categorization. The experimenter invoked a mutually exclusive, exhaustive dichotomy, and placed the subjects in one of these two social categories. As a result of that categorization, subjects favored ingroup members with greater resources.

The Tajfel experiments, now referred to as the *minimal group paradigm*, tell us that the following conditions are not necessary for establishing bias against outgroups: (1) historical enmity, (2) competition, (3) aggression induced by frustration, (4) physical differences, (5) religious differences or important value differences of any sort. Some elaboration is required on this last point. There is some ambiguity as to whether perceived differences matter in the Tajfel paradigm. In another set of experiments, the researchers attempted to create categorical divisions that had no substance to the subjects (Billig and Tajfel 1973). Thus, subjects were put through a set of procedures similar to the under- and overestimator paradigm; however, rather than being labeled under- or overestimators, they were merely labeled as group M or group W types. Billig and Tajfel found that even under these conditions, the usual effects still obtained, suggesting that any categorization, even categorizations seemingly devoid of content, should lead to the same results.

In our view, however, these conclusions are premature. It is not clear, given the design of the Billig and Tajfel studies, that subjects really believed there were no substantive differences between the categories. Indeed, on the basis of the described research, it may well be that subjects did think that there was some meaningful basis for the partition, even though the labels for the partition were M and W. This remains a controversial issue in the minimal group paradigm. Nonetheless, it is safe to say that one can generate substantial bias against an outgroup on the basis of divisions that seem quite arbitrary. This conclusion is quite consistent with the position of Swift and Freud.

Mere Categorization and the Learning of Stereotypes

What role, if any, do stereotypes play in this process of ingroup-outgroup bias?[1] It could be argued that bias against the outgroup generated by the minimal group paradigm (such as the dot-estimation task) is ephemeral, since subjects have no other information about the group except its exclusivity, and that such bias is related negligibly to real-world intergroup conflict. Howard and Rothbart (1980) reason that momentary categorization may itself be short-lived, yet the effects on subsequent perception could be considerable. Specifically, they predict that the categorization generated by the minimal group paradigm implicitly activates the expectation of ingroup superiority ("we" are better than "they"), and that subjects will then selectively remember ingroup and outgroup behaviors in accordance with their perceived superiority (Rothbart, Evans, and Fulero 1979). Howard and Rothbart (1980) used the Tajfel minimal group paradigm to classify college student subjects into under- and overestimators of dots. Subjects were presented with decks of cards in which each card ostensibly contained a statement made by a previous subject in the experiment describing some (very favorable or very unfavorable) behavior he or she had engaged in. Subjects were asked to guess whether

---

[1] We are here defining a stereotype as the image, representation, or perception of a group's attributes.

these statements were written by under- or overestimators of dots. Not surprisingly, subjects perceived the favorable behaviors to be generated primarily by people in their own category and the unfavorable behaviors by people in the opposite category (the outgroup).

In the next experiment, subjects received one deck of cards describing their own group and another deck describing the outgroup. The ratio, or proportion, of favorable to unfavorable behaviors was identical for ingroup and outgroup. Later, using a recognition memory procedure, the kinds of behaviors subjects could remember was assessed. Subjects remembered far more negative than positive behaviors about the outgroup, and far more positive than negative behaviors about the ingroup; in other words, subjects were remembering items consistent with the general expectancy that the ingroup was better than the outgroup (cf. Rothbart, Evans, and Fulero 1979).

In short, merely categorizing the subjects implicitly raised the expectation that "we" are better than "they," which resulted in subjects disproportionately remembering unfavorable behaviors associated with the outgroup. Even though the input suggested no evaluative difference between ingroup and outgroup, the data base that is stored in memory is disproportionally weighted with unfavorable outgroup behaviors. Consider the implications of these findings. If subjects were now asked to do so, they would evaluate the outgroup negatively. If asked why, they would then be able to draw on a number of unfavorable outgroup behaviors as evidence for their negative evaluation. Their memory is correct in the sense that they are accurately remembering the unfavorable outgroup behaviors, but they are not equally good at remembering behaviors from all four cells of the contingency table. They are neither as proficient in remembering favorable outgroup behaviors nor particularly good at remembering unfavorable ingroup behaviors. Thus, starting from a minimal manipulation in which individuals are categorized into mutually exclusive dichotomies, we have quickly moved to a condition in which group members perceive that they behave differently from the other group and can retrieve behavioral evidence from memory in support of these group differences.

The above research suggests that even in the absence of real differences, competition, and aggression, bias against an outgroup can develop. Nonetheless, we live in a world in which groups do often differ in physical appearance, values, and behavior. How do stereotypes function in this real world? How do stereotypes develop, how are they maintained, and how do they change?

One of the most extreme views of the function of stereotypes is associated with the scapegoat theory, which attributes intergroup perception to the internal needs of the observer, rather than to the nature of the stimulus group. It is, as Zawadski (1948) has argued, a pure drive theory that ignores the nature of the stimulus. Despite the appeal of the scapegoat theory, it has received rather little experimental support. There is abundant evidence for displacement of aggression, but little evidence to suggest that ethnic minorities are the "natural target" of aggression. This is not to say that the scapegoat theory is wrong, but that the experimental evidence is not as convincing as one would wish. An additional problem is that the scapegoat theory only predicts hostile attitudes and cannot, without additional assumptions, predict differences in the substantive content of social stereotypes.

A Cognitive Perspective on Stereotyping

Beginning in the early to mid 1970's, the traditional view of stereotyping began to change. The cognitive revolution had a powerful effect on social psychologists, who began to think of people as adequate, but not optimal, information processors. In this view, categories serve useful cognitive functions. While categories are simplifications of the world, they nonetheless allow one to act upon the overwhelming complexity of the external world. This view took precedence in the middle 1970's, but again there were important precursors. In 1922, Walter Lippmann published his book *Public Opinion*, which articulates a view of stereotypes that is quite modern and compelling. Lippmann views stereotypes as maps that simplify the world in a way that permits navigation through complex and uncharted territory. There would be nothing inherently wrong with these simplifications unless, in his words, "these maps sketched in the coast of Bohemia." Maps are acceptable as long as they do not deviate too much from reality. In our view, this is the nub of the issue. Stereotypes are simplifications, and there are benefits to simplifications. The difficulty is that the simplifications should not be grossly erroneous, and this turns out to be a thorny issue.

Errors and Biases in Intergroup Perception

What are some of the sources of error in our perception of groups? First, people perceive more difference between groups than is warranted by the data (Campbell 1956, 1967; Clarke and Campbell 1955). That is to say, category boundaries are perceptually sharpened. We have reason to think that this occurs even with respect to the most innocuous stimuli, such as abstract numbers (Krueger, Rothbart, and Sriram 1988), and there is certainly evidence that this occurs with respect to the perception of human groups as well. People maximize the difference between the boundaries of groups and often treat overlapping distributions of characteristics as if they were non-overlapping. This is a powerful bias that appears at the perceptual level (e.g., Mach bands) as well as at the level of intergroup perception.

Second, related to the first point, we tend to perceive groups other than our own as too homogeneous and monolithic in character. This idea goes back at least to Spinoza's *On the Origin and the Nature of the Emotions* (1677). More recently, we have shown that a group is perceived as more homogeneous by outgroup than by ingroup members, and this is even true when the groups have considerable contact, as do the gender categories *men* and *women* (Park and Rothbart 1982). One way of thinking about this phenomenon is that to women judges, the category *women* is meaninglessly large, and so they are more likely to use and remember information more differentiating than gender, such as occupation, when describing the attributes of a specific woman. But to a male observer (outgroup member) viewing the same woman, the gender information is given more weight than the differentiating information.

Third, stereotypes as causal attributions about the behaviors of human groups are prone to a number of errors. People are likely to confuse evaluation with description. As an example, if one examines the content of stereotypes, particularly with respect to minority groups (including women), one will often encounter terms such as *devious, cunning,* and *deceitful*. These terms may have some validity in the following sense: one of the defining characteristics of minority groups is their powerlessness, and powerlessness, by definition, implies impoverished access to needed resources. Since direct access to resources is blocked, they must be obtained in a circuitous way. But why label the behavior *deviousness* rather than *resourcefulness*? That is, "indirectness in obtaining resources" can be thought of favorably, as resourcefulness, or unfavorably, as deviousness— even though the underlying behavior is the same. One can distinguish, as Peabody has, between the *descriptive* aspect of the behavior, in this instance obtaining resources in an indirect rather than a direct manner, from the *evaluative* component—whether or not one likes the behavior (Peabody 1968, 1984). Stereotypes have both descriptive and evaluative components. The problem is that the evaluative component, which is a judgment that the observer makes about the group, is not perceived as a judgment *about* the group, but as an attribute *of* the group itself. This is what Campbell (1967) calls the "phenomenal absolutism error." Peabody's and Campbell's insights about the distinction between description and evaluation help explain why it is often so unrewarding to argue about what the qualities of a group really are. Often it means arguing about whether a group is, for example, thrifty or stingy, where the difference resides more in evaluation than in the actual behavior of the group.

Another attributional bias erroneously ascribes behavior to the person that is more appropriately ascribed to the setting. As in the devious/resourcefulness example, the behavior may be an adaptation to powerlessness, not an inherent characteristic of minority groups. It is an error to identify something generated by the condition in which a group finds itself as a deep-rooted quality of the group. Commercial avarice was often seen as a characteristic of Jews in the past (Shakespeare's *The Merchant of Venice* being a famous example), but in fact one of the few fields open to Jews in the Middle Ages was moneylending, an occupation forbidden to Christians, who could be excommunicated for charging interest on a loan. Subsequently usury came to be seen as an inherently Jewish trait, rather than as one of the few activities available to Jews.

In other words, the historical circumstance, the setting, or the environment is confused with the inherent dispositions ascribed to the group. This is the basis of important biases in the perception of blacks by whites today. The inferior socioeconomic status of blacks may be perceived as reflecting blacks' capabilities, rather than as a product of historical and contemporary social and economic forces that affect black people.

Stereotype Formation and Change

How are stereotypes formed and how do they change? Stereotypes are formed by general impressions conveyed by socializing agents (media, parents, schools) as well as through direct exposure to group members. It is fair to say that for most groups, our knowledge comes more from these indirect than from direct sources, but the exact mixture of indirect and direct sources depends on the group and the context of intergroup perception.

The two sources of information are not independent of one another, and the exact relationship between the culturally based image of a group and the images that we form on the basis of experience with individual group members becomes a question of paramount importance. It is possible that the cultural image corresponds to the image derived from actual experience with group members. It is also possible that the correspondence is weak, which is more frequently the case. What happens when there is a mismatch between our culturally informed expectations and individual experience?

Developmental psychologists recognize this issue as the classic Piagetian problem regarding the development of conceptual structure. Children form conceptual structures regarding the external world and *assimilate* new experiences into that conceptual structure. Expectations can structure reality. However, the adults' view of the world is not the child's view of the world, and there must be some mechanism by which new experiences that show poor fit to the existing conceptual structure can modify that structure. This is Piaget's principle of *accommodation*. In our view, the dynamic relation between assimilation and accommodation is a useful way to think about the relation between the cultural and experiential component of stereotyping.

The power of assimilation should not be underestimated. Most behaviors that we observe are ambiguous and subject to multiple interpretations (consider the difference between the meanings of the terms *thrifty* and *stingy*). Stereotypes can structure the interpretation of a behavior in a manner consistent with the stereotype (Sagar and Schofield 1980; Rothbart and Birrell 1977). Assimilation is one of the more powerful explanatory concepts in social psychology.

Intergroup Contact as a Means of Stereotype Change

The process of accommodation is more complex, and it relates to an important idea regarding the reduction of intergroup conflict. It should be apparent from the ideas described at the beginning of this chapter that nature has provided us with a plethora of mechanisms for generating intergroup hostility. How many techniques are there for reducing hostility? Unfortunately, only one technique for reducing hostility has been considered in depth, and that is based on the contact hypothesis (see, e.g., Amir 1969; Cook 1985). The contact hypothesis itself has a number of variants, but the basic idea is that antagonistic groups generate unrealistically negative expectations of one another and simultaneously avoid contact. To the extent that contact occurs, the unrealistically negative perceptions of the group members are modified by experience. In other words, hostility is reduced as a result of increasingly favorable attitudes toward individual group members, which then generalize to the group as a whole (Amir 1969, 1976; Cook 1985). Generalization is central to Piaget's concept of accommodation and a key assumption of the contact hypothesis.

The contact hypothesis brings to mind T. H. Huxley's remark about the tragedy that occurs when "a lovely idea is assaulted by a gang of ugly facts." There are roughly equal numbers of studies showing favorable, unfavorable, and no effects of intergroup contact. However, we should be clear about what these findings are. There is evidence that contact can, under proper conditions, generate favorable impressions of individual category members who belong to an unfavorable category. Contact unquestionably can generate favorable attitudes toward *members* of a disliked category. However, do the favorable judgments toward the category members generalize back to the category as a whole? The answer to this question is a strong "rarely," as it is clear that the bulk of the research shows little or no generalization.

Individuation and Categorization—Two Opposing Effects of Contact

These arguments appear in an article we wrote on the cognitive factors that mediate the effects of intergroup contact for an issue of the *Journal of Social Issues* on the contact hypothesis (Rothbart and John 1985). We argued there that when we form favorable impressions of members of a group that we generally regard unfavorably, those individuals are often considered atypical of the category and are not averaged into our judgments about that category. In effect, atypical category members are not category members at all. Consider the following observation by a male rock climber: "There are no good women climbers. Women climbers either aren't good climbers, or they aren't real women." This is an outrageous statement, but it reflects what we think is a powerful and ubiquitous process by which evidence discordant with a concept is functionally isolated, rather than being integrated into that concept, thus allowing the concept to remain intact. This is an old idea and goes back to Freud's concepts of splitting and compartmentalization (Freud 1959b), to Gordon Allport's notion of refencing (Allport 1954), and to R. P. Abelson's ideas about differentiation (Abelson 1959).

The argument we want to make is that there is a reciprocal relationship between individuation and categorization. In our views, it is desirable that members of a category are seen as individuals and that the attributes of the category are no longer assumed to apply to each individual member. The converse of this process, however, is that our (presumably) favorable judgments about category members then do not generalize back to the group, because the individual is, psychologically speaking, no longer a member of the group or category. Rothbart and Lewis (1988) have done a number of experiments that provide at least partial support for this idea.

Conditions for Change

Does this mean that stereotype change is impossible? No. What it does mean is that stereotype change derived from direct contact may occur only under fairly constrained circumstances. We have argued that change occurs when the disconfirming attributes of individual category members become attached to the category as a whole. This will *not* occur when the fit between the category and the individual category members is generally poor. Change ought to occur when the overall goodness–of–fit between the category member and the category is high, but when the category member also possesses a few characteristics disconfirming of the category as a whole. If the person is too atypical of the category (i.e., different from the category in too many ways), then the person's attributes do not become associated with the category as a whole.

Consider an example of a sorority woman who wears a peasant skirt, has long hair, no makeup, wears Birkenstocks, eats tofu, and carries a backpack proclaiming "Abolish Apartheid." Even though the woman is a member of a sorority, she would be viewed as atypical of the sorority, and her attributes would not be averaged into, or amalgamated with, our impressions of sorority women as a group. If, on the other hand, we see a woman who seems in every way a sorority woman (e.g., appears wealthy, wears stylish clothes, cashmere sweater, nylon stockings, high heels, a lot of makeup, highly styled hair) *and* has an "Abolish Apartheid" sign on her backpack or purse, that evidence would be more likely to be incorporated into the category, and this is the argument we proposed.

Since disconfirming attributes are most likely to be associated with the stereotype when these attributes are present in an otherwise typical exemplar, these conditions may be satisfied only rarely. For this reason, the Rothbart and John model predicts considerable stability in our stereotypes, and this prediction is largely confirmed by the longitudinal data to be presented later in this chapter. One of the major implications of the model is that we give too much weight to those individuals who confirm the stereotype and not enough weight to those who disconfirm the stereotype. This in turn implies that only a few stereotype-confirming individuals, against a background of many stereotype-disconfirming individuals, would nonetheless serve to maintain the stereotype.

There is one other possibility regarding stereotype change, but we wish to emphasize that these thoughts are quite speculative. It is possible that broad superordinate categories (for example, women or blacks), might lose their stereotypic power when the useful or functional basis for classification approaches zero. This statement requires elaboration. Consider an earlier point made about outgroup homogeneity: female observers may see a world of difference between a female physicist and a female dancer, but a male observer tends to see only two females. Males tend to view women as women, less so as physicists and dancers. The female observer implicitly views the category *women* as meaninglessly large and shifts to more useful fine-grained subcategories, such as occupation. We suspect that it may be possible to come to view the outgroup more like the ingroup, but this may only occur when there is massively disconfirming evidence for the outgroup stereotype—that is, when "reality" forces the observer to perceive a group in terms of its heterogeneous character and many different "subtypes."

Perhaps recent events may provide a rough analogy for this phenomenon. In 1988, most of us would still have thought of the Soviet Union as a homogeneous entity. Now, given the independence movements in Eastern Europe, we do not think of the Soviet Union as a single entity, but rather in terms of Russia, Ukraine, Belarus, Azerbaijan, Armenia, and so on. Again, it should be emphasized that this view of stereotype change requires massive disconfirming evidence, in which the overwhelming number of individual members of the category are poor fits to the category as a whole, a condition that may be quite difficult to satisfy.

Frequency of Contact

One additional problem posed by any model of stereotype change based on contact with group members concerns the issue of majority-minority contact. Nonwhites constitute a statistical minority in the United States, and their relative infrequency, along with high levels of social and residential segregation, ensures that non-superficial contact will be uncommon. Although change can occur through changes in social norms, as well as through direct contact with group members, the latter may not be an effective means of change if social contact is minimal.

We wish to turn now to a brief consideration of our longitudinal findings, as they apply to racial stereotypes. We have attempted to cover a broad range of issues in the previous sections, and our longitudinal data bear on only a fraction of the issues we have raised. At the end of this chapter we return to some of the broader issues raised previously and speculate about some possible answers.

Assessing Stereotypes: The Katz-Braly Paradigm

Having considered various arguments predicting considerable stability in ethnic stereotypes, what is the evidence for the long-term stability or change in stereotypic beliefs? When Brigham reviewed the literature on ethnic stereotypes in 1971, he found that "unfortunately, longitudinal studies of the stability or change of individual stereotypes over time have not been carried out" (Brigham 1971: 21), and in the early 1980's, when we began work on a large-scale longitudinal study of stereotype change, the situation had not changed. The only available evidence consisted of cross-sectional comparisons of group stereotypes, such as those based on the 1950 and 1968 follow-ups to the original study at Princeton University by Katz and Braly (1933).

Katz and Braly's study of the stereotypes held by a sample of Princeton students was one of the first empirical attempts to measure stereotypes and served as the research paradigm for most subsequent studies. Katz and Braly asked 100 students to select from a list of 84 traits all those they thought were characteristic of each of various groups, including blacks, Germans, Jews, and several others. The students then had to check the five traits they saw as most characteristic of the group. In their subsequent publications, Katz and Braly tabulated the number of students who had checked each trait, and listed only the 12 traits seen as most characteristic by the total sample of subjects. That is, the published studies present stereotypes held consensually by a group of white, upper-class students who had been forced to choose five characteristic traits. The 12 traits that were seen as most characteristic of blacks and Japanese in 1932 are listed in Table 2.1.

Using Katz and Braly's procedures, Gilbert (1951) and Karlins, Coffman, and Walters (1969) conducted follow-up studies at Princeton and compared their findings to the stereotypes held in 1932. By the late 1960's, Karlins et al. noted, the stereotypes of blacks had become considerably less negative; for example, the number of students checking *superstitious* had dropped to 13 percent (from 84 percent in 1932), and the number checking *lazy* had dropped to 26 percent (from 75 percent). These data led Karlins et al. to conclude that the stereotype of blacks had become more favorable. However, stereotyping of blacks did not disappear altogether; rather, the most negative traits were replaced by other, somewhat more benign traits, such as *musical*, *pleasure-loving*, and *gregarious*.

The Katz and Braly technique of stereotype assessment has several serious shortcomings (see, e.g., Brigham 1971). For one, subjects are forced to choose five traits as characteristic, even if they do not find any of them particularly relevant, and subjects cannot express gradations in their perceptions of characteristicness. Moreover, although some traits are central to the stereotype by virtue of being uncharacteristic, such traits are not assessed. Further, the stereotype is defined only at the group (or sample) level; agreement among subjects, expressed as the percentage of subjects checking the trait, is used as a measure of belief strength. Because the individual's personal stereotype is not assessed, temporal changes cannot be assessed longitudinally within the same subject; all comparisons are, by default, cross-sectional in nature. Finally, the data available from the Princeton studies include only the twelve most consensual traits at any given time, making it impossible to examine the relative stability or change for any traits but those that reached the "top twelve" in the previous assessment.

A longitudinal examination of stereotype change therefore requires the

TABLE 2.1

The Twelve Traits Seen as Most Characteristic and Most Uncharacteristic of Blacks and Asians in 1932 and 1987

1932 (Katz and Braly study): Most characteristic	1987 (Rothbart and John study):	
	Most characteristic	Most uncharacteristic
Blacks in General		
Superstitious	Athletic	Scientific
Lazy	Group-oriented	Unpleasant
Happy-go-lucky	Proud	Studious
Ignorant	Energetic	Worldly
Musical	Loud	Unthinking
Ostentatious	Rowdy	Manipulative
Very religious	Talkative	Irresponsible
Stupid	Tough	Lazy
Physically dirty	Musical	Devious
Naive	Showy	Conscientious
Slovenly	Expressive	Open
Unreliable	Friendly	Vain
Asians in General		
Intelligent	Family-oriented	Showy
Industrious	Serious	Boastful
Progressive	Polite	Arrogant
Shrewd	Studious	Ostentatious
Sly	Quiet	Open
Quiet	Reserved	Compulsive
Imitative	Shy	Unimaginative
Alert	Intelligent	Deceptive
Suave	Efficient	Emotional
Neat	Cautious	Excitable
Treacherous	Precise	Materialistic
Aggressive	Truthful	Boring

SOURCES: 1932, Katz and Braly 1933; 1987, Rothbart and John longitudinal study. Note that Katz and Braly reported stereotypes of Japanese Asians only.

assessment of each subject's *personal* stereotypes at several different times, allowing for gradations in the perception of the relevance of the attributes for the group. Moreover, stereotypes are complex and have several different facets; in addition to the favorability of the traits attributed to a group, the perceived similarity of the group to the way the subjects see themselves should also be considered, as well as subjects' desire for contact with members of the group. Finally, an examination of the relation between stereotype change and intergroup contact makes it necessary to assess the amount and quality of relevant contact experiences.

The Rothbart-John Longitudinal Study of Stereotype Change

In 1983, we began an extensive study of stereotype change for the primary purpose of assessing the "longevity" of different kinds of trait attributions to ethnic, social, and occupational groups. On the basis of earlier work (Hampson, John, and Goldberg 1986; Rothbart and Park 1986), we had reason to believe that trait attributions differ from each other in their capacity for disconfirmation. When it became apparent that there were no existing data to test predictions about the differential change of stereotypic trait attributions, we realized that we had to collect our own long-term longitudinal data. We planned to study entering college students who, after leaving home, are in a transitional period and thus open to belief formation and change; we assessed their stereotypes of fourteen groups, varying in size, visibility, ethnicity, social roles, and gender. In addition to an assessment of stereotypic traits, we also included measures of favorability, self-perception, extent and type of contact with group members, and preferences for future contact. This study is unique in providing longitudinal data over almost four years for some very different target groups.

Our longitudinal study provides the opportunity to monitor belief change over a longer period of time and under more naturalistic conditions than is possible in laboratory studies. Here we summarize some initial analyses and findings pertinent to ethnic stereotypes and intergroup contact, focusing on blacks and Asians, the two clearest examples of "racial" categories. Moreover, because, as we argued earlier, "atypical" individuals may be stored elsewhere in memory—for example, as a "subtype" (e.g., black college students) within a larger group (e.g., blacks in general)—we shall report separately on black students and Asian students when appropriate.

Subjects were randomly assigned to describe three of fourteen different groups on the basis of about 45 traits each. Stereotypes were assessed at four different times, but we shall limit this discussion to the first assessment at the beginning of the freshman year and the fourth assessment at the end of the senior year. The traits used to describe the groups were selected from extensive pilot studies, in which we obtained unstructured, "free" descriptions of all the groups of interest. From the terms generated by these subjects, we selected a subset for each group, trying both to cover basic dimensions of person perception and to capture the unique and idiosyncratic characteristics of the different groups. Thus, there is some overlap among the traits rated for each group, permitting between-group comparisons on the same set of traits.

Characteristic and Uncharacteristic Attributes of Blacks and Asians

In addition to the 12 traits from Katz and Braly (1933), Table 2.1 lists the 12 traits our subjects saw as most characteristic of blacks and Asians out of the 45 traits for which we obtained ratings of characteristicness. Subjects' stereotypes, as measured by Katz and Braly's 1932 and our 1987 measures, have changed quite substantially, particularly for blacks, and have generally become more positive. However, the Katz and Braly technique ignores traits seen as relevant but uncharacteristic of a group. As an example, we provide in the third column in Table 2.1 the 12 traits our subjects saw as most uncharacteristic of blacks and Asians in 1987. This analysis unearthed some important components of these stereotypes. For example, blacks were seen as not *scientifically minded*, not *studious*, not *conscientious*, and not *worldly*. Note that these uncharacteristic traits are not that different from some of those seen as characteristic in 1932, such as *ignorant*, *lazy*, *slovenly*, *unreliable*, and *naive*. It is possible that the stereotypes have changed less than is apparent when only the characteristic traits are considered. At the very least, traits along the whole range of characteristicness are needed for a complete appraisal of stereotype change.

Across all traits rated by the subjects, the perception of blacks was slightly favorable, but still significantly less positive than the perception of Asians. However, that difference was attenuated for black students, who were seen almost as favorably as the Asian students.

Intergroup Contact

Interestingly, however, the more positive perception of Asians did not translate into behavioral intentions; when asked to indicate how much they wanted to have contact with members of each of these groups in the future, subjects reported they preferred contact with black students to contact with Asian students. That is, the qualities we admire in others do not necessarily make us seek out their company.

At the end of their freshman year, and again in their senior year, subjects also provided information about the amount and the nature of their contact with these student groups. Personal contact occurred relatively infrequently and did not differ between black and Asian students. On average, subjects reported that they had contact "a few times" (rated on a five-step scale ranging from "never" to "continuously"); similarly, on a measure designed to assess personal closeness via friendship patterns, a substantial proportion of the subjects had only acquaintances but no good friends and no close personal friends among either black or Asian students. However, subjects experienced the contacts they did have as somewhat more positive (i.e., *pleasant*, *feeling secure*, *having positive consequences*) than negative (*unpleasant, insecure, negative consequences*). This lack of personal contact is very relevant to our earlier argument about the difficulty of changing stereotypes through contact when majority-minority contact is so infrequent.

Finally, and unfortunately from the perspective of the contact hypothesis, none of these measures of contact increased substantially from the freshman year to the senior year. Moreover, subjects' interest in future contact with members of either group showed a small but significant decrease. In conclusion, our data suggest that even on the campus of a large, relatively liberal university, white students seem to have little personal contact with blacks and Asians; although contact experiences were rated as relatively positive, neither actual contact nor preferences for future contact increased over time. If there is little actual contact, there is little reason to believe that students would encounter much stereotype-disconfirming information and, consequently, little change should be expected.

Personal and Group Stereotypes and Their Stability over Four Years

In our design, the temporal stability of stereotypes can be examined (unlike in the Katz and Braly design) both at the level of the individual's personal stereotype and at the level of the aggregated group stereotype. The group stereotypes were remarkably stable; the correlations between the mean characteristicness ratings in the freshman and in the senior year, computed across all the traits, ranged from .94 for the two student groups to .95 for the two general racial groups.

The simplest way of illustrating this remarkable level of stability is shown in Figure 2.1. For each trait, we have plotted the subjects' mean characteristicness rating of blacks in the senior year as a function of the mean rating at the first assessment in the freshman year. Almost all the traits are very close to the regression line, suggesting that traits seen as very characteristic at the beginning of the freshman year were also seen as very characteristic in the senior year. The four-year stability coefficients were only slightly lower than the one-week retest reliabilities, which were assessed in an independent sample of subjects and ranged from .96 to .98.

Incidentally, Figure 2.1 also illustrates the kinds of traits seen as most and least characteristic of blacks at the two times. The shading of the circles, indicating favorable and unfavorable traits, confirms our earlier finding that the overall perception of blacks is relatively more positive than negative: there are a larger number of desirable traits on the upper right (the characteristic end of the scale) and a larger number of undesirable traits on the lower left (the uncharacteristic end).

How stable are the personal stereotypes of the individual subjects?

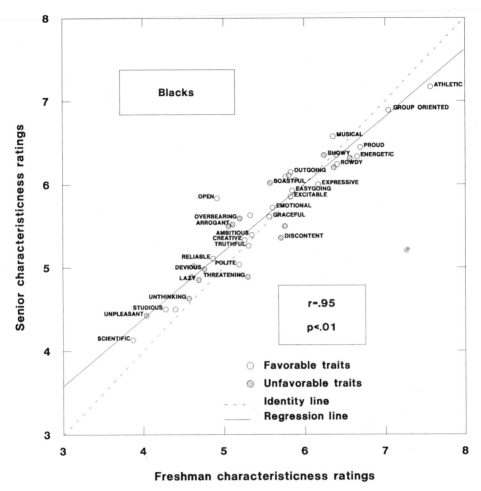

Fig. 2.1. Examples of traits rated as characteristic of blacks in the senior year as a function of characteristicness ratings in the freshman year. (Some circles left unlabeled.)

Within each subject, we correlated the two sets of ratings made almost four years apart across the traits. Averaging these within-subject correlations, the stability of the personal stereotypes was approximately .50 over the four-year interval; this level of long-term stability was clearly lower than the individual retest reliabilities across the one-week interval (average $r = .70$). Moreover, the personal stereotypes were substantially less stable than the group stereotypes ($r = .50$ versus $r = .95$). This difference between personal and group stereotypes emphasizes the need to differentiate clearly between the two levels of analysis. The analysis of the group (or cultural) stereotype indicates extremely high levels of stability for that part of the stereotype that is shared by the individuals in the sample; their individual belief systems, however, are much more changeable over time, an effect that cannot simply be explained by the lower reliability with which individual (as compared to aggregated) belief systems can be measured.

The conclusion that group stereotypes and personal stereotypes should not be confused is highlighted further by our analyses of interjudge agreement on the trait characteristicness ratings. Although Katz and Braly (1933) and subsequent investigators using their technique provided a measure of stereotype "definiteness," their measure does not have a standard metric and is difficult to interpret. The rating format used here allowed us to compute a more conventional index of agreement—namely, the pairwise correlations among the subjects' trait ratings. These correlations were much lower than one might expect on the basis of past research; the correlation between an "average" pair of subjects averaged about .30 for the two black groups, and about .40 for the two Asian groups. Although these correlations indicate that subjects generally agreed about the characteristic traits of these racial groups, there is considerable room for individual differences, and it would be misleading to assume that the same stereotypes are held uniformly by all individuals. If our goal is to understand the psychological processes underlying stereotypes, their stability and their change, then we must examine the personal stereotypes individuals hold, rather than their aggregates. We therefore turn next to a closer analysis of changes in racial stereotypes, with the subject serving as the unit of analysis.

Did the Ethnic Stereotypes Become Less Stereotypic over Time?

To answer this question, we examined the traits included in the ratings of both blacks and Asians. A factor analysis of self-ratings on these items suggested four distinct content domains, which we have labeled *boisterousness* (boastful, arrogant, showy), *warmth* (friendly, open, emotional), *task orientation* (conscientious, studious, ambitious), and *propriety* (polite, truthful). In Figures 2.2 and 2.3, we show the mean ratings for each of these four content domains for the two groups (general and students) of Asians and blacks at the initial assessment and almost four years later at the final assessment.

The main finding from all four panels in these two figures is a rather dramatic difference in the perception of blacks and Asians. The main effect for group was always significant, with blacks being perceived as more boisterous and warm, and the Asians perceived as more task-oriented and higher in propriety.

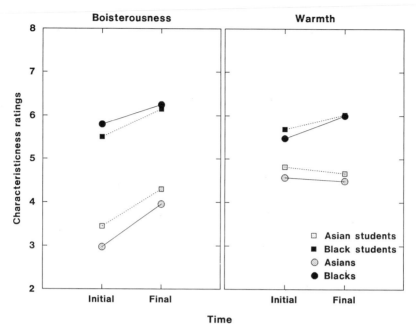

Fig. 2.2. Change in ratings of Boisterousness and Warmth from freshman to senior year for blacks and Asians separately for the student and general groups.

A second issue involves the analysis of the level of the group. Does the perception of the subtype differ from the perception of the more inclusive, general group? Ideally, the two subordinate, more specific groups (i.e., the student groups) should be more similar to each other than each of them is to their respective superordinate groups. At the least, however, the subordinate groups should show the stereotype effect less *extremely* than the general groups. With respect to boisterousness, the black students were seen as less boisterous than the general group, whereas the Asian students were seen as more boisterous than Asians in general. Conversely, for propriety, the Asian students were seen as being less proper than Asians in general, and the black students were seen as more proper than blacks in general. Although this interaction effect between group and level of hierarchical description was significant only for these two trait domains, the effects were similar for the other two trait domains, at least for the group scoring relatively low (i.e., stereotyped at the undesirable pole of the scale). That is, black students were seen as more task-oriented than blacks in general, and Asian students were seen as warmer than Asians in general.

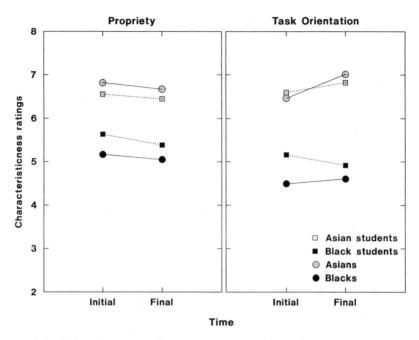

Fig. 2.3. Change in ratings of Propriety and Task Orientation from freshman to senior year for blacks and Asians separately for the student and general groups.

The main purpose of this analysis, however, was to examine whether the initial beliefs became less stereotypic over time. The data for boisterousness are presented in Figure 2.2. There seems to be promising evidence of a reduction in the stereotyping of Asians. In particular, we found that both Asian students and Asians in general were seen as more boisterous at the final assessment than at the initial assessment. However, the findings do not indicate a reduction in overall stereotypicality, because the two black groups were also seen as more boisterous. In other words, we found a main effect of time, rather than an effect that can be attributed specifically to the perception of the groups. Or, alternatively, we would have to conclude that the stereotype was reduced for Asians and increased for blacks.

With respect to the next figure, warmth showed no significant change over time, providing evidence only for the difference between the two groups, and a main effect of level, with the two student groups being seen as slightly warmer than the general groups. Similarly, for propriety, there was no evidence for differential stereotype change; rather, both groups showed a slight decline. Finally, the analyses of task orientation showed evidence for an interaction between group and time of assessment. Unfortunately, however, this effect does not imply a reduction in stereotypicality, but illustrates just the opposite: both Asian groups were seen as even more task-oriented at the final assessment, whereas the black groups remained at about the same level.

Intergroup Contact and Changes in Ethnic Stereotypes

Our measures of intergroup contact were not related to overall stereotype change in any simple or straightforward manner. We found a weak *positive* correlation between amount of direct (personal) contact and stability, suggesting that the overall amount of intergroup contact does not predict change; instead, the more contact the subjects had with a group, the more stable their perceptions of that group were. One possible explanation of this finding is that intergroup contact on college campuses may not elicit much information that is inconsistent with the stereotypes.

A more differentiated appraisal of both contact and the measure of stability versus change, however, did provide evidence for contact effects. Increases in the relative positivity (versus negativity) of the subject's contact with the groups predicted increases in the favorability of that subject's perception of that group, with correlations of about .45 for both the black and the Asian student groups. In contrast, increases in the total amount of contact and in personal closeness to members of the groups were unrelated to increases in the favorability of the final stereotype.

In summary, the comparative analysis of the ethnic stereotypes across an almost four-year-long period show that there was no reduction in the stereotypicality of subjects' beliefs. The few significant changes involved the Asians more than the blacks, and suggest that the Asians were seen as more boastful and even more conscientious at the end of the period under study. In four analyses, we found only one marginally significant interaction between group and time of longitudinal assessment; all other effects involved (a) consistent and strong differences in the perception of the two groups, (b) general changes over time by itself, and (c) effects involving the subtyping hypothesis, with a general tendency for the subordinate groups to be seen as less stereotypically extreme than the superordinate ethnic groups.

More generally, we can draw two general conclusions about the racial stereotypes assessed in our longitudinal study. First, similar to most other stereotypes assessed in our research, the group stereotypes of these racial categories showed extraordinary stability over the four-year college experience. This stability is predicted by a number of models, including the one we propose. The second conclusion is that our research findings are complex and do not permit any simple conclusions regarding overall changes in either the complexity or favorability of racial stereotypes. We have not yet completed our analyses of this large data set, but thus far the simplest conclusion is that we have detected no major shift in group stereotypes over our four-year period.

Conclusions and Implications

What general conclusions can we draw about the nature of intergroup bias and the process of stereotyping? There are four propositions that we suspect are true. First, based on the minimal-group research, any dimension or difference between groups can become the basis for intergroup hostility under the appropriate conditions, and physical differences are definitely not necessary for conflict to occur. The work of Tajfel and many others suggests quite clearly that almost any basis for categorization can become grounds for hostility and conflict between groups. One does not need powerful physical, cultural, or language differences in order for intergroup hostility to develop.

Is it the case, then, that race is not a particularly important kind of social category? Although physical differences between groups are not a necessary condition for intergroup bias, they provide a particularly potent basis for categorization. Physical differences—for example, those associated with race (and gender)—do have a special status because they provide visible markers for category differences ensuring continual activation and reification of categorical differences. The visibility of the basis for categorization has a number of important effects. Visible markers continually serve to remind people of the basis for category differences. We suspect that one of the reasons for the enormously strong effects of competition on intergroup bias (whether in the laboratory or the "real world") is that competition continually reinforces the distinction between "we" and "they" and makes it ever-present.

Moreover, visible differences enable us to act readily on our stereotypes. If an underestimator arrives to buy a car in a neighborhood of overestimators of dots, the "outsider" is not likely to be identified. The genotype of underestimation does not have a readily observable phenotype. But when Yusef Hawkins, a black, walked into white Bensonhurst in New York City to buy a car, his blackness was a marker with tragic consequences.

If we remember our history correctly, the first slaves on North American soil were indentured servants from Ireland. When these white slaves escaped, they blended in with the rest of the population—not the case with black slaves from Africa. It was the visibility of blacks that made the Dred Scott decision functional, which in effect brought the institution of slavery to the free states (McPherson 1988). Physical markers can serve as the basis for reinforcing and perpetuating perceived differences, and may make racial stereotypes more difficult to change than those that are based on nonvisible characteristics. In addition to physical differences serving as a visible marker, there may be another reason why physical differences may be a particularly potent basis for categorization. Rothbart and Taylor (1992) have argued that we may treat some social categories, particularly race and gender, as closer to "natural kind structures" (such as a biological taxonomy) than to artifactual structures (such as the difference between supporters of the Yankees and of the Mets). That is, people may implicitly assume that observable differences in appearance reflect deep underlying genotypic differences that directly influence overt behaviors in a profound and pervasive way.

In stating that physical differences serve as an important category marker, it should not be overlooked that when physical differences provide an imperfect means for differentiating between categories, humans have proved highly creative in supplementing nature's deficiencies. Since physical differences between Jews and Gentiles in Nazi Germany were not readily apparent, the compulsory wearing of a Star of David emblazoned with the word *Jude* created visibility where none existed.

Third, while the basis for categorization can be arbitrary or trivial (and "race" variables such as pigmentation and physiognomy belong in the trivial category), the social reality that becomes correlated with these differences is often far from trivial. To pursue Swift's parody, differences between those who break eggs at the large or small end are trivial in the extreme, but nations were then founded on these differences, wars were fought between these nations, inequality resulted from those wars, and so on. However arbitrary the initial difference, it ultimately becomes correlated with phenomena that are of considerable importance to individual and collective social behavior.

Fourth, and perhaps most controversially, any dimension upon which intergroup hostility is based can become irrelevant *under the appropriate circumstances*. It is important, for psychologists in particular, to realize that patterns of intergroup hostility do change over time. Chinese immigrants brought to the United States in the middle of the nineteenth century to work on the transcontinental railroads were admired for their industry and frugality. In the economic depression at the end of the nineteenth century, the Chinese immigrants tended to congregate in San Francisco, where they were regarded with hostility because they were viewed as unfairly

competing with white Americans for jobs. The attributes of the Chinese
had stayed the same, but the economic circumstances changed and so did
the stereotype—or, more accurately, the valuations of the stereotype.

After World War II, within almost a matter of months, we switched
our animosity from Germany to the Soviet Union. Indeed, the attitudinal
patterns toward the Japanese and the Germans prior to and after the end
of the war changed dramatically. Before the war, the Japanese, being of a
different race, were regarded with more hostility than the Germans, but
after the war, following the disclosures of the Holocaust, Germans were
regarded with more opprobrium than the Japanese.

Changing Racial Stereotypes: A Final Comment

Can racial stereotypes associated with social inequality be changed?
Can white images of blacks and Hispanics become more favorable? In our
view, the answer is yes, but these changes depend upon prior, significant
changes in the social and economic status of these groups. To justify this
argument, we need to be more explicit about how stereotypes function.
Although we have argued that stereotypes are highly resistant to change,
we also believe that they are correlated, however modestly, with social
reality. There are numerous sources of error in our stereotypes, and they
are resistant to change—as the longitudinal data suggest—but they can
change, however glacially. We certainly do not expect a one-to-one correspondence between changes in reality and changes in stereotypes, but
neither do we expect zero change. To the extent that the distribution of
jobs, of social and economic status, between whites and blacks becomes
more equal, it will be mirrored *to some extent* in whites' stereotypes of
blacks. Consistent with an argument we made earlier, dispositional inferiority is inferred from economic inferiority. Important, massive changes
in the social status of disadvantaged groups should be reflected in more
favorable stereotypes. The question, then, resides no longer in the domain
of psychology, but in the domain of those disciplines that are concerned
with effecting social change.

How can we move toward racial equality? This is a problem for social
scientists in general, and it resides more in the domain of economics than
it does in psychology. However, we have never let ignorance stand in
the way of speculation, and we would like to argue that national policies
aimed at full employment, at substituting a negative income tax for the
welfare system, and at instituting serious public works programs would
move in the direction of redistributing income and jobs to disadvantaged
groups. We have not chosen these goals at random, but have tried to think
of policies that would (a) elevate the social status of disadvantaged groups,

and (b) do so in a way that is "color blind" with respect to the beneficiaries of these policies.

The assumption is that stereotypes will not change in a vacuum and have to reflect actual changes in the behavior or status of the disadvantaged groups. While this conclusion reflects some optimism about the prospects for change, the decade of the 1980's does not make us optimistic about the desire of the government, or the country, to eliminate inequality based on race.

3

Personal Attributes of People Described by Others as Intolerant

Harrison G. Gough and Pamela Bradley

Animosities between groups leading to conflict, disparagement, dislike, and even warfare seem to be almost ineluctable phenomena in human history. For example, anti-Jewish feelings are expressed in the writings of the Roman poet Juvenal, who attributed to Jews an unwavering hostility to others, and also by the Roman philosopher and dramatist Seneca, who complained of Jewish "separatism." Even in the Bible, in the Book of Esther, comments appear about the distinctive differences of the Jews in comparison with all other ethnic and religious groups inhabiting the Persian Empire. In the thirteenth century, the scholastic theologian John Duns Scotus suggested that a certain number of Jews be deported to a distant island and maintained there at Christianity's expense to the end of time.

In more recent times, influential claims concerning the superiority of certain races and the inferiority of others have been published. For example, in 1856 the English translation appeared of Comte Joseph de Gobineau's four-volume *Essay on the Inequality of Human Races,* in which he alleged the primacy of whites, and in particular the Aryans, over all others. In 1899, Houston Stewart Chamberlain's *The Foundations of the Nineteenth Century* insisted on the superiority of the Teutons, physically describable as tall, fair, and dolichocephalic. In Britain, Thomas Carlyle and Rudyard Kipling, among others, tended to view imperialism as a beneficent activity that among other things would bring enlightenment to the benighted members of other races.

More tangible expressions of animus have been all too frequent—for example, the Russian anti-Jewish riots of 1881, anti-black riots and lynchings in the United States, the Japanese attack on Korean residents of Tokyo in 1923, and the 1915 expulsion of the Armenians from Turkey, in which it is estimated that over 600,000 died or were massacred. Perhaps the most horrendous example is National Socialism in Germany, under which systematic extermination of Jews was an official policy of the government. During the period from 1933 to 1945, it is estimated that from 18 to 26 million persons were gassed, put to death by lethal injections, starved, or otherwise killed in the concentration camps and crematoria of the Nazis.

Intolerance continues to be a problem in contemporary life, even if its manifestations are less virulent than those of World War II days. One need only call to mind apartheid in South Africa, Arab-Israeli antagonism in the Middle East, the Hindu-Sikh conflict in India, and the many ways in which anti-black and anti-minority feelings are detectable in the United States today.

From the standpoint of social science, the key questions are, why does prejudice exist and how can it be reduced or eliminated? Various theories to explain prejudice have been proposed, including dislike of what is different, transference of hostile feelings to scapegoats, and the tendency to generalize from the imperfections or transgressions of individuals to all members of the same group.

In regard to differences, the notion of ingroup versus outgroup is apropos. What characterizes the ingroup is acceptable, reasonable, and natural, whereas what characterizes the outgroup is alien, strange, and unacceptable. Thus, the "stranger" is distrusted and feared. Albert Camus's novel *L'Etranger* is an excellent psychological analysis of what can happen to a stranger in a time of crisis.

Projection in either conscious or unconscious ways of unwanted and objectionable feelings onto another person or object is at the heart of scapegoating. K. M. Gould (1946) has given many examples of the practice. For instance, the Bhars of India sought to ward off cholera epidemics by frightening the evil spirits of the possession into a water buffalo, which was then driven from the community. In Borneo, natives filled small boats with food so as to attract the evil spirits, and then set the boats adrift. The word *scapegoat* derives from Jewish antiquity, in which the sins of the people were symbolically placed on the head of a goat, which was then allowed to escape into the wilderness.

Stronger scapegoating practices are found in the human sacrifices of the Mayans, the Aztecs, the Yoruba of West Africa, and others. The troubles and wrongdoing of the tribe were transferred to the sacrificial victim, with the shedding of blood intended to propitiate the gods and to expiate its sins.

Stereotyping, or the overattribution of certain qualities to any particular group, can be related to what in cognitive psychology is called *stimulus generalization*. Social stereotypes assume quite specific form, as was shown in the classic study of Katz and Braly (1933), discussed in Chapter 2. They asked 100 college students to select from a list of 84 traits those that were most characteristic of each of ten groups: Americans, Chinese, English, Germans, Irish, Italians, Japanese, Jews, Negroes, and Turks. Germans were consensually described as industrious and stolid, Italians as artistic and impulsive, Irish as pugnacious and quick-tempered, Negroes as superstitious and lazy, and Jews as shrewd and mercenary.

An important query in regard to negative stereotypes is whether or not they will be related to actions. R. T. LaPiere (1934) reports an ingenious study in which he and a Chinese couple traveled across the United States, staying at 66 hotels and eating at 184 restaurants. On only one occasion were they denied service. At the end of the trip LaPiere wrote to the 250 establishments asking whether they would serve Chinese; of the 128 that replied, 92 percent said they would not.

Negative stereotypes may apply even to fictitious groups, as demonstrated in a study by E. L. Hartley (1946), who used a social distance scale (see below) to assess the degree of acceptance of a number of ethnic groups, and included among them three that were nonexistent: "Danireans," "Pireneans," and "Wallonians." Respondents who tended not to accept the real groups also tended not to accept the three fictitious ones, with correlations ranging from .55 to .85 for Danireans, Pireneans, and Wallonians when rejection of them was related to rejection of the authentic groups.

In Hartley's study we move from generalized, undifferentiated analyses of intolerance to the consideration of individual differences in level or degree of intolerance. This is important, because even in cases of intense intergroup hostility there will always be individual differences in the extent to which antagonistic attitudes are accepted and acted on. Certain individuals will be more trusting and benign, whereas others will be more distrustful and punitive. A challenging task for the psychology of personality is to discover what it is about some people that makes them less likely to adopt prejudicial views, and what it is about others that makes intolerance more likely.

To conduct analyses of this kind, some method of calibrating the degree or level of tolerance is required, so that individuals whose views are different in this regard can be examined. One of the earliest measures for this purpose was the social distance scale developed by Emory S. Bogardus (1925) as an operationalization of Robert E. Park's (1924) concept. In the Bogardus scale the respondent is asked to give a reaction to each of these assertions for a typical member of the ethnic group being studied: (1) would admit to close kinship by marriage, (2) would admit to my club as personal friends, (3) would admit to my street as neighbors, (4) would admit to employment in my occupation in my country, (5) would admit to citizenship in my country, (6) would admit as visitors only to my country, and (7) would exclude from country. The closer the degree of personal intimacy indicated by the answers, the smaller the social distance assumed between the respondent and the group under study.

A less direct method of assessment was used by Eugene L. Horowitz (1936), who employed pictures of white and Negro children. In one subtest, 12 of these pictures were ranked in order of preference. In another, the respondent was asked which of the children in the pictures he or she would want as a companion in designated activities. Scores among the various methods of responding correlated significantly with each other, with magnitudes increasing over the age of the children (from 5 to 14 years); this suggested that the strength and configuration of prejudicial attitudes were following a developmental gradient.

The California Public Opinion Study

Techniques for measuring individual differences in intolerance were a primary focus of effort for the psychologists involved in the California Public Opinion Study carried out during and just after World War II. A classic, general report on their work is contained in the book *The Authoritarian Personality* (Adorno et al. 1950). One of their measures was a scale for anti-Semitism (Levinson and Sanford 1944) containing items describing Jews as offensive, threatening, intrusive, and seclusive, plus items stating actions the respondent would take so as to minimize the influence of Jews. Intercorrelations of the subscales for each of these themes ranged from .74 to .86, showing that even logically contradictory beliefs (for instance, seeing Jews as both intrusive and seclusive) were accepted by those with high scores on the scale.

The second scale was for ethnocentrism, with subscales dealing with Negroes, other minorities, and patriotism. These three subscales intercorrelated from .74 to .86, and the full ethnocentrism scale correlated .80 with the anti-Semitism scale.

The third scale was for political and economic conservatism, with emphasis on (1) support of the U.S. status quo, (2) resistance to social change, (3) favoring of conservative beliefs, and (4) conservative preferences for the balance of power among business, government, and labor. Total score on this scale tended to correlate in the .40s with anti-Semitism and in the .50s with ethnocentrism.

The fourth and best known of the measures was that for authoritarianism, designated as the F scale (for "Fascism"). It was hypothesized that this scale, based on antidemocratic values, would tap deep feelings of intolerance and rejection of others and be less dependent on open acknowl-edgement of prejudicial views than the other three scales just discussed. Several other very brief questionnaires were developed for the project, such as those used by Else Frenkel-Brunswik (1948) in her studies of chil-dren, but for the most part the findings for the F scale were central, and it is this scale that has become one of the standard measures in psychology, down to and including present-day assessment.

Initially, the F scale contained 38 items, representing nine categories hypothesized as relevant to antidemocratic values: conventionalism, au-thoritarian submission, authoritarian aggression, anti-intraception (resis-tance to introspection), superstition and stereotype, power and toughness, destructiveness and cynicism, projectivity, and the perception of sexu-ality as ego-alien. Statistical analyses led to the dropping of half of the original items, and the 19 items retained were then augmented by 15 new ones. Subsequent analyses resulted in the dropping of 7 of these 34, and the adding of 3 others, giving rise to the final 30-item scale.

The research program and the measure itself were soon recognized as important. For instance, in the chapter on prejudice and ethnic relations in the 1954 edition of the *Handbook of Social Psychology* (Harding et al. 1954), the work was characterized as an outstanding example of the indi-vidual differences approach. By the 1960's, it was being described as "truly seminal" (Klein, Barr, and Wolitzky 1967), and in the 1970's as "classic" (Scheibe 1970).

Basic analyses in the study pitted high scorers on the F scale (and to a certain extent the other scales) against low scorers, drawing inferences from in-depth interviews, projective tests, and biographical data. The root elements of the authoritarian personality, defined and studied as indicated, included repression as a preferred mode of ego defense, externalization of negative feelings, conventionality of beliefs and values, cathexis of power, and rigidity. Age played a part in this syndrome, as children were in gen-eral less prejudiced than adults. Parental influences, especially the meth-ods of socialization applied by the parents, were also important. Harsh discipline, parental dominance producing submission by the children, and emphasis on conventional practices such as neatness and deference were all associated with higher scores on the F scale. This broad formulation of the authoritarian or prejudiced personality is still widely accepted, and found in current textbooks on personality and social psychology.

Measures to augment or extend the F-scale syndrome followed on the original work. One of the most significant follow-ups was that by Milton Rokeach (1960), who introduced scales for both right and left opinionation, for dogmatism, and for rigidity. Another important deriva-tive was the Machiavellianism scale introduced by Richard C. Christie and Florence Geis (1970). Their Mach-IV 20-item scale is widely used to identify manipulative and exploitative propensities. An interesting recent study (Mullins and Kopelman 1988) has revealed Mach IV to have a median correlation of .41 with four different scales for narcissism. Narcissism, as defined by current psychiatry, consists of grandiosity, fantasies of unlimited power and success, exhibitionism, and disturbances of interpersonal relations such as exploitativeness and feelings of entitlement.

Nevertheless, in spite of widespread and continuing acceptance of work on the authoritarian personality, significant problems have been noted. H. J. Eysenck (1953), for example, believed that two underlying dimensions of (a) liberalism to conservatism and (b) tender-mindedness to tough-mindedness had gone relatively undetected in the studies of Adorno et al. (1950). When he rearrayed the anti-Semitism, ethnocentrism, and F-scale variables in the two-dimensional grid generated by the two axes, high scorers on the three scales were placed primarily in the quadrant for tough-minded conservatism, whereas low scorers were found in the quadrant for radical or liberal tender-mindedness. Thus, Eysenck alleged, the original comparison was principally between strongly prejudiced conservatives and strongly unprejudiced liberals. Left out of the clinical examinations were tough-minded liberals (likely to be intolerant) and tender-minded conservatives (likely to be tolerant).

This line of criticism has remained visible over the years, for example, in the writings of J. J. Ray, who contends that leftists are, in fact, just as prejudiced as rightists (Ray 1984), and who complains (Ray 1990) that scales for conservatism such as that used by R. H. Weigel and P. W. Howes (1985) in their analysis of symbolic racism are "more a leftist's caricature of what conservatives believe than a proper and comprehensive survey of contemporary conservative thought." Bob Altemeyer (1988), on the other hand, has insisted that authoritarianism is solely a right-wing phenomenon.

A second line of criticism of the F scale is that by its harsh wording and unidirectionality (all items are negative in tone), defensive response sets will be triggered in which the form more than the substance of the items will be important. For instance, negative correlations with ability measures are usually found, which could easily arise from the clearer awareness on the part of intellectually able persons that endorsement of such blunt and aggressively worded statements is inadvisable.

The effect of any such influence on a test-taking disposition to deny negative feelings would be to lower the scores of persons who in fact hold and act on prejudicial beliefs, but who are either too intelligent to put them in the uncompromising language of the F scale or simply tend not to agree strongly with any list of attitudinal assertions. In psychometric terms, any such trend will augment the number of "false negatives" generated by the scale, where a false negative is someone who in fact holds intolerant beliefs but whose score on the scale presages otherwise.

A third problem is the fact that the F scale depends wholly on the self-reports of the respondents. Indeed, nearly all of the work done to date on the personality factors associated with intolerance has started with what amounts to self-definition or (to put it more strongly) self-incrimination. What about those people whose intolerance is apparent to others, but who go undetected by self-report measures?

One way to circumvent this problem is to treat the self-report measures as predictors rather than as criteria. Classificatory data in regard to intolerance must then be sought elsewhere. For example, if extensive descriptions of each other could be obtained from spouses, these could be calibrated for the degree of attributed intolerance. Or if similar descriptions of individuals by well-acquainted peers could be gathered, these characterizations could also be coded for manifestation of prejudicial attitudes. In essence, this approach employs observer-based data for estimating degrees of intolerance, rather than self-report data as has typically been done in the past. In the remainder of this chapter, we report a series of analyses in which descriptions by observers are used to establish criteria for intolerance.

Samples

An important consideration in the use of observer-based data is that the observers be closely enough acquainted with the people they are asked to describe so as to make sure that superficial facades and veneers of self-representation can be penetrated. The same self-concealing tendencies that can lead an actually quite intolerant person to achieve a low score on the F scale can just as easily be deployed to mislead a casual observer. For this reason, we wanted samples in which reasonable authenticity of description could be assumed.

The first of our samples consisted of 236 married or enduringly associated couples, in which each partner was described by the other on the Gough-Heilbrun (1983) Adjective Check List (ACL). The 300-item ACL attempts to cover the full range of the personality sphere, such that any consequential trait or syndrome of reaction can be indexed by a cluster of words. The individuals in the sample of couples ranged in age from the early twenties to the mid sixties, with a median age of thirty-eight. The average number of years they had been married or been living together was approximately ten.

Life history interviews were conducted with each of these 472 persons, and each person took a battery of psychological tests and answered questionnaires. The couples were participants in studies at the Institute of Personality Assessment and Research (IPAR) on issues such as population psychology and interpersonal dependency.

The second sample was composed of 194 college males who were members of eight different fraternities at the University of California, and 192 college females who were members of the same number of sororities. The organizations in this sample had agreed to take part in a project seeking normative and interpretational data for a number of tests. Each of the 386 students was described on the ACL by a panel of three peers.

For the couples, each of the 300 adjectives had a 1 or 0 dummy weight, depending on whether it was checked or not checked by the observer. For the students, each adjective was rated on a five-step scale, going from very uncharacteristic of the person being described to very characteristic. These ratings by the three observers were combined into a single appraisal, and the sums for each adjective were standardized within the fraternity or sorority of which the target person was a member. This adjustment put all of the ratings for all of the organizations on an equal footing.

The ACL Intolerance Index

To derive an observer-based ACL Intolerance Index, the 300 adjectives were reviewed by each author separately, and those that seemed to be clearly and unambiguously indicative or contra-indicative of intolerance were noted. We experimented first with a six-item cluster, including the descriptions *intolerant, prejudiced,* and *suspicious* as indicative, and *fair-minded, tolerant,* and *trusting* as contraindicative. The inter-item alpha coefficients of .59 and .52 for the male and female spouses, respectively, were too low to warrant going ahead with this cluster.

We next tried a cluster of fourteen adjectives, for which the alpha reliability coefficients were acceptable, but within which two of the items had marginal relations to the total. We then reduced the cluster to twelve items, all of which had self-evident implications for the tolerance-intolerance continuum, and which generated acceptable alpha coefficients. Specifically, the alpha coefficients for this twelve-item cluster were .73 for the descriptions of husbands by wives, .71 for the descriptions of wives by husbands, .85 for the descriptions of males by peers, and .88 for the description of females by peers.

In this observer-based index there were six indicative items: *cynical, distrustful, intolerant, prejudiced, suspicious,* and *vindictive.* There were also six contra-indicative items: *cooperative, fair-minded, reasonable, sympathetic, tolerant,* and *trusting.*

For the spouses' descriptions of each other, total scores on the Intol-

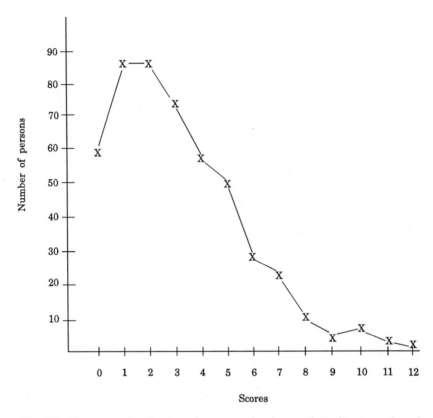

Fig. 3.1. Frequency distribution of scores on the cluster of 12 adjectives selected to assess intolerance, for 472 adults each described by a spouse or partner.

erance Index could vary from −6 (no indicative items checked and all contra-indicative adjectives endorsed) to +6 (all indicative and no contra-indicative adjectives checked). To avoid negative numbers in our tallies and computations, a constant of 6 was added to each sum, giving a range of scores from 0 to 12. Figure 3.1 displays the number of persons at each of the 12 scores.

The range of scores went from 0 (57 persons) to 12 (1 person), with means of 3.24 (standard deviation = 2.50) for males and 2.92 (standard deviation = 2.26) for females. From these means it can be seen that the spouses tended to describe each other more often with contra-indicative than indicative words—that is, as being at least moderately free of observable intolerance. Nevertheless, six males and four females had scores of 10 or above.

For the students, because standard scores with means of 50 were used for each adjective, the possible range went from −300 to +300. A constant of 300 was added to each score to avoid any negative numbers. In this array, the means were 300.04 for the males and 299.79 for the females, near the midpoint, as would be expected, because of the prior standardizing of the adjectives.

Because subsequent analyses were projected in which all 858 subjects would be pooled into a single sample, the ACL Intolerance Index scores were standardized to means of 50 and standard deviations of 10 separately for the 472 adults and 386 students.

The Intolerance Index and the F Scale

Table 3.1 presents descriptive information on a 15-item shortened version of the F scale (Gough and Lazzari 1974) administered to 201 of the couples. This shortened version was developed based on a sample of 255 subjects. Each of the 30 items in the original scale was correlated with total score. Those with largest correlations were designated for retention, guided by the requirements that at least one item from each of the nine taxonomic categories on which the F scale was based should appear in the shortened version. Another consideration was to drop items that were very harsh in tone, or that dealt with time-bound issues. The 15-item version developed in this way correlated .95 with the full 30-item scale in the sample of 255 persons, and in a new sample of 70 subjects produced a correlation of .96.

Examination of the means in Table 3.1 reveals that with only two exceptions, our respondents tended to disagree with the attitudes expressed by the items. The exceptions were for very slight positive endorsement of the statements "Obedience and respect for authority are the most important virtues children should learn," and "What the country needs most, more than laws and political programs, is a few courageous, tireless, devoted leaders in whom the people can put their faith." Neutral responses (that is, a rating of 4 on each) to all 15 items would produce a score of 60, approximately 10 points higher than the observed means of 50.51 for males and 49.38 for females.

Correlations of each item and the total score with the ACL Intolerance Index appear in the last column. Only two of the items had statistically significant ($p \leq .05$) coefficients, and the total score produced a very modest and statistically insignificant correlation of .08. From these findings it is clear that in our sample, scores on the F scale were only minimally related to the ranking of subjects according to the ACL cluster.

The findings do not mean, however, that scores on the F scale were without personological implications. One way to discover these implica-

TABLE 3.1

Average Scores and Correlations with the ACL Observer-based Intolerance Index
for Items and Total Score on the Shortened F Scale

	Average scores			
F-scale item	Male	Female	*Total*	*r*
1. Obedience and respect for authority are the most important virtues children should learn.	4.48	4.18	4.33	.02
2. No weakness or difficulty can hold us back if we have enough willpower.	5.02	5.29	51.6	−.02
3. Every person should have complete faith in some supernatural power whose decisions he obeys without question.	2.70	2.81	2.75	.01
4. What the youth needs most is strict discipline, rugged determination, and the will to work and fight for family and country.	3.65	3.57	3.61	.03
5. Nowadays when so many different kinds of people move around and mix together so much a person has to protect himself especially carefully against catching an infection or disease from them.	2.62	2.41	2.51	.00
6. Young people sometimes get rebellious ideas, but as they grow up they ought to get over them and settle down.	3.93	3.96	3.95	.00
7. What this country needs most, more than laws and political programs, is a few courageous, tireless, devoted leaders in whom the people can put their faith.	4.17	4.24	4.21	.07
8. Sex crimes, such as rape and attacks on children, deserve more than mere imprisonment; such criminals ought to be publicly whipped, or worse.	3.22	3.47	3.35	.04
9. People can be divided into two distinct classes: the weak and the strong.	2.40	3.13	2.27	.11*
10. There is hardly anything lower than a person who does not feel a great love, gratitude, and respect for his parents.	2.73	3.17	2.40	.03
11. Wars and social troubles may some day be ended by an earthquake or flood that will destroy the whole world.	2.67	2.97	2.82	.09
12. Most of our social problems would be solved if we could somehow get rid of the immoral, crooked, and feebleminded people.	2.40	2.20	2.30	.07
13. The wild sex life of the old Greeks and Romans was tame compared to some of the goings-on in this country, even in places where people might least expect it.	3.58	3.40	3.49	−.02
14. If people would talk less and work more, everybody would be better off.	3.99	3.85	3.92	.07
15. Familiarity breeds contempt.	3.06	2.74	2.90	.14**
Total	50.51	49.38	49.94	.08

NOTE: Items were answered on a scale going from 7 = agree strongly, to 4 = neutral, to 1 = disagree strongly. N: 201 males, 201 females (402 total).
*p ≤ .05.   **p ≤ .01.

tions is to correlate the F-scale scores with the 300 adjectival descriptions the spouses gave of each other. With 402 persons in the sample, correlations of .13 or beyond are significant at the .01 level of probability. Five adjectives with positive correlations, hence related to higher F-scale scores, were at this level: *conservative* ($r = .23$), *interests narrow* ($r = .18$), *prejudiced* ($r = .17$), *simple* ($r = .14$), and *nervous* ($r = .13$). It is interesting that the adjective *prejudiced* appears in this list, giving in itself a positive validation. The descriptions pertaining to conservatism, narrowness of interests, and simplicity suggest a theme consonant with the anti-introspective and politically conservative views found among criterion subjects in the original research on the authoritarian personality.

There were 18 adjectives with negative correlations larger than $-.13$, too many to report or assimilate easily. The 10 with largest coefficients were: *reflective* ($r = -.26$), *assertive* ($r = -.21$), *insightful* ($r = -.20$), *idealistic* ($r = -.20$), *unconventional* ($r = -.20$), *individualistic* ($r = -.17$), *complicated* ($r = -.16$), *initiative* ($r = -.15$), *intelligent* ($r = -.14$), and *tolerant* ($r = -.14$). These descriptions, having negative correlations, are all associated with low F-scale scores. The validating term *tolerant* appears in the list, it is reassuring to note. The other terms pick up themes of personal complexity, reflectiveness, and self-assertion.

The description *intelligent* merits specific comment, and can be compared with what happens when both direct and indirect measures of intellectual ability are related to the scale, and to the ACL Intolerance Index. The 402 spouses took the California Psychological Inventory (CPI) (Gough 1987), which contains an Intellectual Efficiency (Ie) scale to assess personological concomitants of intellectual ability. The Ie scale correlated $-.16$ with the Intolerance Index, but $-.42$ with the F scale. It thus appears that an intellectual component is more strongly embedded in the F scale than in the observable syndrome of social intolerance. An experimental College Vocabulary Test was given to 82 of the spouses. Its correlation was .02 with the Intolerance Index, but .22 ($p = .05$) with the F scale. The correlation of .22 also suggests an overweighting of intellectual ability in the F scale.

Attitudes Toward Child Training

Frenkel-Brunswik (1948) found that strict, judgmental attitudes toward children were characteristic of authoritarian personalities, and that they favored firm discipline and control in their child-training practices. To check on this issue, 82 of the spouses (41 of each sex) were administered the Harris-Gough-Martin (1950) Child Training Questionnaire (CTQ). This questionnaire has three sections, one on attitudes toward children

TABLE 3.2

Items from the Child-training Questionnaire Heuristically Related to the Adjective Check List Observer-based Intolerance Index

Item	Mean	SD	r	p
A parent should see to it that his child plays only with the right kind of children (true/false)	0.38	0.49	.17	(.13)
When he doesn't get his own way, my child cries, screams, or storms around. (usually/sometimes/rarely)	1.68	0.63	.23	(.03)
My child resents the discipline that I give him (very much/somewhat/very little)	1.49	0.53	.18	(.10)
A child should never be permitted to set his will against that of his parents (true/false)	0.21	0.28	−.21	(.06)
My child is easy to manage (usually/sometimes/rarely)	2.63	0.48	−.15	(.19)
If my child does not want to do what I ask, I "give in" to him. (usually/sometimes/rarely).	1.48	0.53	−.24	(.03)

NOTE: For items answered as true or false, true = 1, false = 0. For items answered as usually, sometimes, or rarely, usually = 3, sometimes = 2, and rarely = 1. For the item answered very much, somewhat, or very little, very much = 3, somewhat = 2, and very little = 1.

N: 82 parents (41 males, 41 females).

and their control, a second citing specific methods for managing children, and a third presenting vignettes of common problems (such as poor eating), followed by questions about preferred ways of dealing with these problems. The items in parts 1 and 2 of the CTQ were correlated with the ACL Intolerance Index, with results as reported in Table 3.2.

The findings were disappointing, in that only six items reached even heuristic levels of association with the criterion. Even so, the trend in meaning of these items is in agreement with earlier formulations. Our parents ranking high on the intolerance criterion saw their children as difficult to manage, as resentful of parental discipline, and as vociferous in their resistance when wishes were denied. When a child does not do what is asked, it is the lower-ranking person on the Intolerance Index who gives in.

Biodata and Marital Satisfaction

Relationships between the ACL Intolerance Index and biographical data were next explored. Mean age for the 236 men was 31.12 (standard deviation = 5.26), and for the 236 women mean age was 28.56 (standard deviation = 6.20). For all 472 persons, age in years correlated .01 with the Intolerance Index scores.

Years of education were next considered. The means were 13.73 (standard deviation = 1.80) for the men, and 13.46 (standard deviation = 1.76) for the women. The correlation in the total sample between education and the Intolerance Index was .05.

Occupational status was indexed by the Minnesota Occupational Rating Scale (Goodenough and Anderson 1931), which assigns occupations to a seven-step scale going from the professions and top managerial positions (step 7) down to unskilled labor (step 1). For the men, a mean rating of 4.34 was obtained (standard deviation = 1.64). For those women who reported jobs, the mean rating was 4.23 (standard deviation = 1.54). Correlations with the Intolerance Index were −.06 for men, and −.15 for the women; neither coefficient was significant at the .05 level.

Marital satisfaction was reported on a three-step scale, with "3" indicating happy or very happy, "1" indicating unhappy or mostly unhappy, and "2" indicating in-between, not sure, or both happy and unhappy. Mean satisfaction scores were 2.6 for the men and 2.64 for the women, with standard deviations of 0.54 and 0.60, respectively. Correlation between the satisfaction reports of the men and women was .46 ($p < .01$).

Husband's own marital satisfaction correlated −.25 with his intolerance score (that is, with his wife's description of him). Wife's own marital satisfaction correlated −.16 with her Intolerance Index. Both coefficients are significant at the .01 level, although both are low in magnitude. They indicate that the happier the marriage is reported to be, the lower the intolerance attributed to the rater by his or her spouse will be.

Marital satisfaction also appears to affect the ACL descriptions given of the spouse. The husbands' marital satisfaction correlated −.30 with the intolerance score calculated from their descriptions of their wives. The wives' own marital satisfaction correlated −.27 with the intolerance score calculated from their descriptions of their husbands. Thus, for both men and women, more tolerance was attributed to the spouse if the marriage was seen as above average in happiness.

Personality Inventories

The well-known Minnesota Multiphasic Personality Inventory (MMPI) was administered to 192 of the males and 221 of the females, and its scales correlated with the observer-based Intolerance Index as shown in Table 3.3.

No significant ($p \leq .05$) correlations were found for the males, but six significant relationships were noted for females. Females ranked higher on the Intolerance Index also scored higher than others on the MMPI F scale for infrequent and unusual responses, and on the scales for hypomania, psychopathy, schizophrenia, anxiety, and psychasthenia. Within the normal range of scores on these scales, where our subjects were found, the

TABLE 3.3

Correlations of MMPI Scales with the Observer-based
Adjective Check List Intolerance Index

	Correlations	
	Males	Females
L (improbable virtues)	−.03	−.08
F (unusual responses)	.04	.29**
K (cautious responses)	−.13	−.12
Hs + .5K (hypochondriasis)	.02	−.01
D (depression)	.03	.12
Hy (hysteria)	−.09	−.10
Pd + .4K (psychopathy)	.10	.20**
Mf (femininity)	−.06	−.04
Pa (paranoia)	−.08	.11
Pt + K (psychasthenia)	−.09	.15*
Sc + K (schizophrenia)	−.02	.19**
Ma + .2K (hypomania)	.09	.21**
Si (social introversion)	.04	.07
A (first factor, anxiety)	.08	.18**
R (second factor, repression)	−.13	−.11
ES (ego strength)	−.06	−.06

N: 192 males (76 adults, 116 students); 221 females (76 adults, 145 students).
*$p \leq .05$.   **$p \leq .01$.

correlations suggest that observably intolerant women tend to be extra-punitive and impulsive, somewhat indifferent to conventional proprieties, and vulnerable to the experience of anxiety.

In Table 3.4, correlations are given for the Intolerance Index versus the scales of the California Psychological Inventory (CPI) (Gough 1987). Here the patterns of correlations for males and females are quite similar.

For the first seven scales (Do through Em), pertaining to interpersonal skills, self-confidence, and assurance, the coefficients are generally negative, but low in magnitude. Larger coefficients appear in the second cluster (Re to To), which includes measures of pronormative attitudes and the acceptance of internal control. For instance, the So scale for Socialization, which seeks to assess the automatization of societally sanctioned ways of living, correlated −.25 with the Intolerance Index among males and −.18 among females.

In this same sector, the To (Tolerance) scale, originally constructed against the Levinson-Sanford (1944) anti-Semitism scale as a criterion, correlated negatively with the Intolerance Index for both sexes, well beyond the .01 level of significance. In the next sector of three scales assessing achievement motives and intellectual efficiency, all six of the correlations for both sexes were negative, and significant beyond the .05 level.

From the twenty folk measures (Do through F/M) on the CPI profile sheet, it is clear that the strongest predictors of higher scores on the Intolerance Index are those related to the internalization of societal values and self-discipline, all with negative relationships. Then, to a lesser degree, persons with strong intellective–cognitive achievement drives rank lower on the index than do their counterparts. Very modest negative relationships with the index appeared for males only on the scales assessing interpersonal skills and self-assurance.

The next section in Table 3.4 presents correlations for the three structural scales of the CPI. Because these relationships will be elaborated later, in a different way, their functions in the inventory need to be spelled

TABLE 3.4

Correlations of CPI Scales with the Observer-based Adjective Check List Intolerance Index

	Males	Females
Folk scales		
Do (dominance)	−.06	.03
Cs (status)	−.15**	−.04
Sy (sociability)	−.11*	−.03
Sp (social presence)	−.13**	−.06
Sa (self-acceptance)	−.07	.03
In (independence)	−.03	.00
Em (empathy)	−.23**	−.04
Re (responsibility)	−.19**	−.23*
So (socialization)	−.25**	−.18**
Sc (self-control)	−.10*	−.23**
Gi (good impression)	−.12**	−.24**
Cm (communality)	−.09*	−.20**
Wb (well-being)	−.15**	−.28**
To (tolerance)	−.30**	−.28**
Ac (achievement via conformance)	−.17**	−.18**
Ai (achievement via independence)	−.17**	−.13**
Ie (intellectual efficiency)	−.10*	−.15*
Py (psychological mindedness)	−.10*	−.11*
Fx (flexibility)	−.10*	.01
F/M (femininity)	.01	−.08
Structural scales		
v.1 (detachment)	.07	−.14**
v.2 (norm-favoring)	−.11*	−.14**
v.3 (self-realization)	−.21**	−.22**
Special-purpose scales		
Anx (anxiety)	.14**	.22**
Nar (narcissism)	.15**	.28**

N: 430 males (236 adults, 194 students); 428 females (236 adults, 192 students).
*p ≤ .05.   **p ≤ .01.

out here. Over the years, in many factor and smallest-space analyses of the CPI, two primary vectors have repeatedly been identified. The first, dealing with interpersonal orientation, defines a continuum going from involvement and participation at one pole to detachment and privacy at the other. This continuum can be somewhat captured in scales such as Dominance and Social Presence, but a more effective assessment is furnished by the scale called v.1. There is a slight tendency for the more detached or introverted women to have lower scores on intolerance, but this relationship does not hold for men.

The second basic theme in the inventory is one pertaining to normative orientations, generating a continuum going from norm-doubting dispositions at one pole to norm-accepting proclivities at the other. It can be assessed to a certain extent by scales such as Responsibility and Socialization, but it is more accurately appraised by the second vector scale, v.2. For both sexes, as reported in Table 3.4, there is a weak trend toward lower intolerance scores for norm-favoring persons.

The v.1 and v.2 scales were constructed so as to be uncorrelated with each other. Conjoint treatment of the two scales thus gives rise to four different categories, in each of which approximately 25 percent of the norm sample of respondents for the CPI are located. Each of these categories represents a way of living, or lifestyle. The Alpha lifestyle combines involvement and affiliation with the acceptance of norms. The Beta way of living combines detachment with pronormative views. The Gamma category brings together a participatory mode with dubiety about the way most groups function and about the way in which economic and other rewards are allocated. The Delta lifestyle derives from a preference for distance and privacy, with doubts about the legitimacy of normative sanctions.

For each of these lifestyles, there are specific, characteristic ways in which potential can be realized. Alphas, for instance, when functioning at their best are natural leaders, capable of charismatic appeal to followers. Betas can be saintlike in their virtue and selflessness. Gammas, because of their insight into the imperfections of social structure, and into the flaws in all intellectual constructions, can be creative innovators. Deltas, struggling inwardly with the inherent contradictions of life, can produce reconciliating visions in art, music, literature, and other liberating pursuits.

At their worst, persons of each lifestyle will be problems both to themselves and to others. Alphas can be dictatorial and invasive. Betas can be unutterably banal. Gammas can be asocial and even criminal in their oppositional tendencies. And Deltas can be torn apart by their inner battles.

What is needed in this theoretical system is some way of indicating where any individual is in regard to the avoidance of the pitfalls of his or her type, and the attainment of its potentialities. The v.3 scale, for vector 3, serves this purpose. The higher the score on v.3, the more likely that the respondent has moved in the direction of ego integration or self-actualization. Because the v.3 scale is uncorrelated with both v.1 and v.2, the system allows for self-realization in equal frequency for all four ways of living. Scores on v.3 are expressed in seven categories, going from 1 for the lowest, least effective degree of ego-integration, on up to 7 for the highest. Thus, an Alpha-4 would be someone of the Alpha lifestyle functioning in an average way. A Gamma-7 would be someone of the Gamma type coming close to an optimum degree of self-realization. We should note that for both sexes those respondents who report a stronger sense of personal integration on v.3 have significantly ($p < .01$) lower scores on intolerance.

In a moment, the relationship of this three-dimensional theoretical system to the observer-based Intolerance Index will be explored. Before doing that, however, attention is directed to the two "special-purpose" scales cited in Table 3.4. The organization of variables in the CPI calls first for the twenty folk concepts already discussed. Then come the three structural scales. Finally, there is an open category of special purpose scales, now some fifteen in number, which may be introduced into any analysis as a researcher wishes. The Anxiety (Leventhal 1966) and Narcissism (Wink and Gough 1990) scales were chosen for inclusion because of their hypothesized relevance to the criterion; in fact, both are positively and significantly ($p < .01$) correlated with the interspousal attributions of intolerance.

A Type/Level CPI Analysis

Table 3.5 presents an analysis of variance for the 858 individuals for whom both CPI data and the ACL Intolerance Index were available. To ensure a sufficient number of persons in each cell, grouping by level was needed. Subjects ranking at levels 1, 2, and 3 were pooled, then those at levels 4 and 5 were considered separately, and finally those at levels 6 and 7 were combined. The numbers in each cell, the mean Intolerance Index in standard scores for each cell, and the marginal frequencies, means and standard deviations are all reported.

The F-ratios for both type and level were statistically significant ($p \leq .05$), but that for the interaction of type and level was not. In regard to type, the highest intolerance scores were noted for Gammas, followed by Deltas, Alphas, and Betas. In regard to level, there was a steady downward progression in observed intolerance as level increased. This monotonic

TABLE 3.5

CPI Types and Levels Versus the Observer-based ACL Intolerance Index for 858 Subjects

Type		1 + 2 + 3	4	5	6 + 7	Total
			Levels			
Alpha	N	45	62	47	47	201
	Mean	52.07	48.53	48.35	47.76	49.10
	SD	*	*	*	*	9.35
Beta	N	32	45	31	29	137
	Mean	50.63	48.94	46.63	46.04	48.20
	SD	*	*	*	*	9.40
Gamma	N	77	100	86	57	320
	Mean	52.94	51.68	50.49	48.65	51.12
	SD	*	*	*	*	10.03
Delta	N	63	64	37	36	200
	Mean	54.69	49.10	48.55	46.75	50.34
	SD	*	*	*	*	10.74
Total	N	217	271	201	169	858
	Mean	52.93	49.90	49.04	47.55	50.00
	SD	11.56	9.51	8.75	9.11	9.99

ANOVA for:	df	F	p
Type	3	3.24	.02
Level	3	10.27	.00
T × L	9	0.62	.78

trend held for levels within each type, as well as for the overall means shown at the bottom.

Although the findings pertaining to the relationship between the CPI theoretical model of personality and the criterion of observer intolerance is completely expressed in Table 3.5, it is hard to visualize the trends. Figure 3.2 makes the relationships easier to see.

The standardized baseline of 50 on the Intolerance Index is indicated by the solid horizontal line at that point. Then the four trend lines for each lifestyle are drawn within the figure. All four lifestyles tend to manifest observable intolerance (mean scores above 50) when their levels are low, specifically at levels 1, 2, and 3. At levels 4 and 5, only those in the Gamma category are still being described as above average in intolerance. At levels 6 and 7, the ACL Intolerance Index means are below 50 for all four ways of living.

Note that the Betas, who prefer a private, reflective world in which societal goals (including respect for others) are accepted, are least likely to be described as intolerant, especially at levels 5, 6, and 7. Deltas at levels 1, 2, and 3 are most likely to be viewed as intolerant, but at levels 6 and 7 rank second-lowest to Betas.

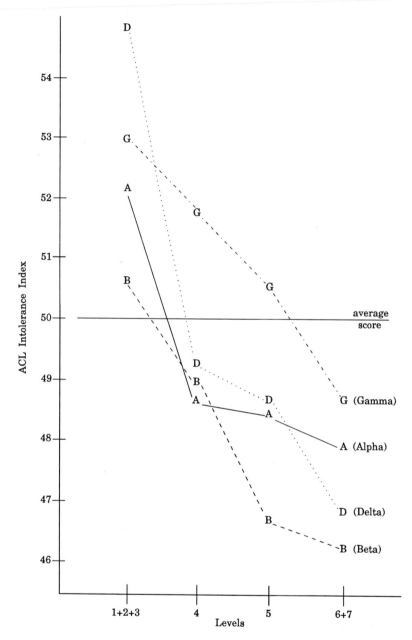

Fig. 3.2. Relationship of lifestyles and level of ego integration, as assessed by the California Psychological Inventory, to scores on the observer-based index of intolerance.

What the figure as a whole suggests is that all persons whose levels of integration are low, and whose functioning is therefore dissatisfying to both self and others, will tend to behave in ways that others perceive as intolerant and distrustful, but that as self-realization improves, observable intolerance diminishes. Intolerance is therefore not a free-standing, isolated personal disposition, but rather an integral part of the way individuals express their feelings of incompleteness and inefficacy.

Case Studies

Finally, to conclude our analysis, we want to present two case illustrations to show concretely how the nomothetic trends reviewed above find expression in the lives of individuals. The highest means for intolerance in Figure 3.2, it will be recalled, were for Deltas at levels 1, 2, or 3. Our first case, therefore, will be a Delta-1 male. His CPI profile is given in Figure 3.3.

At the time of the interview, case Delta-1 was 23 years old, working, like his father, as a truckdriver. He had married his first wife when he was 20, but didn't get along with her at all, and they were divorced within a year. The next year he married his present wife, and they have been together about two years. There are no children from either marriage. Delta-1 has a high school diploma, but never cared much for school. On a list of 77 items for describing an ideal wife, he checked good-looking, physically attractive, sex appeal, neat and clean, and open-minded on questions of morals and ethics, as the five most important. He estimates that he has had sexual relations with around 30 different women.

He describes a typical day as getting up at 6:00 A.M., going to work for eight hours, then coming home and drinking a six-pack of beer before and after supper. Then he watches TV until 9:00 P.M. or so, when he goes to bed. Altogether he thinks he spends around 40 hours a week watching television.

He remembers his father as mean and cold, hitting his children when angry. His mother was overprotective and loved to gossip. His upbringing was strict, based on "an iron hand and a rubber hose."

At age nineteen he was jailed for assault and battery, and for grand theft plus dealing in narcotics. He was also found guilty of carrying a concealed weapon. Since then he has had no further trouble with the law.

He sees himself as a loner, indifferent to others. When asked if he would like children, and what kind of a father he would be, his answer was yes, probably just one, and that he would be a "lousy" father because of his bad temper and impatience. In the interview with his wife, she commented that he would try to be a good parent, but that he probably wouldn't suc-

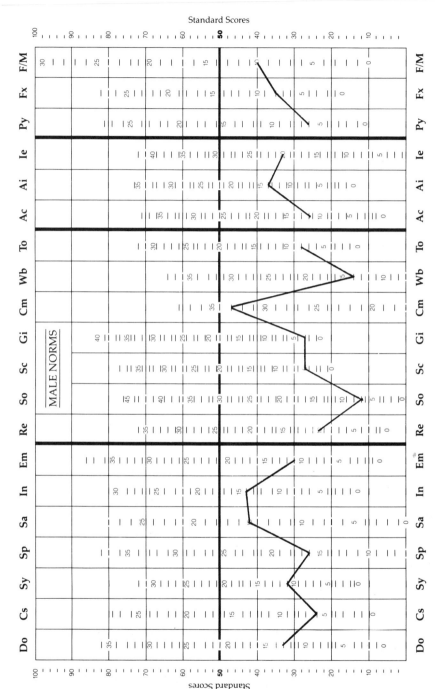

Fig. 3.3. California Psychological Inventory profile form for a Delta-1 male with an ACL Intolerance Index of 11. Reproduced by special permission of the publisher, Consulting Psychologists Press, Inc., Palo Alto, CA 94303, from CPI: *California Psychological Inventory Administrator's Guide*, by Harrison G. Gough, Ph.D., © 1987. Further reproduction is prohibited without the publisher's consent.

ceed. They both feel that their marriage is above average in happiness. His remarks on what is good about it were "knowing that there's someone that cares, who doesn't expect much or try to change me, who accepts me for what I am."

The Delta-1 classification on the CPI indicates a detached, unaffiliative mode of responding to others, along with deep doubts that many of the good things in life will come his way. In the interpersonal domain, he lacks self-confidence and poise and tends to remain on the sidelines. In the realm of values and the internalization of normative guidelines, he is clearly below par, ill-equipped to live by the rules and stay out of trouble. In the achievement domain, he has very little drive for success and poor intellectual skills should he attempt to improve his situation. He is un-insightful about others, poor at coping with change and the unexpected, and traditionally masculine in attitudes and behavior. In this regard, he mentioned in the interview that the only sports he enjoyed were boxing and motorcycling.

From his wife's ACL portrait of him, a score of 11 on the Intolerance Index was obtained. This total converted to a standard score of 83. From what we know about this man, it seems that his intolerance of others originates in his own psychology, not from any ideological, economic, or political basis. We close our discussion of Delta-1 with the character sketch submitted by his life history interviewer.

Mr. Delta-1 is not a happy man. He is alienated from his surroundings, and pays little attention to what goes on around him. He describes himself as a "loner" and asserts that he drinks too much for his own good. Possessed of a "foul temper," he has come to the attention of the police more than once. A lack of self-confidence and purpose in living characterizes this man. Although he is not well educated, he seems to see some aspects of social interaction and the motivations of others with a common sense that is unexpected. He is a hard worker who likes his job because of its variety and absence of routine. He appears vaguely to want to improve his personal situation, but lacks the confidence or knowledge to know where to begin. This liability and his hardened character makes change unlikely. These problems, augmented by his lack of maturity and impulsiveness, presage rocky times ahead.

Case 2, whose CPI profile is shown in Figure 3.4, is a 24-year-old Gamma-2 female of Hispanic background. She graduated from college with a degree in business and now has a good job with a large company. She met her husband when she was in high school and he was a first-year college student. Several years later they began living together and subsequently married. They have no children, and she is not sure that she wants any.

Her husband is also from a minority background, in his case, Chinese. She sees him as competent, but as demanding and critical. She would like

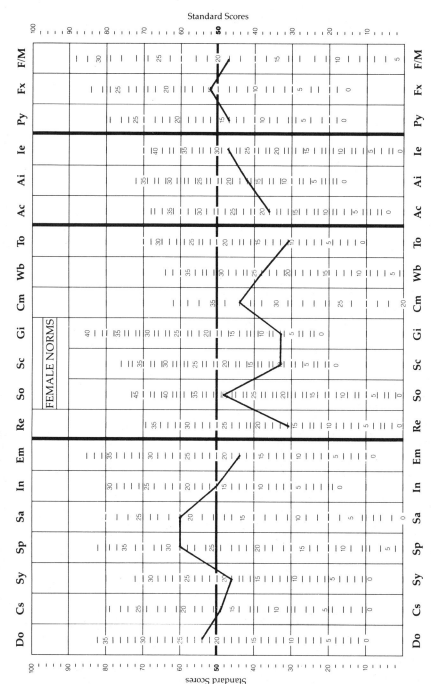

Fig. 3.4. California Psychological Inventory profile form for a Gamma-2 female with an Intolerance Index of 10. Reproduced by special permission of the publisher, Consulting Psychologists Press, Inc., Palo Alto, CA 94303, from CPI: *California Psychological Inventory Administrator's Guide*, by Harrison G. Gough, Ph.D., © 1987. Further reproduction is prohibited without the publisher's consent.

him to be more understanding and spontaneous. He sees their relationship as basically good, but adds that he probably dominates too much and too often tries to impose his will on her. Her mood seems to depend on him—if he is feeling unhappy, she gets depressed; if he is happy, she is happy. To the question, "What would happen if you lost your mate through separation or death?" she replied that she would miss him deeply, and that she doubted whether she would ever remarry. His reply was that it would be a traumatic but not debilitating experience, that he would suffer for a while, but would then look for another person.

Both parents of Gamma-2 were immigrants, and both were eager to do well economically. She described her father as "unbearable to live with," and as being stubborn, too strict, and too bossy. Her mother, on the other hand, was understanding, open-minded, and helpful. The parents did not get along very well and eventually were divorced. Her mother is still important to her, but she rarely sees her father.

While growing up, Gamma-2 was shy at school, associated mostly with children from minority families, and felt that she was discriminated against. In high school she became more self-confident and developed a wider circle of friends. In college she became still more outgoing and expressive, but retained inner doubts about the degree to which she was truly accepted by others.

Her husband's description of her in the ACL produced an Intolerance Index score of 10, equivalent to a standard score of 70. On the CPI profile in Figure 3.4, her lowest score is on the scale for Tolerance. Thus there is evidence both from observer-based and self-report data of a problem in the acceptance of others. But at the same time there are quite positive elements in the profile—for instance, above average scores on Social Presence and Self-acceptance.

Going from left to right on the profile, the small overall elevation on scales in the interpersonal sphere suggests at least moderate feelings of confidence in dealing with others and with social demands. In the realm of interpersonal controls, however, she scores low, in particular on Responsibility, Self-control, interest in creating a good impression (Gi), and Tolerance. The achievement sector is low, particularly for someone with a superior scholastic record in college. An impression is gained of a woman with inner doubts about her own ego strength, but with a veneer of spontaneity and responsiveness that can conceal these worries from non-intimate others. The profile shows the mix of these two facets, and the v.3 scale itself, at level 2, shows that she feels far from being actualized or fulfilled.

We close, as before, with the formulation submitted by her life history interviewer:

Gamma-2 is a vivacious, attractive young woman whose drive and spunk have worked to her advantage in a successful business career. Her strong will, emergent during a difficult adolescence in a racially mixed family, with an over-bearing father and friction-producing sibling rivalries, has left her with a lasting sense that she must always fight for what should be hers.

Perhaps because so much of her energy has gone into perfecting a social persona of competence, she seems on closer scrutiny to be both discontented and shallow. She is only now beginning to wonder if the trappings of success will be satisfying to her in the long run. Also in spite of striving for more spontaneity and adventurousness in her own character, she married a man whose own values of formality and planfulness are dominant in their relationship. Behind her social poise and lively energy, this woman seems to be an emotional, inwardly shy person, whose "dog-eat-dog" world view has kept her from achieving an integrated and resilient sense of self.

Conclusions

We began with an interpersonal observer-based criterion of intolerance, using a cluster of twelve adjectives that functioned in an integrated, consistent way when their inter-item matrix was examined.

Expressed attitudes, including those registered in a shortened form of the F scale, had only moderate relationships to this criterion; however, personal dispositions, in particular those concerned with the internalization of social values, showed significant linkages. Specifically, persons with less conflicted and more pronormative ego controls were seen by others as less prejudiced than their counterparts. Another factor of importance was the self-perceived level of integration. Persons with a good sense of self-realization were seen as more tolerant and fair-minded than those with feelings of incompleteness or unfulfillment.

Finally, in two case vignettes, it was clear that the way in which sociological, psychological, and other factors come together in individuals manifesting different levels of tolerance or intolerance is always distinct and psychologically meaningful. Nomothetic analysis of general trends and relationships is vital, but by itself cannot give a complete picture of how individuals function.

4

Age and Cohort Differences in American Racial Attitudes: The Generational Replacement Hypothesis Revisited

Sue Dowden and John P. Robinson

> There could be no doubt that the races were moving rapidly toward equality and desegregation by 1962. . . . The change had been so rapid, and caste and racism so debilitated, that I venture to predict the end of all formal segregation and discrimination within a decade, and the decline of informal segregation and discrimination so that it would be a mere shadow in two decades.
>
> Arnold Rose, "Proscript Twenty Years Later," in the Twentieth Anniversary Edition of Gunnar Myrdal's *An American Dilemma* (1964)

Since the early civil rights movement, social scientists have generally not been surprised by the continued improvement in the climate of American racial attitudes. This is largely based on the empirical association of racial attitudes with two important demographic characteristics: education and age. Tolerance has not only been more prevalent among respondents with higher levels of education but also with those who are younger.

Thus, as older and less well educated generations die off, their replacement by younger, better educated and more tolerant cohorts should produce a more racially tolerant society. The process could be further ac-

The data utilized in this chapter were made available in part by the Inter-University Consortium for Political and Social Research, the National Opinion Research Center, the Roper Public Opinion Research Center, and the University of Maryland Survey Research Center. Neither the collector(s) of the original data nor the respective institutions bear any responsibility for the analyses or interpretations presented here.

celerated by succeeding generations being socialized into a more tolerant environment.

A clear example of the role of the two factors two decades ago was presented by Angus Campbell (1971), who noted that education level was the most significant predictor of differences in attitudes toward public accommodation rights (Fig. 4.1). Campbell also noted that a breakdown by age groups of attitudes toward the principle of open housing showed steadily increasing percentages of approval among the younger segments of the population (Fig. 4.2). He concluded that such positive trends would in all likelihood continue: "If we knew that these attitudes [of the younger, more educated] would in due course regress to the popular mode, we would not attach any great importance to them, but since our evidence demonstrates that they do not, we must conclude that the infusion of these young people into the bloodstream of American society will have significant results" (Campbell 1971: 161).

The relationship between the values, attitudes, and behavior of generations is closely tied. The older generation are the carriers of existing values and norms in the society, acting as socializing agents to the younger generation. But conflict and tension between the generations arise as young adults assert their independence and respond to other socializing agents, such as their own peers, schools, and, increasingly, the mass media.

Mildred Schwartz's (1967) analysis of racial attitudes during the 1960's resulted in predictions similar to Campbell's. She describes the influence of education and the effect of increased tolerance among younger adults as follows:

All significant population groups are caught up in the same general move, although not necessarily to the same extent. Thus, in each generation, while the older are less tolerant than the younger, the former are more tolerant than their aged peers in the preceding generation. Part of this change is due to education. The passing of older, less tolerant individuals and their replacement by the younger, better educated ones helps account for the incidence of greater tolerance in the population generally. At the same time, each new generation becomes socialized into a more tolerant climate. (Schwartz 1967: 129)

Greater tolerance toward minority groups was one expression of the effect of socialization from the older cohort becoming more extreme in the next generation. M. Kent Jennings and Richard Niemi (1981), using data from a 1960's panel study of students and their parents, found young adults to be more liberal than their parents on most measures of public policy. The relationship between youth and more liberal racial attitudes was more apparent among whites: "Among whites, however, the young were more in favor of school integration, much more favorable when the

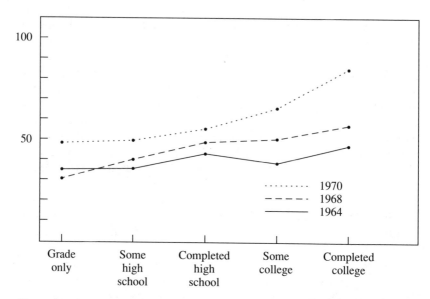

Fig. 4.1. Changes in support of public accommodation rights among whites, by education. From Campbell 1971.

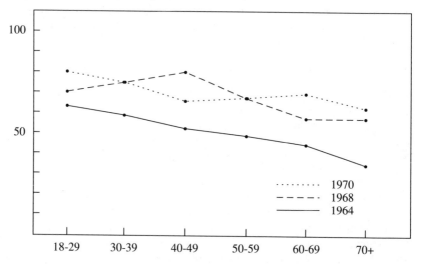

Fig. 4.2. Changes in attitudes of whites toward the principle of open housing, by age. From Campbell 1971.

subject of busing was introduced, and a full step over the 'minority help' scale in the direction of favoring government assistance" (Jennings and Niemi 1981: 322).

Two Models and Hypotheses

Two general models, one based on the life-cycle process and the other on generational replacement, can be seen to underlie expectations that younger whites will be more accepting of changes aimed at equality for blacks. It should also lead us to expect attempts to resolve the dilemmas and contradictions between belief in the principle of racial equality and actual daily behaviors.

The life-cycle model posits that individuals go through a series of stages of life closely associated with age, and that individuals in each distinct life stage are more like each other than to those at different life stages. According to this model, the young adult stage of life is generally a period of more openness to different experiences and of greater willingness to accept new ideas.

Generational differences are also explained by the force of different social contexts operating on each generation. While each generation may experience the same social or historical forces, the experience is different for each succeeding age group. Thus, the impact of World War II was certainly different for those of military age than for their parents. More recent generations would be more affected by school integration, and affected in different ways, than their parents.

A further reason for expecting greater tolerance on the part of younger adults over the past 20–30 years has to do with greater degrees of interracial contact. With strong societal pressures for integrated schools, neighborhoods and workplaces, we should expect increasing social contact on a day-to-day basis. Even though contact should have increased for all age groups, we may expect the youngest adults to report more contact than older age groups because of integrative schooling. In general, the literature on interpersonal contact suggests that people who have more interpersonal contact with a group will have more tolerant attitudes toward members of that group.

In this analysis, changes in three aspects of American social attitudes since the 1960's will be examined: social/interactional, legal/institutional, and racial stereotyping.

1. *Social/Interactional Attitudes.* This aspect encompasses measures of interpersonal contact, particularly as facilitated by institutional changes (school busing, open housing). Measures of this aspect include whether

one has black friends and how one evaluates contact with blacks, as well as interracial contact in school, at work, and in social situations.

2. *Legal/Institutional Attitudes.* The legal remedies available to blacks were the first and necessary steps to eliminate the gulf between the belief in the principle of racial equality and the existing "social reality." Several survey questions are available to examine changing attitudes toward legal and institutional changes over the past forty years. These deal with interracial marriage, open housing, the "right" of whites to keep blacks out of their neighborhoods, and segregation in private clubs. In this analysis, questions that deal with government policy or implementation, such as affirmative action, quotas, or busing, have not been included.

3. *Stereotypes.* The main set of indicators of this dimension assesses perceptions of the societal causes of black educational and employment disadvantages—in particular whether the existing disparities are caused by external societal forces or by genetic or motivational differences.

We first examine the extent of increased interracial contact over the past two decades, with special attention to age and cohort differences in such contact. We then repeat these analyses with attitudes and stereotypes as the dependent variables.

Our main attention in these analyses is to the question of whether there is evidence of continued greater racial tolerance being expressed by the youngest adults—namely, those aged 18–25. Do they continue to express responses to contact, attitude, and stereotype questions that are more tolerant on these matters? Or do we find evidence of equal or less tolerance— evidence that would suggest that the continued improvement in racial attitudes has reached a plateau or is in danger of turning around.

However, we first examine evidence on the extent of interracial contact. As used in this chapter, contact is self-reported, or perceived by respondents. Two dimensions of contact are considered: involuntary contact—the presence of blacks or members of other races in neighborhoods, schools, or the workplace—and more voluntary contact—attending integrated churches, social interaction such as eating together, playing games, having conversation, and so on.

Data Sources

The most comprehensive data set on racial attitudes available for the past twenty years is the General Social Survey (GSS). Conducted by the National Opinion Research Center (NORC) of the University of Chicago and the Roper Center, this unique series of data offers a national sample of over 1,000 adults for every year since 1972. In 1972, block quota sampling was used to select the sample; since that first year, full probability samples have been used. Samples are of the English-speaking population 18 years of age or older, living in noninstitutional housing in the continental United States (GSS Codebook 1990).

Interviews are conducted in person by the field staff of NORC. Many of the questions regarding racial attitudes and perceptions have been asked since 1972; others have been repeated every other year, or more irregularly. To assure sufficient sample sizes, particularly among subgroups such as young adults, the data have been grouped into four time periods: 1972–74, 1975–79, 1980–84, and 1985–88. For this analysis, only the responses of white respondents are examined.

A second national data set, *Monitoring the Future* (MTF), focuses on high school seniors. The study has been conducted in the spring of each year since 1975, replicating the same questions throughout the thirteen-year time span. Using a multistage technique, researchers at the University of Michigan collecting data each spring in approximately 125 public and private schools by self-administered questionnaires (Bachman et al. 1986: 3).

Further data came from two statewide telephone surveys conducted by the University of Maryland Survey Research Center. The Maryland data were collected in 1982 and 1986 under the sponsorship of the Governor's Task Force on Violence and Extremism. Telephone households were chosen by the random-digit-dial (RDD) procedure of sampling; respondents within the household were selected by a rotating procedure based on the number of adults aged 18 or older in the household. The 1986 study included an oversampling (N = 319) of young adults aged 18–25.

Results

Contact with Blacks

Table 4.1 shows the proportions of white respondents by age groups across our four GSS time periods who said that blacks lived in their neighborhood. Starting in the late 1970's, the youngest age group (18–25) were more likely to report blacks living in their neighborhood than the total sample. By the late 1980's, the proportion of this age group reporting living in integrated neighborhoods was 9 percentage points higher than the total sample and at least 6 percentage points higher than that in any other age group.

In the early 1970's, the same levels of integrated neighborhoods were reported by this youngest age group as by the next older age group (26 to 35), but they lagged behind the middle age group aged 36 to 45, 44 percent of whom reported blacks living in their neighborhoods. By the late 1980's, however, the trend had reversed: a majority (54 percent) of

TABLE 4.1
Age Differences in Involuntary Contact and Social Interaction

	1972–74	1975–79	1980–84	1985–88	1972–88 % increase (decrease)
Blacks in neighborhood					
18–25	38%	44%	50%	54%	16*
26–35	38	42	46	48	10*
36–45	44	41	48	46	2
46–55	35	43	48	45	10*
56–65	35	36	42	45	10*
66+	32	35	35	37	5*
Total	37%	40%	44%	45%	8*
N	3,797	5,154	5,071	4,809	
Blacks living close to you (if reported in neighborhood)					
18–25	72%	74%	71%	78%	6
26–35	74	70	71	74	0
36–45	68	70	75	73	5
46–55	67	71	69	72	5
56–65	71	72	69	69	(2)
66+	74	69	70	69	(5)
Total	71%	71%	71%	73%	2
N	1,436	2,117	2,321	2,896	
Blacks attend same church					
18–25	—	32%	40%	42%	10*
26–35	—	32	40	43	11*
36–45	—	40	44	43	3
46–55	—	36	43	40	4
56–65	—	31	39	44	13*
66+	—	32	32	37	5
Total		34%	43%	42%	8*
N		1,103	3,331	2,780	
Blacks home to dinner					
18–25	27%	32%	32%	35%	8*
26–35	26	30	34	34	8*
36–45	24	26	30	33	9*
46–55	22	20	29	29	7*
56–65	15	17	19	18	3
66+	10	8	14	11	1
Total	21%	23%	27%	27%	6*
N	2,582	2,675	3,849	3,327	

SOURCE: General Social Survey, 1972–1990.
*Difference of proportions between 1972–74 and 1985–88 statistically significant at $p > .05$.

the youngest age group reported blacks in their neighborhoods, 6 points more than the next older, 8 points higher than the middle age cohort, and seventeen points higher than the oldest age group.

Table 4.1 next shows the pattern of responses with respect to whether those reporting blacks in their neighborhood perceive these blacks as "living close" to them. The pattern of perceived closeness was different than the perception of blacks in the neighborhood. First, the proportions in the general population remained the same, all being in the low 70 percent range over the four time periods. The pattern across the age groups, however, was more uneven; by the late 1980's, the youngest age group was again more likely than the next older age group (26–35) and the oldest age groups (those over 55) to perceive blacks as living close to them.

Somewhat similar patterns were found for questions on voluntary contacts. When the question of interracial church attendance was first asked in the 1975 GSS, the middle age group (36–45) were more likely to attend integrated churches. While the proportion attending integrated churches in the general population increased (8 percentage points), the proportion in this middle age bracket remained almost the same (increasing 3 percentage points). However, the two youngest age cohorts (18–35) dramatically increased their reports of attendance at integrated churches, so that by the late 1980's there were almost equal proportions in each age group reporting participation in integrated churches.

As shown at the bottom of Table 4.1, the pattern for those who had invited a black home to dinner was somewhat different. Since 1972 the youngest age group (18–25) has been equal or slightly more likely than older cohorts to report a black dinner guest. Significant increases between the early 1970's and late 1980's in the proportions reporting this type of activity were seen in each of the age groups between 18 and 56.

Between 1972 to 1988, then, youngest adults showed at least as much (if not more) increase in perceptions of neighborhood integration, closeness, and interaction as other age groups. By the late 1980's, in fact, they were the only age group in which a majority reported living in integrated neighborhoods.

In the measures of more voluntary contact, there were virtually no differences between the age groups, with the exception of the most senior cohorts.

Thus, across this sixteen-year period, the youngest age group had passed their elders in percentages perceiving physical proximity in neighborhoods and had increased reports of more voluntary contact and interaction to equal proportions of that reported by the older respondents.

Even larger age differences are found in the extent of contact in schools. Self-reports of attendance at integrated high schools for all age groups in

TABLE 4.2

Age Differences in Interracial Contact, Maryland

(whites with at least some high school)

	18–25 (N = 319)	26–35 (N = 223)	36–45 (N = 191)	46–55 (N = 118)	56–65 (N = 98)	66+ (N = 93)	Change
"Was the high school you attended integrated or all one race?"							
All one race	8%	13%	25%	58%	61%	63%	
Integrated	92	87	75	42	39	34	+58%
Don't remember				1		2	
Total	100%	100%	100%	100%	100%	100%	
"Have you done anything social with blacks, like going to the movies, to a sports event, or visiting each others homes?"							
Yes	86%	86%	81%	77%	76%	50%	+36%
No	14	14	19	23	24	50	
Total	100%	100%	100%	100%	100%	100%	

SOURCE: Survey Research Center, University of Maryland at College Park, 1986 survey for the Governor's Task Force on Violence and Extremism.

any given period were not available in the national surveys reviewed in this research.[1] However, surrogate data were available from a 1986 statewide study in Maryland that included a question about the racial composition of the high schools attended by respondents, allowing a cross-sectional comparison for different age groups (Table 4.2).

Among the youngest age group in Table 4.2, those just completing high school in the early to mid 1980's, 92 percent reported attending an integrated high school. The effect of the 1954 Supreme Court decision is clearly seen among older age groups. Of those under 45 at the time of the study, the majority (at least 75 percent) had attended an integrated high school. However, among those older whites who were of high school age prior to the abolition of "separate but equal," substantial majorities (at least 58 percent) had gone to high school only with whites.

Data from this same survey show a similar age pattern in social interaction as seen in the national data set during the late 1980's. As shown in the second part of Table 4.2, the youngest adult age group (aged 18–25 in the Maryland data) were no more likely than the next two older age groups to interact socially with blacks. Compared to the 46- to 55-year-old cohort, however, the difference in reported interaction was statistically significant ($p < .05$).

Table 4.1 indicated that in the late 1980's the youngest age group (18–25) were more likely to report physical proximity to blacks as measured

[1] The General Social Survey asked this question of blacks in 1982. A search of the Roper archives, however, failed to locate a similar question of whites.

by living in integrated neighborhoods, and that they were more likely to perceive those blacks in their neighborhood as physically close. However, if they were churchgoers, they were not more likely to attend integrated churches; nor were they significantly more likely to interact socially with blacks than were older age groups (up to age 55).

The number of young adults available in these national samples remains small. For a closer look at young adults, we turn to the national samples of high school seniors.

Data collected annually since 1976 in the *Monitoring the Future* project from a national sample of high school seniors allow a more in-depth look at the youngest segment of these young adults. Questions measuring availability of contact included neighborhoods, schools, and workplaces; other dimensions of contact were also measured, including quality and frequency of contact.

While some "white flight" did take place, increased physical proximity in the schools was evident in the reports of white students in these samples (Table 4.3). By 1986, 83 percent reported that students of other races had been in their high schools; this proportion had increased by 5 percentage points in high schools since 1976. The point of largest increase had been in elementary schools for these students: 45 percent in 1976 reporting "other race" students in their elementary schools, whereas in 1986 the proportion who remembered their elementary schools as being integrated had increased by 18 percentage points to 63 percent.

Similar results were also evident for contact in the workplace in Table 4.3. By 1986 a majority of this sample of high school seniors (56 percent of those for whom the question of working was applicable) reported working at integrated workplaces, an increase of 12 points over the ten-year period. Given the age of these respondents, these results most likely reflected employment in entry-level positions or service industries, such as fast food restaurants.

TABLE 4.3

Trends in Integration Among White High School Seniors, 1976–1986

	% Reporting integration		
	1976	1986	% Change
In elementary school	45%	63%	+18*
In high school	78	83	+5*
In workplace	44	56	+12*
In neighborhood	35	50	+15*

SOURCE: Bachman et al. 1976–86.
*Differences of proportions between 1976 and 1986 statistically significant at $p > .05$.

TABLE 4.4

Trends of Perceptions of Knowing Blacks and Other Races
Among White High School Seniors, 1976–1986

	% Reporting "getting to know other races a little, some, or a lot"		
	1976	1986	%Change
In school	79%	87%	+8*
On a job	60	72	+12*
On sports teams	54	60	+6*
In clubs	44	53	+9*
In neighborhood	38	52	+14*
In church	31	41	+10*
Doing things like having a conversation, eating together, playing sports	86	90	+4*

SOURCE: Bachman et al. 1976–86.
*Differences of proportions between 1976 and 1986 statistically significant at $p > .05$.

Additional evidence that the proportion of young adults who perceived their neighborhoods as increasingly integrated was also available in this study. Over the ten-year period from 1976 to 1986, the number of white students who reported that their neighborhoods included "other races" increased by 15 percentage points. Similar to the results reported in the General Social Survey, by 1986 50 percent of these students reported living in integrated neighborhoods, even if other races were only a small minority.

The indicators of contact available from these yearly national samples of high school seniors also allow us to examine how well white students feel they "get to know" people of other races in various situations. First, it is apparent from the data in Table 4.2 that of all the areas mentioned, the school remained the point of most opportunity for contact.

In Table 4.4, several potential places for getting to know other races are listed. In each situation mentioned, the proportions of those who reported "getting to know" other races had increased over the ten-year period. The largest increases were evident in the neighborhood (+14 percent) and on the job (+12 percent). The smallest increase, only 6 percentage points, involved contact with other races on sports teams. Among the list of situations offered, fewer young people felt the neighborhoods and churches were the places they went to know other races.

The frequency of contact with the other races in social interaction reported by these young adults also increased. Those who reported "some" or "a lot" of contact with other races increased by 9 percentage points over the ten-year period. This was consistent with the increase seen earlier in the General Social Survey for the youngest age group (a 10 percentage point increase in those attending integrated churches and an 8 percentage point increase in those inviting a black home to dinner).

Institutional Racial Attitudes

Changes among white respondents in support for interracial marriage, for open housing laws, and for other institutional changes are clearly seen in Table 4.5.

However, this move toward more tolerance is true of the white population as a whole. The youngest age group (18–25) showed the smallest increases between 1972 and 1988 in their support for the legal principles supporting interracial marriage and open housing (Table 4.5). In contrast, the older age groups showed double-digit increases over this time period in support for these legal principles. Where the youngest age group did show some significant increases (against keeping blacks out of neighborhoods and for working to change the rule of a restricted social club), their rates of change were usually less than half as large as those of older age groups.

These smaller rates of increase among this youngest age group do not support the hypothesis that demographic replacement will continue to produce increasing proportions of tolerant attitudes in the general population. The increase among young adults is dramatically lower, averaging an increase of only about 5 percentage points, compared to 16 percentage points among older age groups. This lack of change cannot be explained solely as a "ceiling effect," since the proportions of the young adults supporting open housing and open social clubs remained in the 60–70 percent range.

Racial Stereotypes

Much the same picture emerges in the racial stereotype questions examined in Table 4.6. It can be seen that between the late 1970's and late 1980's, the youngest age group show very small changes in assessments of the reasons for the disadvantaged position of blacks. In contrast, most of the older age groups became more positive; most of the positive change in the general population could be attributed to middle age cohorts (aged 35 to 55).

Responses to these stereotyping questions in the 1986 statewide Maryland survey also show this reversal among the youngest age group more clearly. As shown in Table 4.7, 18–25 year-old Marylanders were less likely in 1986 to ascribe external reasons and more likely to ascribe internal characteristics of blacks in explaining black conditions in society relative to older age groups. Thus, on the question ascribing blacks' societal conditions to their "inborn abilities," 15 percent of young adults felt this to be a reason for lower black achievement in jobs, income, and housing, compared to 11 percent of those aged 26 to 55.

TABLE 4.5

Age Differences in Racial Attitudes in the General White Population 1972–1988

	1972–74	1975–79	1980–84	1985–88	1972–88 Diff. in % points
Laws against interracial marriage: (% saying no)					
18–25	82%	86%	84%	86%	+4
26–35	73	81	83	85	+12★
36–45	67	69	77	84	+17★
46–55	59	64	67	71	+12★
56–65	53	50	54	58	+5
66+	35	41	43	49	+14★
Total	61%	65%	67%	71%	+10★
Right to keep blacks out of neighborhood: (% disagreeing)					
18–25	75%	74%	80%	83%	+8★
26–35	68	66	78	84	+16★
36–45	63	60	74	81	+18★
46–55	56	55	71	71	+15★
56–65	47	51	62	64	+17★
66+	43	45	54	59	+16★
Total	56%	58%	68%	73%	+17★
Open housing laws: (% "homeowner cannot refuse")					
18–25	57%	52%	60%	60%	+3
26–35	39	47	57	61	+22★
36–45	35	34	47	57	+22★
46–55	22	28	36	43	+21★
56–65	26	23	31	36	+10★
66+	23	23	27	35	+12★
Total	34%	35%	44%	49%	+15★
Rules of social clubs: (% saying work to change)					
18–25	—	64%	—	70%	+6
26–35	—	53	—	66	+13★
36–45	—	39	—	66	+27★
46–55	—	36	—	53	+17★
56–65	—	31	—	46	+15★
66+	—	24	—	42	+18★
Total	na	42%	na	58%	+16★

SOURCE: National Opinion Research Center 1972–88.
★Differences of proportions between 1972–74 or 1975–79 and 1985–88 statistically significant at $p > .05$.

TABLE 4.6

Age Differences in Racial Stereotypes in the General Population, 1972–1988

	1972–74	1975–79	1980–84	1985–88	1972–88 Difference in % pts
Differences in black/white jobs, income, housing owing to discrimination (% saying yes)					
18–25		51%		51%	0
26–35		48		47	−1
36–45		38		44	+6★
46–55		33		40	+7★
56–65		31		42	+11★
66+		45		44	−1
Total		39%		43%	+4★
. . . lack of educational opportunity (% saying yes)					
18–25		53%		53%	0
26–35		54		55	+1
36–45		50		56	+6★
46–55		45		53	+8★
56–65		50		51	+1
66+		52		51	−1
Total		49%		52%	+3★
. . . inborn ability (% saying no)					
18–25		85%		86%	+1
26–35		88		89	+1
36–45		79		86	+7★
46–55		72		77	+5
56–65		61		70	+9★
66+		49		62	+13★
Total		76%		80%	+4★
. . . lack of motivation (% saying no)					
18–25		46%		50%	+4
26–35		42		47	+5
36–45		32		44	+12★
46–55		30		41	+11★
56–65		28		32	+4
66+		24		28	+4
Total		38%		44%	+6★
Temperature on NES "feeling thermometer" (mean)					
17–25	61	54	63	59	−2
26–35	60	56	62	57	−3
36–45	62	59	63	59	−3
46–55	64	60	61	58	−6★
56–65	62	59	61	57	−5
66+	63	59	60	56	−7★
Total	62	58	62	58	−4★

★Difference of proportions between 1972–74 or 1975–79 and 1985–88 statistically significant at $p > .05$.

TABLE 4.7

Age Differences in Racial Stereotyping in the General Population in Maryland, 1986

Differences between blacks/white income, jobs, housing owing to

discrimination (% saying yes)		lack of motivation (% saying no)	
18–25	41%	18–25	46%
26–35	43	26–35	52
36–45	41	36–45	51
46–55	32	46–55	36
56–65	32	56–65	30
66+	34	66+	32
Total	39%	Total	39%
. . . lack of educational opportunity (% saying yes)		Temperature on NES "feeling thermometer" (mean)	
18–25	44%	18–25	66
26–35	53	26–35	68
36–45	49	36–45	65
46–55	46	46–55	66
56–65	41	56–65	72
66+	47	66+	65
Total	44%	Total	67
. . . inborn ability (% saying no)			
18–25	85%		
26–35	89		
36–45	90		
46–55	89		
56–65	77		
66+	68		
Total	79%		

SOURCE: Survey Research Center, University of Maryland, 1986.

High School Seniors

The older age groups represented in the GSS and the Maryland analyses would have been young adults or of early middle age during the height of the civil rights protests of the 1960's. This leads one to ask whether the falling proportions of tolerance among young adults might be explained by a perceived lack of personal relevance or importance of the issues among today's youth.

The issue of the personal relevance of societal treatment of minorities has also been asked in the *Monitoring the Future* (MTF) project of Bachman et al. (1986). As shown in Table 4.8, the proportions of high school seniors who felt that unfair treatment of minorities should be their concern decreased by 3 percentage points between 1976 and 1986.

This survey also shows a lack of change among these young people across time with respect to several other racial attitudes. By 1986 the white high school seniors sampled were no more likely to indicate that having

TABLE 4.8

Differences in Racial Attitudes Among White School Seniors, 1976–1986

	1976 (N = 2,300)	1986 (N = 2,300)	% Increase (decrease)
Unfair treatment of minorities not my concern (% disagreeing)	71%	68%	(3*)
How would you feel about . . . (% "desirable")			
Having close personal friends of another race	32	33	1
Having job with supervisor of different race	16	18	2*
Having family of different race move next door	25	24	(1)
(Future) children's friends:			
some of other races	38	35	(3*)
Jobs:			
some employees of different race	26	25	(1)
most employees of different race	6	6	0
Neighborhood:			
Neighbors:			
some different race	22	20	(2)
most different race	4	4	0
Children:			
some different race	29	28	(1)
all different race	4	4	0
Those saying all their own race "desirable"			
(Future) children's friends:			
all your race	18	21	3*
Jobs:			
employees all your race	27	27	0
Neighborhood:			
Neighbors: all your race	39	38	(1)
Children: all your race	34	36	2

SOURCE: Bachman et al. *Monitoring the Future* 1976, 1986.
*Difference of proportions between 1976 and 1986 statistically significant at $p > .05$.

friends, neighbors, or co-workers of a different race was "desirable" than the group sampled ten years earlier (Table 4.8). With regard to some items—such as the ones dealing with friends for (possible) future children or neighbors, the proportions of white students who preferred that these be all of their own race increased by 2 to 3 percentage points, a small but statistically significant increase given the large sample sizes. Nevertheless, the overall pattern in these reports of young people in Table 4.8 was of very little, if any, change in the desire for increased contact or interaction with other races.

Summary and Conclusions

Between 1972 and 1988, increased proportions of the American adult white population did support principles of racial equality, as evidenced by the four racial questions (about interracial marriage, open housing, the right to keep blacks out of neighborhoods, and restricted membership of private social clubs) repeated in the General Social Survey. However, less change was evident over this period on measures relating to stereotypes of blacks as a group. Changes in the results of GSS questions about the reasons for blacks' position in society (educational opportunities, discrimination by society, genetic differences, and motivation or willpower) showed only an average increase of 4 percentage points between 1977 and 1988, compared to an average of 10 percentage points over the same time period in support of principles of legal and institutional equality.

Lower rates of increased support for these principles of equality were found among young adults (aged 18–25). This was also the group in which both involuntary and voluntary association with blacks had increased more over time than among older cohorts in the GSS data. Evidence from the annual *Monitoring the Future* studies of high school seniors also showed increases in those attending integrated schools, those employed in integrated workplaces, and those living in integrated neighborhoods in this age cohort. There was also a slight increase in those reporting social interaction with blacks.

Table 4.9 summarizes the percentage point differences for the two age groups for the four attitudinal questions concerning legal rights. These differences clearly show that young adults have contributed very little to

TABLE 4.9

Summary of Changes in Whites' Racial Attitudes and Stereotypes Nationwide, 1972–1988
(% differences)

	White population overall	18–25 age group	26+ age group
Attribution of differences to:			
Discrimination (those saying yes)	+4	0	+4
Educational opportunities (those saying yes)	+3	0	+5
Inborn abilities (those saying no)	+4	+1	+6
Lack of motivation (those saying no)	+6	+4	+7
Temperature on NES "feeling thermometer" (1972–88)	−4	−3	−5
Attitudes on legal equality:			
Opposing laws against interracial marriage	+10	+4	+12*
Opposing right to keep blacks out of neighborhood	+17	+8	+16*
Supporting open housing laws	+15	+3	+18*
Supporting change in the rules of social clubs	+16	+8	+18*

*Differences of proportions statistically significant at $p > .05$.

the overall increased proportions supporting racial equality. Table 4.9 shows that young adults have also lagged behind older adults in changes in views about the reasons for blacks' less favorable position in society.

Two decades after optimistic predictions of increased racial tolerance because of generational replacement, then, young adults lag behind older individuals in their increased support of racial equality. The expectation that young adults will be the forerunners of racial tolerance has been seriously called into question.

Research should continue to look at change over time for different age groups, seeking to identify whether the trends seen in these studies apply to other time periods and other dimensions of racial attitudes. One of the questions that must be examined is the role of contact—both involuntary and social interaction—in racial attitudes. What role, if any, did contact have in the past, and what role, if any, does it play in current racial attitudes?

5

Ethnic Stereotyping:
A Black-White Comparison

Lee Sigelman, James W. Shockey,
and Carol K. Sigelman

Stereotypes, which Walter Lippmann (1922) called "pictures in the head," and which social scientists ever since have defined (though often with additional stipulations) as beliefs about the personal traits of social groups (Ashmore and Del Boca 1981), both fuel and reflect prejudiced attitudes and discriminatory behavior. Research on stereotyping has, for the most part, focused on the beliefs members of a dominant group hold about various minority groups. As discussed in earlier chapters, for example, Katz and Braly (1933) asked Princeton students to select traits typical of several national and ethnic groups from a list, launching a stream of research using the same method and, in some cases, even the same Princeton subject population to trace changes in stereotypes over time (e.g., Karlins, Coffman, and Walters 1969; see also Brigham 1971; Dovidio and Gaertner 1986; John 1990).

Some researchers have extended the study of racial, ethnic, and religious stereotypes by examining how members of majority and minority groups view themselves and one another (e.g., Jackman and Senter 1983; Smedley and Bayton 1978; Triandis et al. 1982). Conspicuously lacking, however, has been attention to minority-group perceptions of other minority groups—an oversight that is unfortunate for several reasons. Determining how members of a particular minority group view other minority groups can greatly expand our knowledge of the social attitudes of the minority group in question. It can also clarify whether there are common dynamics of stereotyping that apply to members of both minority and majority groups. And it can shed light on the extent to which various minority groups can be expected to perceive common cultural and political interests and to form a true "rainbow coalition"—an important consideration in a society where members of one minority group often find themselves living and working alongside members of others.

In this chapter, we seek to determine how positively or negatively black Americans view two other minority groups, Hispanics and Jews, relative to white Americans' views of the same groups.[1] Concerns about black anti-Semitism have grown in recent years, fueled by controversial remarks by the Black Muslim Minister Louis Farrakhan and the presidential aspirant Jesse Jackson. Black-Hispanic relations have also shown signs of strain because the two groups have increasingly found themselves locked in political or economic competition with each other. Even so, little is known about blacks' views of either Hispanics or Jews. Rather, research on racial and ethnic attitudes, following Gunnar Myrdal's (1944) lead, has focused on "what goes on in the minds of white Americans," to the detriment of our understanding of the racial and ethnic attitudes of blacks and other minority groups.

Alternative Perspectives on Black-White Differences in Stereotyping

Stereotypes of Hispanics and Jews, though deeply rooted in the United States, seem to have become less negative over the years (see, e.g., Dworkin and Eckberg 1986; Lipset 1987). In an early study in a Texas border town, Ozzie Simmons (1961) determined that Mexican Americans were viewed by Anglos as unclean, drunken, criminal, deceitful, childlike, and inferior. However, more recent studies have uncovered a mixture of positive and negative stereotypes, with Hispanics being characterized as tradition-loving, talkative, family-oriented, friendly, and hardworking, but also as ignorant, poor, pugnacious, and lazy (Fairchild and Cozens 1981; Guichard and Connolly 1977; Marin 1984; Triandis et al. 1982). Although some researchers find few signs of stigmatization (e.g., Triandis et al. 1982), and some emphasize that few stereotypes of Hispanics are endorsed uniformly by most Anglos (Marin 1984), Hispanics do continue to experience relatively low socioeconomic status and might, like blacks (see, e.g., Jackman and Senter 1983), be subjected to class-based stereotypes, as

---

[1] *Hispanic* and *Spanish American* are, of course, broad terms that encompass an array of subgroups and, because these subgroups arc clustered in various parts of the country, assume different meanings in different regions. Most southwesterners, for example, presumably associate these terms with Mexican Americans, most Floridians with Cuban Americans, and most New Yorkers with Puerto Ricans. While it would have been preferable to have a more precise stimulus concept than "Spanish American," this is the term employed in the Louis Harris survey upon which our analyses are based.

well as to lingering ethnic stereotypes. Moreover, many Hispanics continue to believe that they are perceived very negatively (Casas, Ponterotto, and Sweeney 1987).

White Christians' stereotypes of Jews are now more positive than negative. According to the most common positive stereotypes, Jews are hardworking, intelligent, deeply religious, and friendly (Glock, et al. 1975; Martire and Clark 1982; Quinley and Glock 1979; Wuthnow 1982). However, Jews are still widely perceived as inordinately powerful in business and industry, clannish, ambitious, rich, and, at least in the eyes of a minority, greedy, unethical, and selfish (Glock et al. 1975; Martire and Clark 1982).

What about *blacks'* stereotypes of Hispanics and Jews? Table 5.1 lays out several alternative sets of expectations about black–white differences in stereotypes of Hispanics and Jews.

Cultural Sharing

The starting point for the cultural sharing perspective is that blacks and whites, as members of a single overarching culture, hold many of the same general cultural beliefs. This is not, of course, to assume that there are no important subcultural differences between blacks and whites, for that is simply not the case. But to the extent that a culture has any coherence, its members are bound to share numerous images and perceptions, including, perhaps, common stereotypes of various racial and ethnic groups. Consistent with this idea, research on stereotyping reveals widespread agreement among members of different social groups about the traits of other groups (Brigham 1971). Indeed, in a recent national survey, Asian Americans and Hispanic Americans expressed many of the same stereotyped perceptions of blacks that are widespread among Anglos (Louis Harris and Associates 1989), indicating that the way blacks are viewed may not depend upon one's racial or ethnic vantage point. This same idea constitutes the cultural sharing perspective, which anticipates no black–white differences in stereotypes of Hispanics and Jews.

Minority Solidarity

A second possibility is that blacks, who over the course of U.S. history have grown all too familiar with discrimination, feel an overriding kinship with other groups that are targets of discrimination (see Sniderman, Piazza, Finifter, and Tetlock 1989 for evidence at least partially supportive of this view). It follows from this perspective that blacks should be intensely aware of the pernicious effects of negative group stereotypes and should be sympathetically predisposed toward other groups that have been

TABLE 5.1

Expectations About Black and Whites' Ethnic Stereotypes

	Negative stereotypes of	
Perspective	Hispanics	Jews
Cultural sharing	B = W	B = W
Minority solidarity	B < W	B < W
Racial conflict	B > W	B > W
Vertical conflict	B < W	B > W
Horizontal conflict	B > W	B < W

KEY: B = W signifies that blacks' negative stereotypes of the group in question are expected to be indistinguishable from those of whites; B < W signifies that blacks' negative stereotypes of the group in question are expected to be less pronounced than those of whites; and B > W signifies that blacks' negative stereotypes of the group in question are expected to be more pronounced than those of whites.

victimized by discrimination. Accordingly, blacks should be less likely than whites, the primary purveyors of these negative stereotypes, to stigmatize minority groups, including Hispanics (fellow "people of color") and Jews (fellow targets of age-old hatreds).

The minority solidarity interpretation is certainly plausible, and yet blacks have sometimes been observed to express more anti-Semitic stereotypes and attitudes than whites do, even when black-white differences in level of education and other relevant factors are taken into account (Martire and Clark 1982; but see Glock et al. 1975 for contrary evidence). So we need to consider other expectations as well.

Racial Conflict

Like the minority solidarity perspective, the racial conflict perspective posits a "we-they" mentality, but in this case "we" and "they" are considered to be defined strictly in terms of race. The key to this interpretation is the common tendency to hold more differentiated views of one's own group than of others, since one often can and must make relatively fine distinctions within one's own group, while lumping less frequently encountered outsiders together as "all alike" (Park and Rothbart 1982). Blacks, then, may view Hispanics and Jews, not as their fellow victims of discrimination, as the minority solidarity interpretation stipulates, but above all else as white people—non-mainstream white people, perhaps, but white people nonetheless. Thus Gregory Martire and Ruth Clark (1982) contend that the apparent anti-Semitism of many blacks may reflect generalized negative attitudes toward whites, and the same could also hold for blacks' attitudes toward Hispanics. If whites, like blacks, predominantly categorize Hispanics and Jews as "white people" and if the thinking of both blacks and whites is as fundamentally shaped by the black-white distinction as the racial conflict interpretation assumes, then whites should be less likely than blacks to stigmatize other groups of whites.[2]

While race often plays a pivotal role in shaping intergroup relations, the material sources of group stigmatization must also be taken into account. From the perspective of "realistic conflict theory" (Taylor and Moghaddam 1987), conflicts of material interest provide the key to understanding intergroup hostility. Such conflicts can be vertical—between superior and subordinate—or horizontal—between equals.

Vertical Conflict

In a hierarchical system of rewards, the material interests of the "top dogs" are unlikely to be compatible with those of the "underdogs." Those who are privileged naturally denigrate those who are not, since the ideological justification for privilege necessarily involves the premise that one is more deserving of material wealth than those beneath oneself. The less privileged, for their part, naturally resent those whom they perceive as profiting from unfair advantages. Thus, for example, white Americans have traditionally viewed the depressed socioeconomic condition of black Americans as a product of blacks' inadequate motivation, low intelligence, and other shortcomings, while blacks have placed the primary blame on white racism and discrimination (see Sigelman and Welch 1991 for an elaboration).

Material inequality, then, is apt to be characterized by ill will on both sides. In the present context, this ill will should be borne out, first, in negative stereotypes held by blacks, an underprivileged group, of Jews, an advantaged group many blacks see as instrumental in holding them down. Prior research has shown that blacks' negative stereotypes of Jews center on economic themes, such as the perception that Jews are unethical in business and wield too much power (see, e.g., Martire and Clark 1982; Wuthnow 1982), and it has been argued that black anti-Semitism stems from what blacks perceive as exploitative economic practices by Jews (Marx 1967). At the same time, the vertical conflict perspective downplays the extent to which blacks should be expected to engage in negative stereotyp-

---

[2] A psychoanalytic theory of prejudice and discrimination (see Ashmore and Del Boca 1981) yields the same predictions as the racial conflict interpretation, though the two arrive at their common destination via different routes. From the psychoanalytic perspective, the long-standing frustrations of black Americans should be expected to have generated both a direct hostility toward those whites whom they perceive as oppressors and a displacement of hostility from the perceived oppressors to other groups not seen as sources of the original frustration. Jews would presumably be prominent among the targets of direct black hostility, Hispanics prominent among the targets of displaced hostility.

ing of Hispanics, since blacks and Hispanics occupy adjoining low rungs on the socioeconomic ladder. Social groups generally have more favorable attitudes to other groups that are targets of the same kinds of stereotypes that are applied to them than to groups for which quite different stereotypes prevail (Cauthen, Robinson, and Krauss 1971). Since there are numerous similarities between traditional stereotypes of blacks and Hispanics, but few overlapping stereotypes of blacks and Jews, blacks might be especially sensitive to the unfairness of negative stereotypes applied to Hispanics and reject them. By contrast, the vertical conflict interpretation implies that whites should be less likely than blacks to stigmatize Jews but more likely to stigmatize Hispanics.

Horizontal Conflict

According to the vertical conflict perspective, blacks' stereotypes of Hispanics might be relatively positive, and their stereotypes of Jews relatively negative, because blacks are likely to perceive both themselves and Hispanics as groups oppressed by "mainstream" Americans, including (or perhaps even especially) Jews. However, not all conflicts of material interest are vertical. Indeed, on a day-in, day-out basis, intergroup conflict may be most intense between groups that have the most in common, since such groups so often find themselves in direct competition with one another for jobs, housing, "turf," and a vast array of other scarce resources. That is, negative intergroup attitudes may be especially likely to arise between groups that occupy similar positions in the socioeconomic stratification system. Although in the long run such groups may rise or fall together, in the short run a sense of intergroup rivalry may define their views of one another. To the extent that it does, blacks should be expected to hold especially negative views of Hispanics, because blacks and Hispanics find themselves at the bottom of the socioeconomic ladder competing for jobs, whereas blacks are not in such direct competition with Jews. Whites, on the other hand, should be more likely to stigmatize Jews, while paying relatively less heed to Hispanics.

Summary

It is important to recognize that in almost every "real world" intergroup conflict setting, many of the plausible ingredients of conflict are intertwined (Rothbart 1990). There may be racial differences and cultural differences and economic differences, to name only three, between any pair of groups, and while we can distinguish analytically among such differences, we cannot always disassociate them empirically. Nonetheless, we have framed several sets of hypotheses—some complementary, some contradictory—about the manner in which blacks and whites might differ in their stereotyping of Hispanics and Jews. Blacks are at once members of the broader American culture who might be expected to share with other groups many basic cultural outlooks; a minority group that might be expected to identify with other minority groups; a nonwhite group that might be expected to harbor anti-white sentiments; a socially and economically disadvantaged group that might be expected to resent those above it on the socioeconomic ladder; and a group driven by market forces into competition with other disadvantaged groups, from which negative intergroup feelings might be expected to flow. It may also be true, as Henri Tajfel (1970; summarized by Rothbart 1990) has argued, that none of these forms of intergroup differentiation is strictly necessary for establishing bias against outgroups. Still, depending upon which of these sources of social perceptions and attitudes one views as predominant, one might expect blacks to hold equally negative, more negative, or less negative stereotypes of either Hispanics or Jews than whites do.

Data and Methods

The data for this analysis come from an October–November 1978 national survey conducted by Louis Harris and Associates for the National Conference of Christians and Jews. The survey dealt at length with perceptions of and attitudes toward minority groups, including several questions tapping attitudes toward Hispanics and Jews. Separate national cross-sections of 732 blacks and 1,673 whites were surveyed.[3]

During the interviews, non-Hispanic and non-Jewish respondents were asked whether they agreed with, were uncertain about, or disagreed with fourteen statements concerning Hispanics and Jews.[4] These statements included the following nine:

y_1: "Spanish Americans have worked hard for a better life here."

y_2: "Spanish Americans don't try to learn English."

y_3: "Spanish Americans are deeply religious."

[3] Detailed information about the survey can be found in Louis Harris and Associates 1978. We obtained the data sets from the University of North Carolina Institute for Social Science Research, which, like Louis Harris and Associates, bears no responsibility for our analyses or interpretations.

[4] Since these questions were not asked of Hispanics or Jews, when we refer below to whites' stereotypes of Hispanics and Jews, we mean non-Hispanic and non-Jewish whites' stereotypes of Hispanics and Jews. Since it would be tedious to repeat "non-Hispanic and non-Jewish whites" every time we refer to this group, we simply call them "whites." Readers are enjoined to bear in mind that whites, as the term is used here, do not include Hispanics or Jews.

y_4: "Spanish Americans are highly emotional and apt to fly off the handle."

y_5: "Spanish Americans want to live off the handout."

y_6: "Jews are irritating because they are too aggressive."

y_7: "Most of the slumlords are Jewish."

y_8: "When it comes to choosing between people and money, Jews will choose money."

y_9: "Jews are more loyal to Israel than to America."

The remaining five statements (one about Hispanics and four about Jews) asked whether Hispanics or Jews had, in one way or another, been involved in acts of discrimination, rather than calling for stereotypes of Hispanics or Jews, so these statements are not considered here.

Our primary interest lies in determining whether blacks are more or less likely than whites to engage in negative stereotyping of Hispanics and Jews. The analysis focuses on observations for the two groups of Harris survey respondents (blacks and whites) on the nine stereotype items $(y_1, \ldots, y_9)$ and four independent variables $(x_1, \ldots, x_4)$: religious preference (non-Protestant or Protestant), age, education, and gender. The point of including the exogenous variables in the analysis is, first, to determine whether some of the same personal characteristics that produce stereotyping of outgroups among whites also account for individual differences in stereotyping on the part of blacks, and, more important, to estimate the extent to which black-white differences in stereotyping of Hispanics and Jews remain after differences attributable to religion, age, education, and gender are taken into account.

What does prior research suggest about the impact these factors may have on ethnic stereotypes? Little is known about the impact of gender on the prevalence of ethnic stereotyping, though we suspect that, if anything, women are less likely than men to engage in such stereotyping. Among white Christians, anti-Semitism has been shown to be associated with limited education and advanced age (Martire and Clark 1982; Wuthnow 1982). Indeed, exposure to advanced education in particular, and age as well, have repeatedly emerged as predictors of whites' tolerance of various deviant groups (Corbett 1982; Sullivan, Piereson, and Marcus 1982), presumably because education fosters greater open-mindedness and cognitive complexity and because younger adults have grown up in more tolerant times than older cohorts. Among blacks, the relationship between education (or academic commitment and success among high school students) and anti-Semitic attitudes appears to be weaker than it is among whites (Glock et al. 1975; Martire and Clark 1982), and the relationship between age and anti-Semitism evident among whites has not emerged in research on blacks (Martire and Clark 1982). This may be partially because the sense of alienation from white society and the perception of white discrimination against blacks are more prevalent among younger than among older blacks, and are highest among young blacks with either limited education or advanced education (Schuman and Hatchett 1974). As for religion, whereas in Martire and Clark's (1982) survey, Christian religious orthodoxy did not predict anti-Semitism once education, race, and age were controlled, other research suggests that religiously committed Protestants tend to be especially anti-Semitic (Wuthnow 1982), racist (Gorsuch and Aleshire 1974; McConahay and Hough 1976), and politically intolerant (Sullivan, Piereson, and Marcus 1982). However, while Protestant commitment predicts anti-Semitism and racism among whites, *lack* of traditional religious commitment predicts alienation from white society among blacks (Schuman and Hatchett 1974). There are, then, grounds for suspecting that some of the exogenous variables in our model may register somewhat different effects on blacks' ethnic stereotypes than on those of whites. Other personal characteristics, such as income and social class, do not appear to be strongly related to attitudes toward outgroups (Glock et al. 1975; Martire and Clark 1982; McConahay and Hough 1976).

The analysis of these variables could proceed through estimation of nine separate regression-type models, one for each stereotype item. In that case, each model would include a variable for race (black or white) and the four exogenous control variables, along with appropriate interaction terms between race and the exogenous variables. Or, what amounts to virtually the same thing, we could pursue a multivariate analysis of covariance approach. We hypothesize, however, that a simplified structure underlies the array of stereotype responses, determined by whether the stereotype is of Hispanics or Jews, and by whether it is positively or negatively oriented. This simplification reduces the number of regressions, as well as the number of mean stereotype levels that must be compared. It also requires us to specify the relationship between the observed data configuration and the latent structures underlying it.

Before we can address the issue of black-white differences in the tendency to engage in stereotyping, however, we must consider whether blacks' and whites' views of Hispanics and Jews are cognitively structured in the same way. Questions of this sort have usually been ignored in research on racial attitude differences. For example, researchers undertaking interracial comparisons of anti-Semitism (e.g., Glock et al. 1975; Martire and Clark 1982) have simply assumed that their measures of anti-Semitism are just as appropriate for blacks as they are for whites. But while racial belief systems may well be similarly structured in different groups, this needs to be demonstrated empirically, not simply assumed. Before we can validly compare the degree to which blacks and whites accept negative ethnic stereotypes, we need to ensure that we are comparing common attitudinal dimensions for blacks and whites.

The analytic strategy pursued here incorporates both the measurement or confirmatory factor model for stereotypes of Hispanics and Jews and the structural regression of these latent stereotypes on religious preference, age, education, and gender. The analysis proceeds in three stages. The stages focus, in turn, on the similarity between blacks and whites of (1) the measurement of unobserved stereotypes defined by the model, (2) the structural relationship between the four independent variables and the latent stereotypes, and (3) the mean levels of these stereotyping factors that remain among blacks and whites after accounting for the effects of the exogenous control variables.

Measurement Model

The measurement portion of the model with k latent factors can be written for group g (blacks or whites) as:

$$y^{(g)} = \tau^{(g)} + \Lambda^{(g)}\eta^{(g)} + \epsilon^{(g)}$$

where for group g, $y^{(g)}$ is a (9×1) vector collecting the observed stereotype items, $\eta^{(g)}$ is a $(k \times 1)$ vector of latent variables or factors, $\Lambda^{(g)}$ is a $(9 \times k)$ matrix of factor loadings, and $\tau^{(g)}$ and $\epsilon^{(g)}$ are (9×1) vectors of measurement intercepts and errors respectively. Finally, the (9×9) variance-covariance matrix of the measurement errors is denoted by $\theta_\epsilon^{(g)}$. A similar equation is defined with respect to the exogenous variables, although in the present case no latent exogenous factors are proposed. Thus,

$$x^{(g)} = \xi^{(g)}$$

where $\xi^{(g)}$ typically denotes a (4×1) vector of latent factors, here merely a reproduction of the observed x within each group.

The overall first step in this framework is to determine the number of latent factors and the manner in which they are linked to the nine observed variables. Before considering the impact of exogenous variables or testing for black–white differences in the level of stereotyping, we need to determine that the latent factors are indeed comparable. If they differ, we shall be unable to test for mean black–white differences in stereotyping, and shall be able to proceed no further than a description of the ways in which the measurement structures differ. Thus the value k (that is, the number of latent factors) must be the same for blacks and whites. Next, since all $9k$ elements of Λ are not typically estimated, the pattern of loadings estimated in the measurement equation for whites must be equivalent to that in the black model. If the form of the measurement model is thus equivalent for blacks and whites, we then determine whether the magnitudes of the loadings are the same (i.e., $\Lambda^{(W)} = \Lambda^{(B)}$).

Structural Model and Mean Structure

The structural model in group g relating the exogenous ξ to the endogenous η is written as:

$$\eta^{(g)} = \alpha^{(g)} + \Gamma^{(g)}\xi^{(g)} + \zeta^{(g)}$$

This can be interpreted analogously to a standard regression model, only with the variables on both sides of the equation being unobserved and defined by the measurement model given above. The structural coefficients $\Gamma^{(g)}$ estimate the hypothesized effects of the independent variables on the latent dependent factors. The regression intercepts are represented by $\alpha^{(g)}$. Finally, the $(k \times k)$ matrix $\Psi^{(g)}$ contains the error variances and covariances for the structural model.

In order to examine the means of the latent endogenous (and exogenous) factors, assumptions concerning the errors in the structural and measurement equations must be added. Specifically, the distributions of ϵ and ζ errors are taken to be normal with zero mean and finite variance. In the present case the means of the latent exogenous variables, $E[\xi^{(g)}] = \kappa^{(g)}$, are exactly those of their observed counterparts. The latent endogenous means, however, are functions of the exogenous means (i.e., κ), their relationship to the latent dependent factors (i.e., Γ), and structural intercepts (i.e., α):

$$E(\eta^{(g)}) = \alpha^{(g)} + \Gamma^{(g)}\kappa^{(g)}$$

To show that mean stereotype levels are equal for blacks and whites, it is sufficient (but not necessary) to show that none of the terms on the right-hand side of this equation differs between blacks and whites. If $\Gamma^{(W)} = \Gamma^{(B)}$, and $\kappa^{(W)} = \kappa^{(B)}$, but $\alpha^{(W)} \neq \alpha^{(B)}$, then differences in group means do not depend in a direct way on the exogenous variables. Otherwise, overall differences could be owing in part to the means of the exogenous variables as well as the magnitude of each exogenous variable's effect on the latent stereotyping factor. In such a case, differences in α between blacks and whites represent black–white differences on mean stereotype factors when all exogenous variables take the value 0.

Ordinal Measurement Scale

If all the observed variables were measured on a continuous scale, then efficient estimates of model parameters could be obtained by the method of maximum likelihood. However, in the present case, each of the nine stereotype items is observed as an orderable trichotomy (i.e., agree, uncertain, disagree). Treating such data as though they were continuous can produce highly inefficient estimates and would almost certainly violate the assumption of multivariate normality necessary to obtain the maximum likelihood estimates (Jöreskog and Sörbom 1986).

An alternative procedure is to assume that the data are a collapsed or discretized realization of an unobserved standard normal variable. Rather than analyzing observed covariances or correlations, we can then estimate polychoric correlations—those computed among the unobserved normally distributed variables—and use them to identify the model. Weighted least squares estimation based on the polychoric correlation matrix produces efficient estimates of the parameters in the measurement model defined above, provided that a properly constructed weight matrix is used.[5] The assumption of normality no longer pertains to the observed variables, but only to the associated unobserved constructs.

In multiple-group analyses incorporating mean structures, estimates of the observed variable means must be included as data. This is not a straightforward task when the variables are ordinal, but given the underlying normality assumption, each category can be assigned relevant normal scores in the following manner. First, with the proportion of cases observed in each of the three categories, normal scores are assigned to the two cut points separating the three categories. These, in turn, are used to obtain weighted means of the normal scores within each category.[6] To compare the group means, the transformation to normal scores is accomplished without reference to groups. Since the mean of the normal scores on any variable is zero by definition, if the transformation were performed separately for blacks and whites, every variable would have a zero mean for both blacks and whites, rendering comparison impossible. Thus, normal scores are obtained for the combined sample, and the groups are then separated and the group-specific means obtained.

Results

Normal Scores and Means

The normal scores calculated for responses to each of the nine stereotype statements are displayed in Table 5.2. The normalization to an underlying mean of 0 and variance of 1 is evident, but since the observed distributions are not necessarily normal, the middle score is not constrained to 0. Table 5.2 also reports the group means for blacks and whites. As a

---

[5] See Muthén 1984 for technical details.
[6] Kenneth Bollen (1989: 439–41) describes this procedure.

TABLE 5.2

Perceptions of Jews and Hispanics, 1978
(item category scores and black-white means)

Statement[a]	Normal score transformations and relative response frequencies			Normal score	
	Disagree	Uncertain	Agree	Blacks	Whites
y_1	−1.534 .138 .169	−0.617 .273 .205	0.624 .589 .625	−.011	.005
y_2	−0.797 .466 .518	0.315 .281 .222	1.253 .253 .260	.034	−.012
y_3	−1.571 .144 .146	−0.395 .534 .362	0.903 .322 .493	−.147	.073★
y_4	−1.182 .186 .341	−0.138 .401 .271	0.972 .411 .388	.128	−.064★
y_5	−0.715 .458 .601	0.523 .369 .239	1.506 .172 .160	.125	−.063★
y_6	−0.780 .356 .588	0.302 .345 .146	1.209 .299 .266	.188	−.093★
y_7	−1.113 .186 .390	0.093 .407 .435	1.267 .407 .174	.347	−.173★
y_8	−1.025 .133 .484	−0.035 .292 .210	0.975 .575 .305	.414	−.206★
y_9	−1.041 .126 .475	0.063 .494 .250	1.138 .379 .276	.331	−.165★

SOURCE: Louis Harris and Associates 1978.

NOTE: The first entry in each cell is the normal score transformation—the weighted mean of scores computed from the combined sample (N = 1,831; N of blacks = 609; N of whites = 1,222); the second entry is the percentage of black interviewees giving a particular response; and the third entry is the percentage of white interviewees giving a particular response.

★The t-test for difference of means is significant at $p < .05$.

[a] See text for description of items.

rough attempt to measure baseline differences in item means, the normal scores are treated as the true category values and t-tests are performed. According to the results shown in the two rightmost columns of Table 5.2, the hypothesis of group differences fails only for the first two items concerning stereotypes of Hispanics ("Spanish Americans have worked hard for a better life here" and "Spanish Americans don't try to learn English").

On two of the three remaining Hispanic stereotype items and on all four of the Jewish stereotype items, the mean score of blacks is significantly higher than that of whites.

Measurement Structure

In order to test for black-white differences in the level of stereotyping in the context of the model described above, the factor structure must be examined for blacks and whites. We begin by estimating a highly constrained model that admits no association of any kind among the nine observed endogenous variables, nor between these and the four observed exogenous variables. This model provides an appropriate baseline from which to consider the structural relationships of interest, since it assumes, as a null model, that the data can be accurately reproduced without such relationships. The fit of this model (denoted Model A) and those that follow are reported in Table 5.3. Given the extremely poor fit of Model A (with a likelihood ratio χ^2 value, denoted L^2, of 4,403.97 on 144df, $p < .000$), it is clear that a substantial degree of variation and covariation remains to be accounted for.

To explain these associations and how they differ, a single factor could be defined as underlying the nine stereotype items. Substantively, however, this pattern does not seem plausible, since the stereotype items focus on two different groups: Hispanics (y_1–y_5) and Jews (y_6–y_9). At a minimum, then, two factors seem likely. However, our analyses indicated that a two-factor model also displays a very poor fit. An alternative is to subdivide the five Hispanic stereotype items, two of which (y_1 and y_3) refer to behaviors positively valued in American culture, while three (y_2, y_4, and y_5) focus on negatively valued behaviors. We can then fit a three-factor model in which the first factor is interpretable as positive stereotypes of Hispanics and the second as negative stereotypes of Hispanics, while the third includes the four Jewish stereotype items, all negative in orientation.

TABLE 5.3

Fit Statistics for Various Models

Model	χ^2	df	p	GFI-B[a]	GFI-W[a]
A	4,403.97	144	.000	.806	.700
B	129.69	92	.006	.991	.996
C	145.99	100	.002	.988	.992
D	174.63	106	.000	.988	.992
E	175.26	108	.000	.988	.992
F	178.63	109	.000	.988	.992

[a] Goodness-of-fit indexes for black and white samples respectively.

In order to estimate this model well, the items stating that Hispanics are hard-working (y_1) and highly emotional (y_4) must be included on both latent factors for Hispanics. The model so defined (referred to as Model B) provides a substantial improvement in fit to the data ($L^2 = 129.69$ on 92df, $p = .006$). The success of Model B in describing the data strongly implies that the factor structures have the same pattern for blacks and whites. Model C assumes the same pattern of factor association as Model B, but further restricts the values of the loadings to be invariant across the two groups (i.e., $\Lambda^{(W)} = \Lambda^{(B)}$). This hypothesis fits the data reasonably well ($L^2 = 145.99$ on 100df, $p = .002$), with only a small deterioration in fit relative to Model B. Thus there is evidence that a three-factor structure of stereotypes underlies the nine observed responses, a structure equivalent for blacks and whites.

Next we consider whether the intercepts of the measurement equations are the same for blacks and whites. This model (D) again slightly weakens the fit to the data ($L^2 = 174.63$ on 106df, $p < .001$). While the difference in fit is significant, the overall fit relative to the naive baseline model remains impressive. In fact, Model D accounts for 96 percent of the total (structural) association of interest (as represented by the fit of Model A). Thus we view the fit of Model D to be quite acceptable, even though it technically fails to provide a statistically significant fit.[7]

Estimated Measurement Coefficients

Before comparing the mean stereotype values for blacks and whites, let us review the parameter estimates obtained under Model D (see Table 5.4). Of the estimated factor loadings, all but two run in the anticipated direction. For example, for both blacks and whites, all four observed items related to stereotypes of Jews load positively on the third latent factor. For both blacks and whites, too, the three items that load on the latent factor denoting negative stereotypes of Hispanics all display the appropriate sign, y_1 by loading negatively, and y_4 and y_5 by loading positively. The lone pair of anomalies occurs on the latent factor for positive stereotypes of Hispanics, on which y_4 ("Spanish Americans are highly emotional and apt to fly off the handle") unexpectedly loads positively for both blacks and whites. This same item also loads positively on the latent factor for

---

[7] The criterion of statistical nonsignificance is itself somewhat controversial, since even tiny departures from the posited model, aggregated over hundreds of observations, can yield a statistically significant χ^2 value. Thus a χ^2-to-df ratio of no greater than 3:1 has been proposed, and often employed, as a more reasonable benchmark in empirical work than a nonsignificant χ^2 value (see Wheaton, Muthén, Alwin, and Summers 1977). According to this rule of thumb, all the models tested here except Model A display an acceptable fit to the data.

TABLE 5.4

Parameter Estimates for Measurement Model D

Statement	λ_{i1}	λ_2	λ_3	τ_i	θ_ϵ
		Blacks			
y_1	1	−.798*	0	0	.550*
y_2	0	1	0	0	.778*
y_3	1.497*	0	0	0.027	.642*
y_4	1.853*	1.802*	0	−0.054	.351*
y_5	0	1.574*	0	−0.016	.449*
y_6	0	0	1	0	.646*
y_7	0	0	0.877*	0.008	.728*
y_8	0	0	1.363*	0.020	.342*
y_9	0	0	1.001*	0.008	.645*
		Whites			
y_1	1	−.798*	0	0	.570*
y_2	0	1	0	0	.707*
y_3	1.497*	0	0	0.027	.765*
y_4	1.853*	1.802*	0	−0.054	.326*
y_5	0	1.574*	0	−0.016	.299*
y_6	0	0	1	0	.591*
y_7	0	0	0.877*	0.008	.686*
y_8	0	0	1.363*	0.020	.240*
y_9	0	0	1.001*	0.008	.590*

NOTE: Values reported as single digits are fixed under the model.
*Parameter significant at $p < .05$.

negative stereotypes of Hispanics. Nor can this unexpected positive loading on the positive stereotypes of Hispanics factor readily be dismissed as
being of inconsequential magnitude, since this is the item with the highest
loading on each Hispanic factor. How can we explain the positive loading
of this item on both a positive and a negative stereotypes factor? It may
be that this item inadvertently introduced two dissimilar stereotypes, one
of healthy emotionality and the other of aggressiveness, and that some
respondents reacted strongly to the former, some strongly to the latter,
and still others strongly to both; we hasten to add, however, that this
interpretation is highly speculative.

Two additional sets of parameters are included in the measurement
equations. The τ coefficients represent the intercept in each of the nine
equations in each group. Note that the intercepts have been set to 0 on the
same items with fixed 1.0 loadings. This defines the location of each latent
variable. Further, the intercepts are constrained to be equal for blacks
and whites under Model D. In conjunction with the equivalence of factor
loadings discussed above, these restrictions produce an equivalent scale on
each measurement equation for blacks and whites. Given this, none of the
estimated intercepts differs significantly from zero. This is not surprising,

however, since we standardized each variable in the analysis to a combined mean of zero prior to fitting the model.

The final component of interest in the measurement model is the matrix of variances and covariances among the measurement equation error terms (θ_ϵ). Model D specifies that all the error covariances are zero, so Table 5.4 reports only the diagonal elements (i.e., the error variances). For items denoting positive evaluations of Hispanics, the estimated error variance is greater among whites than it is among blacks. However, the variance estimates are greater for blacks than whites for the negatively oriented items regarding both Hispanics and Jews. Though they are not large, these differences imply that the model does a slightly better job of measuring negative evaluations among whites and positive evaluations among blacks.

Estimated Structural Coefficients

The structural portion of the model includes the estimated relationships between the exogenous and endogenous variables (Γ), the relationships among the endogenous variables (β), and the matrix of variances and covariances among the error terms in the structural regressions (Ψ). The specification of Model D and all the other models considered here excluded any causal relations between endogenous factors, thereby eliminating β from consideration; that is, we did not assume that any one latent stereotype factor was causally prior to any other. Nor were any constraints across groups invoked. The estimates are reported in Table 5.5.

Of the exogenous variables, let us first consider the impact of religious preference (here indexed as non-Protestant [0] versus Protestant [1]) on the level of stereotyping. Among whites, Protestants were less likely than non-Protestants to harbor negative stereotypes of Hispanics, but more likely to hold negative stereotypes of Jews. However, the estimates provide no evidence that religious affiliation affected stereotyping of either Hispanics or Jews on the part of blacks. Thus, consistent with prior research, we find indications that the religious roots of stereotyping differ between blacks and whites. In terms of age, ethnic stereotypes were more widespread among older people, regardless of which latent stereotype factor we considered. That is, the tendency to hold both positive and negative stereotypes of Hispanics and negative stereotypes of Jews increased as a function of age, suggesting that it is stereotyping per se rather than negative stereotyping in particular that is a function related to age. However, this relationship held only for whites. Again, then, we observed a black-white difference in the determinants of ethnic stereotyping, with the extent of stereotyping being more predictable among whites

TABLE 5.5

Parameter Estimates for Structural Model

| | Γ *coefficients* | | |
| | Latent endogenous variable | | |
Observed exogenous variable	Hispanic-positive	Hispanic-negative	Jewish-negative
Protestant	−.041	−.012	−.064
	−.063*	.011	.087*
Age	.028	.042	.042
	.038*	.058*	.116*
Education	−.031	−.027	−.064*
	.011	−.112*	−.222*
Gender	−.037	.086*	−.006
	.003	.001	−.042*

| | Ψ *and* α *coefficients* | | | |
Latent endogenous variable	Ψ	Ψ	Ψ	α
Hispanic-positive	.155*			.003
	.100*			
Hispanic-negative	−.092*	.211*		.059
	−.091*	.264*		.005
Jewish-negative	.038*	.078*	.345*	.345*
	−.041*	.162*	.322*	−.111*

NOTE: Throughout the table, the first entry in each cell is the coefficient for blacks; the second entry is the coefficient for whites.

than among blacks. Education exhibited no impact on the level of positively oriented stereotypes of Hispanics, but in general tended to lessen negative stereotypes of Hispanics and Jews—an effect that held for both blacks and whites. And contrary to our expectations, white women were likely to hold more negative stereotypes of Jews than were white men, although (in line with our expectations) negative stereotypes of Hispanics were more pronounced among black men than among black women.

The final structural components of the model are the error variances and covariances from the structural equations. For both blacks and whites, the least variation among the errors is estimated for positive stereotypes of Hispanics. For the negative factors, greater error variance is apparent in whites' than in blacks' stereotyping of Hispanics, but the opposite is true for stereotypes of Jews. This implies that the model does not predict negative stereotyping as effectively as positive stereotyping, and this is especially the case for negative stereotyping of Jews.

According to the covariances shown in Table 5.5, the direction of covariation among the error terms of latent factors is generally as anticipated. The single exception is that among blacks, the error term from the

TABLE 5.6

Estimated Latent Factor Means Under Model D

Group	Hispanic-positive	Hispanic-negative	Jewish-negative
	Unstandardized values		
Blacks	.001	.063	.347
Whites	.027	−.014	−.156
Difference	−.026	.077	.503
	Standardized values		
Blacks	.003	.059	.345
Whites	.016	.005	−.111
Difference	−.013	.054	.456

equation predicting positive stereotypes of Hispanics varies directly with the errors associated with negative stereotypes of Jews. However, when these estimates are standardized within each group (i.e., transformed into correlation coefficients) or calibrated on a common metric across groups (Jöreskog and Sörbom 1989: 238–39), the negative relationship between these error terms is revealed as the weakest of the observed relationships.

Estimated Mean Structure

We can now directly address the basic issue motivating our analysis: How does the extent of ethnic stereotyping among blacks compare to that among whites, independent of the impacts of religious affiliation, age, education, and gender? The black and white means for the three latent stereotyping variables, computed under Model D, are reported in Table 5.6. The values are obtained as predicted values under the estimated structural model for $E(\eta)$ discussed earlier. Recall that Model D does not restrict any of the relevant structural components, so the group means are not restricted across groups. Thus unrestricted, these means indicate that whites tended to be slightly more accepting than blacks were of positive stereotypes of Hispanics, somewhat less accepting of negative stereotypes of Hispanics, and much less accepting of negative stereotypes of Jews.

Before we make too much of these intergroup differences, though, we must deal with a final methodological issue. The mean differences shown in the top half of Table 5.6 reflect, in part, black-white differences in exogenous mean values and in the relationships between exogenous and endogenous factors, rather than simply differences in the endogenous tendencies to hold stereotypic viewpoints. One common way of dealing with this problem is to standardize the group comparisons by utilizing the mean values on the exogenous variables for one of the groups. Here, rather than using the exogenous variable means for either blacks or whites, we take a slightly different approach. Earlier we discussed the standardization of the data set to the combined mean for blacks and whites on each variable. Once accomplished, the combined adjusted mean becomes 0 for all exogenous and endogenous items. If the standard for comparison is now taken to be the combined population of black and white respondents, then the mean of each endogenous factor is a function of only the structural constant, α.

The standardized values for blacks and whites, shown in the bottom half of Table 5.6, reveal the same pattern of differences as the unstandardized values did, albeit with the magnitudes of the differences slightly reduced. That is, regardless of whether these differences are standardized or not, the white-black gap in mean stereotypes is substantially larger in reference to Jews than Hispanics. To test the significance of the group differences in stereotypes of Hispanics, we estimate a new model in which the structural intercepts on both Hispanic factors are constrained to be equal for blacks and whites. This model (Model E) produces an L^2 value of 175.26 on 108 degrees of freedom. The difference relative to Model D is not significant at the .05 level, indicating that the black and white latent means for Hispanic stereotypes are equivalent. The next logical step (Model F) is to test whether all four of the Hispanic stereotype means equal zero, while the means on the Jewish stereotype factor remain unconstrained. With little loss in fit ($L^2 = 178.63$ on 109df), the model implies that the four Hispanic means are not different from zero. Since the variables have been designed to have an overall mean of zero, the actual value obtained is less important than the findings that blacks and whites have equal means on both Hispanic stereotypes, and that the mean positive and mean negative Hispanic stereotypes are equal as well. It is, then, safe to treat the black mean on each latent factor for stereotypes of Hispanics as identical to the white mean on the same latent factor, and to treat the mean on the Hispanic-positive factor as equivalent to the mean on the Hispanic-negative factor. Additional constraints imposed on the intercept for the Jewish stereotype equation dramatically weaken the model's fit, indicating that blacks' and whites' negative stereotypes of Jews cannot be considered equivalent. Thus, while the means on both Hispanic stereotype factors are not significantly different for blacks and whites, the black and white means on the latent factor for Jewish stereotypes are not equal to one another.

Discussion

It is well to recognize that this analysis is based on surveys conducted more than a decade ago, in 1978. That being the case, it seems possible that the findings reported here are already outdated. However, while stereotypes of social groups do change over time, we know of no reason to suspect that wholesale changes occurred in blacks' or whites' attitudes toward Jews or Hispanics during the 1980's. Indeed, even during the 1960's and 1970's, years of dramatic transformation in Americans' racial and ethnic attitudes, changes in group stereotypes tended to be fairly gradual.[8]

More problematically, perhaps, our analysis focuses on responses to only nine items, and these items are couched in a simple agree-disagree format. Many prior studies of stereotyping have employed lengthy checklists of purported group traits, and some of the issues of identification encountered here might have been lessened, and the validity of the factors would likely have been enhanced, had we been able to draw on a similar array of items. Even then, however, we could have faced problems, since adjective checklists and agree-disagree items have also been criticized as insensitive and, in some ways at least, misleading means of tapping group stereotypes (see especially Jackman and Senter 1983).

Within the context of these limitations, we believe that our analysis sheds new light on racial and ethnic stereotyping, especially as they involve minority groups as perceivers as well as targets. We should emphasize, first of all, a finding that has previously been taken for granted but is of some significance: that the structure of blacks' ethnic stereotypes is similar to the structure of whites' stereotypes. It could certainly have been otherwise—for example, if blacks had lumped Hispanics and Jews together as members of a largely undifferentiated category of "whites," while whites were distinguishing between Hispanics and Jews. More substantively, we have found that blacks are neither more nor less likely than whites to engage in stereotyping, positive or negative, of Hispanic Americans. On average, though, blacks do accept more negative stereotypes of Jews than non-Jewish whites do.

What does this pattern of results tell us about the alternative sets of expectations with which we began? Of the five perspectives laid out in Table 5.1, none exactly anticipates the observed configuration of black and white means on the three ethnic stereotype factors. The minority solidarity interpretation, which predicts more negative stereotyping of both Hispanics and Jews by whites than by blacks, is incorrect on both counts. The horizontal conflict interpretation also misses the mark badly with its predictions of greater white than black negative stereotyping of Jews and greater black than white negative stereotyping of Hispanics. The racial conflict and vertical conflict interpretations both correctly predict that negative stereotyping of Jews is more pronounced among blacks

---

[8] See, for example, Gregory Martire and Ruth Clark's (1982) comparison of stereotypes of Jews in the early 1980's with those uncovered by Gertrude Selznick and Steven Steinberg (1969) in the early 1960's.

than whites. However, both also predict black–white differences in the tendency to stereotype Hispanics, with the racial conflict perspective anticipating greater, and the vertical conflict perspective lesser, stereotyping of Hispanics by blacks than by whites. And while the cultural-sharing interpretation correctly predicts the lack of any significant black–white difference in the tendency to stereotype Hispanics, it fails to foresee the significant black–white difference in negative stereotypes of Jews.

Clearly, then, no simple interpretation—or at least none of the simple interpretations considered here—adequately accounts for the pattern of intergroup contrasts and similarities we have observed. Though less theoretically and conceptually parsimonious, either a relaxed version of one of these interpretations or a hybrid of two or more of them may thus be appropriate. For example, there may be value in a somewhat relaxed version of the racial conflict interpretation, in which both blacks and whites are presumed to consider Hispanics a race apart, neither black nor white, and to reserve their negativism for one another. The observed pattern of findings seems consistent with such an interpretation. As for hybrid interpretations, in our view the likeliest candidate would be a mixture of the racial conflict and vertical conflict perspectives. Such a hybrid interpretation would distill from the former the negative feelings many blacks hold toward nonblacks and from the latter the positive ties many blacks feel to other disadvantaged groups. Unlike the other interpretations, both of these predict that blacks will hold more negative views of Jews than whites do, either because blacks perceive a racial conflict of interests between themselves and whites or because they perceive a vertical or class conflict between themselves and more advantaged groups, such as Jews. If both of these dynamics are operating, black antipathy toward Jews would have an especially strong basis. Meanwhile, whites would tend to perceive similarity between themselves and Jews, on both racial and socioeconomic grounds. However, since the racial conflict and vertical conflict interpretations offer diametrically opposed readings of black–white differences in stereotyping of Hispanics, our finding of no racial differences in stereotyping of Hispanics could represent a counterbalancing of the two predispositions. That is, blacks may simultaneously regard Hispanics as part of the larger class of whites and still recognize a common bond with Hispanics as fellow members of a disadvantaged class. Meanwhile, whites may feel some kinship with Hispanics as fellow whites but also derogate this socioeconomically "inferior" and culturally "different" group, much as they do blacks.

Of course, other grounds for black–white differences in stereotyping of Jews can also be cited. We believe that it makes considerable sense to argue, as Gary Marx (1967) has done, that negative black attitudes toward

Jews stem from perceptions of economic exploitation by Jews. Owing to historical patterns of immigration and migration, disadvantaged blacks have often moved into urban areas in which Jews run businesses and own dwellings. Historically, then, many blacks may have experienced a vertical conflict with Jews that non-Jewish whites have experienced less often. Even though Jews played important leadership and support roles in the civil rights movement, such vertical conflict has doubtless fostered intergroup resentments. More recent events, such as anti-Semitic remarks by black leaders and Jewish opposition to "affirmative discrimination" programs, have fanned the flames.

Although two of the Jewish stereotype items in the Harris survey tap economic themes and reveal clear black-white differences (the statements that most slumlords are Jewish and that Jews will choose money over people), black-white differences are also apparent on the two other items, which are less directly related to the theme of economic exploitation (the statements that Jews are more loyal to Israel than to the United States and that Jews are irritating because they are aggressive). Thus black stereotyping of Jews is not entirely restricted to issues involving economic exploitation, even though such issues may be at the heart of it.

Further analyses are needed to test these possibilities. While we cannot fully evaluate the relative merits of the several interpretations offered here or the potential analytic utility of the speculative approaches we have just been discussing, we can conclude that blacks have more potential bases— racial, socioeconomic, education, and cultural—for anti-Semitic stereotypes than they do for negative Hispanic stereotypes, and that blacks also have more potential basis for anti-Semitic stereotypes than do non-Jewish whites.

6

Dimensions of Whites' Beliefs About the Black-White Socioeconomic Gap

James R. Kluegel and Lawrence Bobo

Supportive white opinion offers no guarantee that government action to correct racial inequities will follow, yet it seems to be a necessary condition (Burstein 1979). It is more certain that public opposition, or even indifference, is sufficient to make the course difficult for existing programs and to deter the development of new policies or programs. In the recent history of government efforts to right racial wrongs, politicians have quickly retreated from support for such policies as busing or affirmative action when the white public has expressed opposition. At present, in an era of seeming indifference among the white public, politicians have been at best reluctant to do anything, and at worst equally willing to ignore racial inequality.

As efforts to redress racial inequalities shifted from the status arena to the political and economic arenas, so too has the relative importance of different aspects of white opinion. How the white public understands the causes of the black-white socioeconomic gap now may have the greatest political significance. In keeping with William Wilson's (1978) thesis about the sources of objective socioeconomic differences between blacks and whites, one might propose a corresponding declining significance of beliefs and attitudes about race per se, and an increasing significance of beliefs about the sources of socioeconomic differences between blacks and whites. A small, but growing, body of research directly examines the public's interpretation of the black-white socioeconomic gap (Apostle et al. 1983; Bobo 1989; Kluegel 1985, 1990; Kluegel and Smith 1982, 1983; Sniderman and Hagan 1985; Welch and Sigelman 1989; Wellman 1977). This research provides a broad descriptive picture of whites' and recently of blacks' explanations of the socioeconomic gap (Welch and Sigelman 1989), a rudimentary analysis of social correlates and causes of these explanations, and a tracking of trends (Kluegel 1990). Other research has shed light on whites' beliefs about the black-white economic gap indirectly, through incorporating questions about its sources in scales measuring "symbolic" or "modern" racism (McConahay 1986; Sears 1988). Research to date is principally based on two sets of questions, employed respectively in the National Election Studies (NES) series and the General Social Survey series (GSS). Although these two sets share questions about the influence of the same major causes of the black-white socioeconomic gap, they differ in potentially important ways. Prior research has addressed neither the implications of these differences for analyses of these different questions nor the more general issue of their validity overall. In this chapter we report the results of research that addresses these issues by examining the dimensional structure underlying existing measures of whites' beliefs about the causes of the black-white socioeconomic gap.

Structuralism and Individualism

It is reasonable to assume that most people are aware of the large economic gap between blacks and whites. As with all matters of race relations in the United States, this gap is highly salient—commonly reported and analyzed in both print and television news media, and visible in numerous ways in daily life. Thus most whites must come to some understanding of it, if only to justify doing nothing about it.

Prior research has focused on two broad types of popular understandings of the black-white socioeconomic gap, often labeled "structuralist" and "individualist." Edward Jones offers a useful conceptualization of these two views, distinguishing between two broad models. "Model 1" (structuralist) is system-blame; seeing racial disparities as the result of "individuals who react in prejudiced ways, the historical legacy of denial, oppression, and legislative, judicial, educational, and economic arrangements which have thwarted and oppressed black Americans" (Jones 1986: 290). "Model 2" (individualist) is individual-blame; seeing racial disparities as the result of "inferior performance of blacks, which is in turn attributed to their inferior character, culture, or genes" (ibid.: 291).

Jones's broad conceptualization may be further differentiated by type or degree of structuralism or individualism. People may be quite weak structuralists, seeing current disparities as the product only of prejudiced individuals acting in the remote past, and not as the result of contemporary institutional arrangements. In contrast, strong structuralists see current disparities as the product of both historical and contemporary forces, and of prejudiced individuals and institutional arrangements that perpetuate discrimination.

Depending upon its constituent elements, two explanations that nominally fit under the "structuralist" heading may have quite different implications. For example, since prejudice is widely perceived by whites to be abating (Welch and Sigelman 1989), those who attribute the black-white socioeconomic gap to prejudice alone may be quite content to have the government take no action to promote economic equality because they believe that the "problem" will go away with the simple passage of time (Kluegel 1985). In contrast, those who attribute this gap to ongoing institutional arrangements should be much more likely to support active "structural" intervention by the government.

Likewise we might distinguish between different types or degrees of individualism. Perhaps the most important of these is that between the "genetic" versus all other types. Perceiving the black-white gap as the product of blacks' innately inferior intelligence would seem to preclude support for any change. Indeed, such whites tend to see the black-white socioeconomic gap as intractable and to express strong opposition to current programs that attempt to close it (Kluegel 1990). On the other hand, explanations that appeal to either "character" or "culture" may be more open to programs for reducing the black-white gap. Though both of these explanations have censorious elements, and though both may preclude support for structuralist interventions by the government, they may allow for "individualist" solutions such as educational or job-training programs.

The possibility of different kinds or degrees of structuralist and individualist thinking poses an important question about existing measures. Specifically, we need to ask of each item employed, which kind or degree of structuralism or individualism, respectively, is being measured by responses to a particular question. Because the wording of questions differs substantially between the NES and GSS sets, it is quite possible that questions from the respective sets nominally measuring the same thing do not do so in fact.

Structuralism and Individualism Versus Prejudice and Symbolic Racism

To what extent does research on whites' explanations of the black-white socioeconomic gap produce an independent contribution to our knowledge about white racial attitudes? Alternatively, how much overlap is there between the concepts of individualism and structuralism on the one hand and of racial prejudice and symbolic racism on the other? In studying whites' beliefs about the black-white socioeconomic gap, are we simply researching old concepts under new names?

A clear area of overlap exists between certain items used in the GSS and NES sets and traditional racial prejudice. Each set includes an item proposing lack of inborn ability as a cause of the black–white socioeconomic gap, and the NES series also includes an item attributing this gap to "differences brought about by God." People who attribute the gap to innately inferior intelligence (GSS and NES) or to a supernatural force (NES) by most conceptions would be called racially prejudiced (Jones 1972; Pettigrew 1982).

The NES and GSS series each include items with individualist content, referring to lack of will or motivation on the part of blacks, that have a conceptually more ambiguous status. Each item may be seen as simply another indicator of traditional racial prejudice, an expression of historically prevalent stereotypes about the inborn personality traits affecting the willingness of blacks to work (cf. Bobo 1988). Each one also may be taken as an indicator of symbolic racism, as an indirect expression of anti-black affect based on new or persistent sources of racial animosity. Indeed, reference to whites' beliefs about the willingness of blacks to work hard is made directly in one influential definition of symbolic racism: "Symbolic racism represents a form of resistance to change in the racial status quo based on moral feelings that blacks violate such traditional American values as individualism and self-reliance, the work ethic and discipline" (Kinder and Sears 1981: 416).

To complicate matters more, attribution to lack of will or motivation might derive more from prevailing stratification ideology than from racism. It may not reflect animosity toward blacks, and in this sense may be, in the words of Paul Sniderman and Michael Hagen (1985), an "equal opportunity interpretation." Some whites may attribute the status of all "have–nots" to personal failings, regardless of race or other social characteristics.

The relationship of structuralism to symbolic racism is of particular interest. Some definitions and measures of symbolic racism include perceptions of discrimination against blacks and other items with structuralist content (McConahay 1986; Sears 1988). Symbolic racism theory has been the subject of much discussion and controversy (Pettigrew 1985; Sniderman and Tetlock 1986). It is not our purpose in this chapter to contribute further to the debate about symbolic racism, but to investigate the place of beliefs about the causes of the black–white gap within the content domain commonly given the shorthand label of "symbolic" or "modern" racism. Nevertheless, there is important reason to question the assumption in symbolic racism theory that individualist and structuralist explanations reflect the same underlying factor.

A strong theoretical case can be made for the independence of structuralism from prejudice and symbolic racism. A compelling argument can be made on logical grounds for the asymmetry of the relationship between structuralism on the one hand and prejudice and symbolic racism on the other. We expect that whites who are prejudiced against blacks will also deny the influence of structural factors. Following Thomas Pettigrew's (1979) discussion of the "ultimate attribution error," we also expect whites who hold anti-black affect, whatever the source, to be likely to deny that the black–white economic gap derives from structural ("situational") sources.

However, there is no logical basis for expecting that the absence of prejudice or of anti-black affect from any source necessarily leads to the acceptance of structuralist explanations. It is a long leap indeed from simply not feeling hostility toward blacks to seeing black–white economic differences as the product of structural factors. In addition, even if individual blame is not the product of anti-black affect as proposed by symbolic racism theory, there still is no reason to expect that denying individual blame is sufficient to engender structuralism. As William Ryan (1976) has argued, not only do people seem to be quite comfortable in denying individual blame without accepting structural explanations, but they may be strongly motivated to do so. Denying individual blame not only permits one to believe that one is racially sensitive, but in a sense is costless. Accepting structural explanations may question the justice of one's own privilege, and may thereby have potential personal and group economic costs if structural solutions are implemented.

In the analyses that follow, we shall test to see how many of the proposed dimensions of whites' racial attitudes discussed above in fact underlie the commonly used measures of whites' beliefs about the black–white socioeconomic gap. In keeping with the above discussion, we shall pay particular attention to the conceptual underpinnings of motivation-based attributions for the black–white gap, and to the independence of individualism and structuralism factors.

Data

We employ data from three sources: (1) the General Social Survey (GSS) series for 1977, 1985, 1988, and 1989 (Davis and Smith 1989), (2) the National Election Survey (NES) for 1986 (ICPSR 1986a) and (3) the 1981 ABC News / *Washington Post* survey (1981 poll) (ICPSR 1986). All are nationally representative surveys of adults (aged 18 and older) with from 1,400 to 2,300 respondents. We restrict our attention to nonblack respondents in each survey. Since most nonblack respondents are white, we refer to them as "whites" throughout.

The GSS series and the 1986 NES data permit us to do comparative analyses of the two major sets of questions about the black-white socio-economic gap for roughly the same point in time. The GSS data, however, permit only limited analysis of the dimensional structure of the survey's questions about the black-white socioeconomic gap, since the only other racial belief questions asked concern traditional racial prejudice. Because the ABC / *Washington Post* survey asked the same set of questions employed in the GSS among a wide array of race relations questions, we use these data to provide a broader analysis of the conceptual underpinnings of the GSS items.

Measures

Explanations of the black-white socioeconomic gap in Tables 6.1 and 6.2 give wordings and response distributions for items from each survey that directly or indirectly involve explanations for the gap. Where possible, reading for these items over time also are given. In each table, items are grouped according to which of the dimensions discussed above—traditional prejudice, individualism or structuralism—they appear to indicate. This grouping also reflects the common treatment of these items in prior research.

The top panel of Table 6.1 ("Direct Items") contains items from the 1972 and 1986 National Election Surveys that directly concern the black-white socioeconomic gap. The bottom panel ("Indirect Items") contains items from the 1986 NES that indirectly refer to this gap and are of the type commonly employed in measures of symbolic or modern racism (McConahay 1986; Sears 1988).

The top panel of Table 6.2 gives the wording and response distributions for questions from the General Social Survey series and ABC / *Washington Post* survey that directly concern the black-white socioeconomic gap. The bottom panel arrays questions from the 1981 poll that indirectly involve this gap. The top two items in this panel (Blacks' Fault and Accept Welfare) are also of the type commonly employed in symbolic racism scales; the others concern discrimination against blacks in general (Whites Keep Down and Police Don't Discriminate) and in specific areas (Education Discrimination through Wage Discrimination).

Two major observations may be drawn from Tables 6.1 and 6.2. First, all measures give a consistent picture of a generally stable, high level of individualist explanation of the black-white socioeconomic gap among white Americans. Second, though the level of structuralism also has been stable during the past two decades, different items seem to give markedly different estimates of its prevalence.

In keeping with evidence for the decline of traditional prejudice in

TABLE 6.1

Question Wordings and Percentage Distributions for Responses to National Election Studies (NES) Survey Items Concerning the Black-White Socioeconomic Gap, 1972 and 1986

		Response categories[a]				
		AS	A	N	D	DS
Direct Items						
Prejudice:						
Blacks come from a less able race and this explains why blacks are not as well off as whites in America. (Less Able)	1972	9%	22		25	43
	1986	3	11	12	21	52
The differences are brought about by God; God made the races different as part of His divine plan. (Supernatural)	1972	31	24		12	33
	1986	16	14	13	12	45
Individualism:						
Black Americans teach their children values and skills different from those required to be successful in American society. (Different Values)	1972	13	36		33	18
	1986	11	28	26	24	11
It's really a matter of people not trying hard enough. If blacks would only try harder, they could be just as well off as whites. (Not Try Hard)	1972	29	38		22	11
	1986	20	34	14	19	12
Structuralism:						
Generations of slavery and discrimination have created conditions that make it difficult for blacks to work their way out of the lower class. (Slavery and Discrimination)	1972	30	42		16	12
	1986	21	40	9	18	12
A small group of powerful and wealthy white people control things and act to keep blacks down. (Powerful Whites)	1972	11	31		32	25
	1986	18	14	13	12	44
Indirect Items[b]						
Individualism:						
Most blacks who receive money from welfare programs could get along without it if they tried. (Don't Need Welfare)		25	35	14	18	6
Over the past few years blacks have gotten less than they deserve. (Deserve More)		3	15	23	38	20
Irish, Italians, Jewish and many other minorities overcame prejudice and worked their way up. Blacks should do the same without any special favors. (Overcome Prejudice)		33	34	12	16	5

[a] The 1972 NES response categories are: (AS) Agree a great deal (A) Agree somewhat (D) Disagree somewhat (DS) Disagree a great deal. The 1986 NES response format is: (AS) Agree strongly (A) Agree somewhat (N) Neither agree nor disagree (D) Disagree somewhat (DS) Disagree strongly.

[b] From the 1986 NES only.

TABLE 6.2

Question Wordings and Percentage Distributions for Responses to the General Social Survey (GSS) and 1981 Poll Items Concerning the Black-White Socioeconomic Gap

GSS question
On the average blacks have worse jobs, income, and housing than white people.
Do you think these differences are . . . (% responding "Yes")

	Year					
	1977	1981[a]	1985	1986	1988	1989
Prejudice:						
. . . because most blacks have less inborn ability to learn. (Inborn Ability)	26	21	21	21	21	19%
Individualism:						
. . . because most blacks just don't have the motivation or willpower to pull themselves out of poverty. (Lack Motivation)	66	59	61	64	61	63
Structuralism:						
. . . mainly due to discrimination. (Discrimination)	41	39	42	41	39	38
. . . because most blacks don't have the chance for education that it takes to rise out of poverty. (Education Lack)	50	56	52	51	52	54

1981 poll items	% agree/ % yes
Individualism (% agree)	
Discrimination has unfairly held down blacks, but many of the problems which blacks in this country have today are brought on by blacks themselves. (Blacks' Fault)	78
Blacks would rather accept welfare than work for a living. (Accept Welfare)	35
Structuralism	
Black people are not achieving equality as fast as they could because many whites don't want them to get ahead. (Whites Keep Down)	51
These days police in most cities treat blacks as fairly as they treat whites. (Police Don't Discriminate)	69
In your area would you say blacks are discriminated against or not in:	
Getting a quality education? (Education Discrimination)	6
Getting decent housing (Housing Discrimination)	17
Getting unskilled labor jobs (Unskilled Discrimination)	10
Getting skilled labor jobs (Skilled Discrimination)	21
Getting managerial jobs (Managerial Discrimination)	26
The wages they are paid in most jobs? (Wage Discrimination)	13

[a] Responses to the GSS question about the causes of the black-white socioeconomic gap from the 1981 poll respondents.

general (Schuman, Steeh, and Bobo 1985), there has been a decline in "genetic" attributions for the black-white socioeconomic gap between the 1970's and 1980's. Some of the difference in response distributions for the NES items between 1972 and 1986 may reflect the absence of a middle response category in 1972.[1] However we interpret the meaning of the "neither agree nor disagree" response, though, it is significant that the proportion of whites who disagree with the inferior ability explanation of the black-white socioeconomic gap (Less Able) has increased between 1972 and 1986 (Table 6.1). GSS and 1981 poll data (Table 6.2) confirm this decline, showing a drop from 26 percent endorsement among whites of "less inborn ability to learn" to 19 percent endorsement in 1989. The percentage disagreeing with the supernatural explanation (Supernatural) also declined between 1972 and 1986 (Table 6.1).

The response distributions for items offering individualist explanations other than those commonly thought to reflect traditional prejudice show that about two-thirds of white Americans blame blacks personally in some measure for the black-white socioeconomic gap. Personal blame is strongly implied in items indirectly referring to the black-white gap, in agreement with statements that fault blacks for accepting welfare payments (Don't Need Welfare, Table 6.1, and Accept Welfare, Table 6.2); for not overcoming prejudice like other minorities (Overcome Prejudice, Table 6.1); for bringing problems on themselves (Blacks' Fault, Table 6.2); and in rejection of the statement that "blacks have gotten less than they deserve" (Deserve More, Table 6.1). Direct questions concerning the black-white gap from the GSS and NES series also indicate that the substantial majority of white Americans perceive that blacks suffer from a lack of motivation or will, and show that the prevalence of this type of individualism has been virtually constant since the early 1970's. In 1972, 33 percent of whites disagreed with the "not trying hard enough" (Not Try Hard, Table 6.1) explanation of the black-white gap. In 1986, the figure was 31 percent. In 1977, 66 percent agreed that "most blacks don't have the motivation or willpower" needed (Lack Motivation, Table 6.2). In 1989, this figure was 63 percent.

If we were to take each of the NES and GSS questions that directly attribute the black-white socioeconomic gap to "discrimination" as the sole indicator of "structuralism," we would get quite different estimates

---

[1] The switch of response format from a four-point scale in 1972 to a five-point scale in 1986 (adding a "neither agree nor disagree" category) confounds claims about change based on NES data (Table 6.1). The "neither agree nor disagree" response may have at least two meanings. It may be chosen by respondents who have no opinion about an area of questioning or by respondents who truly hold a middle position on an issue, perhaps agreeing somewhat with both choices presented in a particular question.

of its prevalence. In 1972, only 28 percent, and in 1986, only 30 percent of whites disagreed with the attribution of this gap to "generations of slavery and discrimination" (Slavery and Discrimination, Table 6.1). In contrast, in 1977, only 41 percent, and in 1989, only 38 percent agreed that the black–white socioeconomic gap was "mainly due to discrimination" (Discrimination, Table 6.2).

The other "structuralist" items also give widely varying estimates of the prevalence of structuralism. A stable one-half of whites endorse the lack of a chance for education (Education Lack, Table 6.2). About one-third of white respondents agree that the black–white socioeconomic gap is owing to the actions of "powerful and wealthy whites" (Powerful Whites, Table 6.2). The 1981 poll data show low levels of perceived discrimination in one's own area (1981 poll items, Table 6.2), ranging from 6 percent of whites agreeing that there is discrimination against blacks in obtaining a quality education (Education Discrimination) to 26 percent agreeing that there is discrimination in getting managerial jobs (Managerial Discrimination).

The differences among items that have structuralist content may derive from the openness of questions to weak structuralist attributions. The NES item proposing "generations of slavery and discrimination" as a cause of the black–white socioeconomic gap may be the most open to weak structuralism, since people who perceive that the current gap reflects racial prejudice and discrimination in the past only may agree with it. The wording "conditions that make it difficult" also may allow people who perceive discrimination as a readily surmountable obstacle to agree with this NES item. In contrast, the GSS discrimination item seems to imply stronger structuralism in two respects. First, the use of the term *mainly* implies that discrimination is a stronger force than implied by the phrase *make it difficult* used in the NES. Second, the absence of a historical reference may imply to respondents that the GSS question concerns contemporary discrimination. The 1981 poll questions may elicit the lowest level of agreement because they refer to specific contemporary discriminatory practices, seemingly ruling out attribution of the current black–white gap to historical discrimination only.

Racial Prejudice

Several items measuring traditional racial prejudice are available in the GSS series, but only two questions were asked in all four of the survey years used in this paper. However, they are commonly employed in measures of racial prejudice, and concern approval for a law banning racial intermarriage (Racial Intermarriage), and support for racial segregation in housing (Housing Segregation).[2]

Several questions employing a similar format to a scale of "sympathetic identification" developed by Howard Schuman and John Harding (1963) are used in analyses of the 1981 poll data. These questions ask respondents to identify certain actions as indicating prejudice or "just common sense."[3] We shall show subsequently that these items behave as if what is common to them is traditional racial prejudice.

Dimensional Structure

We begin by testing the baseline hypothesis that correlations among the racial belief items within each survey can be accounted for by a single factor. This hypothesis fits an early form of symbolic racism theory, predicting that racial beliefs and attitudes lie along a single continuum (Bobo 1983). Should the single factor model fail to produce a satisfactory fit, we proceed to add additional factors, as suggested by the conceptual perspectives discussed above.[4]

Model-Fitting Tests

Table 6.3 gives model-fitting results for analyses of each year of the GSS data independently.[5] As shown here, in no year does a single factor

[2] Analyses of the dimensional structure of GSS items were also carried out with two additional prejudice indicators in the 1977 and in the 1985 data: (1) approval of bringing a black person home to dinner, and (2) agreement-disagreement with the statement "Blacks shouldn't push themselves where they are not wanted." The results in all important respects are the same with the smaller and larger sets of prejudice items.

[3] The specific questions are: "1. Some people say that for whites to avoid driving through large black neighborhoods only makes common sense, but others say it is an expression of prejudice. How about you, would you say it is common sense or prejudice for whites to avoid driving through large black neighborhoods? (White Avoid) 2. For whites to move out of a neighborhood when blacks begin to move in? (White Move) 3. For whites to change their child's elementary school when the number of blacks increases? (White Flight) 4. For parents to prevent their children from dating someone of another race? (White Date) 5. For an employer to expect whites to work harder than blacks? (White Try)."

[4] As we test for different dimensional configurations, we assume, with one exception, a "simple structure," with each item loading on only one factor and no correlations among the errors. The exception to simple structure is allowing the items proposing lack of motivation as the cause of the black-white socioeconomic gap (Don't Try Hard; Lack Motivation) to load on two factors, a prejudice factor and one other. We do this because of the potentially ambiguous meaning of answers to this question discussed previously. After we have achieved a satisfactory accounting of the dimensions underlying a set of items, if needed, we elaborate models further by adding parameters for loadings of a given item on more than one factor and for correlations among the error terms.

[5] Model-fitting tests and parameter estimates were obtained by using LISREL VI (Jöreskog and Sörbom 1986). All results are based on maximum likelihood estimators.

TABLE 6.3

Model-fitting Results for Tests Using General Social Survey Data on Whites' Explanations of Black-White Socioeconomic Gap

Model	Likelihood ratio chi-square	df	Fit index	Adjusted fit index	p
1977					
1. Single factor	233.60	9	.93	.85	.000
2. Two factors	6.63	5	1.00	.99	.250
1985					
1. Single factor	99.54	9	.94	.87	.000
2. Two factors	9.62	7	.99	.98	.211
1988					
1. Single factor	45.92	9	.96	.91	.000
2. Two factors	7.35	6	.99	.98	.290
1989					
1. Single factor	44.97	9	.96	.91	.000
2. Two factors	2.09	7	1.00	.99	.955

model (Model 1 for each year) provide an adequate fit to the matrix of correlations among the two indicators of traditional prejudice and the four attribution items. Thus we estimated Model 2.

In keeping with arguments for the conceptual independence of traditional prejudice from both individualism and structuralism, a Prejudice factor is defined in Model 2 by the two traditional prejudice items (Racial Intermarriage and Housing Segregation) and by the item attributing the black-white gap to inborn ability differences (Inborn Ability). Because there is only one indicator of individualism in the GSS data, it is not possible to test for a separate individualism factor. For the purpose of comparison with subsequent analysis of the 1981 poll data, Model 2 assumes that individualism and structuralism fall along the same continuum, defining a second factor (Structuralism) by the Discrimination, Education Lack, and Lack Motivation items. Model 2 includes a parameter for a loading of Lack Motivation on both the Prejudice and Structuralism factors, and correlated errors as suggested by the pattern of residual correlations.

Table 6.4 gives model-fitting results for analyses using the 1981 poll data (top panel), and the 1986 NES (bottom panel). Before reporting the model-fitting results, we note here that the 1986 NES item attributing the black-white gap to "values and skills different from those required to be successful" is essentially uncorrelated with all other racial beliefs. It behaves as though most respondents did not understand it and answered randomly. The high percentage who respond "neither agree nor disagree" and the nearly bell-shaped distribution of responses overall strongly suggest that this is a poorly understood question. We therefore excluded it from all analyses of the 1986 NES data.

The single-factor model (Model 1 in each panel) again does not provide an adequate fit to either matrix of correlations among racial belief items.[6] Thus we proceeded to test a two-factor model (Model 2 in each panel) corresponding to a more recent formulation of symbolic racism theory (McConahay 1986), with one factor defined by traditional prejudice items and the other by all other racial belief items. Following symbolic racism theory, this specification assumes that structuralism and individualism reflect the same underlying causes. In the analysis of the 1981 data, the traditional prejudice factor is defined by the "sympathetic identification items" and the item attributing the black-white socioeconomic gap to race differences in inborn ability. The second, symbolic or modern racism factor is defined by all other items. In the 1986 NES analysis, the first (prejudice) factor is defined by two items, Supernatural and Less Able. The second or "symbolic racism" factor in the NES analysis is defined by all other items.[7] The model-fitting results in Table 6.4 do not support the more recent symbolic racism specification in either survey. Though the fit indices show the two-factor model has a better fit than the single-factor model in each survey, in neither case is it at all an adequate one.

We next specified and tested a three-factor model (Model 3) in the 1981 poll data. Following our arguments for the conceptual independence

TABLE 6.4

Model-fitting Results for Tests Using 1981 Poll and 1986 National Election Survey Data on Whites' Explanations of the Black-White Socioeconomic Gap

Model	Likelihood ratio chi-square	df	Fit index	Adjusted fit index	p
1981 Poll					
1. Single factor	1,952.74	152	.79	.74	.000
2. Two factor	1,269.51	151	.87	.84	.000
3. Three factor	867.50	148	.92	.89	.000
4. Four factor	534.47	145	.95	.94	.000
5. Four factor plus	309.33	140	.97	.96	.000
1986 National Election Survey					
1. Single factor	289.59	20	.90	.83	.000
2. Two factor	195.39	18	.94	.88	.000
3. Three factor	160.97	16	.95	.89	.000
4. Two factor plus	20.15	13	.99	.98	.092

[6] The fit indices reported here are the goodness-of-fit index and the adjusted goodness-of-fit index described in Jöreskog and Sörbom 1986.

[7] Both symbolic racism factors as constituted in these models fit with David Sears's specification of a "reasonably clear consensus on the content of symbolic racism (Sears 1988: 56). He distinguishes three relevant categories: (1) antagonism toward blacks' demands for change (2) resentment of special favors for blacks in the economic arena, and (3) denial of continuing discrimination.

of structuralist attributions from traditional prejudice and individualism, we identified a prejudice factor as in Model 2, and split the symbolic racism factor into two components, individualism and structuralism. The individualism factor is defined by Lack Motivation, Accept Welfare, and Blacks' Fault. The structuralism factor is defined by the remaining items, including the series on discrimination against blacks in specific areas.

Though Model 3 provides a substantial improvement in fit over the two-factor model (Model 2) for the 1981 poll data, fit statistics also indicate the need to add a fourth factor. Model 4 tests a four-factor model that splits the structuralism factor into two separate factors. One factor is identified by the specific discrimination items. The other is defined by all other items that involve structuralist attributions (Police Discriminate, Whites Keep Down, Discrimination, Education Lack). Model 5, the final model, adds selected parameters to allow for multiple loadings of items and correlated errors—parameters to be discussed shortly.[8] Though we are not able to reject the null hypothesis for the final model, fit statistics indicate that there is nothing substantial to be gained by adding parameters beyond those included in Model 5.

We also tested for a three-factor model in the 1986 NES data. Model 3 specifies loadings corresponding to an individualism, a prejudice, and a structuralism factor.[9] Model 3 only gives a slight improvement in fit over Model 2. In addition, the correlations among the factors estimated under Model 3 further argue against a three-factor specification, since they— and especially the correlation between the structuralism and individualism factors—are too high to permit independent parameter estimation. Thus Model 4, the final model, builds on the two-factor specification in Model 2 by adding parameters for multiple loadings and correlated errors.

Parameters for the Best-fitting Models

Table 6.5 gives the factor loadings and values for correlations among the error terms estimated under the final model specified in Table 6.4 for each of the surveys. Table 6.6 gives the correlations among the factors estimated under the respective final models.

We draw attention to three aspects of the factor loadings in Table 6.5.

[8] Modification indices were used as a guide to adding parameters for multiple loadings or correlated errors. There are several limitations to their use (Bollen 1989). We examined numerous re-specifications of the final model, and these findings are highly robust over alternative approaches to specifying additional parameters.

[9] The Prejudice factor is defined by Supernatural and Less Able. The Individualism factor is defined by Don't Need Welfare, Deserve More, Overcome Prejudice, and Don't Try Hard (also loading on Prejudice). The Structuralism factor is defined by Powerful Whites and Slavery and Discrimination.

TABLE 6.5

Factor Loadings and Correlated Errors from the Best-Fitting Models

General Social Survey:

				Factor				
		Prejudice				Structuralism		
Item	77	85	88	89	77	85	88	89
1. Housing segregation	.77	.65	.76	.74	.00	.00	.00	.00
2. Racial intermarriage	.57	.67	.59	.57	.00	.00	.00	.00
3. Discrimination	.00	.00	.00	.00	.55	.58	.55	.54
4. Inborn ability	.45	.55	.42	.49	.00	.00	.00	.00
5. Education lack	.00	.00	.00	.00	.68	.53	.58	.58
6. Lack motivation	.24	.28	.32	.20	−.41	−.50	−.33	−.49

Correlated errors
1977: $r_{2,4} = .111$, $r_{4,6} = .141$ 1988: $r_{4,6} = .135$

1986 National Election Survey:

	Individualism	Prejudice
1. Don't need welfare	.67	.00
2. Deserve more	−.77	−.40
3. Overcome prejudice	.75	.00
4. Powerful whites	−.32	.53
5. Supernatural	.00	.68
6. Not try hard	.71	.06
7. Slavery and discrimination	−.71	.42
8. Less able	.00	.54

Correlated errors
$r_{2,6} = .118$ $r_{7,8} = .137$

1981 poll:

	Prejudice	Individu-lism	Discrimi-nation	Struc-turalism
1. Inborn ability	.35	.21	.00	.00
2. Accept welfare	.31	.46	.00	.00
3. White avoid	.41	.00	.00	.00
4. White move	.44	.00	.00	.00
5. White flight	.46	.00	.00	.00
6. White date	.40	.00	.00	.00
7. White try	.43	.00	.00	.00
8. Police discriminate	.00	.00	.00	.41
9. Education discrimination	.00	.00	.46	.00
10. Housing discrimination	.00	.00	.67	.00
11. Unskilled discrimination	.00	.00	.60	.00
12. Skilled discrimination	.00	.00	.74	.00
13. Managerial discrimination	.00	.00	.68	.00
14. Wage discrimination	.00	.00	.65	.00
15. Whites keep down	.00	.00	.00	.63
16. Discrimination	.00	.00	.00	.57
17. Education lack	.00	−.23	.00	.35
18. Lack motivation	.04	.69	.00	.00
19. Blacks' fault	.00	.53	.00	.00

Correlated errors
$r_{4,5} = .23$ $r_{12,13} = .17$

First, we note that the Lack Motivation item loads on both the Prejudice and Structuralism factors in analyses of GSS data. Though in all of the survey years this item loads more strongly on Structuralism than on Prejudice, in two years a correlation between the error terms for Inborn Ability and Lack Motivation is needed to achieve an acceptable fit. The problematic behavior of the Lack Motivation item in the GSS, contrasts with its singular and substantial loading on Individualism factors in both the 1986 NES and the 1981 poll. The loading of Lack Motivation on the Prejudice factor and the correlation of its error term with that for the Inborn Ability item may result from the lack of other indicators of individualism. In the 1986 and 1981 data there are several measures of individualism, and it is thereby possible to identify a separate Individualism factor in each case. However, the use of a single indicator of individualist explanations of the black-white gap in the GSS series does not allow us to estimate a separate individualism factor.

Second, the NES items commonly taken to indicate structuralism, Powerful Whites and Slavery and Discrimination, in fact behave like indicators of individualism. More so than indicators of attribution to historical or institutional causes, these items seem to indicate simple denial of blacks' personal blame for the black-white gap. Moreover, these items each have large loadings on the Prejudice factor, in a direction opposite than expected. The results in Table 6.5 show that in addition to denial of individual blame, for some whites, agreement with the Slavery and Discrimination and Powerful Whites items reflects traditional prejudice. We can only speculate about the thinking that motivates prejudiced whites to agree with these items, but these results clearly argue against using them as indicators of the prevalence of structuralism among whites.[10]

In addition to Lack Motivation in the GSS and Slavery and Discrimination and Powerful Whites in the 1986 NES, two other items have noteworthy loadings on two factors. In the 1986 NES, Deserve More has substantial loadings on both Individualism and Prejudice. In the 1981 Poll data, Accept Welfare loads on both the Prejudice and Individualism factors.

From Table 6.6 we see that there are significant, though moderate correlations among Prejudice, Individualism, and Structuralism of the expected signs. Prejudiced whites tend to be more individualist and less structuralist in their view of the sources of the black-white socioeconomic gap, and individualists tend to deny structural causes. Prejudice and Individualism are essentially uncorrelated with Discrimination.

[10] The Slavery and Discrimination item may be open to interpretations that see historical practices such as slavery negatively affecting the innate characteristics of current generations of blacks. Indeed, as reported in the media, this view has been expressed lately by some notable public figures.

TABLE 6.6

Correlations Among Factors from the Best-Fitting Models

General Social Survey:

	Prejudice (1977)	Prejudice (1985)	Prejudice (1988)	Prejudice (1989)
Structuralism	−.42	−.44	−.47	−.53

1986 National Election Survey:

	Individualism
Prejudice	.53

1981 poll

	Prejudice	Individualism	Discrimination	Structuralism
Prejudice	1.00			
Individualism	.37	1.00		
Discrimination	.06	−.15	1.00	
Structuralism	−.26	−.44	.62	1.00

We have seen in Table 6.4 that a model estimated from 1981 poll data assuming that measures of individualism and structuralism load on the same factor fits poorly, arguing that the symbolic racism prediction of a single factor underlying individualism and structuralism does not hold. The moderate to weak correlation shown in analysis of the 1981 poll data between the Individualism factor on the one hand and the Structuralism and Discrimination factors on the other reinforce this argument.

Sociodemographic Determinants

The moderate to weak correlations among Prejudice, Individualism, Structuralism, and Discrimination also suggest that these factors may be differentially determined. Table 6.7 gives results of analyses that address their potential differential determination, arraying coefficients for the partial effects of sociodemographic variables on these factors for each survey. They are estimated from structural equation models with latent traits incorporating the measurement structures of the final models as specified in Table 6.5.

The data in Table 6.7 provide evidence that further supports the claim that structuralism is a dimension of whites' racial beliefs distinct from both traditional prejudice and individualism. The substantially larger R^2's for equations predicting Prejudice and Individualism show that Prejudice and Individualism are much more strongly shaped by sociodemographic variables than is Structuralism (in either the GSS or 1981 poll data) or Discrimination. The differential effects of education account for a large share of this difference. Whereas education has strong partial effects on Prejudice

TABLE 6.7

Standardized Partial Regression Coefficients for the Effects of Sociodemographic Variables on Racial Belief Factors (separately for the combined General Social Surveys, 1986 National Election Survey, and the 1981 Poll)

General Social Surveys:

Sociodemographic variables	Factors	
	Prejudice	Structuralism
Age	.32*	−.07
Education	−.35*	.18*
Gender (female)	−.05	.11*
Income	−.06	−.10*
South	.24*	−.18*
R^2	.39	.09

1986 National Election Survey:

Sociodemographic variables	Factors	
	Individualism	Prejudice
Age	.07*	.11*
Education	−.38*	−.45*
Gender (female)	−.02	.02
Income	−.04	−.12*
South	.18*	.16*
R^2	.22	.36

1981 poll

Sociodemographic variables	Factors			
	Prejudice	Individualism	Discrimination	Structuralism
Age	.32*	.10*	.06	−.14*
Education	−.30*	−.23*	.03	.10*
Gender (female)	−.11*	−.03	−.03	.08*
Income	−.05	.01	.00	−.06
Rural vs. Urban	−.02	−.05	.06	.01
R^2	.26	.08	.01	.04

*$p < .05$.

and Individualism, its effects are much weaker on Structuralism, and its effect on Discrimination is statistically insignificant.

Discussion and Conclusions

Our results show three distinct dimensions underlie responses to the commonly used questions on the sources of the black–white socioeconomic gap. Questions concerning the attribution of the black–white socioeconomic gap to inborn ability or to a supernatural force may best be seen as an aspect of traditional prejudice. In the GSS data the Inborn

Ability item consistently loads across years on the same factor as commonly employed measures of racial prejudice. Though the same measures of traditional prejudice were not available in either the 1981 poll or the 1986 NES, the factors defined by the Less Able, the Supernatural, and other items behave like measures of prejudice in how they are affected by sociodemographic variables. In both surveys, these are affected by age and education in the expected directions, and the 1986 NES data show the expected regional difference in prejudice.

Though Lack Motivation loads on both the structuralism and prejudice factors in the GSS data, overall these results suggest that it is best seen as an indicator of individualism. In both the 1981 poll and the 1986 NES, where multiple measures with individualist content were employed, the respective motivation items unequivocally load on an individualism factor. The results from the GSS analyses may be an artifact of having only a single measure of individualism available, and the corresponding inability to test for a separate individualism factor.

The Education Lack and Lack Motivation items from the GSS clearly help define a separate structuralism factor in both the GSS and 1981 poll analyses. However, the items in the NES series that nominally measure structuralist attributions simply do not appear to do so. Instead, they seem better interpreted as indicating denial of individual blame rather than affirmation that the black-white gap is owing to institutional or historical structural causes. That they also are confounded with prejudice makes interpretation of them highly problematic. Strong consideration should be given to asking different questions about potential structural sources in future National Election Surveys.

There is both something old and something new to be found in analyses of questions concerning the black-white socioeconomic gap. The old lies in our findings that certain items provide alternative indicators of traditional prejudice, and that the individualism dimension underlying the motivation items (Not Try Hard and Lack Motivation) has characteristics consistent with symbolic racism theory. Two findings concerning individualism are particularly noteworthy. First, whites are at the least substantially more willing to express negative opinion about blacks' willingness to work hard than they are to endorse beliefs commonly understood as components of traditional racial prejudice. Second, prejudice and individualism are quite similarly affected by sociodemographic factors. Though prejudice and individualism are distinct factors, the line between them appears to be easily crossed, producing a source of ambiguity in interpreting responses to questions with individualist content—as seen in this study in the several items that have dual loadings on individualism and prejudice factors. Findings concerning the two "welfare" questions

(Don't Need Welfare and Accept Welfare) are particularly telling in this regard. The 1981 poll "welfare" question (Accept Welfare) loads on both Individualism and Prejudice, and only a minority (35 percent) of whites agree that "blacks would rather accept welfare than work for a living." In contrast, the 1986 NES "welfare" question (Don't Need Welfare) loads on Individualism only, and the majority (60 percent) of whites agree that "most blacks who receive money from welfare programs could get along without it if they tried." Most whites appear to classify the former statement as racially prejudiced, while most whites seemingly do not see the latter statement in the same terms.

The most important new information to be gained about white beliefs from analyses of the black-white socioeconomic gap is about structuralism—or perhaps more correctly about the lack of structuralism. Regrettably, the poor quality of NES "structuralist" items means that we cannot use these otherwise rich data to analyze the determinants of structuralism among whites. However, we can draw certain conclusions about structuralism from our analyses of the GSS and 1981 poll data.

Overall, there are markedly smaller differences among sociodemographic groups in structuralism than in the expression of prejudice. This holds especially for age and education group differences. There are much larger differences between the young and the old and between the less and more educated in the expression of traditional prejudice than in adherence to structuralist explanations for the black-white gap. This finding helps to explain a much noted paradox (Bobo 1988; Jackman and Muha 1984; Pettigrew 1985; Schuman, Steeh, and Bobo 1985; Schuman and Bobo 1988) that on the one hand, white Americans increasingly endorse racial equality in principle (Dovidio and Gaertner 1986; Firebaugh and Davis 1988; Schuman, Steeh, and Bobo 1985), while continuing to show little or no support for policies to alleviate racial inequality.

White Americans may have become less prejudiced, in the traditional sense, with the passage of time and the increase in the average level of education, but these results show that neither factor has been or likely will be sufficient to lead to greater structuralism. Since structuralist explanations are crucial for support of structural interventions needed to further economic equality (Apostle et al. 1983; Kluegel 1990; Kluegel and Smith 1986; Sniderman and Hagen 1985), there is no reason to expect that declining traditional prejudice brings with it increased support for policy to bring about racial economic equality.

We cannot make causal inferences about the relationships among the dimensions underlying whites' beliefs from these data, but the pattern of correlations among them fits a conjecture that structuralist explanations are reached by a kind of stair-step progression. Prejudice leads to individual blame of blacks for the black–white economic gap, but the absence of prejudice does not necessarily lead to the absence of individualist attributions. Individualist attributions may largely preclude structuralist ones, but the absence of individualism does not necessarily lead to the presence of structuralism. The findings of this and other research showing that a minority of whites reach the end of this progression argue for the urgent need to learn more about the factors that inhibit structural explanation of the black–white socioeconomic gap and, perhaps more important, about factors that may encourage it.

7

Middle-Class Blacks and the Ambiguities of Success

Jennifer L. Hochschild

"In the beginning," wrote John Locke, "all the world was *America*" (1980: 29). Locke was referring specifically to the absence of a cash nexus in primitive society. But the sentence evokes the newness, infinite possibility, limitless resources that are the essence of "the American dream." The American dream is commonly invoked to characterize everything from young families' desire for a home in the suburbs to undocumented immigrants' desire for amnesty. What links the many invocations is the assumption that being able to pursue success is an unmitigated good.[1] The only troubling feature of the American system for the pursuit of success, in conventional understanding, is that poverty, race, nationality, gender, or some other illegitimate barrier handicaps some people. The solution to this problem, of course, is to eliminate those barriers. Once the possibility of success is available to all, it is as unproblematic as any broad ideology can be.[2]

I do not propose directly to challenge this common and powerful be-

My deep thanks for their help on this topic to Derrick Bell, Monica Herk, Jacquelyn Mitchell, Russell Nieli, Noah Pickus, Earl Smith, Clarence Stone, Julie Strawn, Susan Welch, and Roger Wilkins. Some have not seen this chapter in manuscript, so they are more than usually absolved of any responsibility for its contents.

[1] In this chapter I am loosely equating "the American dream" with the pursuit of success (primarily, but not exclusively, material success). In the book to which this chapter is a preliminary, tentatively entitled *Race, Class, and the American Dream*, I provide a more rigorous definition of the American dream and a more formal treatment of the meaning and implications of success for various groups of Americans.

[2] I recognize the enormously complex political and philosophical arguments hidden under these few sentences. But if I stop to pursue them, I shall never get to the main point of this paper.

lief. I propose instead to explore how well it accords with the experiences of one group, middle-class African Americans. I have two goals—generally, to suggest that achieving success is not as unqualifiedly good as most Americans assume, and, in much more detail, to analyze the distinctively problematic features of black "success."

Middle-class blacks are a good test case of the American ideology of success because they seem to vindicate it in several ways. The recent growth of a substantial black middle class is typically taken to show that white Americans have abjured the practice of prohibiting blacks from participating in the pursuit of success. In addition, the American dream is obviously an attractive ideology whose ideals have shaped American society—otherwise African Americans would not have moved so quickly into the mainstream middle class once they were allowed to. Thus the new presence of blacks in mayors' offices, Big Ten universities, Wall Street law firms, and Fortune 500 headquarters shows that the American dream is encompassing, attractive, and within everyone's reach.

But Americans should not be so quick to congratulate themselves that the problems of race have been solved by an extension of the ideology of success to all. At a minimum, the most complacent interpretation of the success of middle-class blacks is surely wrong, since the entry of African Americans into the mainstream middle class comes only after arduous conflict and at considerable cost. Beyond that point, I remain uncertain about how deep a challenge is warranted. After all, many middle-class blacks *have* succeeded, at least some with the help of supportive whites. But at this point the evidence is sufficient to speculate that those who have benefited from the American ideology of success really do *not* intend to include, and will not allow success to extend to, more than an unthreatening handful of African Americans.

Thus middle-class blacks may exemplify either the difficult, but ultimately triumphant, march of the American ideology of success or its limits and hypocrisy. This chapter cannot resolve that question, but it does provide evidence for a more direct and systematic look at it than has hitherto been the case.

We first need more precision on the nature and extent of my subject. Most generally, I am focusing on "the new black middle class"— white-collar workers who are not necessarily descendants of the traditional black elite, who usually work and sometimes live in predominantly white settings, and who at least tentatively accept (if not fully embrace) the "integrationist" rather than the "separatist" mode of coping with white Americans (Landry 1987).

Conventional criteria of class or status more specifically indicate my subject.[3] In terms of education: in 1990, 44 percent of blacks over age 25 had at least some college education, compared with 53 percent of whites (U.S. Department of Education 1991: 127). In terms of occupation: in 1989, 56 percent of employed black women and 31 percent of employed black men held white-collar jobs[4] compared with 73 percent and 50 percent of employed white women and men respectively (U.S. Bureau of the Census 1991a: 400). In terms of income: in 1990, 25 percent of black households, compared with 44 percent of white households, had incomes of $35,000 or more (U.S. Bureau of the Census 1991b: 197–98).[5] In terms of self-identification: 41 percent of a 1988 black sample, compared with 56 percent of whites, described themselves as being in the middle or upper-middle classes. (Harris 1989: 141, 238; see also Vanneman and Cannon 1987: 129, 231).

A final criterion, mobility, is more complicated, but essential for portraying the "new black middle class." In 1962, researchers could "uncover no evidence of class effects on occupational or income achievements that could rival the effect of race on [jobs or income]. . . . Race was such a powerful variable that even the more modest of the class effects that stratified whites were canceled by the skin color of blacks" (Hout 1984: 308; Blau and Duncan 1967; Duncan 1969). In other words, middle-class blacks generally could not pass their status on to their children. However, between 1962 and 1973 blacks began to resemble whites in the importance of family background for determining intra- and intergenerational mobility. In particular, black men from relatively advantaged backgrounds enjoyed the greatest amount of upward mobility (Hout 1984). We have no comparable data since 1973, but we do know that "successive cohorts of black men have had higher levels of occupational status relative to their fathers"

[3] Black scholars sometimes argue that African Americans' unique history implies a distinct definition of "middle class." For example, the black middle class has historically included "working-class" occupations such as those of barber, Pullman porter, and factory worker, or has been defined by lifestyle and values rather than by achievement and possessions. Thus "objective" indicators of education, income, and head of household's job status explain none ($R^2 = 0.03$) of the variation in blacks' self-identification by class, although they explain a respectable amount ($R^2 = 0.28$) of the variation in whites' self-identification (Jackman and Jackman 1983: 83; see also Stricker 1982). Here the precise boundaries of the black middle class do not much matter, although the whole debate over who is in the middle class can itself be seen as evidence of the strain felt by this new generation of "winners." For different purposes, however, the question of how to demarcate classes may be crucial since different definitions of classes yield considerably different outcomes on both attitudinal and behavior variables across the races (A. Wade Smith 1985).

[4] In Census Bureau terms, these job categories were "managerial, professional, technical, sales, and administrative." For cautions about assuming that male and female white-collar workers really occupy jobs of similar status, see Sokoloff 1989 and Reskin and Roos 1990.

[5] Incomes over $50,000 were reported by 12 percent of black and 26 percent of white households.

(Hauser 1990: 16). Thus members of the black middle class now appear to have about the same chance as members of the white middle class to improve their own position and pass it on to their children.

In short, between one-quarter and one-half of African Americans have reached the socioeconomic middle class, compared with well below one-tenth three decades ago and roughly one-half of whites at present. Many of these people have white superiors, subordinates, clients, and neighbors. That too is new. Let us turn, then, to the consequences of the fact that a substantial portion of the black population seems to be well on the way to achieving the American dream.

The Costs of Success for Middle-class Blacks

We can begin to discern the costs of success for middle-class African Americans by reading the words of the journalist Leanita McClain, who rose from public-housing-project poverty to the editorial staff of the *Chicago Tribune*. She committed suicide, at age 32, less than four years after writing the following:

> I am a member of the black middle class who has had it with being patted on the head by white hands and slapped in the face by black hands for my success. . . . We have forsaken the revolution, we are told, we have sold out. . . . The truth is, we have not forgotten; we would not dare. We are simply fighting on different fronts and are no less war weary, and possibly more heartbroken, for we know the black and white worlds can meld. . . .
>
> My life abounds in incongruities. . . . Sometimes when I wait at the bus stop with my attaché case, I meet my aunt getting off the bus with other cleaning ladies on their way to do my neighbors' floors. . . . But I am not ashamed. Black progress has surpassed our greatest expectations. . . .
>
> I have made it, but where? Racism still dogs my people. . . . I run a gauntlet between two worlds, and I am cursed and blessed by both. I travel, observe, and take part in both; I can also be used by both. I am a rope in a tug of war. If I am a token in my downtown office, so am I at my cousin's church tea. . . . I have a foot in each world, but I cannot fool myself about either. . . . I know how tenuous my grip on one way of life is, and how strangling the grip of the other way of life can be. (McClain 1986: 12–14)

Most successful blacks, of course, do not kill themselves; nor did McClain's suicidal despair have to do only with her dual identity (Campbell 1984; Klose 1984; Page 1986). Nevertheless, her story should give us pause.[6]

---

[6] Similarly horrific examples of the costs of success for middle-class blacks are the cases of Edward Mann, Leonard Avery, and Lonnie Gilchrist, each of whom responded to what he saw as the unmitigated racism of his corporate employer by randomly shooting fellow

One could save the unblemished image of the American dream if McClain were alone in her anguished response to success, or if her tragedy were entirely personal and independent of context. However, neither claim is warranted. The evidence on both points is more anecdotal and less systematic than one would like, but its cumulative impact is, I believe, persuasive.

A curious survey research finding begins to suggest the extent of the costs of success for African Americans. Unlike whites, for whom socio-economic status is closely associated with subjective quality of life, blacks do not report greater happiness or more satisfaction with their lives as their economic position improves (St. George and McNamara 1984; Jackson, Chatters, and Neighbors 1986; Ellison and Gay 1990). Most researchers interpret these results to suggest that religion, family, and friends matter more or differently for blacks than for whites, or that poor blacks lower their expectations to fit their possibilities more than poor whites do. With-out denying these hypotheses, let me suggest another: middle-class blacks find their lives much more problematic than middle-class whites do, so the comfort that a broader education, better job, and more money usually bring to whites is denied to similarly situated blacks.

Survey data can establish the breadth of successful blacks' distress, but not its content and historical context. For that we must turn, among other places, to the testimony of blacks themselves.

Economic Strains

Some members of the black middle class are insecure about their class position itself, feeling only "one paycheck away from poverty." A black couple whose two professions and real estate investments yielded an an-nual income over $70,000 in the early 1980's worried that "send one kid to school, and you might as well be on welfare. . . . A guy could have a good job and after an affirmative action cut, could have nothing." This couple saw the term "middle class" as divisive and misleading: "We need to eradicate the boxes people tend to put us in. We're all in the same boat. There's really no difference" (Riley 1986). They are not unique; 34 per-cent of middle-class black respondents in a 1983 *Los Angeles Times* survey felt "economically vulnerable," and 38 percent claimed to "belong to the 'have-nots,'" compared with 24 percent and 19 percent respectively of white middle-class respondents (Lewis and Schneider 1983: 13).

Another class-based strain has less to do with income per se than with

---

employees. We must beware of making too much of a few dramatic examples—whites, too, go on killing sprees, and most blacks do not—but these cases provide at least a rhetorical reminder that success may come at too high a cost.

its consequences for political attitudes. In the past two decades, middle-class blacks have become less liberal than poorer blacks in their preferences for social welfare policy and government expenditures (Parent and Stekler 1985: 529–33; Dawson 1986; Welch and Combs 1985; Welch and Foster 1987; Parent 1984; Lichter 1985; Gilliam and Whitby 1989; for disagreement, see Seltzer and Smith 1985). Young blacks who perceived their personal financial situation to be improving led a dramatic increase in approval of President Reagan's job performance from 1984 to 1986 (Williams 1986: 4–7).[7] In 1986, black support for a second presidential campaign by Jesse Jackson declined as education, occupation, and income rose (Harris and Williams 1986: 6). African-American support for President Bush is similarly disproportionally strong among those with high incomes and considerable education (Oreskes 1990).

Middle-class blacks' increasing fiscal and political conservatism parallels middle-class whites' relative conservatism compared with poor whites, and is not itself grounds for distress. However, their social and political context makes this shift deeply problematic for some middle-class blacks. Poor blacks and civil rights veterans accuse well-off conservative blacks of being sellouts—Uncle Toms and Oreos—corrupted by their desire to get and keep the white man's wealth and power. Harold Cruse is a representative accuser: "The new black middle class . . . is an *empty class* that has flowered into social prominence *without a clearly defined social mission*. . . . [It is] mindless of its own potential or else reticent to mobilize it. . . . It is an indulgent 'Me' generation . . . [with] puny . . . intellectual, scholarly, and creative output" (Cruse 1987: 389–90; italics in original). Manning Marable concurs; during the 1980's "black actors opportunistically seized the subordinated roles which were given to them. . . . Corporate black Reaganites are even more dangerous than [Thomas] Sowell, because their blatant and vigorous support for conservative public policies is rooted not in any ideological commitment, but purely in their own vicious desire for money and their hunger for power" (Marable 1982: 7, 9).[8] Others apparently concur: in a 1984 national survey, almost twice as many well-off as poor blacks (62 percent to 36 percent) denied that "black people who have

[7] This survey gives contradictory results for direct measures of the relationship between blacks' socioeconomic status and their support for President Reagan. Higher-income and better-educated blacks endorsed him more than poorer and less well educated blacks, but blue-collar workers gave him higher approval ratings than professional, business, or clerical workers. These results are all bivariate relationships; I know of no multivariate analyses of these data.

[8] These accusations are not new; in his characteristically more tactful language, Martin Luther King, Jr., called on "the Negro haves . . . to rise up from its stool of indifference, to retreat from its flight into unreality and to bring its full resources—its heart, its mind and its checkbook—to the aid of the less fortunate brother. . . . The salvation of the Negro middle class is ultimately dependent upon the salvation of the Negro masses" (King 1967: 132).

'made it' are doing a lot to improve the social and economic position of poor blacks" (Tate et al. 1988: 129).[9]

Some members of the black middle class dismiss these charges: "Guilt about the ghetto is passé. A lot of blacks won't admit that. But most of us have a lot of other things on our minds" (Brashler 1978: 140). Others dismiss them for the opposite reason—they and their friends *are* committed to improving the lives of poor blacks (Logan 1986; Wilkins 1989; Raspberry 1990; Ifill and Maraniss 1986). But others, perhaps a majority, fall somewhere in between, searching for ways simultaneously to avoid selling out, to maintain their newfound status, and to respond enough but not too much to the siren call of communal responsibility. In short, given the common black sentiment that "none of us are free if some of us are not," middle-class African Americans are especially susceptible to calls for sacrifice that, if they are made to whites at all, simply roll off the backs of many.

These class-based tensions reinforce one another. The more insecure one's own middle-class status, the harder it is to extend oneself to help those worse off, no matter how deep one's concern. Moreover, the most insecure members of the black middle class may be precisely those most concerned, since they are most likely to have left the ranks of the poor recently and to have left family and friends behind (Martin and Martin 1978).

Another strain directly related to middle-class status further confounds the first two. Since the 1960's, at least part of the black community has come to define black identity in opposition, not merely to some amorphous white identity, but specifically to white middle-class values. Working hard, saving money, acceding to authority, doing well in school, maintaining a stable two-parent family—all those mainstream, Protestant, bourgeois values came to be associated in the eyes of some blacks with illegitimate white dominance and intolerable black submission. Therefore succeeding in a white-dominated society means becoming white—something no self-respecting black chooses to do. Conversely, honoring one's blackness means rejecting conventional success. Wrestling with this "polarity of images" is painful: "There is no forward movement on either plane that does not constitute backward movement on the other. . . .As I spoke about class, . . . I was betraying race. Clearly, the two indispensable parts of my identity were a threat to one another" (Steele 1988: 43). And destructive:

Learning school curriculum and learning to follow the standard academic practices of the school are often equated by the minorities with . . . "acting white"

---

[9] Similarly, as many well-off as poor black Atlantans (39 percent and 41 percent respectively) agreed in a 1981 survey that "non-poor blacks do not care about poor blacks in the city" (Center for Public and Urban Research 1981).

while simultaneously giving up acting like a minority person. School learning is therefore . . . perceived *as a subtractive process*: a minority person who learns successfully in school or who follows the standard practices of the school is perceived as becoming acculturated into the white American cultural frame of reference at the expense of the minorities' cultural frame of reference and collective welfare. (Fordham and Ogbu 1986: 7–8; see also Zweigenhaft and Domhoff 1991)

We have no good evidence on how many blacks feel this conundrum. But again, in the absence of systematic data, we may speculate that it is precisely the newest entrants into the middle class who are most beset with fears that they are betraying their identity and community. Small wonder that Leanita McClain felt like a "rope in a tug of war."

Strains of Professional Status

Their professional success is itself the source of another cluster of stresses for members of the new black middle class. One scholar, for example, found the very content of her chosen profession inimical to her integrity as an African American:

The central dilemma of my professional training . . . [was]: I am a black child—one of the subjects whose behavior needed an alternative explanation [to the "deficit theory" she had been taught]. By enrolling in graduate school, I was embedding myself in an environment that denied the complexity of my experience. . . . I expected to develop new methods through activity that was based on the premises and methods of the very system I questioned. If I were successful, I might have to regard myself as a failure. (Mitchell 1982: 34)

Having negotiated that substantive hurdle, she faced an even more difficult behavioral one. As a scholar, her problems have

increased and intensified. . . . A role and identity conflict has crystallized: I am expected somehow to be an objective social scientist yet have a black perspective. This role is a contradiction, and I have begun to experience feelings of anxiety and futility, emotions that paralyze and inhibit my creativity and productivity. . . . It is of little consequence that we may be recognized and respected for our contributions and scholarship; our ever-present visibility never allows us to experience complete membership in white academia. At the same time, these marginal feelings begin to affect our ethnicity as well. We thus experience double marginality, belonging to and feeling a part of two worlds, yet never at home in either. (Mitchell 1982: 37–38)

As she progresses in her career, Mitchell identifies yet more conflicting pressures. African American students make complicated emotional demands, against which even the most sympathetic professor must struggle in the interests of professional integrity. Members of the community expect the black professor to conduct research of direct benefit to them; colleagues expect the black professor both to conduct "pure" scholarly research and to mentor black students; black scholars "often use criteria far harsher than traditional university standards to judge each other's behavior." As a consequence, "whether the faculty member is seen as loyal to the ethnic group or as loyal to the university, he or she is not seen as an individual. . . . This dilemma becomes the primary element of our visibility and the source of great stress; the self is obscured by the social category. . . . We deny ourselves, . . . unable to . . . demand . . . space . . . to pursue individual interests and needs" (Mitchell 1983: 24–25). Stress, especially with regard to reward and recognition, skyrockets (Earl Smith 1989).

Black corporate managers and public officials report analogous strains, each with a twist appropriate to the distinctive setting. Some corporate managers find themselves constantly looking over their shoulders, second-guessing their decisions, wondering if they are being sabotaged by resentful subordinates or patronized by uncomfortable superiors. Besides a lot of stiff necks, this strain leads to excessive caution, occasional outbursts out of proportion to the immediate provocation, and eternal vigilance in the search for racism.

Edward Jones describes the trajectory from excitement to self-consciousness to perplexity to fury to ultimate confidence and effectiveness in his initial foray into corporate management. He reports "a lack of closeness, support, and protection. . . . It became obvious that no matter how much I achieved, how hard I worked, or how many personal adjustments I made, this system was trying to reject me" (Jones 1973: 111). Jones focuses usefully on perhaps the most troubling feature of being a black in a white professional world—subtly pervasive racism, or at least the *perception* of subtle but pervasive racism: " 'What do they expect?' I thought. 'They know that I am bound to run into prejudice; yet no one lifts a finger when I am treated unfairly. Do they expect a person to be stupid enough to come right out and say, 'Get out, blackie; we don't want your type here'? This surely wouldn't happen—such overt behavior would endanger the offending person's career" (ibid.: 111–12). Many black professionals see most whites they deal with as more or less prejudiced; individual whites, each of whom deals with the black professional in only a small subset of his or her total encounters, see no such pervasive pattern.[10]

Furthermore, say black executives, the problem goes far beyond simple

[10] For example, a 1978 survey of 4,200 managers in ten large corporations consistently found blacks much more likely than whites to report that minorities face informal social ostracism, penalties for mistakes, exclusion from communication networks, resistance from subordinates, assumptions about cultural and personal inferiority, and more (Fernandez 1981).

racial prejudice to concrete discriminatory acts. In large corporations, black executives face "glass ceilings" when it comes to promotion, are the first to be laid off when businesses retrench, and are hired only for visible but nonauthoritative positions (Fernandez 1981; Davis and Watson 1985; Jones 1986; Collins 1989). Banks redline black neighborhoods and thereby deny loans to black businesses and their customers; white businessmen are reluctant to trade with African Americans; products marketed by black-owned firms are assumed to be appropriate only for black users (Mitchell 1988; Wartzman 1988; Morganthaler 1988; Hylton 1989; Bradbury, Case, and Dunham 1989).

Black public officials are similarly beset. First and most simple are perceptions of racial discrimination, expressed by 42 percent of one sample of state employees (Hopkins 1980; see also Bosworth 1989). Beyond that bedrock problem, black officials, like black academics, feel compelled simultaneously to represent their presumed constituency, define their own independent position, and effectively negotiate an inherently difficult setting. Black officials are especially distinguished, however, by the extraordinary pressure they face to "represent blacks," even if they are not so inclined or disagree with the particular request. One administrator in a public institution describes the consequences of not recommending reappointment for a black faculty member. The relevant committee had voted unanimously to deny reappointment, but she, as the publicly visible leader of the organization, was the focus of the ensuing challenge:

The aggrieved applicant elicited the support of blacks in the community who led several angry protest marches into the school and clinical agency where she and I held joint appointments. I found myself on the boundary between the school and the angry black leaders who yelled obscenities at me for allowing myself to be taken in by "the system" that was "kicking out" the only member of the faculty who cared anything about the black community. The one other black faculty member was on leave of absence, therefore I was the only black faculty around at that time, and I felt totally alone. I became the target for a great deal of hostility over a period of several months. (Dumas 1980: 213)

Dumas believes that black women are especially likely to be placed in such a difficult situation, but probably most African American administrators face the same structural cross-pressures:

The agency goes out in search of the "Super-Black." . . . The new Black is selected in part because he meets the agency's political needs—one of which is working out some response to the black community. . . . This Black is also proof that affirmative action is being pursued. . . . Note that the Black is brought in to serve the interests of the bureaucracy. It would be a mistake for the Black to miss this point and to think that his or her coming in is due to a desire to make the agency more responsive to the black community. (Howard and Roberson 1975: 234)

The temptation to play "trouble extinguisher" is powerful: "Blacks are expected to be part of the team, to observe certain amenities on the job, and to project general cordiality. . . . If the Black administrator . . . does assert a militant stand, he finds himself isolated and often unable to bring together the cooperative pattern necessary to carry through any reforms. So the way in and up the agency is very likely to be the path of supporting the status quo" (Howard and Roberson 1975: 234–35; see also Herbert 1974).

Black elected officials face similar tensions, along with the added complexity of having the mass public for a boss. Whites typically perceive them to be "represent[ing] the interests of the black community ahead of the entire city's" (in a 1972 survey, 45 percent of white officials and 42 percent of white citizens agree, compared with 10 percent of black officials and 27 percent of black citizens [Cole 1976: 114]) even though whites do not make the analogous attribution to white officials. In addition, they are fighting an uphill battle, since their constituency is generally poorer, smaller, less politically connected, and possibly more impatient for immediate results than the typical white constituency.

Black elected officials usually make one of two choices in this situation. They "run on race," using patronage, assertions of black pride and distinctiveness, and accusations of racism to keep their constituents loyal and active. Recent examples include George Forbes of Cleveland, Congressman Gus Savage of Chicago, and Mayor Marion Barry of Washington, D.C. Or they become "crossovers," deliberately downplaying racial issues and seeking to appeal to a wide, often majority white, constituency through their character, experience, or policy positions. Recent examples include Mayor Tom Bradley of Los Angeles, Governor Douglas Wilder of Virginia, Mayor Norman Rice of Seattle, Congressman Alan Wheat of Kansas City, Missouri, and Mayor David Dinkins of New York.

Each strategy has flaws. The first only has a chance of working, of course, if the elected official has a predominantly black constituency; even in that case, it often "works" only in the narrow sense of ensuring reelection and providing some jobs. The official quickly discovers that to do much more for his constituents, he must ally with, in the case of mayors, for example, the downtown (white) business leaders and a few well-placed blacks. The mayor's reward for this pragmatism, however, is often the accusation of selling out and the discovery that there is no monolithic black community with a single interest. He quickly faces a dilemma: programs to satisfy the economic interests needed to keep the city functioning— mainly, fostering downtown development—directly contradict promises he has made to those who elected him—mainly, to improve the quality of residential neighborhoods (Reed 1987; Stone 1989).

"Crossover" politicians who eschew distinctive racial commitments face different problems, as Minister Louis Farrakhan's comment about Governor Wilder suggests: "America is willing to use safe black men, non-threatening black men who will not rock the white boat by crying out for justice for black people" (*Newsweek*, January 1, 1990). Black scholars are sometimes only slightly less blunt:

> Black politics is not maturing and may be degenerating. . . . Blacks are interested not only in the symbolic benefits of descriptive representation in terms of "more black faces in high places," but also substantive representation in terms of the articulation and implementation of their progressive policy preferences. . . . It will be a hollow victory if in order to achieve equitable descriptive-symbolic representation blacks are required to sacrifice their substantive policy agendas. The new black politician would then be a shell of himself. (Smith 1990: 160–61)

Most crossover politicians vigorously deny any role conflict—"Black and white citizens put me here to do the job as elected state's attorney. I don't set the black agenda."—but they can hardly claim to rest easy—"The more successful you are, the more dangerous you are to people who don't want you to rise up. Right now people are plotting Alex Williams' demise. I know it. I'm a threat to them. If my guard isn't up, I'm going to get trouble from them" (Williams 1989: 20, 43).

Some of these problems, of course, are common to all politicians, who must constantly juggle constituents with competing demands in the face of too few resources and too many opponents. But the common problems are often worse for blacks, and the refrain of "You can't succeed in white America and remain a real black" is probably uniquely difficult to cope with.

I have saved for last a problem perhaps faced by many black professionals because it is deeply controversial among African Americans themselves. This is the issue variously described as "rumors of inferiority" (Howard and Hammond 1985), the "disbelieving anti-self" (Steele 1989, 1990), "the victim mentality" (Kemp 1990), and "the undermining of self-confidence" (Loury 1986). These writers argue that blacks appointed to high-level positions through the use of affirmative action criteria will not only receive little respect from whites but will also doubt their own capacities. After all, both black recipients and white observers are presumed to think, if high-level blacks were truly talented enough to warrant their position, they would have attained it without the boost of considerations of racial compensation.

Furthermore, in this view, the very existence of affirmative action policies perpetuates the perception on both sides of the color line that blacks are victims and whites are masters. But African Americans will never escape subordination until they escape victim status, and that includes rejecting all its supposed advantages, such as affirmative action policies. Orlando Patterson put the point first and best:

There can be no moral equality where there is a dependency relationship among men; there will always be a dependency relationship where the victim strives for equality by vainly seeking the assistance of his victimizer. No oppressor can ever respect such a victim, whatever he may do for him, including the provision of complete economic equality. In situations like these we can expect sympathy, even magnanimity from men, but never—and it is unfair to expect otherwise—the genuine respect which one equal feels for another. (Patterson 1973: 52)

In Patterson's hands, this perspective implies "constructive public rebellion," in which blacks and other ethnic groups with "a potentially common class interest" create "a total, almost revolutionary change in American society." More typically, it is a plea for renunciation of government handouts and an argument against the "outmoded" traditional civil rights leadership.

What matters here is neither the truth of this claim nor its policy implications, but whether black professionals in fact suffer from affirmative action appointments. Unfortunately, we do not know. We have no systematic analysis of whether high-level blacks feel more insecure about their capabilities than do high-level whites, or whether they interpret what insecurity they feel to be a consequence of affirmative action. Nor am I aware of systematic evidence on when whites denigrate affirmative action appointees, or whether such appointees can overcome initial denigration by demonstrated accomplishments. Disputes over affirmative action have generated an extremely high ratio of claims to evidence, and here I can do nothing to right that imbalance.

Strains over Social Relations with Whites

A third cluster of tensions revolves around desirable and possible social relations with whites. Most simply, newly mobile blacks are lonely. One young woman speaks for all:

When I was 15, my dad was transferred from Baltimore to New Jersey. It was a big change for my family. . . . We moved to this all-white suburban community. . . . We were the only blacks around. A few people were friendly, but it wasn't Baltimore. . . . At school, the students were very cold. It took a long time for me to make friends, but I managed it and graduated from the high school; it was a good school. My dad seemed not to mind so much being the only blacks there, but my mom really resented it. My parents didn't socialize or have a dinner party for two years. My mom began to meet black people on the commuter train, and so things got better. We used to get so excited when we saw another black person. It was lonely. My [eight-year-old] sister seemed to do all right. She had many white friends, and she goes back to the bar mitzvahs and parties. Now my dad has been transferred back to Baltimore. My mom is happy. My sister misses her friends, and in Baltimore most of her friends are white. (Jaynes and Williams 1989: 195–96)

This artless story captures many features of middle-class African Americans' social life. On the one hand is the fear or perception of persistent, if subtle, racism. In a recent movie, an elegant black woman in a glittering cocktail dress describes herself as "the obligatory second," invited to a high-toned Washington party so that the hosts will not be accused of tokenism. Real-life blacks make the same observation, albeit with less wit; by the mid 1970's, the higher the status of blacks, the more they distrusted whites, the less optimistic they felt about civil rights progress, the more social and criminal injustice they saw, and the more racial prejudice and discrimination they perceived (Denton and Sussman 1981; Hagen and Albonetti 1982; Lewis and Schneider 1983; Bowman, Quick, and Hatchett n.d. [c. 1983]; Parent and Stekler 1985; Adams and Dressler 1988). To the degree that we can tell from the scanty and unreliable data available, this is a reversal from the 1950's and 1960's, when well-off blacks were more sanguine about race relations and opportunities for blacks than were poorer blacks (Banks 1950; Westie and Howard 1954; Brink and Harris 1966).

On the other hand is the fear, sometimes expressed by the same people, of too much integration. As one Washington hostess explains the distance between black and white party-goers, "Blacks often want to keep control over the degree of closeness they have with whites. So they will keep it at the business level, the fundraiser and benefit, and will not open their homes. This is an old ambivalence that disappeared in the 1960s and 1970s but is more operative now" (Trescott 1985: H1). Parents worry that in desegregated schools their children will forget their roots and history, will fail because they are "too busy being only one thing—black," or will misbehave because white teachers "program [them] for failure" (Gaines-Carter 1984, 1985; Latimer 1986; Arocha 1986). Executives fear that they must deny their most distinctive characteristics to fit into cold, rationalistic, "up-tight" white corporations and country clubs (Beckham 1980; Davis and Watson 1985).

Stresses Specific to Black Women

Another cluster of stresses is specific to African American women. Sometimes interpreting subtle signals is not the problem: a Peace Corps volunteer told the *Washington Post* that a black member of Congress "tried to force me to have sex with him." When she refused, "He told me I was a traitor to the black movement if I didn't go along." The congressman dismissed, but did not deny, the charge (Kosova 1990).

But gender problems are usually less crude, if no less harmful. Black women professionals report pressure to be less successful, or at least less aggressive, on the grounds that their accomplishments exacerbate white society's continued emasculation of black men (Dumas 1980; Minerbrook 1990). Of 6,200 self-selected respondents (97 percent women) to a 1980 survey by *Essence* magazine, only 37 percent saw black men as supportive of black women. Seventy-two percent believed black men and women to be in competition with one another; 82 percent agreed that black women encounter sexist attitudes and behaviors from black men as much as from white men; and 52 percent agreed that "sex discrimination will persist long after race discrimination is eliminated" (Braithwaite 1981: 92–94).

Examples abound. Shirley Chisholm retired from the House of Representatives in 1983 because, she claimed, she was sick of her black male colleagues: "I love a good fight and people know I love a good fight. But what hurts me more than anything is the brothers in politics. . . . If the brothers would stop attacking me so much and stop giving out wrong statements about me, I'd continue. . . . But they won't get off my back. After all, I'm only human and how much can I take of this constant pressure and lies?" (Giddings 1984: 340). "Black males here tend to go to the white man when they need something in my area of responsibility, even though I'm in charge. I get more respect from white males and females," an academic administrator reports (Mosley 1980: 304).

These women may well be reading the situation correctly. In a 1980 poll of 155 middle-class black men, 56 percent agreed that "Black women seem to have more opportunities today than Black men"; 42 percent agreed that "many Black women, without realizing it, have helped to keep the Black man down because of their low regard for him"; and 31 percent agreed that "for perhaps the last fifty years there has been a growing distrust, even hatred, between Black men and Black women." Asked to indicate "the *major* problem facing the relationships between Black men and women today," 16 percent chose "lack of respect" and 6 percent chose "too much competition" (Cazenove 1983: 344–45).

But relations with white co-workers are hardly frictionless. For example, black women feel caught in the "paradox of 'underattention' and 'overattention,'" in which their race and gender cause them to be called upon to articulate "the woman's view" *and* "the minority view," but then to be ignored by colleagues when serious decisions are actually made (Sandler 1986: 13).

Even relations with similarly situated white women pose stresses for black women professionals. For over a decade, feminist journals have been filled with black women's angry accusations and white women's soul-searching and guilt-ridden replies on the issue of racism among American feminists. As one woman puts it, "How do Black females react to a call for unification with a group which heretofore has been a source of subjugation and humiliation for them?" (Hemmons 1980: 285). For the *Essence* respondents, at least, the answer is "fairly positively"; 67 percent agreed that feminist issues are relevant to black women (Braithwaite 1981). Nevertheless, even black feminists mistrust white feminists, for personal as well as political reasons:

White women are very standoffish. They don't invite me over to their houses or call me up on the phone. But they do invite me to monthly meetings. Basically, what they're saying is, "We need your money, but we don't want to be bothered with you otherwise."

Black women were left out of the women's movement because it was basically a white upper-class women's movement, the goal of which was to get their "share of the pie." For example, when white women were out in the labor market, they had to have someone care for their kids. They did not seem to consider that their maids might wish to fulfill themselves. Once on a television program, I saw a C-R [consciousness-raising] session composed of wives of corporate executives. . . . One woman said she could afford to have someone come in and take care of her child. I'm certain that person who took care of her child was a black woman. (Eichelberger 1977: 17, 21)

A white feminist's effort to grapple with these charges best captures the central point: "It is only possible for a woman who does not feel highly vulnerable with respect to other parts of her identity, e.g. race, class, ethnicity . . . etc., to conceive of her voice simply or essentially as a 'woman's voice'" (Lugones and Spelman 1983: 574). White feminists' focus on the vulnerability of their gender is, to black women, a luxury that they are denied. From that perspective, it is hardly surprising that even white feminists seem, at best, untrustworthy allies.[11]

Finally, black female professionals must deal with clients, customers, or students who are at best unused to seeing people like them in positions of authority. One lawyer's story will suffice: "A woman obtained my name from the American Bar Association and sent her husband to me. . . . When he arrived and I introduced myself, and he saw that I am Black, he said, 'I knew you were a woman, but this is too much,' and he turned and left" (Leggon 1980: 195).

11 An interesting confirmation of Elizabeth Spelman's observation lies in Jackman and Jackman's demonstration that "subordinate status is experienced more sharply than is dominant status" (1983: 81).

The Strain of Being Black in a White Society

A final set of anxieties, more purely philosophical or ideological, re-volve around the issue of what it means to be a black in a predominantly white society. The simplest version is the feeling that each individual must uphold the standard for all blacks:

I [a young doctor] tried very hard to fit into the activities of the hospital. I knew that some top people in the profession were watching me. I felt that some of them expected me to fail. Others wanted me to be a perfect showcase black. In either case I felt that if I did well I would be opening doors for other blacks, if I didn't I would be closing doors which were just beginning to open for us. (Thompson 1986: 22; see also Palmer 1983)[12]

A more complex version is the feeling that one must defend all blacks in trouble with white society, no matter what they have done to call down this trouble. African Americans sometimes argue that convicted criminals are political prisoners, that unwed teenage mothers on welfare are no different than single professional adoptive mothers in their forties, that drug sellers are only responding to an inhospitable labor market, that Tawana Brawley "was telling the truth. . . . Something bad happened to her. . . . She is afraid. I think she is being threatened by law officials" (McFadden 1988: 32).

A recent striking example of this phenomenon occurred after Mayor Marion Barry of Washington, D.C., was arrested for drug use. Many blacks continued to support him or were outraged at his arrest.[13] Few black professionals would speak on the record about him—"You want me to talk after what white folks did to Barry? Shoot, they might spend 35, 40 million to catch *me*!"—but some at least share the common D.C. view

[12] A student at Princeton University tells a similar story:

"I can't begin to describe the tension I sense in a classroom when I—the only black student in the class—speak. Before I open my mouth, I have to carefully edit in my mind everything I want to say. If I fumble with my words or say something that isn't exactly right, I see some turn away in embarrassment. . . . When this happens, I leave the room feeling as though I've further damaged young white America's perception of black students.

"On the other hand, if what I say is well-orchestrated and sounds plausible, I see two reactions: one of surprise on the face of the other students that I could articulate and relate to such a mainstream topic, and another of relief, from those students who were hoping that I wasn't as one-dimensional as they had thought. When this sort of thing happens, I get a warm feeling inside, the feeling that comes from knowing you have represented your people adequately in the eyes of the disillusioned majority." (Malebranche 1989)

In my view, this student exaggerates, at least partly because no student ever pays such careful attention to the words of another. But the feeling remains, whether fully warranted or not.

[13] A *Washington Post* poll found that of 661 District of Columbia residents, 20 percent of the blacks but only 6 percent of the whites agreed that "law enforcement officials were out to get Marion Barry any way they could"; 42 percent of the black but only 14 percent of the white respondents felt that federal investigators "would not have tried as hard to arrest the mayor if he were white" (Morin 1990).

that "they [whites] want a white man in that chair. They really think the drugs will end, things will calm down if they get a white man in there" (Britt 1990: F1). A more sophisticated response argued that Barry was indeed at fault for smoking crack, but that his downfall was the consequence of "bearing the burden of being the black mayor of the white man's plantation," as one newspaper headline put it. In this view, "racism was truly eating away at Barry, as he frequently made known. That he dealt with it poorly by allegedly using cocaine proved his point, because racism does nothing if not make the victim destroy himself" (Milloy 1990: A16).

The relevant issue here is not whether Barry or Brawley deserve condemnation, support, both, or neither. Two other points are at issue. The first is contained in a response to whites who are "incredulous" at Barry's supporters: "To see this one instance in isolation is a luxury for whites, while blacks who have witnessed favoritism in prosecution are more prone to think this might fit the same template. Our view of reality, after all, is seen through the prism of our own . . . experiences" (Gilliam 1990: D3). The second point is simpler, but no less important: to feel that one must defend every member of one's race who gets into trouble must be a terrible burden to carry around.

The strongest version of the "one for all" phenomenon is the pressure that successful blacks feel to endorse black nationalism or separatism while struggling to live reasonably integrated lives. Some scholars worry that, for example, the resurgence of interest in Malcolm X and the search for an Afrocentric worldview are unproductively romantic and nostalgic. But they worry also that speaking their minds could foster their students' already dangerously high levels of frustration and despair, and could provide openings for hostile whites. In addition, they themselves are often in despair over intransigent racism and the condition of poor blacks. Thus scholars tone down negative book reviews and weaken their criticisms in classrooms, but seldom speak of this strain and even less often write about it. It does not, however, go away.

I could continue, but surely by now we have enough evidence to argue that at least for some members of the new black middle class, success is not an unmitigated blessing. Let us turn, then, to a brief discussion of how to evaluate the nightmarish components of attaining one's dreams.

Evaluating the Costs of Success

Five questions need answers before one can confidently evaluate this litany of stresses. How many middle-class blacks feel these tensions, how strongly, and in what combinations? Are these strains unique to blacks or are they common to all upwardly mobile Americans or, alternatively, are they common to all members of the middle class in the 1980's?

Are these strains historically new or have middle-class blacks always felt them? Finally, how "real"—that is, warranted by "objective" evidence— are they?

It would take several more papers to answer these questions with precision, so here I shall settle for general answers and hints of the direction my more precise answers would take.

First, not all middle-class blacks feel these stresses. It would be as easy to find upbeat quotations and to look at the other side of survey questions as it was to find the evidence I have focused on. Fifty years ago, to give only one example, it would have been unheard of for a black "highly paid vice president of a large corporation" to report: "I have had some success. I was well-trained, . . . prepared . . . for the *real world*. I know how to get along with my white and black subordinates as well as my superiors. I work hard. I get results. I make my boss look good. I get promotions when my turn comes" (Thompson 1986: 82; italics in original). Nor would it have been possible a few decades ago to survey well-off black youths living in predominantly white suburbs, much less to conclude that they have "positive attitudes about themselves, their communities, . . . their schools . . . [and] both Blacks and Whites" (James Banks 1984: 16).

We simply do not know how many middle-class blacks feel the anxieties I have described, how intensely they feel them, and in what combination. One could begin to answer these questions by reanalyzing the 1980 National Survey of Black Americans, the 1984 National Black Election Study, NORC General Social Surveys, the Gallup surveys for the Joint Center for Political Studies, and other recent large and sophisticated polls of African Americans. But to my knowledge no one has done that work. Luckily, all we need here is the very general and uncontroversial answer that "many" middle-class blacks feel these tensions intensely. That completely banal observation suffices for my central claim: the ideology of success is more problematic than Americans want to believe, even— perhaps especially—when its obvious flaw of explicit exclusion of some group is remedied.

The second question, whether these strains distinguish middle-class blacks or are common to all newly successful groups, begins to explicate my other main claim—that blacks incur a particularly problematic set of costs when they attain success. Certainly the issue of the connections among success, community, and integrity is not unique to blacks. Much of America's best literature and most poignant oral histories revolve around the question of what one must give up and take on to succeed (e.g., Mangione 1942; Terkel 1980; Morrison and Zabusky 1980; Simon 1982, 1986; Novak 1972; Rodriguez 1982; Rivera 1982). This corpus of work suggests two broad conclusions.

On the one hand, African Americans and most immigrants seeking the American dream face the same basic questions: What are the steps to and costs of success? How can I make dominant whites accommodate me and my people instead of always the reverse? What shall I do with success? The particulars of what one must give up—language, religion, culture, community—vary across groups and historical moments, as does the meaning of success and the difficulty of achieving it. Nevertheless, the issue of how to succeed by the insiders' standards while maintaining one's identity and integrity is always the same.[14]

On the other hand, African Americans face greater psychological and political barriers to success than most immigrant groups have done. Racist and ethnocentric though white Americans have historically been, still no group (except native Americans, whose story is quite different) has faced the depth of enmity and height of obstacles that blacks have. And no group (again excepting native Americans) has faced so constantly the devastating charge that to succeed in the dominant community is to fail your own. Thus the external barriers and the internal ambivalences faced by African Americans are of a different order of magnitude than they have been for any immigrant group over a long period of time.

The third question, how middle-class blacks and whites in the 1980's compare, points to the same conclusion. Middle-class whites have indeed recently faced many of the same strains as middle-class blacks. Both races have, after all, been subject during the past two decades to the same economic slowdown (Levy 1987) and the same shift in the national mood from public to private involvements (Hirschman 1982). But the same context means something quite different to a group struggling for upward mobility and a group striving to maintain its long-standing status. Of course, broad racial categories break down quickly here, since some whites are moving upward from poverty and some black families have enjoyed middle-class status for generations. But a broad generalization seems reasonably safe: to the degree that blacks and whites have felt the same anxieties in the 1980's, blacks have felt them more deeply and been more harmed by them.

The fourth question, historical change within the black community, moves us to the challenge I raised in the introduction but said I could not answer: does the success of the new black middle class demonstrate the triumph of the American ideology of success or its limits? We can

[14] A small bit of evidence for this proposition comes from Everett Hughes's classic evaluation of the contradictions of upward mobility: "[When] new kinds of people in established professional positions are assessed by others, . . . that assessment of their statuses and the role activity associated with them is likely to be made on the basis of both universally accented technical criteria and in terms of 'auxiliary' characteristics carried over from such other social contexts as race and sex" (Hughes 1945: 353).

begin to address this question by noting that successful blacks' difficulty in negotiating white America is not at all new. We need only remember W. E. B. Du Bois's famous depiction of the "peculiar sensation, this double-consciousness, this sense of always looking at one's self through the eyes of others, of measuring one's soul by the tape of a world that looks on in amused contempt and pity" (1986 [orig. 1903]: 363–64). Many of the particular tensions I have described are also not new. Harold Cruse mostly echoes Malcolm X, to whom the black bourgeoisie was merely "the brainwashed, white-minded, middle class minority, who are ashamed of being black, and don't want to be identified with the black masses, and are therefore seeking to lose their black identity by mixing, intermarrying, and integrating with the white man" (Clarke 1969: 284; see also Hare 1965; Cruse 1967; Frazier 1957). Similarly, conflict over black women's role outside the household goes back to the days of slavery, as do the troubles of successful African Americans caught between the demands of powerful whites and the needs of less-successful blacks (Litwack 1961; Genovese 1972; Gutman 1976).

Nevertheless, some features of the 1980's are new. Members of the new black middle class are more centrally located in traditionally white institutions than ever before. That means that many more blacks face these tensions than ever before—too few easily to overcome social and professional isolation, but too many to be dismissed by whites as simply an unthreatening aberration. Whites are therefore under pressure to change their racial assumptions and behaviors, and the available locations for racial conflict, anxiety, and simple uncertainty multiply.

Two possibilities emerge at this point. A benign "tipping point" could occur, when enough blacks occupy socially and occupationally prominent positions that whites no longer remark their presence, and blacks feel that the society sometimes accommodates them instead of always the reverse. That point is closer than it has ever been in American history, but it is hardly visible on the horizon. Alternatively, the closer blacks come to *really* breaking down three and a half centuries of racial walls, the more whites might resist and the greater the degree of ensuing interracial conflict and intraspychic strain (see Chapter 8 in this volume and Bell 1985).

Neither alternative was a realistic possibility any time before the 1980's. Thus historical comparisons are only partially apt, since the slow accretion of quantitative change has created a qualitatively new situation.

Addressing the fifth and final question raised above—how "objectively valid" African Americans' insecurity and perceptions of racism are—will provide some evidence useful for an analysis of which alternative seems most likely. Two caveats: first, blacks' perceptions of racism and insecurity warrant concern in their own right, regardless of how "valid" they are. The feeling that "they're just looking for something to hold against you, so you have to be very careful what you go public with" (Davis and Watson 1985: 6) is a terrible burden to carry around, whether or not it is "true." Second, there can be no clear-cut distinction between "truth" and "perceptions." Black professionals who believe their every move is monitored in the expectation of failure may well behave in ways that lead them to be monitored, or to fail. Families who fear being "one paycheck away from poverty" may invest their money so conservatively that they never acquire enough wealth to have a comfortable financial cushion. Whites may say things or take actions that they see as racially untainted, but that produce a reaction that pushes them in the direction of racial stereotyping.

Nevertheless, we can distinguish relatively more and less accurate perceptions, beginning with financial well-being. On the one hand, to claim that "there's really no difference" between well-off and poor blacks is simply irresponsible. In the aggregate, middle-class blacks have been doing better and poor blacks worse over the past four decades. In 1947, the poorest nonwhite quintile received 4.3 percent of total nonwhite income and the wealthiest quintile received 45.3 percent. By 1987, that gap had grown: the poorest fifth were now down to 3.2 percent and the wealthiest fifth had acquired 48.3 percent (U.S. Bureau of the Census 1989b: 43).[15]

On the other hand, blacks with high incomes are nowhere nearly as well off as whites with similar incomes. Black households with annual incomes of $22,500 to $29,999 have a median net worth of $11,300; similar white households are worth on average $35,700. For black and white households with annual incomes of $45,000 to $59,999, the median net worths are $35,900 and $74,000 respectively (Oliver and Shapiro 1989: 12; see also U.S. Bureau of the Census 1986).

Whites also earn more income from their wealth; 52 percent of white wealth but only 27 percent of black wealth is invested in interest-bearing assets or property (Oliver and Shapiro 1989: 14; see also U.S. Bureau of the Census 1986; Blau and Graham 1989). Newly wealthy blacks acquire less wealth and property from their families than whites with similar incomes, and apparently spend more of their income to acquire the goods (especially cars and houses) that their white peers acquired through inheritance (Landry 1987).

Even the incomes of African Americans are less secure than those of

[15] Whites followed the same pattern to a lesser degree. In 1947, the shares of total white income held by the poorest and richest quintiles were 5.5 percent and 42.5 percent respectively. In 1987, those figures had shifted to 5.1 percent and 42.9 percent. Data are not reported in published tables for blacks alone; they make up about 90 percent of "nonwhites." Data are not broken down by race at all in subsequent Census Bureau reports.

comparable whites. Middle-class black families depend more on earning two incomes, and more of their annual income comes from the wife's earnings (Brimmer 1987). Blacks also depend more on public employment to enter and remain in the middle class. "Between 1960 and 1970, fully 60% of the increase in black professional and managerial employment (compared with 40% for whites) occurred in the . . . public sector. By 1970 over one-half of all black professionals and managers were directly employed by the government, compared with slightly over one-quarter of similarly situated whites" (Erie 1980: 310; see also Brown and Erie 1981; Hout 1984). Public employees are less likely than private employees to get (legal) opportunities to acquire great wealth, and they are often less likely to have long potential promotion ladders.

Blacks do in fact fall from middle-class status frequently enough for their economic insecurity to be well-founded: 21.3 percent of privately employed and 7.2 percent of publicly employed black professionals in 1962 had fallen to the status of manual laborers by 1973 (Hout 1984: 317–18; no data are reported for whites).

Finally, middle-class black men continue to earn lower returns on their education and labor market experience than do comparable whites. The value of an additional year of college education for white men in 1960 was $.78 per hour of employment; for similar black men the figure was $.56. In 1980, white men earned $.96 and black men earned $.69 for each additional year of college. Each year of labor market experience added $.38 to white men's and $.14 to black men's earnings in 1960, and $.51 and $.21 to white and black men's earnings respectively in 1980 (Farley and Allen 1987: 333).[16]

In short, if middle-class African Americans compare themselves with poor African Americans, any complaints are crocodile tears. But if they compare themselves with apparently similar whites, their insecurities are warranted.

Perceptions of white racism may be equally well grounded, but the data are much less definitive. Glass ceilings, for example, may be real (U.S. Department of Labor 1991). We have already seen that returns on schooling and experience are lower for black than for white men, and even the recent increase in the number of black professionals may be less than meets the eye: "Black occupational advancement in the 1970s is not particularly

[16] The figures are reversed for women. White women earned $.59 and black women $.62 for each additional year of college in 1960. The figures for 1980 were $.64 and $.79 respectively. With regard to labor market experience, white women earned $.03 and black women earned $.04 for each additional year of work in 1960. In 1980, the figures were $.06 for white and $.11 for black women. Thus the real discrepancies in returns on human capital, especially with regard to the effects of seniority, lie between men and women, not between blacks and whites (Farley and Allen 1987: 333).

impressive. . . . Although a higher proportion of blacks could be found among the professional and technical occupations in 1980 than in 1972, they were concentrated in jobs at the lower end of the professional pay scale" (Westcott 1982: 31). Black professionals' pay increases were small relative to those of whites; the black/white ratio of earnings for white-collar workers actually declined from 91 percent in 1973 to 86 percent in 1980 (ibid.: 35 [these data do not control for age or seniority]; see also Sokoloff 1989; Reskin and Roos 1990). The "average job authority of black men is markedly lower than that of white men," even after controlling for personal characteristics of employees, and "black men receive a lower income return to authority than do whites, with the discrepancy in income return being especially pronounced at higher occupational status levels." Thus "the exclusion from authority . . . on the average across occupations . . . accounts for approximately one-third of the total black-white income gap" (Kluegel 1978: 285).

Discrimination is harder to pinpoint outside the economic realm, but it persists. Government employee organizations with many minority members are less effective in wage negotiations than those with few minorities because community interest groups are more hostile toward them and more active against them (Billeaux 1988). Federal courts continue to find school districts, state and local governments, and employers guilty of intentional segregation.[17] Whites make racial distinctions in controlled experiments despite their own self-perceptions as racially neutral and despite social norms against such distinctions (Crosby 1980; Pettigrew and Martin 1987). Teenagers, less well socialized than their elders, express stereotypes even on surveys: 35 percent of the nonblack students in one high school applied "negative imagery" (the adjectives were "lazy, snobbish, stupid, selfish") to the black students, compared with scores for other groups ranging from 32 percent of the non-Italian students rating Italians negatively to 16 percent of the non-Irish and non-Jewish students rating Irish and Jewish fellow students negatively (Lichter and Lichter n.d. [c. 1989], table 5).[18]

[17] See, e.g., *United States v. Yonkers Board of Education*, 624 F. Supp. 1276 (U.S. District Ct. S. D. New York), November 20, 1985.

[18] Conversely, blacks received the lowest percentage of "positive imagery" ratings (the adjectives were "friendly, honest, polite, hardworking, smart, kind, emotional, and religious"); 22 percent of nonblacks rated blacks favorably, compared with 32 percent of non-Jews rating Jewish students favorably, and 36 percent of non-Italians rating Italians favorably. Fully 31 percent of blacks rated blacks unfavorably, and blacks rated blacks more unfavorably than they rated any other group except Italians (33 percent). 46 percent of blacks rated blacks favorably; blacks rated blacks more favorably than they rated any other group (the next highest was Italians, at 34 percent). This odd pattern with regard to black evaluations of Italians may be explained by the fact that there were more Italian students (N = 257) in the school than any other ethnic group except blacks (N = 318). The survey was conducted a

But not everything that blacks perceive to be racism necessarily is. And the point is not whether discrimination exists—it surely does—but whether it is as pervasive as some middle-class blacks claim and whether it is rising or falling. Only when we answer those questions will we be able to tell whether the dramatic growth of the new black middle class can continue its trajectory or whether whites will contrive to stop it in its tracks. And only then will we be able to tell whether all the strains I have described are the apparently inevitable concomitants of achieving the American dream or the surface manifestations of an underlying struggle to the end.

---

few weeks before white residents of Howard Beach attacked several black men, killing one (Lichter and Lichter n.d. [c. 1989], tables 5 and 6).

8

The Inevitability of Oppression and the Dynamics of Social Dominance

Jim Sidanius and Felicia Pratto

"Is Martin Luther King's dream that people be judged by the content of their characters rather than by the color of their skins really possible?" "Is political equality between men and women actually achievable?" "Is democracy, as defined by political equality between individuals regardless of race, creed, sex, nationality or other random social categorization, really within the realm of human possibility?" Let us pose these questions more generally and query, "Can multi-ethnic, and multi-group societies be other than oppressive?" We submit that in an effort to answer "yes" to these questions, some American theorists have looked at American racism from a particularly American, and thereby unnecessarily constrained, perspective (see e.g., Kluegel and Smith 1986; Sears 1988).

We believe that special explanations for *American* racism are inadequate and incomplete, in part because they fail to consider American racism within the broader context of the dynamics of group oppression in general. We refer to such things as the long-term European persecution of Jews, conquistadores' and missionaries' exploitation of Native Americans, Israelis' failure to recognize Palestinians, the Anglo-Irish conflict, and so on ad infinitum. Although each ethnic group has its own deeply held beliefs to justify ethnic oppression (although sometimes called nationalism, ethnocentrism, racism, national security, etc.), the cultural specificity of these beliefs cannot serve to explain the pervasiveness of oppression. Moreover, none of the beliefs justifying ethnic oppression account for the almost universal second-class status of women. What all of these forms of oppression have in common is that they are group-based hierarchies. We suggest that the many forms of group-based oppression, plus the culturally shared justifications for them (in, for example, religions) are as pervasive as they are because they have been of survival value for the human group throughout its evolutionary history. We explicate the human characteristics and individual and social processes that we believe contribute to group-based social hierarchy, drawing on social comparison and social identity theories, neoclassical elitism theory, research findings within the fields of political socialization, public opinion, psychophysiology, and reasoning from evolutionary psychology. This approach is called social-dominance (SD) theory (Sidanius, Devereux, and Pratto 1992; Sidanius and Liu 1992; Sidanius and Pratto 1992; Sidanius, Pratto, Martin, and Stallworth 1991).

We begin with the observation that all human societies throughout recorded human history have been hierarchically organized.[1] Given this relatively uncontroversial statement, SD theory then makes four basic assumptions:

(1) Human social systems are predisposed to form *group based* social hierarchies. This type of social hierarchy consists of, at least, a *hegemonic group* at its top and a *negative reference group* at its bottom.

In complex, multi-ethnic and multi-group societies, hegemonic groups are most easily recognized as those groups whose proportional representation in decision-making positions within powerful social institutions shows the steepest degree of increase with increasing power of the institution. This principle can be regarded as another manifestation of R. D. Putnam's law of increasing disproportion (see Putnam 1976). Similarly, a negative reference group is most easily recognized as that group whose proportional representation in decision-making positions within major social institutions shows the sharpest decrease as the power of the institution increases. This group-based social hierarchy must be distinguished from an individually based meritocracy in which an individual's social rank is solely a function of his or her individual achievements.

(2) Hegemonic groups will tend to be disproportionately male.

We can also refer to this as *the iron law of andrarchy*. As with hegemonic groups in general, Putnam's law of increasing disproportion will also apply with respect to male-female differences. Males will tend to dominate in positions of political power and the degree of this dominance will increase with increasing levels of political power.

(3) Most forms of social oppression (e.g., racism, sexism, nationalism, classism) can be regarded as manifestations of the same human predisposition toward the establishment and maintenance of group-based social hierarchy.

(4) Social hierarchy is a survival strategy that has been selected by most if not all species of primates, including homo sapiens.

---

[1] Although the universality of hierarchy throughout human history is a generally accepted notion, there are those who dispute this (see, e.g., Gimbutas 1989).

Here it is assumed that the establishment of group-based dominance systems has proven itself to be useful very early on in the evolutionary development of primates. Among the useful functions that social hierarchy might serve are:

(a) *Social hierarchy could serve as a principle of scarce resource allocation.* For example, within an economy of scarcity, an environment in which the species homo sapiens probably evolved, there might often not be enough food to sustain the entire proto-human troupe. Therefore, a strictly equal distribution might, not infrequently, lead to general starvation. On the other hand, although a distribution principle based on social rank might lead to the death of low-ranked individuals, it would at least increase the chances of troupe survival as such.

(b) *Everything else being equal, social hierarchy might serve to reduce internal social conflict.* This will be because of the tendency of those with lower social status to defer to and obey those with higher rank.

(c) *Social groups that are hierarchically organized will have a competitive advantage over social systems that are not hierarchically organized.* If we conceptualize the proto- and early human troupe as an ambulatory "attack and defense unit," willing and prepared to exploit opportunities to attack weaker and/or less well organized troupes, while at the same time prepared against attack from rival troupes, then it is clear that, everything else being equal, military success will go to that troupe that has better military organization. Good military organization always implies hierarchical and well-functioning chains of command. Social groups that have hierarchical chains of command already in place will therefore have a competitive advantage.

If, as we postulate, hierarchies have had survival value during the course of human evolution, there ought to be human characteristics, some relatively constant, and others brought out in group interaction, that contribute to hierarchical social organization. In explicating SD theory, we explain the social and individual processes that we believe contribute to formation and maintenance of group-based hierarchy, and those individual characteristics that contribute to these processes. The overall framework of the model appears in Figure 8.1.

The process of forming and maintaining social hierarchy is driven by two proximal mechanisms: (a) aggregated institutional discrimination and (b) aggregated individual discrimination. *Aggregated institutional discrimination* results from institutions such as courts, schools, banks and financial houses, committees of various sorts, legislative bodies, and so on, distributing things of social value in a discriminatory manner. By *social value* we mean any thing or set of things that is highly valued in a given social system (e.g., money, promotions, university positions, titles, sea shells). This distribution can be described as "discriminatory" to the extent to

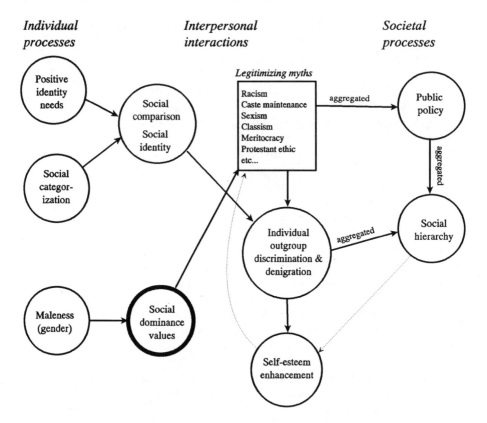

Fig. 8.1. Social-dominance model.

which it is differentially allocated to different social groups. It is to be expected, almost by definition, that institutions will allocate greater value
to hegemonic groups than to negative reference groups.

By *individual discrimination* we refer to the case of simple, individually
based differential allocation of value by individual A against individual B
based purely on B's group membership. One of the factors contributing
to individual discrimination is the need for positive self-identity; there is
empirical evidence that one of the immediate benefits that individual A
derives from discriminating against individual B is enhanced self-esteem
(see Lemyre and Smith 1985). Since one's feelings of self and self-worth
are substantially derived from the social comparisons one makes between
"self" (defined in terms of "individual" and/or "group self") and "other,"
one's positive feelings of self will be enhanced if the outcomes of such
comparisons lead to relative "gain" for the "self." In other words, such

comparisons are inherently zero-sum games and are often facilitated by an act of discrimination against a member of an "outgroup," especially if this individual is a member of a "negative reference group." When such cases of discrimination are aggregated over many individual encounters over many years, the degree of power and prestige of group A will begin to diverge from that of group B. One of the results of this continual social comparison is that, in general, the higher an individual's social rank, the greater his or her self-esteem should be.

Both institutional and individual acts of discrimination will be greatly facilitated by the use of *legitimizing myths,* that is the entire class of attitudes, values, beliefs, or ideologies that serve to provide intellectual and moral justification for, and thus social legitimacy to, the unequal distribution of value in social systems. In this sense, SD theory is, in essence, a functional theory of social attitudes, values, ideologies and beliefs. However, besides the widely accepted notion that attitudes, values and beliefs serve functions for the *individuals* holding them (see Katz 1960), SD theory also assumes that attitudes, values, ideologies, and beliefs also serve functions for *social systems* as well. The extent to which these myths are shared is the extent to which discrimination can exist with relatively little social tension resulting.

Legitimizing myths come in at least three ideological flavors: left-wing, right-wing, and centrist/liberal. Examples of right-wing legitimizing myths would be such beliefs as the nineteenth-century theories of European racial superiority, notions of the "White Man's Burden," the divine right of kings, the theory of papal infallibility, the Monroe Doctrine, and Manifest Destiny. Probably the best example of a left-wing legitimizing myth is Lenin's theory of the leading and central role of the Communist Party. This maintains that since communists are the only ones who truly understand the "real interests" of the working class, they are the only ones who should control state power. Finally, examples of centrist/liberal legitimizing myths would include such beliefs as the theory of meritocracy, the Protestant work ethic, social Calvinism and social Darwinism.

Besides differing in ideological orientation, legitimizing myths can also differ in their degree of *robustness* or *potency*. Legitimizing myths are robust to the extent to which they are well-anchored, attached to and consistent with other centrally integrating conceptions of the "moral" and the "true." For example, the "centrist" legitimizing myth of "meritocracy" or the "Protestant work ethic" is presently a robust and potent legitimizing myth in contemporary U.S. society because it is so consistent with Americans' general notions of morality and fairness (see Kluegel and Smith 1986) and theories of social mobility that it has taken on the appearance of self-evident "truth." On the other hand, the theory of European moral and intellectual superiority, which appeared equally self-evident not long ago, is no longer very potent because it is no longer consistent with what modern society considers to be scientific "truth" or with modern notions of "fairness" or "democracy."

We have postulated an individual and group difference variable that should be related to individual discrimination, adherence to legitimizing myths, and support for institutional discrimination, *social dominance orientation*, or what we also sometimes refer to as the *generalized imperial imperative.* This construct refers to the degree to which people desire and strive for superiority of the ingroup over the outgroup and oppose egalitarianism.

The SD model posits that males will be significantly more dominance-oriented than females. This greater male dominance orientation is assumed to be a function not only of the differential socialization of males and females, but also a function of certain genetic and hormonal differences between the sexes as well.[2] For example, there is strong experimental evidence to indicate that the levels of agonistic and dominance-oriented behavior in males are affected by androgenization of the fetal brain and its subsequent sensitivity to testosterone and other androgens (see Kelly 1985; Dearden 1974). The role that more dominance-oriented persons (males) will play is that of *hierarchy enforcers* within social systems. This is obviously not to imply that all males will be more dominance-oriented and aggressive than all females, any more than one can state that all males will be taller than all females. If we use the term *agonism* to refer to the combined state of competitiveness, aggression, and dominance orientation, then the SD paradigm merely implies that, everything else being equal,

$$E(agonism)_\delta > E(agonism)_\circ.$$

Finally, the SD model assumes that, everything else being equal, the level of oppression in any social system will tend to reach some equilibrium point short of genocide. This is to say that a certain level of oppression is assumed to increase the survivability of a social system, while "too much" oppression will tend to decrease the survivability of a social system. Therefore, in social systems that are relatively stable, we expect that an *oppression equilibrium* or an *oppression asymptote* will be found at the point that simultaneously: (a) satisfies the need to maintain as hierarchical a society as possible, (b) but that does not at the same time come into critical conflict with other central values and beliefs within the social system, and (c) does not create socially destabilizing hardships for major sections of the negative reference group(s).

---

[2] For evidence concerning the covariation between hormonal functioning in females and the fluctuation of certain intellectual abilities and dominance orientation see Hampson and Kimura 1988, Kimura 1983 and 1987, and Christiansen and Knussmann 1987a and 1987b; see also fuller discussion of this work below.

One of the factors assumed to contribute to the establishment of this oppression equilibrium is a curvilinear relationship between social status and social-dominance orientation. It is expected that general dominance orientation will tend to increase with increasing levels of social status. However, after a certain point, it is expected that this relationship will begin to level off and even decrease. Thus, among the elite members of the hegemonic group, there will be somewhat lowered levels of social-dominance orientation. However, this tendency will tend to be restricted to those members of the hegemonic elite who have enjoyed high status and power for a relatively long time: that is, patricians. Patricians will enjoy higher levels of self-esteem and tend to feel quite personally secure in their hegemonic roles. This sense of personal security and general well-being will then permit them the luxury of feeling and exhibiting greater sympathy for less fortunate others through lowered general ethnocentrism and through acts of noblesse oblige. This heightened level of "social nurturance" will generally not be found among "nouveaux riches" or other upwardly striving members of the hegemonic group. Owing to the disproportionate amount of social influence enjoyed by patricians, their more "liberal" attitudes toward negative reference groups will tend to act as a braking mechanism on the overall level of oppression, which will in turn help guide the social system into oppression equilibrium.

Social-Dominance Theory and Other Models

Two-Value Theory

SD theory shares a number of assumptions with other general models of political and social behavior. To begin with, it shares a limited similarity to and has been greatly influenced by Milton Rokeach's two-value theory of political attitudes (Rokeach 1979). The two-value theory assumes that almost all political attitudes and behavior are driven by two fundamental values, *social equality* and *individual freedom*. The similarity between the two models is embraced by the central role given to the concept of egalitarianism. Although the concept of "social dominance" is slightly larger than Rokeach's notion of egalitarianism/anti-egalitarianism, the two concepts are nevertheless strongly related. The use of this construct is the only real point of overlap between the two models.

Social-Identity and Downward-Comparison Theories

Social-dominance theory makes a number of assumptions that are quite similar to those found in social-identity theory (SIT; see Tajfel 1978, 1982a, 1982b), particularly with regard to the ego-enhancing functions of downward social comparisons (see also Crocker and Schwartz 1985; Crocker et al. 1987; Hakmiller 1966; Taylor and Lobel 1990; Wills 1981, 1987). However, there are also some important differences between the SIT and SD models. SIT and downward-comparison theories posit that outgroup comparisons are made to enhance self- or ingroup esteem. Given that members of low-status groups cannot compare themselves favorably to members of higher-status outgroups, they may avoid this by not engaging in comparisons with higher-status outgroups. Clearly, they should not engage in outgroup favoritism. Furthermore, outgroup favoritism will be especially unlikely on the part of members of low-status ingroups who cannot either escape or defect from such low-status groups.

We question these conclusions. When the hegemonic group controls social discourse and the media, it must be very difficult for negative refer-ence groups members to avoid outgroup comparisons. Also, as S. Hinkle and R. Brown (1990) have pointed out, and as a good deal of evidence testifies, outgroup favoritism is not an uncommon occurrence. The most famous illustration of outgroup favoritism is found in K. B. Clark and M. P. Clark's (1947) doll study, in which black children were found to favor white over black dolls. The conclusion that Hinkle and Brown (1990) reach, which is consistent with the Clark and Clark results, is that ingroup favoritism will tend to occur when the ingroup occupies *equal or higher* social status than the outgroup, whereas outgroup favoritism will occur when the ingroup occupies lower social status than the out-group. This is particularly likely to happen when the status hierarchy is perceived to be both stable and legitimate. Although these findings are difficult to reconcile with both SIT and downward-comparison theory, they are most congruent with and even derivable from social-dominance theory. The reason for this theoretical congruence lies at the heart of SD theory's most basic assumption: that *all social systems will converge toward the establishment of stable, group-based social hierarchies.* Given this assumption, it would then seem perfectly reasonable and even necessary for members of high-status groups to discriminate against members of low-status groups, while members of low-status groups will tend not to discriminate against, but rather to discriminate in favor of and defer to, members of high-status groups. While such a strategy (e.g., "Uncle Tom-ing") might ensure survival or better treatment for a low-status individual, it also facilitates domination by the hegemonic group. In this analysis, the leaders of the American black power and South African black consciousness movements were correct in recognizing that black self-denigration served to support the white-dominated hierarchy and that "black pride" could be a power-ful tool in dismantling it. Likewise, white southerners who asserted that all was peaceful until "outside agitators" attempted to convince blacks to stop deferring were correct. The refusal of blacks to accept their "station" was and must necessarily be conflict-producing and socially destabilizing.

As the previous examples imply, general lower-status deference does not imply that lower-status groups will be totally passive, uncompetitive and acquiescent toward hegemonic groups; rather, when the legitimizing myths are functioning as they should, this counterpressure from lower-status groups will tend to be weaker and more fragmented than the pressure from hegemonic groups. This *discriminatory asymmetry* maintains the stability of the hierarchy. If members of low-status groups were to discriminate against members of high-status groups to the *same extent* that they are discriminated against, this would tend to produce high levels of social conflict and social instability, ultimately leading to a state of "Lebanese politics" in which each group is in almost constant and brutal conflict with every other group and in constantly shifting and complex alliances. Such a social system would be extremely unstable and ultimately incapable of surviving.

Realistic Group-Conflict Theory

There are also a number of superficial similarities between SD theory and realistic group-conflict theory (see Bobo 1983, 1988; Jackman and Muha 1984; Sherif 1967). Both view the output of social policy as resulting from group rather than individual conflict and both see political ideology and sociopolitical attitudes functioning essentially as legitimizing myths providing social justification for the hegemonic position of one social group over another. However, the two models differ quite fundamentally in terms of their analysis of the etiology of and ultimate goals of the group conflict.

First, realistic group-conflict theory takes a relatively traditional "class" or "structural" rather than an "evolutionary" approach to the analysis of the group conflict, such that under the proper environmental circumstances, conflict between groups can be severely attenuated if not completely eliminated. SD theory views group conflict as having less to do with "structural" features of the economy or culture than as being primarily driven by a ubiquitous human drive toward domination and group-based hierarchical social organization.[3]

Secondly, realistic group-conflict theory maintains that conflict among groups is primarily driven by "realistic" competition for scarce, material resources (e.g., wealth, housing, university positions, jobs). Although SD theory does not deny the fundamental importance of concrete resource competition, the SD model maintains that even when the basic necessities of life are satisfied, group conflict will persist, in part because of the desire to enhance and/or maintain social prestige, social status, and self-esteem

---

[3] This is not to imply that group conflict is impervious to structural characteristics, but simply that group conflict is not dependent upon structural characteristics.

of one group at the cost of another. Thus, contrary to realistic group-conflict theory, *SD theory predicts that a dominant, hegemonic group will be quite willing to decrease its absolute level of material wealth so long as it increases the difference between its own wealth and the wealth of a subordinate group*. Consistent with the empirical findings of the minimal-groups literature, in the allocation of resources, ingroups will tend to *maximize group differences* even at the cost of absolute ingroup profit. This is congruent with the SD notion that the attainment of social prestige is necessarily a zero-sum game, and can therefore only be realized by one group at the expense of another (see Tajfel and Turner 1986; Wills 1981).

Given the broad nature of SD theory, it is not possible to test the model in any definitive manner within a single empirical study. Instead, we attempt to triangulate upon the plausibility of the model by examination of several of the model's predictions within four independent data sets using subjects from five different parts of the world, including Western Europe, Latin America, Asia, the Middle East, and the United States.

Empirical Support

The data sets included: Sample 1, a random sample of 5,342 U.S. and foreign students from the University of Texas at Austin collected in 1986;[4] Sample 2, a mail survey of 723 UCLA undergraduates collected during the spring of 1988; Sample 3, a random sample of 783 Swedish gymnasia students collected from the county of Stockholm, Sweden, in 1979;[5] and Sample 4, 192 UCLA undergraduates recruited for a minimal-groups and social-dominance experiment during the fall of 1989.

In the following discussion, we illustrate the plausibility of the SD paradigm by examining various relationships and hypotheses derivable from the basic model. To do this, depending upon the specific nature of the data available to us, we have employed either direct measures of our central concept of *social-dominance orientation*, or close surrogates of this concept such as *anti-egalitarianism* and *caste-maintenance orientation* (to be defined below).

Simple Beginnings: A Demonstration of Ethnic Status and Social Rank

The entire reasoning of SD theory rests on the simple assumption that different ethnic groups may reliably be ranked along a single social

[4] For more details concerning this sample, see Sidanius 1989.
[5] See Ekehammar, Sidanius, and Nilsson 1989.

status continuum. Anthropologists and sociologists have asserted this in nearly every culture studied. As an additional demonstration, we asked some UCLA students (Sample 2) the following question: "There are many people who believe that the different ethnic groups enjoy different amounts of social status in this society. You may not believe in this for yourself, but if you had to rate each of the following groups as such people see them, how would you do so?" The subjects were asked to rate the different groups on a seven-point scale from 1 (Low Status) to 7 (High Status).

The results of these ratings showed that people had little trouble in distributing ethnic groups along a single social status dimension. Furthermore, the allocation of groups to ranks was quite consistent with what one would expect. The median ratings of the groups were: European Americans, 7; Asian Americans, 5; Mexican Americans, 3; African Americans, 3. The distribution of the ratings is shown in Table 8.1.

In addition, the intraclass correlation coefficient showed that the reliability of the mean social status ratings across all subjects was quite high indeed ($r = .99$).

Self-esteem and Social Status

It will be recalled that SD theory predicts a monotonic relationship between social rank and self-esteem; the higher one's social rank, the higher one's self-esteem should be. Among other reasons, self-esteem is expected to increase with social rank because the greater one's rank, the more often one is able to make favorable social comparisons with other individuals and groups.

Self-esteem was measured on the ten-item Rosenberg Self-esteem Scale (Rosenberg 1965) ($\alpha = .89$), while social rank was measured by respondents' self-classification into one of nine social status categories, ranging from "lower working class" to "upper upper class." The distribution of the social status categorizations and their relationship to self-esteem is shown in Figure 8.2.

As can be seen in Figure 8.2, there was a moderately weak, but statistically significant and monotonic, trend to this relationship consistent with the SD paradigm. The higher the social status, the greater the self-esteem ($r = .15$, $p < .01$).

Caste-Maintenance Orientation, Gender, and Ethnic Status

Another central assumption of SD theory is that all complex, multiethnic societies will tend to be group-based hierarchies. One of the implications of this assumption is that multi-ethnic societies will also converge toward caste systems. There has been a good deal of debate over the defi-

TABLE 8.1

Social Status Ratings of Four Ethnic Groups by 715 UCLA Students

Count	Value	
		European American Status Rating (median = 7.00; SD = .772; N = 715)
1	2.00	
2	3.00	
13	4.00	X
64	5.00	XXXXXX
227	6.00	XXXXXXXXXXXXXXXXXXXXXXXXX
408	7.00	XXXXXXXXXXXXXXXXXXXXXXXXXXXXXXXXXXXXXXXXXXXXXX
		Asian American Status Rating (median = 5.00; SD = 1.167; N = 715)
9	1.00	X
14	2.00	XX
67	3.00	XXXXXXXX
156	4.00	XXXXXXXXXXXXXXXXXXXX
283	5.00	XXXXXXXXXXXXXXXXXXXXXXXXXXXXXXXXXXXXX
146	6.00	XXXXXXXXXXXXXXXXXX
40	7.00	XXXXX
		Mexican American Status Rating (median = 3.00; SD = 1.202; N = 710)
58	1.00	XXXXXXX
204	2.00	XXXXXXXXXXXXXXXXXXXXXXXXXXXX
228	3.00	XXXXXXXXXXXXXXXXXXXXXXXXXXXXXXX
153	4.00	XXXXXXXXXXXXXXXXXXX
46	5.00	XXXXXX
12	6.00	XX
9	7.00	X
		African American Status Rating (median = 3.00; SD = 1.354; N = 715)
54	1.00	XXXXXXX
157	2.00	XXXXXXXXXXXXXXXXXXXX
211	3.00	XXXXXXXXXXXXXXXXXXXXXXXXXXX
156	4.00	XXXXXXXXXXXXXXXXXXX
101	5.00	XXXXXXXXXXXXX
19	6.00	XX
17	7.00	XX

NOTE: Each X represents approximately eight subjects. Ratings were made on a scale from 1 (very low status) to 7 (very high status).

nition of *caste*. Some have argued that the term should apply only to India, while others have maintained a less restrictive definition (see Cox 1948; Davis, Gardner, and Gardner 1941; Drake and Cayton 1945; Dollard 1937; Myrdal 1944; Pohlman 1951; Willie 1979). Taking a less restrictive approach, we define a caste system as *any social system consisting of endogamous social groups arranged along a single social status hierarchy*.

To maintain separate castes, there can be very few cross-caste, socially sanctioned sexual relations. SD theory posits two mechanisms for the maintenance of sexual caste boundaries. First, higher-status persons should be more interested in guarding their caste's separateness and so be more in favor of caste maintenance than lower-status persons. Second, as men are more dominance-oriented than women and serve as "hierarchy enforcers," they should also be more favorably disposed toward hierarchy maintenance via sexual caste separation than females. To test these two hypotheses, we used Sample 1 from the University of Texas and defined a concept we refer to as *caste-maintenance orientation*, or sexual apartheid: attitudes toward (a) interracial dating and (b) interracial marriage ($\alpha = .82$). Although *caste-maintenance orientation* is related to general racism, previous empirical research within other samples (see Brigham, Woodmanese, and Cook 1976) and prior factor analysis of this sample has disclosed that *caste-maintenance orientation* (or anti-miscegenation) falls out as a separate dimension.

We examined *caste-maintenance orientation* as a function of sex (male versus female) and ethnic group (African American, Mexican American, Asian American, and European American). The results of this analysis can be found in Figure 8.3, where the four ethnic groups are ordered along a

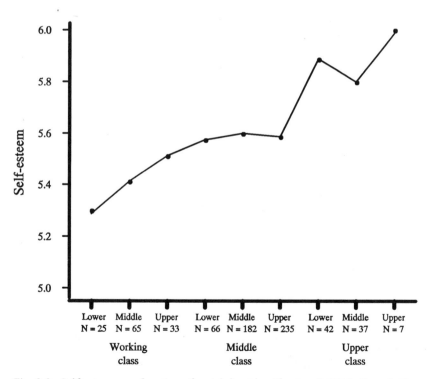

Fig. 8.2. Self-esteem as a function of social class identification (UCLA, Sample 2).

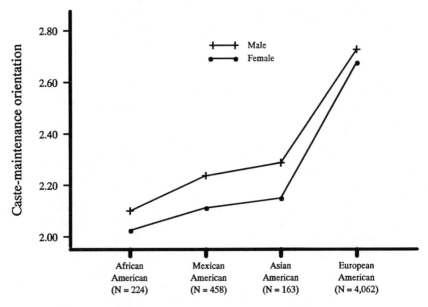

Fig. 8.3. Caste-maintenance orientation as a function of gender and ethnic status (University of Texas, Sample 1).

social status dimension (which reflects our Sample 2 mean ratings and results from a national probability sample [Bobo 1989]).

As expected, the results of a two-way ANOVA and the data in Figure 8.3 show that: (1) within each ethnic group, males were significantly more caste-maintenance-oriented than females (F [1, 4906] = 6.1, p < .02), and (2) the ethnic groups displayed relatively sharp differences in caste-maintenance orientation (F [3, 4906] = 65.9, p < .001). The nature of these ethnic group differences was clearly consistent with expectations; the higher the social status of the ethnic group, the greater the caste-maintenance orientation. Furthermore, inspection of Figure 8.3 discloses that there was no evidence of an interaction effect between sex/gender and ethnic status (interaction F < 1). That is, the degree of the difference between males and females was relatively constant across ethnic groups.

This lack of a significant interaction between sex and ethnic group is significant in and of itself. If one were to interpret the main effect for sex/gender as purely a function of socialization (i.e., the "cultural-deterministic argument"), then it is also reasonable to assume that this should reflect itself in slightly greater or lesser differences within certain ethnic groups compared to others (e.g., Mexican American versus European American). However, the fact that there was not even a tendency toward interaction in this very large sample makes the strictly cultural-deterministic argument somewhat implausible.[6]

The International Generalizability of Male Caste-Maintenance Orientation

To be truly useful, the SD paradigm must be able to display cross-cultural robustness as well as replicability within American culture. Therefore, it is desirable to be able to demonstrate the robustness of SD-generated predictions in foreign populations as well. We recall from Figure 8.3 that within each of the four U.S. ethnic groups, males were more *caste-maintenance-oriented* than females. SD theory asserts that this pattern will not only be restricted to groups within American culture but will be internationally generalizable. To uncover whether or not this assertion can be supported by data, we examined males and females socialized in different parts of the world. To begin, we examined the caste-maintenance orientations of 435 foreign students who were part of Sample 1. These students came to the United States for university study from countries in four different parts of the world: (1) Asia (N = 163), (2) Latin America (N = 99), (3) the Middle East (N = 33), and (4) Western Europe (N = 63). We also include a category of students who gave their ethnicity and country of origin as "other" (N = 87). If the "male-hierarchy-maintenance" hypothesis of SD theory is correct, even across these very disparate countries and cultures, we should find that: (a) males are more caste-maintenance-oriented than females, and (b) there should be no statistically significant interaction between nationality or ethnic group and sex. This is only to imply that the difference in caste-maintenance orientation between males and females should be constant (within sampling error) across nationality/culture.

We analyzed the data using a 2×5 ANOVA design (sex by national/ethnic group), and the results can be seen in Figure 8.4.

Interestingly, the five national/ethnic groups did not display statistically significant differences on caste-maintenance orientation ($F\,[4, 435] = 1.42$, n.s.). However, consistent with the prediction of SD theory, there was a weak, yet statistically significant, gender effect; males were significantly more caste-maintenance-oriented than females ($F\,[1, 435] = 5.22$, $p \leq 0.03$). The only exception to this general trend of greater male caste-maintenance orientation was found for the European group; however, this exception was apparently not significant, because SD theory's second

---

[6] More will be said about sex differences later.

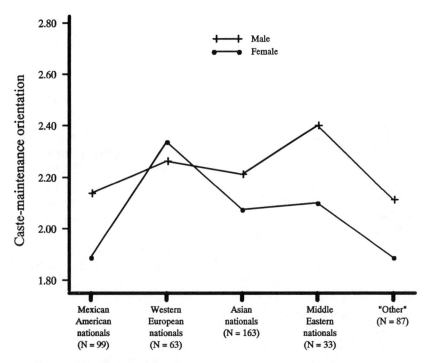

Fig. 8.4. Caste-maintenance orientation as a function of gender, nationality, and "other" group status (University of Texas, Sample 1).

prediction was also confirmed. The data indicate that there was no statistically significant interaction between nationality or ethnic group and sex (F [4, 435] < 1).

A second attack on the international generalizability of male caste-maintenance orientation was achieved by use of the Swedish sample. This sample offered only one item tapping the caste-maintenance dimension ("interracial marriage" from the S7 scale; see Sidanius 1976). Obviously, use of a single item lowers the reliability with which we can measure any latent continuum. On the other hand, the fact that this measure has relatively low reliability, and is therefore more subject to random error, implies that it will also be more difficult for us to reject the null-hypothesis. In this sense, we are posing a rather severe test of our hypotheses.

In view of the ethnic homogeneity of the Swedish sample, we examined opposition to interracial marriage as a function of gender and social class. Again, we expected that (a) males would be significantly more opposed to interracial marriage than females, and (b) there would be no significant interaction between gender and social class. This again simply implies that greater male opposition to interracial marriage (or support of group boundary maintenance) should be constant across social class.

Figure 8.5 shows that, despite the single-item measure, Swedish males were still significantly more opposed to interracial marriage than Swedish females at every level of social status (F [1, 765] = 25.36, $p < 10^{-4}$). Furthermore, and consistent with the previous findings, the results showed no significant interaction between gender and social status (F [2,765] < 1).

Ideological Asymmetry

The fact that caste-maintenance orientation increases with increasing ethnic status in Sample 1 can be interpreted in at least one of two ways. First, one can view this as a reflection of a purely symmetrical "rational actor" strategy: for those at the higher end of the social status continuum, "out-marriage" or "out-dating" is more likely to involve a lower-status person and therefore to result in a "loss" of status; whereas low-status persons could "gain" status from "out-marriage" and "out-dating." Seen from this perspective, individuals at different levels of the social status hierarchy should be expending equal or "symmetrical effort" at either

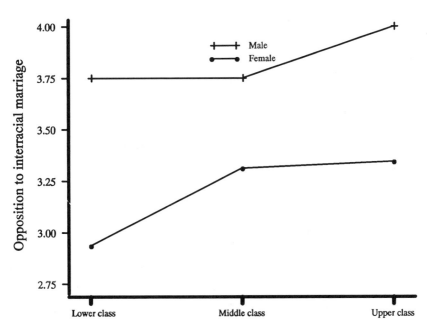

Fig. 8.5. Opposition to interracial marriage as a function of social class and gender among Swedish students (Sample 3).

caste maintenance (for high-status individuals) or "caste equality" (for low-status individuals).

However, if low- and high-status groups were expending equal effort in the conflict over caste maintenance, this conflict would tend to be destabilizing and serve to dismantle the social hierarchy. SD theory therefore predicts that under normal circumstances, people at various levels of the social status hierarchy will expend *unequal* effort in either maintaining or challenging the status structure. Higher-status persons should be *more* interested in maintaining the status hierarchy than lower-status persons are in challenging it. This would be consistent with experimental evidence that ingroups tend to discriminate *against* outgroups of equal or lower status, while they discriminate *in favor of* outgroups of higher status (see Brown 1978; Hinkle and Brown 1990; Sachdev and Bourhis 1985, 1987; Skevington 1981; van Knippenberg and van Oers 1984). The SD perspective assumes that the net effect of this discriminatory asymmetry will be to maintain and stabilize social hierarchy. Furthermore, because social discourse, including persuasion of lower-status members of the "correctness" of caste maintenance, is one of the chief tools for hierarchy maintenance, the relationship between adherence to hierarchy-legitimizing myths and caste-maintenance orientation should be stronger among higher- than lower-status persons. Not only will higher-status groups be more interested in maintaining status boundaries than lower-status groups, but this greater interest will also manifest itself in a greater utilization of ideology or "legitimizing myths" to achieve this purpose. As a result, we expect that *the greater an ethnic group's social status, the stronger the connection between caste-maintenance orientation and political ideology will be.*

We tested this hypothesis using the large Texas data set (Sample 1) with a simple causal model in which gender drove *caste-maintenance orientation* and *political ideology*,[7] and *caste-maintenance orientation* drove *political ideology*. If we arrange the four U.S. ethnic groups (i.e., European Americans, African Americans, Mexican Americans, and Asian Americans) from the Texas sample along a social status hierarchy, we should observe a systematic increase in the strength of the causal path between *caste-maintenance orientation* and *political ideology* with increasing social status. Using a multigroup, manifest variables LISREL (Jöreskog and Sörbom 1984) analysis, we began by estimating fully saturated models (see Fig. 8.6). The covariance matrices were used as input and the coefficients found in Figure 8.6 therefore represent the regression slopes.

Starting from the fully saturated models in Figure 8.6, we examined

[7] Political ideology was defined by use of a five-step political self-rating ranging from "very liberal" to "very conservative."

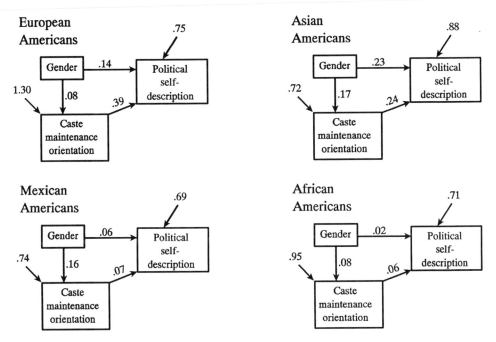

Fig. 8.6. Saturated models showing hypothetical functional relationships between gender, caste-maintenance orientation and political ideology for four ethnic groups (University of Texas, Sample 1).

three hypotheses in a hierarchical manner. The hypotheses correspond to Models A, B, and C and concern each of the three slopes between the constructs in Figure 8.6. Model A assumes that the slopes between gender and political ideology will be the same, within sampling error, for all four ethnic groups. Model B assumes homogeneity of slopes between gender and caste-maintenance orientation across all ethnic groups. Model C assumes slope homogeneity between caste-maintenance orientation and political ideology across ethnic groups. According to SD theory and the ideological asymmetry hypothesis, Model C should be rejected (see Table 8.2).

Using a likelihood ratio test with the nested models, the results disclosed that both Models A and B could not be rejected. In other words, the slopes relating gender to caste-maintenance orientation and to political ideology appeared to be equal across the four ethnic groups. However, restricting the slopes between *caste-maintenance orientation* and *political ideology* to be equal across all four groups (Model C) yielded a large and statistically significant increase in the χ^2 value (67.77, $p < 10^{-5}$). This indicates that

TABLE 8.2

Hierarchical, Likelihood Ratio Test of Three Nested Models of the Causal Relationships Between Sex, Political Ideology, and Caste-Maintenance Orientation Across Four Ethnic Groups

Model	Differences statistics	df	χ^2	p	Decision
A	Ho*: $\gamma_{11} = \gamma_{12} = \gamma_{13} = \gamma_{14}$	3	2.08	.556	Accepted
B	Ho**: $\gamma_{21} = \gamma_{22} = \gamma_{23} = \gamma_{24}$	3	1.07	.794	Accepted
C	Ho***: $\beta_{11} = \beta_{12} = \beta_{13} = \beta_{14}$	3	67.77	10^{-5}	Rejected

*γ_{1j} = Slope between gender and political self-description for ethnic group$_j$.
**γ_{2j} = Slope between gender and caste-maintenance orientation for ethnic group$_j$.
***β_{1j} = Slope between caste-maintenance orientation and political self-description for ethnic group$_j$.

these slopes do differ significantly. Furthermore, the plot of the slopes as a function of the median social status ratings of each ethnic group shows a very clear linear trend (see Fig. 8.7). These results are clearly congruent with the expectations of the SD paradigm.

The fact that the dependence of political ideology on caste maintenance increases with increasing social status is consistent with the findings of other research teams. For example, G. W. Mercer and E. Cairns (1981) found that political ideology was significantly correlated with anti-Catholic attitudes among Protestants in Northern Ireland but was not significantly correlated with anti-Protestant affect among Northern Irish Catholics. Furthermore, H. M. Bahr and B. A. Chadwick (1974) showed that anti-Indian affect was significantly associated with political ideology among American whites but was not associated with anti-white affect among native Americans. The asymmetry hypothesis is also consistent with Edward Carmines and James Stimson's (1982) findings that for white Americans, political ideology is very much concerned with the issue of race.

Structural Asymmetry and Political Party Preference

The SD paradigm and the structural asymmetry hypothesis offer another way of looking at political conservatism in the working class, or the question of why large sections of poor and working-class people so often support conservative and upper-class political candidates (see Stacey and Green 1971; Lipset 1959). Whereas Marxists would explain this behavior in terms of the dynamics of "false consciousness," the SD model explains it in terms of the hierarchy-maintaining function of structural asymmetry. Assuming that a significant portion of voting behavior in Western Europe in general, and Sweden in particular, can be conceived of in terms of "group conflict" (i.e., the wealthier classes against the poorer or working classes), it is then quite reasonable to expect that poorer people will tend to support left-wing parties and wealthier people will tend to support more conservative parties (see, e.g., Centers 1949). However, if we conceive of European, multi-party elections in terms of "ingroup-outgroup" dynamics, where conservative parties are the "ingroup" for high-status people, while left-wing parties are the "ingroup" for low-status people, a wealthier (higher-status) person voting for a conservative party or a poorer (lower-status) person voting for a left-wing party may be viewed as "ingroup favoritism."

Given the structural asymmetry hypothesis, wealthier people should also display a significantly greater level of ingroup favoritism in their voting behavior than lower-status (i.e., poorer) people. We tested this prediction with Sample 3 (Sweden) by dividing the sample into two social status groups, high-status and low-status, and then examining the degree to which low-status (lower third on SES) Swedes and high-status Swedes (highest third on SES) supported their respective ingroups (i.e., left-wing parties (communists and social democrats) and "bourgeois" parties re-

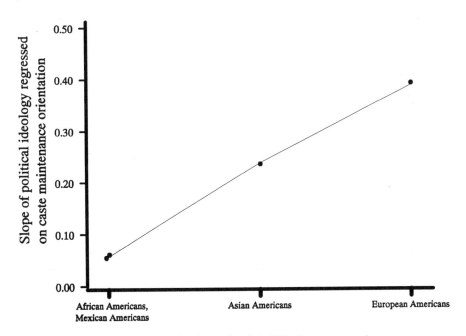

Fig. 8.7. Relationship between the slope of political ideology regressed on caste-maintenance orientation as a function of the rated social status of four ethnic groups (University of Texas, Sample 1).

TABLE 8.3

*Frequency of Ingroup Support as a Function of Social Status
Among Swedish Respondents*

	Social status	
	Low	High
Support of ingroup	97 (61%)	134 (81%)
Support of outgroup	62 (39%)	32 (19%)
Total	159 (100%)	166 (100%)

NOTE: Test of independence of social status and support for groups, $\chi^2 = 14.41$, df = 1, $p < .001$. Support of ingroup was defined as preference for communist and social democratic parties among low-status respondents and as preference for "bourgeois" parties among high-status respondents.

spectively; see Table 8.3). As the data in Table 8.3 indicate, the structural asymmetry hypothesis was again confirmed. A significantly greater proportion of high-status individuals supported their "ingroup" (81 percent) than was the case for low-status individuals (61 percent; $\chi^2 = 14.4$, df = 1, $p < .001$).

Structural Asymmetry, Deference, and the Exercise of Terror

Since the structural asymmetry hypothesis holds that, all else being equal, lower-status individuals will tend to defer to higher-status individuals, the question that naturally follows is, why? This question does not concern the aggregate, structural reason because SD theory assumes that the answer lies in the maintenance of hierarchical and structural integrity; rather the issue turns on the *individual's* motivation for displaying this deference.

There are at least two reasons why lower-status individuals might defer to those of higher status. As has been suggested by B. G. Stacey and R. T. Green (1971), lower-status people might be thoroughly convinced that higher-status people really are worthier, wiser, nobler, and simply "better" than themselves. This is particularly to be expected when the legitimizing myths are "robust,"[8] and the social hierarchy is stable.

A second possible individual motivation for lower-status deference is *systematic terror*—that is, the use of violence or the threat of violence against low-status individuals by high-status individuals. There are two major varieties of systematic terror, *vigilante terror* and *institutional terror*. Examples of vigilante terror are the activities of the Ku Klux Klan and similar informal organizations so common in the United States between the late 1870's and 1924. *Institutional terror* refers to violence or the threat of vio-

[8] See definition of "robust" legitimizing myths above.

lence by the various institutions of the state (e.g., police, army, courts, etc.). Under normal circumstances, systematic terror will be most often exhibited when a member of a negative-reference group or caste publicly violates a status boundary between himself and the hegemonic group and thereby steps "out of his place." What is seen as one of the most egregious ways in which lower-status individuals "step out of place" is when negative-reference-group males accost hegemonic females or when negative-reference-group individuals (male or female) commit acts of violence against hegemonic individuals (male or female). It is circumstances such as these that will often lead to the most extreme forms of systematic terror, including disfigurement and death. We refer to this as the *out-of-place principle*.

When the out-of-place principle has been violated, even when competing and contradictory norms and values such as "due process of law" hinder naked forms of vigilante terror, this terror will only manifest itself in less obvious and more institutionalized ways. One of the most effective means of exercising more subtle, institutional terror is through the operations of the legal system. Because social systems are expected to put a premium on the maintenance of stable social hierarchies, according to the out-of-place principle, acts of aggression by lower-status or negative-reference-group individuals against members of higher-status or hegemonic groups should be among the most severely punished "crimes" to be observed.

Many data consistent with the out-of-place principle can be found in the analysis of real courtroom decisions in the United States. For example, there is convincingly consistent evidence indicating that when blacks murder whites, they are not only more severely punished than whites who murder blacks (i.e., a case of simple discrimination), but more to the point, they are also more severely punished than when they murder other blacks (see Arkin 1980; Barnett 1985; Bensing and Schroeder 1960; Bienen et al. 1988; Bowers 1983; Bowers and Pierce 1980; Ekland-Olson 1988; Foley 1987; Foley and Powell 1982; GAO 1990; Garfinkel 1949; Green 1964; Gross and Mauro 1984; Johnson 1941; Keil and Vito 1989; Kleck 1981; Klein 1989; Klemm 1986; Lewis, Mannle, and Vetter 1979; Murphy 1984; Nakell and Hardy 1987; Paternoster and Kazyaka 1988; Radelet 1981; Radelet and Pierce 1985; Radelet and Vandiver 1983; Riedel 1976; Smith 1987; Vito and Keil 1988; Zeisel 1981).

A concrete example of this pattern of institutional terror can be found in a study by R. Paternoster (1983), who showed that when blacks killed whites, prosecutors in South Carolina were *40 times more likely* to request the death penalty than when blacks killed other blacks! Furthermore, and quite consistent with SD theory and the out-of-place principle, there is research indicating that this effect might have more to do with social status than with race per se. For example in a relatively sophisticated study, R. A. Farrell and V. L. Swigert (1978) examined the discriminability of low- and high-status offender-victim combinations in murder cases. The study included 444 defendants and 432 victims of criminal homicide between 1955 and 1973 in a large urban jurisdiction in the United States. Status was defined using D. J. Treiman's (1977) classification system. The occupational status of offenders and victims were dichotomized, resulting in four offender-victim status categories. Farrell and Swigert then examined the ability of five variables to distinguish among these four offender-victim categories: (a) use of private attorney, (b) trial by jury, (c) bail, (d) offender's prior record, and (e) final conviction severity. The results of the analysis disclosed that punishment severity made a statistically significant contribution to the ability to distinguish among the offender-status–victim-status categories. Low-status murderers of high-status victims received the most severe punishment of any victim-offender status combination.

Examining Other Causal Assumptions of Social-Dominance Theory

In addition to accounting for some important social structure phenomena, we have begun to examine the plausibility of SD theory by directly testing some of the causal assumptions embedded in the model. We began by examining data from white UCLA students (N = 203; Sample 2).[9] Because at the time we collected Sample 2, our research team was just starting to develop the SD model, the scores from this first SD scale are called SDO_1 (see Table 8.4; more fully developed measures of SD are described later). The alpha reliability of this scale was satisfactory (α = .84).

The variables from Sample 2 were used as manifest variables to model the theoretical relations shown in Figure 8.1. The structural depiction of the causal relationships between gender, group identification, social-dominance orientation, the Protestant ethic, caste-maintenance orientation, racism, political and racial policy attitudes (e.g., affirmative action and busing) is found in Figure 8.8. As can be seen, the legitimizing myths (Protestant ethic, caste maintenance, political ideology, and racism) are considered to be largely driven by social-dominance orientation (SDO_1), and SDO in turn is a function of gender and group-centeredness.[10]

---

[9] For a more detailed description of the data set and of the causal paths, see Sidanius, Devereux, and Pratto 1992.

[10] The concepts were defined by the following items: *racism* (α = .88): (1) a black president, (2) blacks are inherently inferior, (3) civil rights activists, (4) white superiority, (5) racial

TABLE 8.4

The SDO₁ Scale Used with Sample 2

---

1. Some people are just more worthy than others.
2. Increased economic equality.
3. Increased social equality.
4. Winning is more important than how the game is played.
5. Getting ahead in life by almost any means necessary.
6. Equality.
7. If people were treated more equally, we would have fewer problems in the country.
8. It is not really a big problem if some people have more of a chance in life than others.

NOTE: Respondents rated how positively or negatively they felt about each item on a scale from 1 (very negative) to 7 (very positive).

The most critical results disclosed that these SD expectations were all essentially confirmed:

(1) Social-dominance orientation had relatively large positive connections with the entire cluster of legitimizing myths, including the Protestant ethic ($\beta = .43$), political ideology ($\beta = .45$), racial policy attitudes ($\beta = .23$), racism ($\beta = .53$), and caste-maintenance orientation ($\beta = .43$).

(2) Opposition to ameliorative racial policy initiatives such as affirmative action and busing was found to be significantly related to the entire cluster of legitimizing myths and SDO.

(3) Gender was significantly related to two factors contributing to hierarchy maintenance. Males were more dominance-oriented than females ($\gamma = .23$) and more strongly ingroup identified ($\gamma = .21$; see n. 10).

Besides all the statistically significant bivariate relations predicted by the theory, the model as a whole provided a statistically acceptable and relatively strong fit to the empirical data ($\chi^2 = 15.27$, df = 12, adjusted

---

equality, and (6) blacks; *protestant ethic* ($\alpha = .49$): (1) "Most people who don't get ahead in life probably work as hard as those who do," (2) "Most people who don't get ahead in life should not blame the system; they have only themselves to blame"; *political ideology* ($\alpha = .85$): (1) socialized medicine, (2) increased taxation of the rich, (3) laissez-faire capitalism, (4) socialism, (5) "In terms of foreign policy issues, how would you describe yourself politically?" (seven-point scale from "very liberal" to "very conservative"), (6) "In terms of economic issues, how would you describe yourself politically?" (seven-point scale from "very liberal" to "very conservative"), (7) "In terms of social issues, how would you describe yourself politically?" (seven-point scale from "very liberal" to "very conservative"); *racial policy attitudes* ($\alpha = .78$): (1) affirmative action, (2) racial quotas to achieve integration, (3) civil rights, (4) racial integration, (5) school busing, (6) helping minorities get a better education is good for all of society. *Group centeredness* was operationalized by asking two questions: (a) "How often do you think of yourself as a member of an ethnic group (e.g., blacks, whites, Latin-American, etc.), and (b) "How close do you feel you are to members of other ethnic groups?" The comparative group identity variable was then defined as (a)−(b).

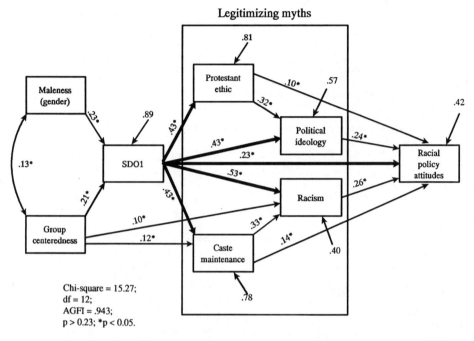

Fig. 8.8. Test of the structural assumptions of social-dominance theory (UCLA, Sample 2).

goodness-of-fit index [AGFI] = .943, p > .23). These results stand in contrast to attempts to fit the data by use of alternative symbolic racism (see Sears 1988), Protestant ethic (see Kluegel and Smith 1986), or political ideology models, none of which were found to provide statistically acceptable fits to the data (see Sidanius, Devereux, and Pratto 1992).

There is one further point worth mentioning about the results in Figure 8.8 concerning the relationship between the Protestant ethic and opposition to affirmative action and busing. Several commentators have implied that the reason white Americans are opposed to these racial policy initiatives is because they are perceived as violating norms of fairness, justice, meritocracy, or the Protestant ethic. The results in Figure 8.8 provide some support for this claim because there is a direct path between the Protestant ethic and opposition to these racial policies (β = .10). However, it must also be observed that this is the *weakest* of all direct effects. There is even stronger support for the position that white opposition to these policy initiatives is primarily a function of classical racism (β = .26), social-dominance orientation (β = .23), and caste-maintenance orientation (β = .14). Furthermore, the size of the total effect of SDO on racial policy attitudes (i.e., both direct and indirect) is rather substantial (total effect = .64).

To show that SD theory can predict other policy attitudes and apply outside the United States, we tested a general model with Swedes (Sample 3), using support for the military as the most endogenous variable. Since the military in many societies is a tool for enforcing the social order (including, at times, dominance over other societies) and symbolizes strength and victory, we expected support for the military to be related to SDO.

SD theory posits the following kinds of relations among the variables in Figure 8.9: (a) support for the Swedish military will be directly affected by ethnocentrism, political-economic conservatism (PEC), and anti-egalitarianism; (b) ethnocentrism and PEC will be significantly driven by anti-egalitarianism; and (c) anti-egalitarianism will be significantly driven by gender.[11]

For the most part, the results of the structural equation analyses were consistent with the expectations of SD theory and all theoretical paths were statistically significant:

(1) Support of the Swedish military was related to PEC (β = .31), ethnocentrism (β = .23), and anti-egalitarianism (β = .08).

(2) Ethnocentrism and PEC were both significantly related to anti-egalitarianism (β = .40, .48, respectively).

(3) Anti-egalitarianism was found to be significantly related to gender, with males being significantly more anti-egalitarian than females (γ = .25).

However, in order to produce a model with a statistically acceptable fit to the data, it was necessary to add some additional paths, including paths between gender on the one hand and ethnocentrism (γ = .22) and PEC on the other (γ = .09) and a path between ethnocentrism and PEC (β = .12). These changes were still quite consistent with the general spirit of SD theory in that: (1) not only were males more dominance-oriented than females, but even controlling for anti-egalitarianism, males were found to be more ethnocentric and politically conservative; (2) even controlling for gender and anti-egalitarianism, political-economic conservatism was still significantly related to ethnocentrism. The more ethnocentric the subjects, the greater their level of conservatism. This larger model was found to

---

[11] The variables in the Swedish data set were defined in the following manner: *ethnocentrism* (α = .74): (1) white superiority, (2) racial equality, (3) mixed marriage, and (4) tighter control of foreigners; *sex* (males = 2, females = 1); *political economic conservatism* (PEC) (α = .82): (1) increased socialization, (2) socialism, (3) capitalism, (4) nationalization of private companies, (5) increased democracy on the job, (6) NATO (7) social welfare, and (8) the United States; *support for the military* (α = .68): (1) increased support of the military, and (2) decreased weapons development.

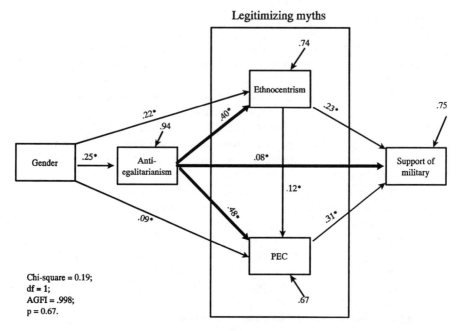

Fig. 8.9. Test of the structural assumptions of social-dominance theory with Swedish students (Sample 3).

give a very tight fit to the empirical data, as well as being congruent with the SD paradigm ($\chi^2 = 0.19$, df = 1, AGFI = .998, $p = .67$, see Fig. 8.9).

An Experimental Demonstration

As will be recalled from the introduction to this chapter, social-dominance theory has been heavily influenced by social-identity theory and the minimal-groups paradigm. In that experimental paradigm, it has been found that the mere cognitive classification of an individual into an in-group is sufficient to produce discrimination against and denigration of outgroups and outgroup members, even in the complete absence of prior history with the group or any of its members. Jim Sidanius and his colleagues have recently replicated the simple minimal-groups experiment using a sample of UCLA undergraduates (Sample 4, N = 192), but with the addition of a more fully developed social-dominance scale (SDO2; see Table 8.5). The reliability of this more comprehensive SD scale was satisfactory ($\alpha = .84$).

For the most part, the standard minimal-groups experiment was conducted, in which the subjects were first given a questionnaire and then a perceptual test in which they were to estimate the number of dots flashed on a screen for a brief period. After the perceptual test, the subjects were told that, on the basis of their performance in the perceptual test, they were either "overestimators" or "underestimators." Of course, these were fictitious groups and the actual assignment of subjects to groups was random. After completing a number of other intermittent tasks, the subjects were asked to make a number of judgments about "overestimators" and "underestimators." These judgments included:

Relative Outgroup Denigration. The subjects were asked to make evaluative ratings of both "underestimators" and "overestimators" along eight evaluative scales. The task read: "To what extent does each of the following characteristics apply to your impression of overestimators/underestimators?" The scales were: Able, Intelligent, Kind, Cold, Dis-

TABLE 8.5

Items in the SDO₂ Scale

1. Some groups of people are just more worthy than others.
2. Increased social equality.
3. Winning is more important than how the game is played.
4. Getting ahead in life by almost any means is necessary.
5. This country would be better off if we cared less about how equal all people are.
6. Equality.
7. If people were treated more equally, we would have fewer problems in the country.
8. It is really not a big problem if some people have more of a chance in life than others.
9. Competition.
10. To get ahead in life, it is sometimes necessary step on others.
11. This country would be better off if inferior groups stayed in their place.
12. The world was provided with enough resources to take care of all its people.
13. Being at the top is the ONLY place to be.
14. It is important that our country continue to be the best in the world.
15. Sometimes war is necessary to put other countries in their place.
16. In an ideal world, all nations would be equal.
17. This country must continue to lead the Free World.
18. I'd give almost anything to get rich.
19. It's about time that we put Japan in its place.
20. We should do anything necessary to increase the power of our country, even if it means war with smaller countries.

NOTE: *Instructions read*: Which of the following objects or statements do you have a positive or a negative feeling towards? Besides each object or statement place a number from "1" to "7" which represents the degree of your positive or negative feeling. Remember, your first reaction is usually the best.

7 = Very positive	4 = Neither positive	3 = Slightly negative
6 = Positive	nor negative	2 = Negative
5 = Slightly positive		1 = Very negative

honest, Sociable, Assertive, and Trustworthy. Using these ratings, *relative-outgroup-denigration* scores were computed on the basis of the differences between ingroup versus outgroup ratings along each of the scales. Exploratory factor analysis of these scales revealed two major dimensions of these evaluations: Ability (i.e., Intelligent, Able, Assertive) and Warmth (Cold, Sociable). Given the fact that the subjects were university students, the ability dimension was judged to be the most relevant and was used in the analyses following.

Outgroup Social Distance. Assessed by four questions, this measured the degree to which subjects felt ingroup-outgroup membership was relevant in professional and social relations.[12]

Perceived Group Difference. Assessed by asking, "In general, how much difference do you think there is between overestimators and underestimators in personality characteristics?"

Perceived Outgroup Variance. Assessed by the question "How much variability do you think there is among (overestimators/underestimators)." The response scale ranged from 1 (mostly the same) to 7 (extremely variable).

Strength of Group Identification. Measured by asking subjects, "How likely do you think it is that you have been correctly classified as an overestimator or underestimator?"

Self-esteem. Measured on the well-known Rosenberg (1965) Self-esteem Scale ($\alpha = .88$).

The causal relationships among these variables were modeled in accordance with the assumptions of social identity and social-dominance theory as found in Figure 8.10.

According to SIT, which is incorporated into the SD paradigm, the mere categorization of self into an ingroup is sufficient in and of itself to prompt discrimination and outgroup denigration. These expectations were largely confirmed in the results of this experiment. The results showed that the more the subjects felt that they were correctly classified into their ingroups, the more they: (a) perceived differences between ingroups and outgroups ($\gamma = .23$), (b) engaged in relative outgroup denigration ($\gamma = .25$), and (c) were in favor of social distance toward the

---

[12] The questions read: (1) "From what you know so far, do you think that people's tendency to be overestimators or underestimators should be measured as part of the job application process?" (2) "Do you think that it would be useful for you to know whether a person is an overestimator or underestimator while choosing a friend?" (3) "Do you think that it would be useful for you to know whether a person is an overestimator or underestimator when deciding whether to date someone?" and (4) "Do you think it is important for overestimators and underestimators to interact as much as possible or is it more important that people be given the opportunity to interact with other members of the same group?" All questions were answered on seven-point scales.

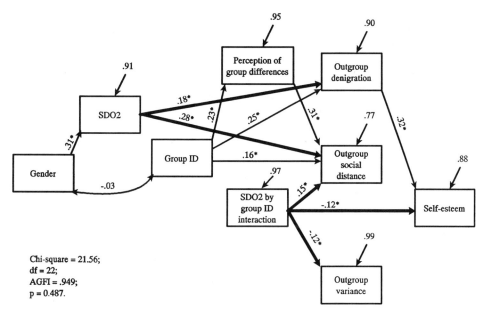

Fig. 8.10. Causal model of minimal-groups experiment, including social-dominance orientation (UCLA, Sample 4).

outgroup ($\gamma = .16$). Consistent with the expectations of SD theory, it was also found that: (a) males had significantly higher social-dominance scores than females ($\gamma = .31$), and (b) the greater one's dominance orientation, the greater the outgroup denigration and outgroup social distancing ($\beta = .18$ and $\beta = .28$ respectively).

It is interesting to note that, even when controlling for the main effects, the evidence also indicated that a mild, yet statistically significant, interaction between social-dominance orientation and degree of group identification led to slightly increased levels of social distancing of outgroups ($\beta = .15$) and lower levels of perceived outgroup heterogeneity ($\beta = -.12$).[13] This latter path indicates that the combination of greater SDO and increased ingroup identification led to perceptions of lower outgroup variability.

The last major path worthy of comment is the relatively strong connection between outgroup denigration and positive self-esteem ($\beta = .32$). This connection is theoretically consistent with SIT, downward-comparison theory (see Wills 1981, 1987), and SD theory. However, its specific interpretation within the context of this experiment must be

[13] For a discussion of interactions in causal models, see Cohen and Cohen 1983: 369–71.

somewhat circumspect. Because self-esteem is a long-standing and relatively stable construct, we seriously doubt that it is liable to be significantly affected by the minimal-groups manipulation. Rather, we interpret
this path to indicate that persons who have a tendency to believe that
their reference groups are intellectually superior to others will also tend
to enjoy heightened self-esteem as a result of long-lasting and continuous
intergroup and interpersonal comparison processes.[14]

Finally, it is also worth noting that not only are these individual paths
theoretically congruent with the SIT and SD paradigms, but the entire
model fits the empirical data well (χ^2 [22] = 21.6, AGFI = .949, p =
.487). Most significant of all, however, these results support the notion
that not only is mere group membership sufficient to trigger outgroup
denigration and discrimination as SIT maintains, but social-dominance
orientation will contribute to these results as well. The greater one's SDO,
the greater one's denigration of outgroups, even groups with which one
has no experience and that do not even really exist.

The Connection Between Political Conservatism and Racism

A long vector of research findings attests to a correlation between
political-economic conservatism on the one hand and racial prejudice and
ethnocentrism on the other hand (see, e.g., Adorno et al. 1950; Bahr and
Chadwick 1974; Dator 1969; Eysenck 1951, 1971, 1975, 1976; Eysenck
and Coulter 1972; Eysenck and Wilson 1978; Kerlinger 1972; Sidanius
and Ekehammar 1976, 1979, 1980; Sidanius, Ekehammar, and Ross 1979;
Tursky et al. 1976; Wilson 1973a, 1973b; Wilson and Bagley 1973; Wilson
and Lee 1974). Besides models that have explained the connection between
these constructs as flowing from the fact that they are both reflections of
general conservatism (see Wilson 1973a), only authoritarian-personality
theory has attempted to explain why these two constructs are related (see,
e.g., Adorno et al. 1950).

Social-dominance theory offers a third and perhaps more parsimonious
explanation. This explanation simply states that political-economic conservatism and racism (and caste-maintenance orientation) will be positively associated because they are all reflections and manifestations of the
same drive toward group-based dominance (SDO). Structural equation
models offer us a relatively simple and straightforward manner in which
to test this.

We posited two models to test using the UCLA data set (Sample 2):

---

[14] On the other hand, it is possible to interpret this correlation in the reverse causal
order—that is, students with high self-esteem will tend to view themselves as intellectually
superior to others. Both interpretations are perfectly consistent with the data, and it is not
possible for us to disentangle them with the data at hand.

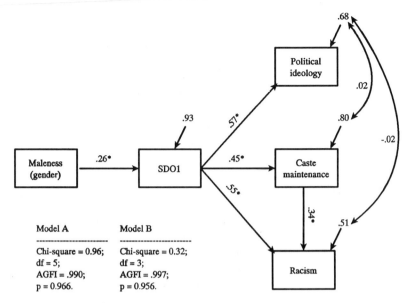

Fig. 8.11. Test of spuriousness in the covariance of political ideology versus racism and caste-maintenance orientation (UCLA, Sample 2).

model A, in which gender drives SDO₁, which in turn drives PEC, caste-maintenance orientation, and racism, and where racism is thought to be affected by caste-maintenance orientation ($\chi^2 = 0.96$, df = 5, AGFI = .994, $p = .966$), and model B, which makes the same assumptions as model A and also assumes that there will be correlations between the error terms for political ideology on the one hand and caste-maintenance orientation and racism on the other hand ($\chi^2 = 0.32$, df = 3, AGFI = .997, $p = .956$; see Fig. 8.11). If social-dominance orientation is not adequate to explain the correlation between the political and racial constructs, then model B should offer a statistically significant improvement in fit over model A. However, comparison of the two chi-square coefficients reveals that for a loss of two degrees of freedom, the χ^2 value is only improved by 0.64, a result that is clearly not significant. In other words, model B does not fit better than model A. This implies that social-dominance orientation is perfectly adequate to explain the correlations between political ideology and the various types of racism (i.e., racism and caste-maintenance orientation). The correlation between these two constructs appears to be spurious.

Summary and Broader Implications of Social-Dominance Theory

In this chapter we have introduced a new and very general model with which to conceive of the dynamics of intergroup relations and its functional relationship with sociopolitical attitudes, including racism in the United States. Among other concepts, the theory proposes that social attitudes that in one way or another are directly relevant to intergroup relations are also strongly driven by social-dominance orientation. This orientation is primarily concerned with the dominance or superiority of one group over others. The SD approach also assumes that all human social systems will have a tendency to converge into *group-based social hierarchies* and that most forms of social oppression, including racism, sexism, nationalism, and classism, can also be viewed as different manifestations of the same underlying psychosocial processes.

In the course of our empirical illustrations of some of these processes, we have examined social-dominance orientation and closely related variables (e.g., caste-maintenance orientation, anti-egalitarianism) as they relate to social status, political ideology, attitudes toward the military and intergroup marriage, and denigration of minimally defined outgroups. Although work within this theoretical paradigm is just beginning, the results for social comparison processes and attitudinal processes thus far look encouraging.

Broader Implications

We can now therefore return to the questions with which we began this discussion—namely, are racial justice, gender equality, and political democracy really possible? Social-dominance theory clearly implies that none of these goals is likely to be achieved. Furthermore, the SD approach implies that even if, for example, African Americans suddenly ceased to function as America's "negative reference group," they would only be replaced by some other group serving the same role, perhaps undocumented workers or the "homeless." Indeed, in parts of the United States where blacks have been relatively uncommon, such as the West in the early part of this century, Mexican Americans and Asian immigrants have served as negative reference groups, experiencing a similar set of oppressive conditions to blacks (e.g., forced labor, lack of land ownership, exclusion from voting).

Clearly, how one views the attainability of "democracy" itself depends upon exactly how one defines the term. For example, *Webster's Third New International Dictionary* (1986) gives as its fifth definition of democracy: "political, social or economic equality: the absence or disavowal of hereditary or arbitrary class distinctions or privileges." To the extent that "equality" and the absence of "arbitrary class distinctions or privileges" are inherent and necessary features of "democracy," the SD model maintains that such a state will probably never be attained. The fact that no truly egalitarian society has yet been found to exist throughout all of recorded human history is, perhaps, a more powerful and eloquent support for SD theory than any array of statistical coefficients could ever be. If, on the other hand, one divorces any notion of political or social equality from the definition of *democracy* and substitutes the concept of the citizen's opportunity to choose among competing elites, hegemonic groups, oligarchies, or aristocracies (i.e., polyarchy; see Dahl 1971), then a substantial number of states are truly "democratic."

Second, the SD approach suggests that rather than regarding prejudice and discrimination as pathological or quasi-pathological conditions of the body politic, as has been predominantly the case within the social sciences since the demise of National Socialism, we should instead regard prejudice, discrimination, and oppression as *normal* or default conditions huddled at the very heart and soul of politics as a process of human interaction. In many ways, the difference between traditional models of prejudice and discrimination and the SD approach is similar to the conflict between the *contingency* and *inherency* models of collective political violence (see Eckstein 1980). Contingency models consider political violence an unusual condition, demanding an answer to the question "Why?" Inherency models, by contrast, consider political violence a "normal" mode of human interaction, and when violence does *not* occur in conflict situations, ask instead, "Why not?" Applied to the domain of general intergroup relations, rather than reacting with surprise to instances of racial, ethnic, and sex discrimination, the SD model will lead one to always expect discrimination against lower-status outgroups, in the limit;[15] the lower the social status, the more discrimination to be expected.

Third, the SD model would lead us to suspect that any consciously manufactured, social policy effort directed at the eradication of inequality and discrimination between hegemonic and negative-reference groups (e.g., blacks in America, Turks in Germany, "untouchables" in India) such as affirmation action, busing, and equal-housing and anti-discrimination laws will not only fail to achieve their publicly stated goals, but the efforts themselves will be ultimately unsustainable. The major reason for this is not that these public policies violate basic norms of fairness or the Prot-

---

[15] By the term *in the limit*, we refer to long-range outcomes. For example, as with any statistical relationship, we cannot say that a specific white individual will discriminate against a specific black individual. However, given a statistical relationship greater than 0, we can predict that, in the long run, the average white will discriminate against the average black. In other words, we can be sure of discrimination "in the limit."

estant ethic, as many American theorists suggest (see, e.g., Sears 1988; Kluegel and Smith 1986), but rather because they tend to violate status boundaries between hegemonic and negative-reference groups. Any effort designed to alter status boundaries between hegemonic and negative-reference groups will be met with extreme resistance, and when these efforts are to be executed by elements of the hegemonic group itself, they are ultimately doomed to failure. Therefore, from the SD perspective, the recent spate of U.S. Supreme Court decisions (a) striking down minority set-asides (*Richmond v. Croson*), (b) shifting the burden of proof from employers to employees in job discrimination cases (*Wards Cove v. Antonio*), (c) allowing claimants to attack consent decrees that purportedly support "reverse discrimination" (*Martin et al. v. Wilk et al.*), (d) restricting the application of Title VII of the 1964 Civil Rights Act to apply to initial contracts rather than "post formation racial harassment in employment" (*Patterson v. McLean Credit Union*), and (e) ruling that a lower court decision striking black venirepersons from a black defendant's trial was not evidence of racial discrimination (*Tompkins v. Texas*) have the effect of "reaffirming" status differentials between hegemonic whites (particularly white males) on the one hand and blacks on the other, and should be seen as a return to a "normal" politics. In other words, the end of "the second Reconstruction," which we are now witnessing, will lead to a result not terribly different from the end of the first Reconstruction: the clearly reestablished social domination of blacks by whites. In sum, the SD model views the hope or expectation that anti-discrimination laws or policies will either eliminate or very greatly reduce discrimination against negative-reference groups as being simply naive and overly optimistic.

Fourth, within the SD model it is expected that political and status equality between males and females will be *extremely* difficult, if not impossible, to achieve. This is not only because males, without exception, comprise the hegemonic group in all major social systems and will therefore resist such status reallocation, but also because, in the limit, males are inherently more aggressive and dominance-oriented than females. Even using the reasoning of modern feminist thinkers (e.g., Gilligan 1982), there is good reason to believe that females, on average, are more oriented toward the maintenance of close personal relationships, social nurturance, and the "private sector" rather than the exercise of power and the domination of others as executives within large organizations in the "public sector" (e.g., multinational corporations, government bureaucracies, and the military). The SD model posits the same kinds of differences between males and females but also assumes that these differences are, in part, determined by genetic as well as sociocultural factors. If it is true that females are inherently oriented toward nurturance and the "private sector," while males are oriented toward dominance and the "public sector," it is difficult to see how females will ever achieve political parity with males without some *extraordinary* effort on their part, ceaselessly applied.

Of course, it is also clear that the seriousness with which one takes the immutability of male political dominance is intimately connected to one's theory of this phenomenon's etiology. If one adopts a strictly environmental or cultural deterministic view (see e.g., Bleier 1984), then there is nothing compelling about the SD arguments. If, on the other hand, one views these gender differences as a very complex interaction between cultural and genetic factors, then the situation changes quite substantially. Although we must all recognize that we lack the technology to separate the "nature" from the "nurture" components of human behavior in general and with regard to gender differences in particular,[16] there is some very recent and intriguing evidence dealing with the nature of some gender differences that is worthy of serious consideration. For example, there is consistent and mounting evidence of a direct correlation between androgen levels and aggressive and dominance-oriented behavior in human males (see Dabbs and Morris 1990; Ehrenkranz, Bliss, and Sheard 1974; Christiansen and Knussman 1987b; Jeffcoate et al. 1986; Rejeski et al. 1989; Olweus et al. 1988; Bradford and Bourget 1987; Salvador et al. 1987; Susman et al. 1987; Baucom, Besch, and Callahan 1985; Dent 1983; Elias 1981; Mazur and Lamb 1980; Scaramella and Brown 1978). Two examples are illustrative. First, A. Mazur and T. A. Lamb (1980) reported three experiments showing that a male's testosterone level changes when his status changes, rising when he achieves or defends a dominant position, and falling when he is dominated. Second, K. Christiansen and R. Knussmann (1987b) examined the relationship between serum concentrations of testosterone (T-sub[ser]), 5alpha-dihydrostestosterone (DHT), and the level of free testosterone in saliva (T-sub[sal]) and the behaviors exhibited on projective and standardized tests in 117 healthy men. These tests included measures of aggression, including sexual aggressiveness and dominance. The results showed all three androgens had reliable and positive correlations with the self-ratings of spontaneous aggression. Dominance had a positive and significant correlation to T-sub(ser) and DHT, and DHT was negatively related to restraint of aggression. Furthermore, the ratio of DHT to T-sub(ser) was also found to be correlated with interest in sexual aggression. It must be added, however, that although these results are highly suggestive and generally supportive of SD theory, further work still needs to be done in order to firmly establish the *causal* connection

[16] This assumes that the "nature versus nurture" question is meaningful at all, which we seriously doubt.

between androgen levels in males and social-dominance orientation as it is being defined here.

Lest we be misunderstood, we should like to emphasize what we are *not* saying:

(1) *Although the SD model clearly implies that gender-egalitarian, multi-group, multi-ethnic, and truly democratic societies are probably not attainable, this does not imply that movement toward more democratic forms of social organization is not possible at all.*

Obviously social systems are dynamic. A cursory glimpse at various societies around the globe will quickly reveal that some societies are a good deal more equitable and democratic than others. For example, using any number of criteria, Sweden would probably have to be considered one of the most democratic societies in the modern world. It is one of the very few countries in the world that allow foreign residents to vote in local elections and where women comprise about 23 percent of the national legislature (Riksdag). In most parliamentary states women constitute only about 5 percent of the national legislature (Putnam 1976). However, if Swedish women enjoyed true parity with Swedish men, then 51 percent rather than 23 percent of the seats in parliament would be occupied by them. Given this fact and the dynamic nature of social systems, there are at least two clusters of questions that immediately follow: (a) "How much equality is really achievable; does Sweden represent the most equitable and democratic society achievable or is it merely an anemic shadow of the possible?"; and (b) "What are the parameters of equality and democracy? That is to say, besides the obvious factors of history and tradition, what are the conditions and forces that will tend to make one social system more democratic than another?" These are just some of the questions that social–dominance theory needs to deal with in the future.

(2) *We are not suggesting that negative reference groups will always acquiesce to oppression. What we are suggesting is that under normal circumstances, the pressure from below will not equal the pressure from above.*

This structural asymmetry is necessary in order for group-based hier-archies to remain relatively stable. However, when low-status persons do decide to risk the negative consequences of defiance (which clearly in-clude death) to change the social order, they may be effective. However, after a relatively short period of "quasi-egalitarianism," the social system is bound to return to a hierarchical, stable equilibrium once again.

(3) *With the possible exception of male-female relationships, we are not implying that any given social group is "destined" always to be a hegemonic group while other groups are destined always to be negative-reference groups.*

So far, at least, SD theory does not address the question of why particular groups rise and fall within dominance hierarchies at particular times.[17] What we are suggesting is that, although the particular actors may change their roles within the context of constantly changing plots, the drama's basic theme remains the same. This theme is group-based hierarchy and oppression, forever mutating, ever-present.

In conclusion, then, we would argue that SD theory offers a number of potential advantages over more traditional approaches to the study of the politics of group relations and the formation of political attitudes and behavior. First, there is reason to believe that it is consistent with empirical observation from a very wide number of domains, including laboratory experiments, survey data, and the distant and recent history of warfare and intergroup conflict. Second, this model integrates and is consistent with a number of heretofore unconnected literatures in the fields of: (a) social comparison and social identity theory within contemporary social psychology (see, e.g., Brewer 1979; Lemyre and Smith 1985; Tajfel and Turner, 1986), (b) contemporary and neoclassical elitism theory (see Domhoff 1967; Michels 1962; Mosca 1939; Mills 1956; Parenti 1986; Pareto 1901, 1935; Putnam 1976), (c) the sociobiology and ethology of group conflict and ethnocentrism (see Eibl-Eibesfeldt 1989; Reynolds, Falger, and Vine 1987; van den Berghe 1978a, 1978b), (d) laboratory work within neuropsychobiology (Christiansen and Knussman 1987a, 1987b), (e) survey research connecting racism and general political ideology (see, e.g., Carmines and Stimson 1982), and (f) contemporary thinking within economic and military history (see, e.g., Kennedy 1987). Third, like realistic group-conflict theory, and as opposed to symbolic racism theory, and U.S. dominant-ideology theory (see Kluegel and Smith 1986), the SD model is quite general in scope. Its generality is not only inherent in the fact that it may be applied to different cultures and historical contexts, but also because it may be extended to many different kinds of group conflict as well.

---

[17] However, within the context of interstate dominance systems and read from an SD perspective, Kennedy 1987 provides some thought-provoking suggestions as to why particular actors move up and down dominance systems at particular times.

9

The Politics of the American Dilemma: Issue Pluralism

*Paul M. Sniderman, Philip E. Tetlock,
Edward G. Carmines, and Randall S. Peterson*

The American experience has presented itself in many guises, but no aspect of it has been as persistently divisive, and as morally searing, as the issue of race. The issue of race is not the only blemish on the American experience, but thanks to the civil rights movement of the 1960's, it has become, for our time, the preeminent *moral* blemish. So it is well to weigh what political arguments over race signify. What do they mean now? What are the arguments over race and politics actually about?

Since Gunnar Myrdal's monumental *An American Dilemma* (1944), one reading of the American experience has been dominant. On this reading, the issue of race hinges on a conflict; a conflict between liberty, equality, and the American idea of fair play on the one side and prejudice, self-interest, and habit on the other. That this was once an accurate reading we do not deny; that it remains the right reading we question.

What distinguishes the contemporary argument over race—what makes conflict over it both unavoidable and anguishing—is precisely that the American dilemma has become a genuine dilemma. Or rather a set of dilemmas. For we shall demonstrate that a dominant feature of the contemporary politics of race is issue pluralism. Rather than a single issue of race, there are many of them.

Why does it mean to speak of "issue pluralism"? Most fundamentally, that there is no longer one conflict at the heart of arguments over racial issues, but a number of them, and the values that come into conflict can change from one policy domain to another. The politics of employment are not the same as the politics of housing, and neither are interchangeable with the politics of affirmative action. Of course, a common thread runs through racial policy issues: a bigot will oppose policies aimed at assisting blacks whatever the details of the particular policy or domain from which it is drawn. But the thread tying race policies together is slenderer than commonly supposed. Still more crucially, we want to suggest that what distinguishes the present-day politics of race from Myrdal's is precisely that issues of race have become a genuine dilemma; a genuine dilemma in that many of them require people to choose, not between the American creed and race prejudice, but rather between competing values that belong to the creed itself.

Issue Pluralism

It is now a commonplace that citizens tend to possess conspicuously modest levels of consistency in their opinions on specific political issues (Converse 1964). Indeed, given the minimal levels of political attention and information exhibited by ordinary citizens, it seems only natural that their opinions on politics should be only minimally consistent. But although minimal consistency about issues of public policy tends to be the rule, plainly there are exceptions; and the most striking exception, P. E. Converse (1964) has argued, is the issue of race.

Why should race be an exception? Why is the average citizen capable of figuring out what goes with what on racial policy issues even though the very same person picks positions on other issues—for example, employment and defense—apparently at random?

The answer is intuitively obvious, at any rate after Converse proposed it. Given the importance of Converse's argument, we shall reproduce it in detail. Imagine a set of questions, to be asked in a public opinion survey:

Should blacks be kept out of professional athletics?

Should the government see to it that blacks get fair treatment in jobs and housing?

Should the government cut down on its subsidies for peanuts and cotton, which are raised mainly by blacks in the South?

Should the government give federal aid only to schools that permit blacks to attend?

Should state government be able to decide who can vote and who cannot, even though it may hurt the position of blacks in the South?

It is not difficult, after examining the content of these questions, to see that even a politically unsophisticated person could give consistent answers to them. Each question explicitly refers to blacks: dislike blacks, and you oppose their being helped; like them, and you favor it. It is not necessary that you know a lot about politics, only that you know how you feel about blacks. For the average citizen, questions about different racial policies "would tend to boil down for many respondents to the same single question: 'Are you sympathetic to Negroes as a group, are you indifferent to them, or do you dislike them?' The responses would be affected accordingly" (Converse 1964: 235).

Put more systematically, the suggestion is that social groupings can serve as central objects in belief systems, providing a focus and frame of reference that evoke a politically consistent response even in the absence of knowledge of politics. It is thus not necessary to know details of one or another policy dealing with a salient group, let alone overarching political concepts like liberalism or conservatism: it suffices to know that a policy aims to assist or deprive a salient group.

We want to suggest that this line of reasoning—let us call it the "racial affect" hypothesis—provides an apt characterization of racial politics during the 1950's and 1960's, when the civil rights movement defined the politics of race, but a misleading one of the politics of post–civil rights racial issues in the 1980's and 1990's. By way of a starting point, Table 9.1 illustrates the thinking of white Americans about racial issues drawing on a national survey of the general population conducted nearly two decades ago.[1] The extent to which Americans react consistently to pairs of racial issues is indexed by the common correlation coefficient: the larger its value, the limit being 1.0, the greater the consistency.

The top triad of issues in Table 9.1 capture the heart of Myrdalian racial politics. First, there is the core issue of segregation itself, with respondents being offered three options—desegregation, strict segregation or "something in between." Filling this out are two parallel issues, one centering on whether the government should support the right of black people to go to any hotel or restaurant they can afford, and the other on whether it should lend its support to the integration of schools. The intercorrelations of positions across the triad of issues is high—strikingly so by the standards of public opinion data—on average, approximately .4.

There was thus a tight—by public opinion standards—cluster of opinion about the primary issue of whether blacks were entitled to equality under the law a generation ago (cf. Carmines and Stimson 1982, 1989). The positions that people took on the correlative issue of whether the federal government should throw its weight behind efforts to improve the life circumstances of blacks was also an aspect of the argument over

---

[1] For the record, we analyze only the attitudes of white Americans, not because the opinions of blacks do not matter to us, but because our aim is to understand the roots of opposition to assistance for blacks.

TABLE 9.1

Intercorrelations Between the Racial Policy Attitudes of Whites
(1972 National Election Survey; N = 960)

	Des	PubA	ScI	EqE	Aid
(De)segregation	1.0				
Public accommodations	.43	1.0			
School integration	.36	.40	1.0		
Equal employment	.26	.35	.50	1.0	
Aid minorities	.30	.31	.29	.29	1.0

race a generation ago, although to judge from the correlation coefficients in Table 9.1, a secondary aspect.[2] All the same, the positions that white Americans took had an impressive measure of consistency to them, with substantial numbers supporting or opposing key racial issues to achieve racial equality across the board.

So much by way of background. For the question that concerns us here is the character of post–civil rights racial politics: How do Americans think about racial policy issues now, a generation after the civil rights laws of 1964 and 1965?

American thinking about issues of race is more complex now than it was a generation ago; more complex and centered on different issues. The questions that were center-stage in arguments over race in the 1950's and 1960's have moved off to the wings. The contest over segregation— over legally sanctioned, explicitly codified racial inequality—has ended, notwithstanding a ragbag of holdouts. New racial issues now command attention; new issues that are neither tied together tidily in a single package nor connected closely to the traditional civil rights programs.

To give some sense of the variety of new racial issues, and the complexity of the public's reactions to them, we have ransacked a number of recent surveys and packed their results into Table 9.2. They include the 1986 National Election Study, the premier national political survey, conducted every two years by the Institute of Political Studies at the University of Michigan and specially focused, in the year we have selected, on issues of race;[3] the 1986 General Social Survey, the premier national survey oriented to sociology, conducted annually by the National Opin-

---

[2] The median correlation for the "secondary" issues—equal employment and aid to minorities—is .29.

[3] The National Election Studies were conducted by the Institute for Social Research, University of Michigan, under a grant from the National Science Foundation, and were made available through UCDATA, University of California, Berkeley, and the Inter-University Consortium for Political and Social Research. We are, of course, responsible for the analysis and interpretation of the data.

TABLE 9.2

Constraint Across the Racial Policy Attitudes of Whites

A. 1986 National Election Studies survey
(N = 634)

	FedS	EqO	Aid	AAJ	AAS
Federal spending	1.0				
Equal opportunity	.24	1.0			
Aid blacks	*.40*	.30	1.0		
Affirmative action–jobs	.29	.18	.23	1.0	
Affirmative action–school	.23	.16	.27	*.43*	1.0

B. 1986 National Election Studies survey
(N = 507)

	ScI	Emp	EqO	Aid	AAJ
School integration	1.0				
Guarantee employment	.22	1.0			
Equal opportunity	.26	.30	1.0		
Minority aid	.26	*.38*	*.46*	1.0	
Affirmative action–jobs	.31	.22	.32	.32	1.0

C. 1986 General Social Survey
(N = 1,470)

	SpBl	Bus	HlpB	Hous	IYC	BPres
Gov't. spend blacks	1.0					
Busing	.14	1.0				
Help blacks	.34	.19	1.0			
Housing	.18	.22	.15	1.0		
Integrate your child	.18	.12	.14	.16	1.0	
Black president	.21	.08	.17	.21	.28	1.0

D. San Francisco–Oakland Bay Area
(N = 699)

	HeB	Hou	Job	Con	AAC	Bus
Help blacks	1.0					
Housing	.22	1.0				
Job opportunity	*.43*	.24	1.0			
Minority contracts	.28	.14	.23	1.0		
Affirmative action–college	.30	.14	.21	.27	1.0	
Busing	.23	.15	.23	.24	.24	1.0

ion Research Center;[4] and, finally, the 1986 San Francisco–Oakland Race and Politics Survey, the first of a series of studies on the racial attitudes of Americans exploiting the new technology of computer-assisted survey interviewing.[5]

[4] The General Social Survey data were collected by the National Opinion Research Center, under a grant from the National Science Foundation, and were made available through the UCDATA Program, University of California, Berkeley, and the Inter-University Consortium for Political and Social Research. We are, of course, responsible for the analysis and interpretation of the data.

[5] The Race and Politics Study was funded by the National Science Foundation grant

First the results from the 1986 National Election Studies. Americans' reactions to a number of racial issues are taken into account, including integration of schools; government assurance of fair treatment in employment for blacks; government assistance to improve the social and economic position of blacks; government guarantees of equal opportunity for blacks; and affirmative action, variously targeted. (Some questions were asked of one half of the sample, randomly selected, some of the other half, so the results for the 1986 NES study are shown in two separate matrices.)

Looking at the top section of Table 9.2, one cannot help but be struck by the change over time in the average size of correlation coefficients indexing consistency in positions taken across pairs of racial issues. As against a mean value of .35 in the 1972 NES survey, the mean correlation across pairs of racial issues taking account of all 1986 surveys is .24—a marked reduction translated into proportion of variance shared.

We do not mean to suggest that there is no longer consistency in the thinking of Americans about racial issues; still more crucially, we do not mean to suggest that opinions about *certain* racial issues are not tied together—we shall focus on these in just a moment. But we do mean to observe that it would be simply incorrect to suggest that most Americans now are responding to issues of race as if "they boil down for many respondents to the same single question: 'Are you sympathetic to Negroes as a group, are you indifferent to them, or do you dislike them?'" (Converse 1964: 235).

But why do Americans nonetheless react to some issues of race as though they are centrally raising the same question, and what might that question be, since it manifestly cannot be simply how they feel toward blacks? The answer has to do with the *politics* of racial issues, and it is fairly easy to pick out if one concentrates on the particular issues Americans think are closely related, judged by the uncommonly large size of the correlation of positions taken on them.

The racial issues that belong together—in the minds of white Americans—stand out, the coefficients summarizing the consistency of Americans' positions on them having been italicized in Table 9.2.[6] Consider the largest, .43, located in the fourth column and the fifth row of section A. There is surely no mystery here: the coefficient indexes the extent to which people are consistent in their reactions to affirmative action applied to employment and affirmative action applied to college admission: it cannot be puzzling why an opponent of preferential treatment in one context

SES-8508937. The study was conducted by the Survey Research Center at the University of California, Berkeley.

[6] Coefficients larger than .35 have been italicized to call attention to the similarity of results across studies.

might be an opponent of preferential treatment in another. Or consider the swarm of the next largest coefficients, all hovering in the neighborhood of .40. They summarize reactions to whether the government should assure equal opportunity for blacks; whether the government should make every effort to improve the social and economic position of blacks; whether the government should see to it that blacks get fair treatment in jobs; and whether the federal government should spend more money to assist blacks. Surely there is no mystery here, either. For each of these issues is explicitly posed so that they have in common, not only a reference to blacks, but also a reference to whether the government has an obligation to assist blacks in dealing with their problems. And it is Americans' differences over the propriety and prudence of government assistance, as much as their differences over the desirability of assisting blacks, that account for these issues being tied together and evoking a consistent response.[7]

Another window on the thinking of Americans about contemporary racial issues is offered by the General Social Survey. The issues covered include the level of spending to be devoted to problems of blacks, busing, the responsibility of government to improve the living standards of blacks, and, finally, "open housing" laws. The pattern of intercorrelations, displayed in section C of Table 9.2, corresponds nearly exactly to the pattern of results from the 1986 National Election Survey. On the one hand, the consistency of people's positions across the full range of racial issues tends to be far from stunning: the correlation between attitudes toward busing and government responsibility to improve the living conditions of blacks, for example, is .14. On the other hand, citizens have far more tightly knit opinions about issues of race that hinge on the role government should play: thus, the correlation between the positions taken on whether government should help improve living conditions of blacks and whether spending in behalf of blacks should be increased, far from being modest, is a substantial .34.

A final window on contemporary attitudes about racial issues is offered by the Race and Politics Study, also conducted in 1986. The sample is not a national one, being instead focused on the San Francisco–Oakland Bay Area; but the coverage of racial issues is more comprehensive, and includes questions on whether government spending should be increased to assist blacks or blacks should rely on themselves; whether there should be fair housing laws or, alternatively, homeowners should be free to refuse to sell to someone because of race or color; whether the government should

[7] For a fuller presentation of evidence on this point, see Paul M. Sniderman and Thomas Piazza, "The Scar of Race" (MS, Survey Research Center, University of California, Berkeley).

assure fair treatment in employment for blacks; whether there should be set-asides in federal contracts to ensure that a certain number of them are awarded to minority contractors; whether there should be racial quotas for university admission; and whether children should be bused to school to achieve racial integration. Given that the coverage of issues is extensive in the Race and Politics Study, it is the more impressive that the pattern of results parallels, indeed corresponds nearly perfectly to, those of the 1986 National Election Survey and General Social Survey. Again the overall pattern is plain: the tendency of Americans to react to racial issues in an across-the-board fashion is quite weak; the mean intercorrelation of positions across pairs of racial issues is only .24. And again there is the same exception to the overall pattern: the correlation between government spending to assist blacks and government assurance of fair treatment in employment in jobs for blacks is .43. In short, when Americans react to contemporary issues of race with consistency, it is as much because of politics as race.

Beyond this, it is revealing that the weakest correlations in Table 9.2 tend to be found between issues located not just in different domains but also in different eras of racial politics and policy. Thus, in the 1986 National Election Survey, attitudes toward school integration are only moderately correlated with attitudes toward the newer issues focusing on government-sponsored economic assistance for blacks. Similarly, busing is only moderately correlated with the "help" and "spend" for blacks items in the General Social Survey. Finally, in the Bay Area Study, the two lowest correlations are between open housing and minority contracts and affirmative action respectively. Moreover, in this survey, the correlation between open housing and busing is only .15. These issues are in different policy domains obviously, but they were also prominent in different periods of our racial history. School integration was central in the 1950's and early 1960's during the traditional civil rights struggle, followed by open housing in the mid to late 1960's, then by busing in the 1970's, and, most recently, by affirmative action. The set of issues focusing on government assistance to improve the economic and social condition of blacks covers several of these periods but has been most prominent during more recent years. The point is that connections between these issues tend to be far from strong, reflecting the fact that they were prominent at different times, as well as being located in different policy domains. The politics of race has clearly evolved over time.

Issue-Framing and the "Spending" Experiment

But what, more exactly, does it mean to say that the heart of the American dilemma now is political as well as racial?

Citizens are presented with issues of public policy, not as they individually may wish to define them, but as they have come to be structured through the process of political competition. Issues, that is to say, come prepackaged; and one reason this matters is that they are not always packaged individually, carefully separated and labeled one by one, but tend frequently to be bundled together.

The "bundling together" of issues is carried over in the study of attitudes toward racial issues (Carmines and Stimson 1982, 1989). Different elements are combined: a concern to assess whether a person wishes to see blacks receive assistance or not; a focus on a particular method (or mode) of their receiving assistance; a recommendation that an agent (the federal government, for example) see to it that the assistance is delivered. And the response a person gives—whether he or she favors or opposes assistance for blacks or—is made to the bundle of elements as a whole, not to each separately, one at a time. How, then, is it possible to tell which of the bundled-together elements Americans are taking into account?

This question, we have become persuaded, must be addressed if we are to get a grip on what issues of race are in fact about now. Consider a standard finding: conservatives tend to be more opposed to government assistance for blacks than liberals (see, e.g., Carmines and Stimson 1982; Sears and Kinder 1971; Sniderman, Brody, and Kuklinski 1984). But what is the reason for this? Is it because conservatives are racists and oppose assistance out of an irrational hostility to blacks? Because they are suspicious of government intervention in all forms? Or because of some combination of prejudice and political conviction?[8] And insofar as all these elements are empirically correlated because they are causally linked, can we ever disentangle which of them is cause and which effect?

Analytically, a number of racial issues can be thought of as consisting of two components. One—and this is the one organizing discussions of American attitudes—centers on discrimination: should we dedicate ourselves to getting rid of racial barriers for blacks? Another element centers, not on whether an effort is called for on behalf of blacks, but rather on how that effort should be made. The object, we want to suggest, is to separate the two.

But how is this separation to be accomplished? Or, more exactly, how

[8] For a new perspective focusing on the analysis of racial double standards, experimentally determined, see Sniderman et al. 1991.

is it possible to manage this without being either hopelessly artificial or self-defeatingly transparent?

As a first approximation, we designed the "spending" experiment. Taking advantage of the Indiana State Poll, conducted by the Survey Research Center at Indiana University[9] and based on the Computer-assisted Survey Instrument (CASES) developed by the Program in Computer-assisted Survey Methods at the University of California at Berkeley, we devised two versions of a question assessing attitudes toward government assistance for blacks. The first—or standard—version was adapted from the National Election Studies. It ran as follows:

Some people think that the government in Washington should increase spending for programs to help blacks get more jobs. Others feel that blacks should take care of their own problems. Which makes more sense to you:

—the government should spend more

or

—blacks should take care of their own problems.

In addition, there was a second version of the question. This "pure" version was developed to focus not on the means by which blacks were to obtain more jobs, but rather on the objective—to break down unfair racial barriers. It ran as follows:

Some people think that the government in Washington should *do more to make sure that blacks are not discriminated against* in getting jobs. Others feel that blacks should take care of their own problems. Which makes more sense to you:

—the government should do more

or

—blacks should take care of their own problems.

For convenience the key phrase that differs in the "pure" second version has been italicized. Notice that, this phrase aside, the two versions are essentially identical: both focus on more jobs for blacks; both ask whether government should do more or blacks should take care of their own problems.

The two versions, "standard" and "pure," were each asked of one half of the sample, the two versions, of course, being randomly assigned. This randomization is the key to our analysis. Since the assignment to the standard or pure version is made on a random basis, the two halves of the

[9] We should very much like to express our appreciation to the Survey Research Center, Indiana University, and its director, John Kennedy, for the excellent job they did in carrying out this survey.

TABLE 9.3

*Correlation Among Whites in Indiana Between Ideological Self-
Identification as Conservative and Opposition to Government
Assistance for Employment for Blacks Depending on the
Framing of the Issue, 1991 (N = 579)*

	r
Frame A: Spend to help blacks (N: 292)	.31
Frame B: Special effort to help blacks	
(N: 287)	.09
	.19

sample are necessarily alike in every relevant respect, chance variations aside, ensuring that any difference in the reactions of the two halves is to be attributed to the framing of the policy.

Let us start by considering the connection between conservatism and the issue of increasing government spending to help blacks get more jobs. Table 9.3 reports the correlation between attitudes toward more spending and ideological self-identification. The self-identification measure follows a common format, asking people whether they think of themselves as liberal, moderate, or conservative.[10] Look first at frame A of Table 9.3, which reports the correlation between conservatism and opposition to increased government spending to help blacks get more jobs: the correlation is quite sizable; to be exact, .31. Now, by way of contrast, consider frame B of Table 9.3. There, the correlation between conservatism and opposition to increased government effort to fight racial discrimination in jobs appears. Plainly, the relation between ideological orientation and racial policy preference is smaller; indeed, it is trivial—less than .10—which is statistically insignificant at the conventional .05 level.[11]

This is a striking result; for it means that a good part of the opposition of conservatives to programs to help blacks get more jobs is political, and not simply racial. By political we mean the familiar and deep-rooted differences between a conservative and a liberal about how the public business is best carried out. We do not mean to suggest that this dissolves arguments over racial policy—to suggest, that is, that the liberal and the conservative understanding of race as an issue is "essentially" the same,

[10] The actual text of the question runs as follows: "When it comes to political views that people hold, do you think of yourself as liberal, moderate, conservative, or don't you think in those terms?" The fourth category—those who reject an ideological designation—has been set aside for a moment; it is analyzed in Table 9.5.

[11] Nor is this an artifact of a restriction in variance, or so-called ceiling effect: in fact, only 54 percent support government doing more to fight racial discrimination in jobs—a point to which we shall return.

with the two differing only over the means they judge feasible and necessary. In their understanding of race as an issue, the left and the right differ on many points: both may wish to end unfair barriers to blacks getting jobs, but for example disagree profoundly on what defines unfairness, even about what constitutes discrimination. Does a showing that blacks are "underrepresented" in a line of work suffice? Or is a more direct demonstration of discrimination called for? Is it necessary that discrimination be intentional? Or does it suffice that blacks wind up being disadvantaged? Beyond this, it is essential to point out that even if the issue of government spending is surgically separated from the issue of government help for blacks to find jobs, it does not follow that conservatives will be as enthusiastic in their support as liberals. For even if the objective is to fight discrimination, the conservative is still being asked to support a more active and interventionist government, and the more deeply imbued he or she is with conservatism, the more reluctant he or she will be.[12]

Commitment to Racial Equality and Consistency Across Racial Policy Domains

It is important to push the inquiry to a deeper level. Suppose the results of the spending experiment are pointing in the right direction. This suggests in turn that specific racial policies may comprise at least two distinguishable facets—one centering on the objective of assisting blacks, the other on the means of doing so. The hypothesis we want to advance is this. Insofar as racial policies in different domains focus on the common objective of assisting blacks, then reactions to them are more likely to be consistent; insofar as questions about means come to the fore, the positions Americans take on them tend to be less consistent, being influenced by considerations not simply of race but also of politics.

To determine whether this is so or not, the "two-facet" experiment was performed. The root idea behind the experiment is to see how attitudes across racial policy domains hang together depending on how they are framed. As we have already remarked, the question on government efforts to help blacks to get more jobs was framed in two ways. In addition, a question assessing attitudes toward affirmative action was framed in two ways. One—the standard—version, ran as follows:

Some people say that because of past discrimination, qualified blacks should be given preference in hiring. Others say that such preference in hiring of blacks is

---

[12] By way of example, separating out the most educated, the correlation between ideological self-identification and using government to fight racial discrimination in employment is .27.

wrong because it discriminates against whites. What about your opinion? Are you for or against preferential hiring and promotion of blacks?

—for preferential hiring and promotion of blacks

or

—against preferential hiring and promotion of blacks.

Again a second—or "pure"—version of the policy was framed, to see the reactions of people when the issue was more directly framed on the desirability of helping blacks. Specifically, the strategy was to eliminate the reference to "preference" and "preferential treatment," substituting instead the idea of trying harder. To be exact, the pure version of affirmative action ran like this:

Some people say that because of past discrimination, *a special effort should be made* to consider qualified blacks for jobs. Others feel that such a special effort is wrong because it discriminates against whites. What about your opinion? Are you for or against making a special effort?

—for making special efforts.

or

—against making special efforts

Again the crucial change in the framing of the issue is italicized. And again it should be emphasized that, this change aside, the policy remains the same. The focus is still affirmative action, and to emphasize this both versions of the policy warn, explicitly and identically, that some feel proceeding in this way "is wrong because it discriminates against whites."

As we have seen, the extent to which Americans tend to react consistently to issues of race in different policy domains, either favoring or opposing them across the board, tends to be fairly limited. But it does not necessarily follow that they do not have a genuine attitude about whether blacks should be helped or not, setting aside the policy issues of how they should be helped. On the contrary, it is reasonable to hypothesize, and we would strongly argue, that the average citizen has a quite definite view on whether government help should be provided for blacks. What we should like to determine, therefore, is the extent to which citizens have consistent reactions to racial issues *across* policy domains insofar as the issues are framed primarily in terms of assisting blacks or not. Table 9.4 accordingly lays out a set of correlation coefficients summarizing consistency of racial policy preferences across policy domains, for all combinations of the two versions—pure and standard—of the two policies, employment assistance and affirmative action.

The results are arresting, and deserve to be carefully set out. Each

TABLE 9.4

Correlation Among Whites in Indiana Between Attitudes Across Policy Domains Depending on the Framing of the Issues, 1991 (N = 782)

		Give preference to blacks in hiring	Make special effort to consider blacks in hiring	Total
Frame A:				
Spend to help	r	.29	.40	.33
blacks	N	(197)	(189)	(386)
Frame B:				
Special effort	r	.09	.48	.32
to help blacks	N	(184)	(212)	(396)
	r	.20	.44	.33
	N	(381)	(401)	(782)

policy was framed in two ways: the standard version, complete with complicating considerations of politics, and the pure version, focused more one-sidedly (though not necessarily completely) on the objective of assistance for blacks. Consider therefore the contrast between the two extreme variations: on the one hand, when people are being asked their opinions across policy domains on racial issues where the political element is as salient as the racial; and on the other, when they are invited to give their opinions across policy domains on racial issues where the issue of race is more completely in the center of attention. To see the difference the framing of racial issues makes, it is necessary only to examine the first column of Table 9.4. For the difference could not be more dramatic. On the one hand, when the political as well as racial element is salient, the correlation in the positions people take on the issues of job assistance and affirmative action is statistically insignificant—to be exact, only .09; on the other hand, when people are presented with the "pure" versions of both issues, then the correlation is an eye-popping .48.

But there is an additional lesson about the politics of race embedded in Table 9.4, possibly as important as the first. Consider the column of the table that shows the correlations of positions across policy domains for respondents who were asked the "special effort" version of affirmative action. Plainly, the correlations are quite high, and this is true whether the issue of job assistance is framed in terms of spending more money or doing more to fight discrimination. It is essential to emphasize this result, for it suggests that coalitions can be built across issue domains so long as the "New Agenda," with its divisive emphasis on quotas and preferential treatment, is excluded.

Taking the results so far, we have seen that the contemporary arguments over race are not merely about race but, at least as vitally, hinge on politics. What we want to do now is to take the interplay of ideology and issue-framing one step further.

Issue-framing, Political Ideology, and Political Sophistication

As we have seen, a person's ideological orientation can supply a decisive cue conditioning his or her reaction to a racial policy, although, as we have also seen, whether ideology supplies a cue can hinge on the framing of the policy. But the question can be turned around: if the influence of ideology is dependent on the framing of a racial issue, is the impact of the framing of an issue dependent on ideology?

Affirmative action is a strategic issue to explore, not least because its framing so manifestly matters: put in terms of "preferential treatment," only one of five whites in our study were in favor of it; in contrast, put in terms of "special effort," one in every two support it. And, of course, it is perfectly obvious that the way an issue like affirmative action is framed influences people's reactions to it: so we have seen that the impact of political ideology depends on whether the issue of government efforts to get more jobs for blacks is put in terms of increasing spending or fighting discrimination. In contrast, what has gone unexplored is whether the impact of variously framing an issue itself varies with political ideology.

Who should be most affected by the framing of an issue? Having a political outlook, being in some marked degree liberal or conservative, serves as an anchor: it gives direction, coherence, and a pattern to one's thinking. So far as this holds, it seems reasonable to argue that the various ways an issue can be put matter more to those without a political orientation and less to those with one.

Let us call this the "anchor" hypothesis. Two implications of the hypothesis deserve to be drawn. It is, to take the first point first, obvious what it means to have an ideological orientation: a person is liberal or conservative, in varying degrees. But just what does it mean to say that person is without an ideological orientation? A straightforward stance is unwillingness to categorize oneself in ideological terms, and approximately one-third of the public fall into this category. A more oblique alternative is declining to classify oneself as liberal or conservative, instead placing oneself in between, as a "moderate" or "middle-of-the-roader." It is surely not obvious, on the face of it, however, that those who classify themselves as moderate in outlook are as lacking in orientation or direction as those persons who are unable, or unwilling, to classify themselves at all; nonetheless, it is an issue worth examination.

A second aspect of the argument deserves to be spelled out, and that concerns the relationship between ideological orientation and political sophistication. It has been established that the impact of ideology is contingent on the level of political sophistication: the more politically aware and sophisticated a person is, the more likely that his or her opinions on a policy issue will be shaped (where appropriate) by an ideological outlook on politics. And it may seem only natural to conclude that the more politically sophisticated people are, the more likely their ideological orientations are to anchor them in place.

The problem we are considering here is different from the standard analytic problem, however. The issue itself—or more exactly, how the issue is framed—is one of the independent variables to be taken into account, and the question that needs to be considered accordingly is, under what condition does the framing of an issue most affect the positions taken on the issue? The answer, we want to suggest, has a slightly paradoxical flavor: the less politically sophisticated people are, the more likely it is that they will be anchored by an ideological orientation, in the event that they have one, since the more politically sophisticated a person is, the more attentive and responsive he or she will be to the way a policy has been framed.

To assess whether our line of reasoning is valid, Table 9.5 lays out a correlation matrix summarizing the difference it makes on how the policy of affirmative action is framed in terms of the positions people take on it, with a larger value of the coefficient indicating that the framing matters more, a smaller that it matters less. To gauge the impact of political ideology, and in particular to determine whether how a policy is framed matters more for those who lack an overall political orientation than for those who have developed one, correlations are calculated separately for self-classified liberals, moderates, conservatives, and, finally, for those who reject an ideological description of themselves, whether liberal or conservative. Finally, to gauge the impact of political sophistication, and in particular to determine whether how a policy is framed matters differently depending on how politically sophisticated a person is, correlations summarizing the connection between the framing of affirmative action and the positions people take on it are calculated separately by level of education.[13]

Consider first the impact of having an ideological orientation. The results are decisive: on the one side, the correlation between how affirmative action is framed and the position taken on it is a modest .20 for conservatives and a still more modest .14 for liberals; on the other side, for those who reject the use of ideological terms altogether the correlation is a quite

---

[13] Education is used here as a proxy of political sophistication. For an argument at length on this usage, plus qualifications, see Sniderman, Brody, and Tetlock 1991.

TABLE 9.5

Relationship Between the Framing of the Issue of Affirmative Action and the Position Taken on the Issue, by Political Ideology and Level of Education, Indiana Whites, 1991
$(N = 900)$

Education		Liberal	Moderate	Conservative	Reject ideological self-description	Total
				Political ideology		
High school	r	.12	.30	.15	.36	.26
	N	(67)	(132)	(113)	(155)	(467)
Some college	r	.05	.22	.25	.43	.25
	N	(23)	(72)	(43)	(68)	(206)
College degree	r	.27	.59	.26	.56	.45
	N	(40)	(90)	(53)	(44)	(227)
	r	.14	.37	.20	.40	.30
	N	(130)	(294)	(209)	(267)	(900)

robust .40. And as for the question of whether people who classify them-selves as moderate or middle-of-the-road are not in fact actually without an orientation, the correlation summarizing the impact of how affirmative action is framed and issue preference is .37, which differs only trivially from the coefficient for those who explicitly say they are not ideological at all.

But if the impact of framing varies with having an ideological orienta-tion, it also varies with political sophistication—or more exactly covaries with both sophistication (as indexed by formal education) and ideologi-cal orientation. Consider first the pattern for those without an ideological orientation: among respondents who classify themselves as moderate, the correlation between framing and position is .30 for those with a high school education or less, as compared to a quite astonishing .59 for those with a college degree; among respondents who reject any ideological ori-entation outright, the figures for least and most educated are virtually identical to those for the moderates.

But is it the case that how an issue is framed matters most for the most sophisticated if they in fact have an ideological orientation? Evidently so. Compare the size of the correlations for the least and most educated lib-erals and for the least and most educated conservatives. For the former, the figures are .12 and .27 respectively; for the latter, virtually the same, .15 and .26. In short, and not a little paradoxically, how the policy of affirmative action is framed is most consequential for the most sophisti-cated who lack an ideological orientation, and matters substantially and approximately equally for the least sophisticated who lack an ideology and the most sophisticated who possess one.

Affirmative Action and Stereotypes About Blacks: The "Mere Mention" Experiment

The positions white Americans take on racial issues, as we have seen, vary with the domain of policy the issue falls within. Their positions also depend on how a racial issue is framed. And, finally, the impact of the framing of the issue itself depends upon whether citizens possess an ideological orientation and are politically sophisticated. It is not customary to highlight the complexity of Americans' thinking about racial issues in this way, and so we should like to take advantage of the opportunity before us to explore one final aspect of this complexity.

This final aspect is one we should personally prefer to avoid, but it is at the center of contemporary racial argument, and it is necessary to confront it squarely to understand how the American dilemma has become a genuine dilemma.

The issue we must explore is affirmative action. Consider a familiar argument. Why do some (white) Americans oppose affirmative action? Because they dislike blacks and are racist? How can this be proven? Statistically regress—that is, try to explain—the variation in people's attitudes toward affirmative action in terms of their feelings toward blacks, taking into account at the same time, of course, other possibly relevant factors. And following this analytic line, the results are seemingly straightforward: the more people dislike blacks, the more likely they are to oppose affirmative action (see, e.g., Kinder and Sears 1981).

Surely this must be true. It must be the case that a racial bigot, a person who despises blacks, will be *less* willing to lend a helping hand to blacks, let alone go so far as backing affirmative action, than a person who feels warmly and sympathetic toward them. But granted that a dislike of blacks can lead to opposition to affirmative action, is it possible that the causal relationship can also work the other way around? Is it possible, that is to say, that opposition to affirmative action can lead to dislike of blacks?

This reverse hypothesis—dislike of affirmative action leading to dislike of blacks—has long seemed to us, among others (e.g., Rieder 1985), a distinct possibility. As public opinion surveys have shown, affirmative action was opposed by overwhelming majorities of white Americans when it was introduced,[14] and is opposed by majorities as large, or still larger, nearly two decades later (Kinder et al. 1989). And setting quantitative evidence to one side, one would have to be obtuse indeed *not* to notice the resentment and vexation that many express on encountering a newspaper

---

[14] It should be observed, for the record, that majorities of blacks also tend to oppose affirmative action, particularly if the person to receive the benefit—whether getting a job or getting admitted to college—would not have done so on his or her own merits.

story, for example, about a fireman being promoted to captain on declaring that he was not of Italian but of Hispanic origin (*Washington Post*, December 11, 1990). Having seen how morally offended some are, how it angers them, when their sense of what is fair is violated by affirmative action, we think it necessary to take seriously the possibility that their very dislike of affirmative action may lead some in consequence to dislike blacks; an interesting irony.

But how is it possible to tell if affirmative action leads to dislike of blacks as well as the other way around? A standard survey assessing people's feelings toward blacks and affirmative action can establish a correlation between the two. But as for establishing scientifically that it is dislike of blacks that leads to affirmative action rather than the other way around, that is a fool's errand: it is impossible to determine this authoritatively in a conventional survey.

To overcome the difficulty, it is necessary to transcend the limitations of the standard survey and exploit the potential for innovation of computer-assisted interviewing. Accordingly, we have devised a special experiment, the first we believe to investigate whether affirmative action may be undercutting public sympathy and respect for blacks.

The experiment was conducted by the Survey Research Center at the University of Kentucky, drawing on a random sample of the Lexington Municipal Area.[15] The sample, which consisted of whites only, was randomly assigned to two conditions. Half of the respondents were asked to describe blacks and offered a variety of adjectives for the purpose— "lazy," "family-oriented," "irresponsible," and so on. Half of the adjectives were positive; half negative. After each adjective was mentioned, respondents were asked if they strongly agreed, somewhat agreed, somewhat disagreed, or strongly disagreed that the adjective described blacks. They were then asked their opinions on affirmative action.

In contrast, the other half of the sample were asked their opinions on affirmative action first. The interviewer began by saying: "In a nearby state, an effort is being made to increase dramatically the number of blacks working in state government. This means that a large number of jobs will be reserved for blacks, even if their scores on merit exams are lower than those of whites who are turned down for the job. Do you favor or oppose this policy?" And having recorded their responses, the interviewer went on to ask them to describe blacks, going through exactly the same

[15] We want to express thanks to the Survey Research Center at the University of Kentucky, Lexington, which did an excellent job in carrying out the survey, and to Mark Peffley of the University of Kentucky and Jon Hurwitz of the University of Pittsburgh, who bore the primary weight, and deserve the major credit, for designing the survey.

TABLE 9.6

Support Among Whites in Kentucky of Black Stereotypes as a Function of the Mention of Affirmative Action (N = 251)

% agreeing that blacks are:	Mention of affirmative action	
	Yes (N = 128)	No (N = 123)
Arrogant	35.0%	28.6%
Lazy	29.4	20.0
Irresponsible	40.5	24.8
Violent	33.1	42.2

descriptive adjectives as with the first half of the sample, set out in exactly the same way.

It is well to emphasize that the "manipulation" consisted entirely in the mere mention of affirmative action. Nothing else was done. If simply asking a question about affirmative action can increase dislike of blacks even in the slightest degree, the consequences of the public battle over quotas and preferential treatment during the past two decades can only be imagined.

Table 9.6 records the percentage of people endorsing negative stereotypes of blacks as arrogant, lazy, irresponsible, and violent.[16] Results are shown for all four, although it is surely farfetched to expect that the mere mention of affirmative action would lead people to derogate blacks in every conceivable respect—for example, in perceiving them to be violent.

As inspection of Table 9.6 shows, the results of the "mere mention" experiment are provocative indeed. Proportionately more respondents who were asked first about affirmative action agreed with three of the four negative stereotypes of blacks. So 40 percent of those asked first about affirmative action described blacks as irresponsible, as compared with 25 percent of the control group. The size of the differences, it should be observed, are modest; indeed, the differences observed for the stereotypes "lazy" and "arrogant" are only marginally significant. But having remarked this, it is unfortunately necessary to point out that not only is the pattern of the results consistent, but still more decisively, if the size of the Kentucky sample even approached that of the standard opinion survey sample, the results in Table 9.6 would easily meet the standard threshold of statistical significance.

[16] In addition to the negative descriptors, a large number of positive descriptors (for example, "family-oriented") were also included in the stereotype measure.

The New American Dilemma

Having set out our specific findings, we want to say a word about their larger implications. The place to start is the vocabulary that all of us, naturally and without a moment's pause, use in talking about race.

How serious, thoughtful observers are accustomed to ask, does the issue of race continue to be? What progress, if any, has been made on it? The questions are natural to ask—indeed, so much a part of ordinary discourse that we do not always stop to consider just what they presuppose. But recalling our findings, we can see now that the key assumption undergirding these questions is problematic. For it is deeply misleading to speak of *the* issue of race. The consistency of positions that Americans take across racial issues is far too modest to speak of *the* issue of race. Hence our thesis of "issue pluralism": the issue of equal access to housing is only marginally related to that of employment in the minds of white Americans; and that means that the politics of the two issues differs, not of course in every respect, but in some strategic and politically relevant ways. We cannot trace out these ways here,[17] but at least one implication of issue pluralism—of the relative autonomy of different racial issues—demands to be set out. It *necessarily* cannot be the case that white reactions to the array of contemporary racial issues are dominated by racism; *necessarily* because if racism did dominate in this way, then the positions they take across the array of racial issues would be correlated at a level higher than we observed—higher, indeed, by orders of magnitude.

Issues of race have become political, but in a complicated and deeply uneven way. Some are saturated with ideology because they belong to the larger department of issues over which liberals and conservatives have battled since the New Deal. Others, like affirmative action, more complexly echo ideology if only because of their unpopularity, their support among the larger public being essentially confined to the—small—part of the public uncommonly interested in public affairs and uncommonly sympathetic to liberal ideas. And still other issues, like fair housing, are fought out on still different grounds.

The willingness of (white) Americans to embrace policies to assist blacks, as we have seen, is remarkably sensitive to how these issues are framed, and it is essential to consider the implications of the importance of issue-framing.

Most crucially, the values engaged by racial issues depend on how they are framed. Racial issues are about race, but by no means entirely and sometimes only peripherally: they are also about other concerns, as im-

---

[17] For a discussion of the political implications of issue pluralism, see Sniderman and Piazza, "Scar of Race" (cited n. 7 above).

portant to the ordinary citizen as considerations of race. Myrdal's reading of the American dilemma represented the conflict over race as asymmetrical with respect to the American creed: on one side are arrayed the values of the creed—liberty, equality, justice, fair play; on the other, prejudice, self-interest, sexual jealousy, and habit. Indeed, it was precisely the asymmetry of the conflict, with the dominant values of the culture concentrated on one side, that underpinned Myrdal's optimism over the longer run: surely, he reasoned, the central values of the American creed would win out eventually.

On our reading, however, what distinguishes contemporary arguments over issues of race is that the conflict is more nearly symmetrical. On many (though not all) issues of race, a variety of values are in play, only one of which—and by no means the most important—is racial equality (Merriman and Carmines 1988). The variety of values in play is a potentially pivotal aspect of the contemporary politics of race, worth stressing. The point is not simply that on many issues of race there are now competing values but, more fundamentally, that the values that the objective of racial betterment finds itself in conflict with frequently differ radically from one domain of racial policy to another, and more than occasionally from one way of framing a particular policy to another. And so far as this holds, it is a mistake to represent the politics of race as consisting simply in a battle, say, between liberal and conservative values—as central as this battle is. To say that the politics of race is pluralistic is not to say that it is kaleidoscopic. There is a structure to arguments over race, and stepping back from the details of the tables, one can make out its outline.

By way of contrast, consider a familiar stylization. There are, we are told, two agendas of race—the "old" and the "new" (Lipset and Schneider 1978). On this view, the division is chronological: on the one side falls the race politics of the 1950's and 1960's, centered on the assurance of equal rights and the principle of race-neutral policies; on the other, the race politics of the 1970's and 1980's, focused more narrowly and controversially on affirmative action and the principle of race-conscious policies. Without minimizing the heuristic merits of the "two-agenda" suggestion, we have become persuaded that there are not two agendas but three, and that rather than being strictly successive in time, the signature of the contemporary politics of race is precisely that all three are on the table simultaneously.

An economical characterization of the three agendas would run roughly like this. First, there is the original equal-treatment agenda, hinging on the role government should play in fighting discrimination, defined as intentional penalizing of blacks because they are black. Second, there is the "social welfare" agenda organized around the role that government should play to improve the social and economic position of blacks. Finally, there

is the "race conscious" affirmative action agenda—an array of policies
covering everything from employment practices, educational admission,
the awarding of government contracts, and the race norming of tests for
the awarding of school scholarships—animated by the idea that the distribution of benefits should take into account the race of the beneficiary. The
politics of the three agendas, we are persuaded, differ in pivotal ways, if
not necessarily at the level of elite politics, then at any rate, and crucially,
at the level of mass politics.

In suggesting that there are a number of different racial agendas, we
are aware we are swimming upstream: the prevailing wisdom not only
suggests that distinctions among types of racial issues are unnecessary,
but that whole classes of racial issues have been effectively settled. In this
view, race prejudice has gone underground and now tends to express itself
only indirectly and subtly. Thus, Donald Kinder and David Sears contend
that "white America has become, in principle at least, racially egalitarian—a momentous and undeniably significant change" (Kinder and Sears
1981: 416).

This view trivializes the problem of prejudice and discrimination. Explicit support for legalized segregation has dwindled, with Jim Crow endorsed by only a relative handful of white Americans (see, e.g., Schuman,
Steeh, and Bobo 1985). But this is a far cry from saying that raw prejudice has been contained publicly, and politically can express itself only or
chiefly on putatively nonracial grounds—through opposition to affirmative action as ostensibly a violation of fairness, for example, or opposition
to government benefits for blacks on the grounds that blacks have violated
the work ethic. It simply is a mistake to suggest that resistance to the use of
government to eliminate deliberate discrimination and prejudice against
blacks has disappeared. The issues on all three agendas are live issues—
and this most definitely includes those on the "equal treatment" agenda.
Moreover, large numbers of white Americans hold frankly derogatory
opinions of blacks (Sniderman et al. 1991). And not only do they hold
them, they are perfectly willing to express them—to say, "Most blacks
who are on welfare programs could get a job if they really wanted one,"
for example, or to charge that "black neighborhoods tend to be run down
because blacks simply don't take care of their property."[18] And, even set-

[18] To cite illustrative figures from the Race and Politics Study: 61 percent of whites
agree with the welfare stereotype, and 42 percent with the neighborhood irresponsibility
stereotype; these figures are all the more worthy of attention because they come from an
uncommonly liberal part of the country, the San Francisco–Oakland Bay Area. Also worthy
of attention is the fact that the proportion agreeing with negative black stereotypes is still
higher among other minorities: 75 percent of Hispanics and 77 percent of Asians agree with
the welfare stereotype, while 68 percent of the former and 61 percent of the latter agree

ting this aside, the important point politically is that the idea of using government to try to relieve the disadvantages and discrimination suffered by blacks is a closely contested one—even when "extraneous" issues, such as spending of money or the violation of accepted standards, are removed from consideration. As our issue-framing experiments demonstrate, even when the reference to spending more money is removed, and the issue of government effort to assist blacks get more jobs is framed only in terms of fighting discrimination, only 54 percent of respondents are supportive. Or, to give a second example, even when reference to quotas is removed and affirmative action is framed only in terms of making an extra effort to locate qualified blacks, only 51 percent of respondents are in favor.

The politics of the first agenda, Myrdal suggested, consisted in a conflict between the dominant values of the American creed—liberty, equality, and fair play on the one side—and prejudice and self-interest on the other. In contrast, the conflict over the second—the "social welfare" agenda—is pitched not *between* the creed and betterment for blacks, but *within* the creed itself. Myrdal's stylization of the American dilemma is thus not so much a false view as a partial one—but in its partiality a misleading view of the contemporary politics of race.

It is misleading in more than one way, but perhaps particularly in the Myrdalian assumption of the fundamental harmony of the creed. All of its primary components, Myrdal supposed, were working in concert to promote the principle of racial equality. However true that may have been in the 1940's, when the primary issue was legally sanctioned segregation, it is profoundly at variance with the racial politics of the 1980's and 1990's, and most especially insofar as they concern the second or "social welfare" agenda, which pits the social and economic plight of many blacks precisely against the ambivalent attitude of many white Americans toward the welfare state (cf. Hochschild 1981; McClosky and Zaller 1984). The crucial point is thus that the conflict over the second agenda—over federal spending for social services or employment programs for blacks, for example—is rooted in the American creed itself. Both those committed to more activist government and those opposed to it can cite chapter and verse from the creed legitimating their position—slightly different chapters and verses, to be sure, but equally legitimate ones all the same.

If the politics of the second agenda are rooted in the American creed, those of the third agenda show how Myrdal's American dilemma has been turned on its head. Myrdal argued that the dominant values of the Ameri-

---

with the neighborhood irresponsibility stereotype. It is, in short, a mistake to represent race prejudice as a white-black issue.

can creed reinforced the object of betterment for blacks in the 1940's; hence his optimism for the longer run. But the affirmative action, race-conscious objectives of the 1970's, 1980's, and 1990's are at odds with most of the values of creed. Whites in consequence overwhelmingly reject affirmative action, some of them, no doubt, for more than one reason, but fundamentally, and among the majority, because it strikes them as wrong that a person should get a job not because of merit but because he or she is black—a conviction, and this deserves more recognition than it has received, that a majority of blacks share (Lipset and Schneider 1978).

So the *issue* of race has now become the *issues* of race, with one agenda giving way to three and simplicity giving way to complexity of public opinion on matters of race. The complexity of contemporary racial politics comes about because there is now no single, overarching racial agenda but instead multiple agendas, simultaneously competing for public attention, visibility, and government action. And, no less important, these multiple agendas bear no simple relationship to the American creed. Quite the contrary. Only the discrimination agenda can find unambiguous support in the values of the creed: the social welfare agenda both reinforces and contradicts various aspects of the creed; still more divisively, the race-conscious, affirmative action agenda runs against its very grain. Multiple issues and agendas, sometimes relying on, sometimes conflicting with basic American values—this is the politics of the contemporary American dilemma.

10

The Changing American Dilemma: Liberal Values and Racial Policies

Edward G. Carmines and W. Richard Merriman, Jr.

antithetical

Historically, whites' treatment of blacks has represented a deep paradox in American political thought and social practice: how could a society supposedly committed to human freedom and justice be so strongly influenced by racial prejudice and so deeply committed to racial discrimination?

Survey research suggests that white Americans' historical resistance to applying ideals about freedom and justice to racial questions has weakened considerably in the past fifty years. The percentage of white Americans who think whites and blacks should go to the same schools increased from 30 percent in 1942 to 90 percent in 1984. Support among southern whites for integrated schools grew from 2 percent in 1942 to 83 percent in 1984. Whites' support for fair employment practices increased from 42 percent in 1944 to 96 percent in 1972 (Smith and Sheatsley 1984: 15–16). The percentage of whites who agreed that blacks have a right to live wherever they can afford increased from 65 percent in 1964 to 88 percent in 1976. While in 1958 only 37 percent of white respondents said they would vote for a well-qualified black presidential candidate, 81 percent said in 1983 that they would vote for such a candidate (Schuman, Steeh, and Bobo 1985: 74–75).

These increases in levels of white support for the ideals of racial integration and fairness are impressive. But there has not been an equally impressive increase in white support for governmental policies designed to put these ideals into practice. Whites' support for federal efforts to integrate schools reached its peak, at 48 percent, in 1966 and slipped down to 25 percent in 1978; their support for busing reached 21 percent in 1983, but a survey item that invoked the powerful symbol of "neighborhood schools" found white support for busing to be only 9 or 10 percent in 1972, 1976, and 1980; and white support for federal efforts to guarantee fair employment practices stood at 36 percent in 1974 (Schuman, Steeh, and Bobo 1985: 88).

The wide gap between rather high levels of white support for ideals and lower levels of white approval of governmental action to implement these ideals has been a persistent feature of contemporary American racial attitudes. This chapter explores several explanations of this gap. These explanations assert that either racial prejudice, antipathy to the power and intrusiveness of the federal government, or white Americans' commitments to individualist values rooted in America's liberal tradition account for their inability or unwillingness to support governmental efforts to translate their support for the ideals of integration and fairness into support for consonant policies.

We shall show in this chapter that the first two explanations, emphasizing prejudice and aversion to federal power, face several anomalies found in patterns in whites' attitudes about blacks, the federal government, and governmental racial policy. However, these patterns are not anomalous with respect to an account of whites' racial policy attitudes that takes into consideration the influence of liberal individualist values on their policy reasoning. Nevertheless, we shall go on to suggest that the invocation of such individualist values by whites should be regarded with some skepticism, not because these invocations are completely insincere or inauthentic, but because the objective conditions that sustain them are increasingly problematic.

Racial Prejudice and Antipathy to Federal Power

Racial Prejudice

The persistence among whites of racial prejudice and its continued influence on their racial policy attitudes are asserted by proponents of the "symbolic racism" argument (Sears 1988; for further discussion, see Kinder 1986; Sniderman and Tetlock 1986a, 1986b; Carmines and Champagne 1990). This argument asserts that many whites acquire certain attitudes and predispositions toward blacks in early life that influence their responses to racial policies. For whites who have acquired prejudiced attitudes to blacks, racial policies trigger "long-held, habitual responses" that are negative (Sears et al. 1979: 371). Since these policies trigger negative racial affect, they also, it is claimed, trigger opposition to racial policies.

In the "old days," according to the symbolic racism argument, whites who were prejudiced against blacks, and who approved of the continuing subordination of blacks, spoke their minds and acted on their beliefs. But avowals of racial prejudice are no longer fashionable, and racial discrimination is now illegal. These changes in the social environment, it is claimed, do not change the basic psychological process by which racial prejudice issues into opposition to policies that aim to benefit blacks, but these changes in the environment now cause many whites to enlist "previously neutral stimuli" for use in expressing opposition to racial policies. The inconveniences and hazards of transporting students are therefore cited in opposing busing. The alleged unfairness of special attention to, or preferential treatment of, blacks is thus invoked in opposing affirmative action policies. In sum, racial prejudice is triggered by the symbol of blacks and by the symbolic recognition by governmental policies that blacks are important and worthy citizens. The resulting policy opposition is symbolically expressed in acceptable ways through the invocation of nonracial values and concerns.

Mary Jackman's (1978) study of the effect of education on racial policy attitudes reached a similar conclusion. Jackman found that well-educated whites are more supportive of the ideal of integration than whites with less education. But well-educated whites were not significantly more inclined than those with less education to support federal efforts to integrate schools. The better-educated have, Jackman believes, acquired the tolerant veneer that is now fashionable. Those with less education have not yet donned such stylish attitudinal apparel. But the bottom line, it appears, is that when it is time to put up or shut up by supporting integration policy, white Americans, regardless of education, are not ready to support integration. The appearance of progress toward a more tolerant and less prejudiced society is, then, just that: appearance only.

Antipathy to Federal Power

Margolis and Hague (1981) and Kuklinski and Parent (1981) have directly challenged Jackman's argument and, by implication, the "symbolic racism" argument. Both have claimed that Jackman's analysis confounds opposition to racial integration with concerns about the power and intrusiveness of the federal government. They assert that concerns about the power and trustworthiness of the federal government prevent many whites from doing what they might otherwise do: translate support for principles into support for consonant federal policies. These studies exonerate whites, to some extent, of the charge that racial prejudice motivates their opposition to federal racial policies.

Anomalies

Accounts that focus on racial prejudice and antipathy to federal power as the motive in whites' opposition to federal racial policies face several

TABLE 10.1

Racial Affect and Racial Policy Attitudes

Year	γ	Overall policy support	Support among those whose self-placement on NES "Feeling thermometer"[a] was:				
			75– 100	51– 74	50	25– 49	00– 24
			Fair Job Treatment				
1964	−.25	38.8%	51.6%	39.5%	37.3%	25.7%	9.4%
1968	−.22	37.9	50.5	33.9	27.6	24.1	19.0
1972	.04	48.4	50.6	47.1	52.5	45.5	28.8
			School Integration				
1964	−.35	42.7	62.1	45.4	36.1	23.4	14.0
1968	.31	37.5	54.5	34.9	32.5	27.6	7.3
1972	−.11	39.3	42.4	40.4	52.5	28.0	19.3
1976	.25	32.3	40.3	38.0	27.5	21.0	12.1
			Accommodation Rights				
1964	−.36	46.8	65.9	47.5	41.3	30.4	17.0
1968	−.36	55.6	73.2	54.8	52.7	34.5	16.1
1972	−.12	69.3	72.9	69.6	73.0	59.3	44.6
			Busing				
1972	−.07	5.5	7.2	4.0	6.8	2.8	3.1
1976	−.20	6.4	10.5	3.8	3.3	2.4	0.0
1980	−.19	5.6	8.5	6.8	3.8	1.1	0.0
			Aid to Minorities				
1972	−.22	29.5	41.7	30.1	27.1	19.1	1.8
1976	−.26	29.7	42.6	35.6	23.4	18.1	2.4
1980	−.31	17.8	25.1	19.9	14.9	7.9	5.3

SOURCE: National Election Studies.
[a] See Appendix.

anomalies. First, there is the problem of varying levels of white support for different racial policies. Are blacks less obviously the beneficiaries of accommodations rights guarantees than they are of busing? Why, then, was there 70 percent white support for the former and only 6 percent support for the latter in 1972? Was the federal government a less visible ally of blacks in the case of the first policy than the second? In short, if racial prejudice was the sole motivating force behind whites' racial policy attitudes, then all such policies should be equally opposed. But they are not.

Second, surprising policy attitudes are found among those whites most likely to oppose federal racial policies because of racial prejudice or antipathy to federal power. Among whites who in 1972 flatly professed to feel "cold" toward blacks (by placing themselves below 50 degrees on the National Election Studies [NES] "feeling thermometer"), almost 60 percent favored federal guarantees of blacks' accommodations rights (see

Table 10.1). In the same year, as Table 10.2 shows, almost 70 percent of whites who believed the federal government was too powerful favored federal accommodations rights guarantees.

Third, equally surprising attitudes are found if we "control" for avowed racial prejudice and antipathy to federal power by examining, in turn, the policy attitudes of those who profess to feel rather warm toward blacks (over 75 degrees on the "feeling thermometer") and those who are not concerned about the power of the federal government. As Table 10.1 indicates, among those who felt warm toward blacks, only about 9 percent favored busing in 1972, 1976, and 1980. Among whites who did not feel the federal government was too powerful, support for busing ranged from 7 to 10 percent in 1972, 1976, and 1980, as shown in Table 10.2.

If the existence of racial prejudice and antipathy to federal power are not crippling obstacles to majority white support for one racial policy, and if the absence of such negative attitudes is not sufficient to generate

TABLE 10.2

Attitudes About Power of the Federal Government and Racial Policy Attitudes

Year	γ	Overall policy support	Support among those who feel the federal government is:	
			too powerful	not too powerful
		Fair Job Treatment		
1964	−.43	37.0%	24.1%	50.5%
1968	−.32	37.5	30.4	49.3
1972	−.16	48.8	45.7	53.9
		School Integration		
1964	−.40	42.5	30.5	55.1
1968	−.37	36.2	27.5	50.3
1972	−.11	41.1	39.0	44.5
1976	−.44	30.5	25.2	46.4
		Accommodation Rights		
1964	−.50	45.9	30.0	62.5
1968	−.30	55.2	48.3	65.6
1972	−.06	69.2	68.8	70.8
		Busing		
1972	.03	7.1	7.2	6.8
1976	−.15	6.2	5.0	10.0
1980	−.13	4.4	2.3	10.3
		Aid to Minorities		
1972	−.10	33.1	32.2	34.8
1976	−.19	28.9	25.9	38.2
1980	−.25	16.0	13.1	26.6

SOURCE: National Election Studies.

substantial support for another racial policy, what are we to make of arguments about the influence of racism and antipathy to federal power on the racial policy attitudes of white Americans? Obviously, the type of policy being evaluated matters very much. Neither argument can easily account for the fact that different racial policies evoke dramatically different white evaluations, since blacks are the visible beneficiaries of all the policies under consideration and the federal government is the visible executor of the policies.

There is more. The racism argument would lead us to expect that because prejudice endures, its negative impact on levels of white support for racial policies must also persist. But it doesn't. In 1964 the gammas of association between avowed racial affect (as measured by the NES feeling thermometer) and attitudes about federal racial policies were .36 for accommodations rights guarantees, .35 for federal involvement in school integration, and .25 for federal guarantees of fair employment practices. By 1972 the gammas between responses to these survey items were, respectively, .12, .11, and .04 (see Table 10.1). Interestingly, the means and standard deviations of whites' placement on the racial feeling thermometer changed very little during this period. Racial prejudice has persisted, but apparently a number of whites have severed the formerly strong link between their attitudes to blacks and their attitudes to racial policies. The "federal antipathy" argument encounters similar difficulties. In 1964, gammas of association between attitudes about the power of the federal government and federal racial policies were .50 for accommodations rights guarantees, .40 for school integration, and .43 for employment practices. In 1972, the gammas were respectively .06, .11, and .16 (see Table 10.2). Opposition to federal power no longer exerts a significant influence on attitudes toward these racial policies.

Lakatos (1970) argues that a theory should not be discarded simply because it encounters anomalies. We agree. But these anomalies are sufficiently serious to justify at least the examination of an alternative explanation, a task to which we now turn.

Liberal Individualism and Whites' Racial Policy Attitudes

It is a commonplace assertion that the United States is a liberal society. The liberal label, though, is a vexing one to employ. In America it has connoted both the ideology of individualism and limited government and the ideology of government intervention in the social and economic life of the nation. The former we shall call "old" or "classical" liberalism, the latter "new" or "interest group" liberalism.

"Old" liberalism claims that the rights and prerogatives of the individual are paramount. This view can be traced back to John Locke's classical liberalism, which asserted that man enjoyed in a *pre-social and pre-governmental* state of nature certain rights to life and property, the preservation of which required the creation of government and defined government's purpose. Classical liberalism claims that government's appropriate role in a liberally ordered society is to enforce such rules as will allow individuals to pursue their interests unhindered by the unreasonable intrusions of others. These individual interests may be worldly, in which case government must impartially enforce certain rules about the acquisition, secure enjoyment, and disposition of property. Alternatively, these interests may be "otherworldly," in which case government must restrain and discourage zealots who would impair the civil rights of individuals because of their religious beliefs and practices.

The bargain individuals strike in securing the opportunity to unleash acquisitive impulses or follow their own religious consciences is acceptance of the burden of responsibility. If they fail in a fair and free society to attain what they want, they have no legitimate recourse to public authority for redress, assistance, or succor. Consequently, the ideals of self-reliance and responsibility have prominent places in the old liberal catalog of virtues.

Classical liberalism has been an intensely moralistic system of beliefs and values. The Protestant ethic made it imperative for the individual to find a calling and work hard at it, while forgoing the morally corrosive enjoyment of leisure and luxury (Troeltsch 1960; Weber 1958). Certainly this ethic made the trip across the Atlantic. In the United States the importance in political life of individual independence and self-reliance also came to be emphasized. A populace of independent, self-made men was said to serve as a barrier to the constant tendency of political power to encroach on citizens' rights (Berthoff 1979). The moral content of thinking about individual self-reliance became very prominent in the United States in the period from the 1820's to the 1860's, the period during which old liberalism effectively supplanted classical republicanism and became dominant. During this time a measure of daring and a readiness to undertake driving labor were widely regarded as sufficient conditions for considerable economic mobility. Economic success was thus regarded as an individual accomplishment that reflected favorably on the morality of the succeeder. What a lack of economic success was thought to reflect is not difficult to guess (Foner 1970).

Liberalism and Race

Most of the racial history of the United States has been characterized by the contradiction between white Americans' professed commitments to these old liberal values and an implacable racism that prevented the extension to blacks of the protection and promise of those values (for futher discussion, see Merriman and Carmines 1988). Gunnar Myrdal's appreciation of the deep psychological roots of white racism and the economic benefits to whites of black subordination prevented him from making the optimistic assertion that America's racial dilemma would inevitably be resolved in favor of extending old liberalism's protection and promise to blacks (Myrdal 1944). But Myrdal did see that many white Americans were truly committed to these old liberal values and had, as a consequence, no *principled* basis for rejecting blacks' demands for such protection. It was this absence of a principled basis for resisting blacks' demands that was so brilliantly exploited by the rhetoric and tactics of the early civil rights movement.

Old liberal values, in sum, provided a reservoir of support for racial policies designed to ensure "prospective equal opportunity." Such policies mandate, in essence, that "from now on" blacks are to be treated fairly. This means no deliberately engineered dual school systems, no segregation and discrimination in the enjoyment of public accommodations, and no race-based distortions of the rule of merit in employment practices. But some newer racial policies do not share this simple logic of prospective equal opportunity. These are policies of "prospective compensation." They seek to redress past injustices and prevent their perpetuation by altering future social competition in ways favoring blacks.

It is clear that many civil rights advocates saw prospective equal opportunity laws as a "first step" on a long road to racial equality. But it is also clear that many white Americans viewed them as a first and last step that would admit blacks to a competitive society in which they would have to sink or swim "like everybody else." Even such a limited "first step" was a hard one for many white Americans to accept. Racial prejudice, shock at the expansion of federal activity in racial matters, and distaste for the tactics of civil rights activists all had to be surmounted, or put aside, before white Americans could support such policies. Some whites have not accomplished this. But with the help of elite leadership in opinion and action, many whites have now come to support such policies.

Are white Americans likely to support new racial policies of prospective compensation? Will they support busing, affirmative action, and social programs to assist blacks? The answer appears to be no, and a key reason seems to be that many whites believe such policies challenge the old liberal values to which they are committed. Old liberal values are an obstacle that many whites have no intention of getting past.

The 1972 and 1976 NES surveys contain valuable items that illustrate this point. They elicit whites' opinions about the causes of racial inequality

TABLE 10.3

Economic Individualism and Racial Policy Attitudes, 1972

	γ	Policy approval (%) with economic individualism measured by Index 1[a]			
		Low	Low/ Moderate	High/ Moderate	High
Accommodations rights	.38	92.2%	80.8%	72.8%	61.4%
Fair job treatment	.36	76.0	60.8	52.6	39.1
School integration	.39	79.1	50.8	42.3	30.3
Busing	.44	32.7	8.2	3.8	2.1
Aid to minorities	.39	72.0	44.9	31.3	18.5

	γ	Policy approval (%) with economic individualism measured by Index 2[a]		
		Low	Moderate	High
Accommodations rights	.35	90.4%	69.9%	63.9%
Fair job treatment	.34	66.0	53.1	40.0
School integration	.34	61.7	43.5	33.1
Busing	.45	17.1	6.9	1.7
Aid to minorities	.38	58.8	42.0	22.6

SOURCE: National Election Studies.

[a] See Appendix for detail on indices.

and the best way to eliminate it. Merriman and Parent (1983) used three of these items from the 1972 survey to create an additive index of whites' commitment to "economic individualism" and belief that social competition is now fair (see Appendix for texts of items and details of index construction). The expectation, of course, is that whites who emphasized individual black striving as the way to economic success and who doubted the importance of racial discrimination as a barrier to this success would be much less supportive of governmental racial policies than those who emphasized group action by blacks to combat discrimination.

These expectations are borne out, as Table 10.3 shows. The top half of this table shows, for example, that among those white respondents high in commitment to economic individualism, only 18.5 percent supported aid to minorities, whereas this is true of 72 percent of those with low commitment to economic individualism. Similarly, among those respondents with high commitment to economic individualism, only 2 percent approved of busing; this is true of 33 percent of those with low commitment to economic individualism. In short, whites' economic individualism is strongly associated with their racial policy attitudes at a time when racial prejudice and antipathy to federal power are only weakly associated with these policy attitudes (see Tables 10.1 and 10.2). Interestingly, even among those whites most committed to the economic individualist market view

TABLE 10.4

Economic Individualism and Racial Policy Attitudes, 1976

	γ	Policy approval (%) with economic individualism measured by Index 3[a]			
		Low	Low/ Moderate	High/ Moderate	High
School integration	.46	71.1	45.1	41.7	22.0%
Busing	.36	19.0	14.9	8.8	2.4
Aid to minorities	.30	51.8	44.7	35.2	21.5

	γ	Policy approval (%) with economic individualism measured by Index 4[a]		
		Low	Moderate	High
School integration	.30	45.4	35.2	22.7%
Busing	.39	16.0	7.0	2.5
Aid to minorities	.20	38.9	30.7	22.9

SOURCE: National Election Studies.
[a] See Appendix for detail on indices.

of society, and therefore least supportive of government racial policies, there is substantial support for *prospective equal opportunity* policies such as accommodations rights guarantees and federal action to ensure fair employment practices. Federal efforts to ensure school integration were less popular, no doubt because by 1972 school integration had come to connote busing to many whites. Busing and aid to minorities, policies that require the government to exert itself in a multifaceted effort to improve the situation of minorities, show a considerable divergence of levels of support between those who are committed to economic individualism and those who are not.

A very similar pattern is found when using an index constructed with items concerning the situation of the poor. Here the focus is on whether respondents attribute the existence of the poor primarily to societal conditions or to the behavior of the poor themselves. The former represents a low score on economic individualism, the latter a high score. Those scoring high in economic individualism are substantially less likely to favor school integration, busing, or aid to minorities than those scoring low in economic individualism, as seen in the bottom half of Table 10.3.

This same pattern of relationships is found in the 1976 National Election Studies survey, in which the situations of blacks (Index 3) and women (Index 4) are used as indicators of economic individualism (see Table 10.4). Again, those scoring high in economic individualism are considerably less likely to support school integration, busing, or aid to minorities. Thus, for example, the top half of Table 10.4 indicates that among those respondents strongly committed to economic individualism only 22 percent supported school integration, whereas this is true of 71 percent of those with low commitment to economic individualism.

The bottom half of Table 10.4 shows similar relationships when the situation of women is used as an indicator of economic individualism. Again those respondents emphasizing individual initiative as opposed to group action to improve the situation of women are significantly less likely to support these racial policies. For example, only some 23 percent of the former, but over 45 percent of the latter, favor government-enforced school integration.

In sum, whether the situation of women, the poor, or blacks themselves is used as an indicator of economic individualism, the same pattern emerges: those committed to individual striving rather than collective action to improve the particular group's situation are markedly less likely to support these racial policies. Old liberal values in the form of economic individualism seem to provide a fundamental barrier to the widespread acceptance of these policies (see also Feldman 1983).

It appears, then, that many white Americans make a distinction between simple prospective equal opportunity policies and racial policies that commit government to actively undoing the segregative effects of past discrimination, enhancing blacks' access to education and employment, or making special efforts to attack the problem of underdeveloped black human capital. Merriman and Carmines (1988) found this distinction sharply drawn in responses to a 1981 survey conducted by ABC News and the *New York Times*. The analysis focused on the link between support for a hypothetical local fair-housing ordinance and support for a policy that would give blacks governmental assistance that whites in similar economic circumstances would not receive (see Appendix for item texts). Attitudes toward these two policies were almost completely unassociated ($\gamma = -.04$). Among white respondents who opposed the fair-housing ordinance, 76.6 percent also opposed the policy of race-conscious assistance. But even among whites who supported the fair-housing ordinance, 75.3 percent opposed the race-conscious measure.

National Election Studies data show a similar pattern. Those white respondents who support fair housing and accommodations rights give higher than average levels of support for fair employment and school integration, as seen in Table 10.5. For example, in 1964, 39 percent of all respondents approved of federal guarantees of fair employment for blacks. But this increased to 54 percent among those who supported fair housing, and to 69 percent among supporters of both fair housing and accommodations rights. Similarly, to take another illustration, in 1972, 41 percent of the full white sample approved of using the power of the federal govern-

TABLE 10.5

Consequences of Support for Fair Housing and
Accommodations Rights

		Policy Approval (%)	
Year	Overall policy approval (%)	Among supporters of fair housing	Among supporters of fair housing and accommo- dations right
Accommodation Rights			
1964	47.2%	68.1%	—[a]
1968	56.8	69.9	—[a]
1972	69.2	78.4	—
Fair Job Treatment			
1964	39.0	53.5	68.8%
1968	41.6	47.5	60.6
1972	48.8	54.4	64.4
School Integration			
1964	43.2	64.3	79.6
1968	40.6	51.9	65.5
1972	41.1	48.2	59.2
1976	27.3	33.5	—[a]
Busing			
1972	7.1	8.2	10.8
1976	6.1	7.1	—[a]
Aid to Minorities			
1972	33.2	37.2	41.0
1976	29.8	31.3	—[a]

SOURCE: National Election Surveys.
[a] No measure available.

ment to ensure school integration, while this was true among 48 percent of supporters of fair housing and 59 percent of supporters of both fair housing and accommodations rights.

But this carryover effect disappears when busing and aid to minorities are being considered. Thus, in 1972, 7 percent of all white respondents approved of government-enforced busing, only slightly less than the 8 percent who approve of busing among supporters of fair housing and the 11 percent recorded by supporters of both fair housing and accommodations rights. Aid to minorities displays a similar pattern, with little additional support for this policy among supporters of fair housing and accommodations rights.

What all this appears to mean is that white Americans evaluate racial policies, not just in terms of their feelings about the policies' black beneficiaries and federal origin, but also in terms of old liberal beliefs about the legitimate role of governmental action in shaping the outcomes of social and economic competition. White Americans profess to value an individualist approach to getting the good things of life. Many are therefore willing to see the federal government take action to ensure that blacks get a "fair chance from now on." But many whites balk at policies that probe more deeply into what it means, given the racial past of the United States, to be "fair" and that, consequently, seek to do "something more" for blacks than simply promise them prospective equal opportunity.

Conclusion

The confluence of the stream of America's racial history with the stream of its liberal tradition produced two consecutive periods of racial politics with distinctive characters. The first period—extending from the 1940's to the late 1960's—was characterized by a struggle to commit the United States to the extension of old liberal values and protection to black Americans. During this period, the old liberal belief in individuals having a fair chance to make it on their own was invoked by Americans intent on attaining passage of the civil rights legislation of the Second Reconstruction. The prominence of racial attitudes in the racial politics of this period is unmistakable. The struggle was between the old liberal value of fairness and racial prejudices sustaining unfair racial subordination. In the end, the liberal creed triumphed over racial prejudice.

The second period of racial politics began in the mid 1960's and continues to the present. Racial politics during this period has been increasingly dominated by the struggle between advocates of "new liberal" racial policies and policy opponents armed with old liberal values. Debates about programs for the poor, affirmative action in employment and admissions, and set-aside contracts for minority business enterprises have increasingly become part of the racial politics agenda. These debates do not pit the liberal creed against racial prejudice, but instead represent a conflict over different meanings of the creed itself.

In sum, the old liberal values that were such effective weapons during the struggle for a Second Reconstruction are of almost no help today because old liberal values have replaced racial prejudice as the standard appealed to by whites in opposing new liberal racial policies. The problem of discerning whites' real motives for opposing these policies is a terribly difficult one in such a situation. Certainly, more than racial prejudice and antipathy to the power of the federal government are at work.

The invocation of old liberal values on the part of whites in opposing new racial policies is not without deep irony, however. Modern capitalism has created an interdependent economy in the United States, which means that the ability of the average American to find work that provides a living wage, a decent life, and a secure retirement is conditioned by the vagaries of the international market economy, the decisions of bankers, investors, and employers, and the consumptive preferences and capacities of millions of other Americans. Such an economy obviously strips the individual of a significant amount of control over his or her economic circumstances and prospects, as bewildered millions who honored the values of hard work and frugality discovered in the bread lines of the depression era. Americans today live in a society that features a highly interdependent economy that puts the self-making American at risk.

Americans have acknowledged this interdependence through government policy that recognizes the need to shelter individuals (in a limited way) from their vulnerability in such an economy. But Americans have, in fact, gone well beyond this simple acknowledgement. They have become active participants in the creation and sustenance of a polity dominated by interest groups that pursue advantageous treatment for their constituents at all levels of government.

Even as Americans acknowledge their interdependency, even as they assiduously pursue governmental benefits, they remain deeply committed to an ideology of individual responsibility and self-reliance. In part, this commitment reflects objective conditions; as James Holt writes: "A corporation might depend for its existence on federal armament contracts or more distantly the purchasing power generated by governmental expenditures. Yet the men and women who worked for that corporation would be hired, fired, or promoted on the basis of their talents and industry in competition with others" (Holt 1975: 29).

Working hard and competing well still matter. In part, this commitment reflects the limited range of ideologies to which most Americans may turn in understanding their circumstances and the situations of others. As Garry Wills (1979) notes, Americans have no vibrant ideological tradition that exalts U.S. society's ability to care for others.

Thus the irony is that even as the interdependence of the U.S. economy provides less and less sustenance for old liberal values and practices, even as Americans' pursuit of governmental benefits makes them resemble the storied rugged individualists of old less and less, the old liberal view that celebrates economic individualism and exalts the independent, self-made man retains its vitality and is invoked in opposition to new racial policies. Old liberal values were once a powerful ally of the civil rights movement; they are an equally powerful opponent of the new racial policies.

Appendix: National Election Studies Survey Questions

Attitudes to the Power of the Federal Government, Racial Affect, and Fair Housing

Concern About the Power of the Federal Government

What is your feeling, do you think the government is getting too powerful or do you think the federal government is not getting too strong?

—The government is getting too powerful.

—The government is not getting too strong.

Feeling Thermometer

Respondents were asked to assess their feelings toward blacks. The "thermometer" ranges from 0 to 100, with 50 denoting feelings that aren't particularly warm or cold.

Fair Housing

Which of these two statements do you agree with most?

—White people have a right to exclude Negroes (blacks) out of their neighborhoods if they want to.

—Negroes (blacks) have a right to live wherever they can afford to, just like anybody else.

Racial Policy Items

Fair Job Treatment

How do you feel? Should the government in Washington see to it that black people get fair treatment in jobs or leave these matters to the states and local communities?

—See to it that black people get fair treatment in jobs.

—Leave these matters to the states and local communities.

School Integration

Do you think the government in Washington should see to it that white and black children go to the same schools or stay out of this area as it is not its business?

—See to it that white and black children go to the same schools.

—Stay out of this area as it is not its business.

Busing

There is much discussion about the best way to deal with racial problems. Some people think achieving racial integration is so important that it justifies busing children to schools out of their own neighborhoods. Others think letting children go to their neighborhood schools is so important that they oppose busing. Where would you place yourself on this scale?

—Bus to achieve integration.

—Keep children in neighborhood schools.

Accommodation Rights

Should the government support the right of black people to go to any hotel or restaurant they can afford, or should it stay out of this matter?

—Go to any hotel or restaurant they can afford.

—Stay out of this matter.

Aid to Minorities

Some people feel that the government in Washington should make every possible effort to improve the social and economic positions of blacks and other minority groups. Others feel that the government should not make any special effort to help minorities because they should help themselves. Where would you place yourself on this scale?

—Government should help minority groups.

—Minority groups should help themselves.

Four Indices of Economic Individualism

The indices use dichotomized variables, each scored 1 or 2: 1 is assigned to responses that indicate low economic individualism and 2 is assigned to responses that characterize high economic individualism. These scores were then summed to create the various indices.

1972: Index 1—References to Blacks

1. Which of these two statements do you agree with most?

    —Discrimination affects all black people. The only way to handle it is for blacks to organize together and demand rights for all. (Scored 1)

    —Discrimination may affect all blacks but the best way to handle it is for each individual to act like any other American—to work hard, get a good education, and mind his own business. (Scored 2)

2. Which of these two statements do you agree with most?

—It's lack of skill and abilities that keeps many black people from getting a job. It's not just because they're black. When a black person is trained to do something, he is able to get a job.
(Scored 2)

—Many qualified black people can't get a good job. White people with the same skills wouldn't have any trouble.
(Scored 1)

3. Which of these two statements do you agree with most?

—Many blacks have only themselves to blame for not doing better in life. If they tried harder, they'd do better.
(Scored 2)

—When two qualified people, one black and one white, are considered for the same job, the black won't get the job no matter how hard he tries.
(Scored 1)

1972: Index 2—References to Poor People

1. Which of these two statements do you agree with most?

—People who are born poor have less chance to get ahead than other people.
(Scored 1) .

—People who have the ability and work hard have the same chance as anyone else, even if their parents were poor.
(Scored 2)

2. Which of these two statements do you agree with most?

—Many poor people simply don't want to work hard.
(Scored 2)

—The poor are poor because the American way of life doesn't give all people an equal chance.
(Scored 1)

1976: Index 3—References to Blacks

1. Which of these two statements do you agree with most?

—Discrimination affects all black people. The only way to handle it is for blacks to organize together and demand rights for all.
(Scored 1)

—Discrimination may affect all blacks but the best way to handle it is for each individual to act like any other American—to work hard, get a good education, and mind his own business.
(Scored 2)

2. Which of these two statements do you agree with most?

—Many black people who don't do well in life have good training, but the opportunities just go to whites.
(Scored 1)

—Black people may not have the same opportunities as white, but many blacks haven't prepared themselves enough to make use of the opportunities that came their way.
(Scored 2)

3. Which of these two statements do you agree with most?

—The attempt to fit in and do what's proper hasn't paid off for blacks. It doesn't matter how proper you are, you still meet serious discrimination if you're black.
(Scored 1)

—The problem for many blacks is that they aren't really acceptable by American standards. Any black who is educated and does what is considered proper will be accepted and will get ahead.
(Scored 2)

1976: Index 4—References to Women

1. Which of these two statements do you agree with most?

—Many qualified women can't get good jobs, men with the same skills have much less trouble.
(Scored 1)

—In general, men are more qualified than women for jobs that have great responsibility.
(Scored 2)

2. Which of these two statements do you agree with most?

—Women can best overcome discrimination by pursuing their individual career goals in as feminine a way as possible.
(Scored 2)

—It is not enough for a woman to be successful herself. Women must work together to change laws and customs that are unfair to all women.
(Scored 1)

3. Which of these two statements do you agree with most?

—The best way to handle problems of discrimination is for each woman to make sure she gets the best training possible for what she wants to do.
(Scored 2)

—Only if women organize and work together can anything really be done about discrimination.
(Scored 1)

11

Assessing the Presidential Candidacies of Jesse Jackson

Harold W. Stanley

Jesse Jackson's 1988 presidential campaign made strong gains over his 1984 bid. In 1988 he secured 29 percent of the primary votes and nearly 30 percent of the convention delegates. Four years earlier the corresponding figures were 18 and 12 percent. Simple extrapolation of the geometric rates of increase through 1992 would have made Jackson the 1992 Democratic party's presidential nominee, with 47 percent of the primary votes and 75 percent of the convention delegates.

The political accomplishments of the 1988 Jackson campaign are obvious. In 1984 Jackson finished first in only two primaries—Louisiana (where Governor Edwin Edwards had urged Democrats to stay home) and the District of Columbia. The only Jackson caucus victory came in South Carolina, where Jackson, the top-ranking candidate, trailed the "uncommitted" line. In 1988 Jackson placed first in seven primaries and seven caucuses. Campaign finance also showed marked gains. In both years the eventual Democratic nominee spent about one-third of the total all Democrats spent. In 1984 Jackson's expenditures were just under 10 percent of the Democratic totals; in 1988, 21 percent (Federal Election Commission, as reported in Stanley and Niemi 1988: 93 and 1990: 241).

Assessments of Jackson's presidential bids have addressed various questions, among them, whether Jackson's campaign turned on, turned out, and perhaps turned off certain groups of voters (Cavanagh and Foster 1984; Gurin, Hatchett, and Jackson 1989; Zipp 1989); the effect of the rules on Jackson's performance (Ansolabehere and King 1990); how the media covered the Jackson candidacy (Broh 1987); Jackson's effect on the campaign agenda and Democratic party's platform (Moreland-Young 1989); whether and how Jackson's prominence affected voting decisions in the general election (Sears, Citrin, and Kosterman 1987), and the role of the Jackson campaign in the larger context of black political development (Reed 1986).

The current effort has a more restricted focus: analyzing Jackson's quests for the nomination in terms of support secured, voters mobilized, and opposition encountered. The strong gains of the 1988 Jackson campaign were accompanied by disappointments beyond failure to win the nomination. In 1988, as in 1984, the supporters sought by Jackson's Rainbow Coalition proved all too elusive. Rather than an underclass extending across racial and ethnic lines, Jackson's support coalition was predominantly black, with racial diversity provided by affluent whites. While the 1984 Jackson campaign coincided with, and helped to further, markedly greater black voter mobilization in the Democratic party primaries, the 1988 campaign was accompanied by only marginal further advances. Reluctance on the part of some white voters to support Jackson posed obstacles to expanding his political base, but assessment of Jackson's support within the dynamics of the presidential nominating process suggests that the give-and-take of ordinary political competition accounts for some of the opposition he encountered.

Analyzing Jackson's support seems deceptively simple. Yet contextual differences between 1984 and 1988 might help account for Jackson's stronger showing in 1988. Such differences include simultaneous Republican party primaries in 1988 (at least in the early going) but not in 1984, meaning some voters in states without party registration could opt for the Republican rather than the Democratic primary in 1988, leaving the Democratic primary voters more conducive to a candidate of Jackson's left-of-center ideology. Moreover, no Democratic candidate in 1988 could match the strong appeal Walter Mondale had to Democratic voters in 1984. This left Jackson essentially unchallenged for the black vote in 1988 and lessened the competition for the liberal vote. In addition, three candidates survived the 1984 nomination season—Mondale, Gary Hart, and Jackson, but in 1988 only Michael Dukakis and Jackson stayed the course. Insofar as some voters in the later primary states were dissatisfied with the likely nominee, Jackson was the sole beneficiary in 1988, but he shared that role with Hart in 1984. Consideration of such campaign dynamics must inform inferences about Jackson's political base.

The 1988 presidential nomination season had opened auspiciously for Jackson. As the only nationally known candidate in a field of regional ones, Jackson began with the greatest name recognition. In the preliminary national surveys on presidential preferences, once Hart withdrew in spring 1987, Jackson emerged as the front-runner, with pluralities in overall support.[1] In 1988, the early balloting in nearly all-white caucus and primary states showed that Jackson was making greater inroads in gaining white support than he had in 1984. Broadening his 1984 emphasis on racial justice to encompass economic justice, Jackson's 1988 message registered greater appeal among whites. Moreover, Mondale's absence meant Jackson's black support would likely solidify in 1988.

Prospects were promising. Presidential campaigns are highly volatile as candidates such as Jimmy Carter in 1976, Gary Hart in 1984, and George Bush in 1980 and 1988 learned—some to their satisfaction, others to their discomfort. Greater white and black support for Jackson could combine to produce primary wins and, given the dynamics of presidential campaigning, momentum, media coverage, and money could follow in a potent mix. Jackson was expected to do well on Super Tuesday, March 8th, and he did: Jackson's strong support among black voters, surpassing 90 percent, was tellingly revealed, and he carried five states.

A peak point for the Jackson campaign came on March 26th with his unexpected win in the Michigan caucus. While Dukakis, Albert Gore, Jr., and Jackson could each claim five primary victories on Super Tuesday (March 8th), Jackson then surged, while Dukakis and Gore slumped. Jackson doubled the Dukakis vote total in Illinois and won caucuses in Alaska and South Carolina, as well as a primary in Puerto Rico. On the eve of the Michigan caucuses, Jackson and Dukakis were virtually even in the total number of primary votes received and delegates committed (*National Journal*, March 26, 1988, p. 823, and April 2, 1988, p. 906). Jackson's surprising 54 to 29 percent win over Dukakis in Michigan generated considerable comment about Jackson as the likely Democratic nominee. For instance, Bob Beckel, Walter Mondale's 1984 campaign manager, said, "If Jesse Jackson can win in Michigan with its blue-collar and traditional Democratic vote, all bets might be off" (quoted in Muzzio 1989: xxxv).[2]

Jackson's prospects dimmed after the Michigan caucus. Dukakis recovered to win the Connecticut primary in late March and three key primary states in April: Wisconsin, New York, and Pennsylvania. Jackson remained as one of only two contenders, but his campaign fell short of the nomination.

[1] When Hart reentered the race in December, he reemerged, briefly, as the Democratic front-runner (Plissner and Mitofsky 1988: 56; *Public Opinion* 11, no. 1, January/February 1988, pp. 36–39; *New York Times* / CBS News Poll, March 1988).

[2] Unfortunately, but typically, no one conducted an exit poll in Michigan, so such commentary was uninformed by firm data on support patterns there.

The Data

Network exit–poll data are a particularly rich resource for discerning the patterns in presidential primary voting.[3] Large sample sizes for most state primaries furnish details national surveys most often overlook. Exit polls, targeting voters as they leave the polling place, avoid the difficulties surveys have with overreporting the vote—for example, the 1988 National Election Study survey of Super Tuesday shows a self-reported turnout rate double the rate indicated by aggregate figures. The secondary analysis of exit-poll data furnishes firm insights into the groups making up a candidate's base of support, even though exit polls lack extensive sets of questions probing the voter's political beliefs. Exit polls are strong in demonstrating who supports a candidate, even though data on why the candidate receives that support may be in short supply (Bartels and Broh 1989: 587).

One caveat: available exit polls slight the caucuses. Scores of exit polls for primaries contrast sharply with almost no coverage of caucuses except in Iowa (owing to its first-in-the-nation status). In 1984 there was no difference, but in 1988 Jackson fared better in the caucus states, from which he secured 36 percent of the available Democratic delegates, than in primary states, where he got 28 percent (Stanley and Niemi 1990: 96). So focusing on primaries in 1988 examines Jackson's support in a less favorable context.

Jackson's Political Base

The sequencing of primaries and caucuses, particularly the expectations early ones set for subsequent events, is a critical component in accounting for the support a candidate secures (Bartels 1988). Nevertheless, valuable perspectives on candidates' political bases can be gleaned by ignoring this fundamental truth and combining available data to construct a national overview of who supported whom for the presidential nomination.

Table 11.1 shows how groups of primary voters responded to the leading Democratic contenders in 1984 and 1988. The overall composition of the primary voters was virtually the same for the two years, suggesting that the presence of simultaneous Republican primaries in early 1988 but

[3] This chapter relies on different network exit polls, but uses for secondary analysis the ABC exit polls in 1988 in 31 states holding Democratic primaries (N = 56, 576). The ABC polls were made available by the Inter-University Consortium for Political and Social Research. Neither ABC nor the consortium bears any responsibility for the analyses and interpretations presented here.

TABLE 11.1

Vote by Groups in Democratic Party Presidential Primaries, 1984–1988

	1984				1988			
	Share of primary voters	Mondale	Hart	Jackson	Share of primary voters	Dukakis	Jackson	Others
Total	100%	38%	36%	19%	100%	43%	29%	28%
Sex								
Men	46	38	36	17	47	41	29	30
Women	54	39	35	20	53	43	30	26
Race/ethnicity								
White	78	42	43	5	75	54	12	35
Black	18	19	3	77	21	4	92	4
Hispanic	—	—	—	—	3	48	30	20
Age								
Under 30	17	26	39	26	14	35	38	27
30–44	30	30	38	23	31	37	36	26
45–59	24	41	34	18	25	42	30	28
60+	28	52	31	10	30	53	19	29
Religion								
Catholic	—	—	—	—	30	60	18	22
White Prot.	—	—	—	—	36	43	10	47
Jewish	—	—	—	—	7	75	8	17
Party								
Democrat	74	42	33	20	72	43	33	24
Independent	20	28	44	16	20	44	20	34
Ideology								
Liberal	27	34	36	25	27	41	41	19
Moderate	47	41	37	15	47	47	25	28
Conservative	21	37	34	16	22	38	23	38
Union household	33	45	31	19	—	—	—	—

SOURCES: Adam Clymer, "The 1984 National Primary," *Public Opinion* 7, no. 4, July/August 1984: 52–53; *New York Times*, June 13, 1988, B7.

NOTE: Dashes indicate data not available. Entries are derived from exit poll data for 24 contested delegated selection primaries in 1984 and from 33 primary states in 1988. No exit poll was conducted in Louisiana in 1984 or in Montana, Oregon, or Washington, D.C., in 1988. In each year exit poll data are taken from the three major network polls: *New York Times*/CBS News, NBC News, and ABC News. Individual state results are weighted according to the total Democratic primary vote in the state.

not in 1984 did not distort the overall shape of Democratic primary voter characteristics.

What do the exit polls indicate about candidate support patterns? The broad overview of Table 11.1 reveals that Jackson surpassed the other candidates only in the support he received from black voters and, in 1988, in the support from voters under 30. In both years, Jackson's candidacy appealed more strongly to blacks, the young, Democrats, and liberals. Jackson's black support rose from 77 to 92 percent, his support among whites— 5 percent in 1984—rose to 12 percent in 1988. Jackson's gains among black voters figured prominently in his carrying Alabama and Georgia on Super Tuesday. Had another candidate duplicated Mondale's strength by securing the support of one-third of the black voters there, Gore, a close second in each state, would have placed first in both and altered the campaign dynamics following Super Tuesday to Jackson's detriment.

Table 11.2 refines the perspective on Jackson's political base by presenting his vote by race for selected groups of primary voters in thirteen states. Focus first on Jackson's support among blacks. The patterns present in 1984 (lower support among southerners, moderates, conservatives, the older, and the less educated) disappeared in 1988, when Jackson gained 90 percent or more from every category except black Catholics.[4] Perhaps black Catholics had misgivings about backing a Protestant minister for the presidency (Cain, Lewis, and Rivers 1989: 37–38). Even so, at 83 percent, they were no exception in Jackson's monolithic black support in 1988.

Among whites, Jackson's patterns of support in 1984 and 1988 matched up more closely, with gains registered in every group. Liberals, youth, and college graduates constituted the strongest components of Jackson's base among whites. Indeed, liberal whites, at 26 percent, provided the strongest backing for Jackson of any of the white groups. However, Jewish voters, a core group among Democratic liberals, backed Jackson to a lesser extent than did white voters as a whole. The West (in Table 11.2, California) remained Jackson's strongest region among whites. Although not shown in Table 11.2, Jackson secured over 20 percent of the white vote in five states: California, Connecticut, Nebraska, New Mexico, Vermont, and Wisconsin, topping out in Vermont at 32 percent. Among the states, higher white voter support for Jackson showed a positive relationship with the proportion of white voters and liberal voters, as well as with later primaries, in which Jackson remained as the only alternative to Dukakis. A simple model incorporating these three variables accounted for two-thirds of the variance across states in the white vote for Jackson.

Among Hispanics, Jackson also fared better in 1988 than in 1984, gaining almost a third of the vote, up from 17 percent in 1984 (Plissner and Mitofsky 1988: 57). In both years he fared better among Hispanics than among whites. Yet Hispanics made up a mere 3 percent of the 1988 Democratic primary voters overall, surpassing 10 percent of the Democratic

---

[4] Given the sample sizes in exit polls, even slight differences have statistical significance. Although the differences between 91, 93, and 95 percent may lack substantive significance, given concern over the Rainbow Coalition, it merits mention that Jackson's support in the *New York Times* / CBS exit polls was inversely related to education among blacks in 1988 (as shown in Table 11.2). Rather than make much of that relationship, it suffices to note that a similarly combined summary of ABC exit polls in 31 primary states reveals similar levels of support but not the inverse relationship.

TABLE 11.2

Primary Vote for Jackson by Race, 1984 and 1988

		White		Black	
		1984	1988	1984	1988
All states	(13)	5%	13%	77%	92%
Region					
Northeast	(5)	4	13	82	93
Midwest	(3)	4	11	79	90
South	(4)	2	6	68	94
West	(1)	9	25	78	93
Sex					
Men	(47%)	5	14	76	90
Women	(53%)	4	14	78	94
Ideology					
Liberal	(28%)	9	26	82	93
Moderate	(49%)	3	10	76	92
Conservative	(23%)	3	8	75	93
Religion					
Catholic	(25%)	3	11	72	83
Protestant	(36%)	—	13	—	93
Jewish	(6%)	4	8	—	—
Age					
Under 30	(15%)	6	18	83	93
30–44	(31%)	7	21	83	93
45–59	(24%)	4	13	74	93
60+	(30%)	2	6	66	92
Education					
Less than HS	(11%)	1	10	67	95
High school	(31%)	2	8	77	93
Some college	(26%)	5	14	82	93
College grad.	(32%)	9	21	80	91

SOURCE: Martin Plissner and Warren Mitofsky, "The Changing Jackson Voter," *Public Opinion* 8, no. 4, July/August 1988, p. 57.

NOTE: Dashes indicate data not available. Table based on 13 states holding presidential primaries where CBS News and the *New York Times* conducted exit polls in both 1984 and 1988. A comparison of the 1988 Jackson vote in any category in the 13 states presented in this table and all 24 states where exit polls were conducted shows a difference of no more than 2 percentage points. The 13 states are: Alabama, California, Georgia, Illinois, Indiana, Maryland, Massachusetts, New Jersey, New York, North Carolina, Ohio, Pennsylvania, and Tennessee. In 1984, 17 percent of Hispanics voted for Jackson; in 1988, 33 percent did. Numbers in parentheses give the sample size for the category, either a raw count or the category's percentage of the total number of primary voters in 1988.

primary voters only in Texas (14 percent) and New Mexico (33 percent) (Muzzio 1989: xxxvi).

These broad contours of Jackson's support do not follow the lines one associates with the Rainbow Coalition. Rather than "a rainbow coalition of the rejected" "spanning lines of color, sex, age, religion, race, region, and national origin" (Jackson 1987: xiv), the racial mix of Jackson's supporters in the 1988 primaries can be characterized as almost all of the black voters, one-third of the Hispanics, and one-seventh of the whites. Put differently, primary exit polls indicate that the Rainbow Coalition was 67 percent black, 31 percent white, and 3 percent Hispanic. Although disproportionately black, these percentages marked a greater balance than prevailed in 1984, when the corresponding figures were 76, 21, and 3.

If the racial mix of the Rainbow Coalition was lopsided, the class composition was askew too. Two pollsters noted: "Neither the black nor the white Jackson voter represented an underclass. . . . The true elite this Democratic primary season, however, were the white Jackson voters. . . . The higher a white voter's income, the more likely he or she was to vote for Jackson" (Plissner and Mitofsky 1988: 57). ABC News exit polls in 31 primary states do not confirm this positive relationship between white household income and Jackson support. The two network exit polls do agree that, among whites, the highly educated responded most favorably to the Jackson campaign (the ABC percentages for 31 states are within a percentage point of those reported in Table 11.2).

These findings about the demographic makeup of Jackson's coalition, coupled with the conventional wisdom that a party's primary voters are better educated, more affluent, and more partisan than its rank-and-file, suggest that Jackson failed to mobilize the constituency of the powerless he targeted. In light of the previous evidence, this charge seems merited, but the conventional wisdom adds little to it.

The conventional wisdom describing a party's primary voters has a respectable lineage (Ranney 1972; but see Bartels 1988: 140; Geer 1988; and Hagen 1989). Data from 1988 question the conventional wisdom. The Democratic primary voters were contrasted with general election voters in those same states who supported Dukakis or identified with the Democrats. The two sets of voters had essentially similar educational attainment and income distributions (Table 11.3). Differences do appear. These general election voters claimed Democratic partisanship at a higher rate than did primary voters. Proportionately, Democratic primaries attracted fewer young and more elderly people, more blacks, and more Protestants. Democratic primary voters were less liberal and slightly more moderate and conservative. But the switch of eight southern and border states from caucuses to primaries for Super Tuesday in 1988 did not appreciably alter the overall ideological composition of Democratic primary participants (Hadley and Stanley 1989: 34–35). Rather than a mismatch between Democratic participants in the primaries and the general election, with an upper-class tilt toward primary voting, the data for 1988 suggest no differences in education or income, along with unexpected partisan and liberal tilts among Democratic general election voters.

A different reading of the racial composition of Jackson's support em-

TABLE 11.3
Democratic Primary and General Election Voters, 1988

Category	Democratic primary voters	Democratic general election voters	Absolute difference (general election–primary)
Age			
Under 30	16.3%	21.2%	4.9
30–49	44.3	46.4	2.1
50+	39.4	32.4	−7.0
Education			
<High school grad.	9.0	9.3	0.3
High school grad.	28.3	28.7	0.4
Some college	26.8	26.7	−0.1
College graduate	19.1	19.4	0.3
Postgraduate	16.9	15.9	−1.0
Ideology			
Liberal	36.0	42.4	6.4
Moderate	40.5	36.9	−3.6
Conservative	23.3	20.7	−2.6
Income			
<$5,000	6.5	7.5	1.0
$5,000–9,999	8.2	8.9	0.7
$10,000–19,999	17.2	17.2	0.0
$20,000–29,999	19.9	19.3	−0.6
$30,000–39,999	17.5	16.9	−0.6
$40,000–49,999	12.0	11.3	−0.7
$50,000+	18.6	18.9	0.3
Partisanship			
Democrat	74.1	79.4	5.3
Independent	17.0	13.7	−3.3
Republican	7.0	5.1	−1.9
Something else	1.9	1.8	−0.1
Race			
Black	19.9	14.2	−5.7
White	76.2	80.0	3.8
Other	3.9	5.8	1.9
Religion			
Protestant	40.0	34.0	−6.0
Catholic	28.2	32.9	4.7
Jewish	6.0	6.7	0.7
Other	17.7	17.0	−0.7
None	8.0	9.3	1.3

SOURCE: Secondary analysis of ABC News primary election exit polls (including the ABC News Super Tuesday primary election exit poll), February–June 1988.

NOTE: Table indicates the percentage of Democratic primary voters and Democratic general election voters possessing each characteristic. Democratic primary voters are those voting in Democratic presidential primaries in 31 states (N = 56,576). Democrats in the general election are those who either identified as Democrats or voted for Dukakis in the general election in the same 31 states (N = 34,067; for ideology and religion, N = 15,881). Democrats so defined constituted 54 percent of all general election voters. Tabulations were weighted to reflect the aggregate primary turnout in these states.

phasizes the seven primaries that he won. Were his first-place finishes in 1988 attributable to high black population percentages, high white racial crossover voting rates, or bits of both in a crowded field of candidates? Merely to list the primary victories goes some way toward furnishing the answer: Alabama, Georgia, Louisiana, Mississippi, Virginia, Puerto Rico, and the District of Columbia. No exit polls exist for Puerto Rico or the District of Columbia. The remaining five Super Tuesday states are the first five in terms of percentage of primary voters who were black, ranging from 33 to 46 percent (if data were available, the District of Columbia would head the list). Only in Virginia did Jackson's share of the white vote match his national average. In the rest of the states, he received 5 or 6 percent of the white vote. The sizable black voter base in these states was all the more potent given the number of candidates vying for the white vote. Jackson's Super Tuesday victories occurred within the first month of the 1988 nomination season, before several candidates who later fell by the wayside (Gary Hart, Richard Gephardt, Paul Simon, and Al Gore) had been winnowed. Most caucus victories came later. In the caucuses, mobilizing smaller numbers of committed supporters can pay off politically: Jackson took Texas, Alaska, South Carolina, and Michigan in March, followed by the Virgin Islands, Delaware, and Vermont in April.

Voter Mobilization

The 1984 Jackson campaign made voter mobilization one of its major missions (Reed 1986: 11–30), and black participation rose dramatically. Indeed, in seven states for which ABC News exit-poll data are consistently available for the 1980, 1984, and 1988 Democratic presidential primaries (California, Florida, Illinois, New Hampshire, New York, Ohio, and Pennsylvania), an additional 900,000 black voters took part in 1984. This constituted an increased black participation of about 80 percent over 1980. In 1988 such strides in participation remained but were not appreciably increased, inasmuch as fewer than 100,000 additional black voters turned out.[5] (In 1984 and 1988, those black voters who took part in the primaries constituted roughly half the number of black voters who turned out for the general election.) Pointing to voter mobilization is not proof that Jackson's candidacy caused it. Nationally, rates of participation in the general elections followed similar patterns. Black and Hispanic participation rose from 1980 to 1984 but ebbed in 1988 (U.S. Bureau of the Census 1989: 2).

[5] Absolute numbers of black voters were calculated by multiplying the exit-poll estimate of the black voter proportion by the total number of voters in each state's primaries. In absolute numbers in these seven states, white voter participation dipped, falling by about 150,000 from 1980 to 1984, and another 350,000 from 1984 to 1988.

Opposition

Jackson's stronger showing in 1988 than in 1984 raises questions about how much farther Jackson can expand his political base. A consideration of "high negatives," voter resistance, trial heats, and ideology will explore the obstacles Jackson has encountered in expanding his support coalition so far.

"High negatives" are one major problem Jackson has faced. When the *New York Times* / CBS News Poll has asked, in national surveys, "Is your opinion of Jesse Jackson favorable, not favorable, undecided, or haven't you heard enough about Jesse Jackson yet to have an opinion?" those responding "not favorable" have ranged between 33 and 49 percent since 1984. "Favorable" responses have ranged between 15 and 38 percent. Dukakis, by contrast, experienced unfavorable ratings of 14 to 43 percent and favorable responses of 28 to 38 percent during 1987 and 1988. During the fall of 1988, Jackson's favorability ratings matched those of Dukakis (*New York Times* / CBS News Poll Post-Election Survey 1988: 7–8). This may seem to be damning with faint praise, but the Dukakis general election vote share was the Democratic high point for the 1980's. Rather than being a fixed and unchanging problem, Jackson's "high negatives," as the ranges indicate, fluctuate and have occasionally given way to rather favorable ratings.

Some voter reluctance to back Jackson was undoubtedly based on racism. In March 1988, in the midst of the nominating season, the General Social Survey asked, "If your party nominated a black for president, would you vote for him if he were qualified for the job?" Among whites, 19 percent said no, another 5 percent responded that they did not know; in 1958, the percentages were 53 and 10 (Niemi, Mueller, and Smith 1989: 24). Such a possibility can be raised, but it cannot be tested with the exit-poll data available for 1988. A sense of the reluctance to back Jackson—even though the share attributable to racism cannot be determined—can be gathered from questions assessing the impact of Jackson as running mate and trial heats pitting Dukakis against Bush and Jackson against Bush.

Among Democratic primary voters, 86 percent of blacks favored Jackson as Dukakis's vice president, and 30 percent of whites did, but only 18 percent of the white supporters of Dukakis favored Jackson.[6] With few exceptions, press reports on surveys indicated that Jackson as the vice presidential nominee would hurt Dukakis in trial heats with Bush (Bar-

[6] The question was asked in seven primary states in the final third of the nomination process. Sample size was 1,876 for blacks, 10,572 for whites, and 7,448 for white Dukakis supporters.

tels and Broh 1988: 583–85). On the final day of primaries in 1988, ABC surveyed voters in California, New Mexico, and New Jersey on whether picking Jackson as the Democratic vice presidential nominee would affect the voter's general election choice. It would. One-third of Dukakis's supporters indicated that Jackson as running mate would make them less likely to vote for Dukakis, another 11 percent were not sure, 17 percent said it would make a Dukakis vote more likely, and 40 percent said it would make no difference.[7] In short, the proportion less likely to back a Dukakis-Jackson ticket was double the proportion more likely to do so.

Trial heats between Jackson and Bush revealed that large numbers of white Democratic primary voters would back Bush if Jackson gained the Democratic nomination. Faced with a choice between Jackson and Bush in the general election, only 28 percent of the white Dukakis voters would back Jackson, 41 percent Bush, and 31 percent would support neither (Table 11.4). Put differently, almost three-fourths of Dukakis's white backers would not support Jackson against Bush.[8]

Such numbers from hypothetical candidacies and trial heats signify some of the difficulties Jackson faced in expanding his base of support. But such low loyalty levels to Jackson as the presidential or vice presidential nominee should be viewed in the appropriate political context. Rather than being considered as enduring realities carved in stone, these numbers must be placed within the dynamics of the political campaigns from which they emerged. The heat of a nomination campaign, when the contest has narrowed to two or three candidates, is a poor time to expect to find eagerness among each candidate's political supporters to back the hypothetical general election campaign of an opposing candidate. Nomination campaigns typically center on and sharpen the differences between candidates. Having just cast a vote for one rather than the other candidate for the nomination is quite a different context for choice than the one in which a voter decides after a general election campaign between the candidates of different parties. The Carter-Kennedy battle for the Democratic nomination in 1980 and the Mondale-Hart-Jackson contest of 1984 gave evidence of the reluctance of one candidate's backers to unite behind another in the general election. No single summary number for those contests is available, so two examples must suffice: Hart backers in Pennsylvania in 1984, if faced with a choice between Mondale and Reagan, would have decided as follows: 38 percent for Mondale, 30 percent for Reagan, and 33 percent for neither; Hart backers in New Jersey in 1984, if faced with the same choice, would have split 37, 35, and 28, respectively (Smith 1985: 621,

[7] Sample size: 3,740.

[8] The question was asked in eleven primary states (sample size: 11,693) late in the nomination season—states where Jackson received some of his larger shares of the white vote.

TABLE 11.4

Trial Heats, Dukakis or Jackson Against Bush, by Race and Democratic
Primary Vote, 1988

	Dukakis	Bush	Neither
Blacks			
Dukakis voters	88.7%	8.4%	2.9%
Jackson voters	63.4	7.1	29.5
Whites			
Dukakis voters	88.4	10.5	1.1
Jackson voters	77.6	10.2	12.2
	Jackson	Bush	Neither
Blacks			
Dukakis voters	55.1	22.8	22.1
Jackson voters	98.5	0.8	0.7
Whites			
Dukakis voters	27.8	41.4	30.8
Jackson voters	91.7	6.9	1.4

SOURCE: Secondary analysis of ABC News primary election exit polls, February–
June 1988.

NOTE: Questions were as follows: "If the 1988 presidential election were being held
today and the candidates were Jesse Jackson and George Bush, for whom would you
vote?" and "And if the candidates were Michael Dukakis and Bush, for whom would you
vote?" Respondents had the names of each candidate beside boxes to mark. "Neither"
was also a choice with its own box. The questions were asked of 24,121 Democratic primary voters in California, Connecticut, Indiana, Nebraska, New Jersey, New Mexico,
New York, Ohio, Pennsylvania, Wisconsin, and West Virginia. Dukakis and Jackson
combined received 90 percent of the Democratic primary vote in these states. Tabulations
were weighted to reflect the aggregate Democratic primary turnout in these states.

635). Such numbers approach the figures for Dukakis voters reacting to
Jackson as the nominee, suggesting that a portion, perhaps a very large
portion, of the reluctance to back Jackson undoubtedly stems from the
normal give-and-take of politics in the struggle for the nomination.

Even so, evidence of substantial refusal to back Jackson is available
from early in the nomination season. In the sixteen Super Tuesday primary states, ABC exit polls contained a question tapping general political
opposition. The results reveal considerable resistance to Jackson, but some
political figures fared more poorly. Voters were presented with a list of
candidates and asked, "Are there any candidates on the list below you
definitely WOULD NOT VOTE FOR for president? (CHECK ALL THAT APPLY)"
(capitalization in the original). Among white Democratic primary voters
on Super Tuesday, 46 percent checked Jackson, a figure surpassed only by
Hart (49 percent) among Democratic candidates and Pat Robertson (65
percent) among Republican candidates. Robertson, like Jackson a minister
campaigning for president, drew the most negative response from white

Democratic primary voters. Bush, at 45 percent, practically matched Jackson's unpopularity among white Democratic voters on Super Tuesday.[9]

Exit-poll data can document refusal to support Jackson, but assessing various explanations for that opposition is not possible with the limited scope of the data. One explanation for reluctance to back Jackson—ideology—can be demonstrated. Supporters of Jackson and Dukakis both perceived the other candidate as ideologically out of step. Jackson backers who saw Dukakis as too conservative made up 35 percent of the whites and 21 percent of the blacks. An additional 29 and 49 percent respectively were unsure whether Dukakis was too liberal, too conservative, or about right. Backers of Dukakis were more convinced that Jackson was too liberal: 48 percent of whites and 41 percent of blacks thought so. Those unsure were 32 and 25 percent respectively.[10] Dukakis supporters thinking Jackson too liberal (or unsure whether he was) favored Bush over Jackson by a margin of three to one.[11] Given the dynamics of the 1988 campaign, these figures are not surprising, reflecting as they do the Dukakis campaign strategy of running to the right of Jackson. Other factors were at play, but while Dukakis could campaign as centrist in opposition to Jackson, national survey trial heats had Dukakis ahead of Bush in the popular vote (*Public Opinion* 11, no. 6, November/December 1988: 36–40).

Such ideological divisions, part and parcel of ordinary politics, do not bode well for expansion of Jackson's political base if he continues to be viewed by many as "too liberal." Beholders and the beheld both account for such perceptions. While the expectation of widespread changes in such perceptions may be unrealistic, a voter's tendency to project her or his preferred positions onto candidates is well documented. The problem for Jackson is that projection applies principally to the less well known candidates (Bartels 1988: 104–7).

Conclusion

A repetition of Jackson's solid gains between 1984 and 1988 should have made him the Democratic nominee in 1992. Presidential politics is not so simple, however, and extrapolating from two data points does not produce solid predictions. Whether Jackson builds on or falls back from the gains he posted in 1988 turns in part on what he does and on the fields of competitors future contests will draw. Jackson is a familiar candidate.

[9] Sample size: 1,355.
[10] Sample size for Jackson supporters: 1,592 black and 1,991 white; for Dukakis: 167 black and 6,997 white.
[11] Sample size: 3,418.

The mayor's race in the District of Columbia is a case in point: few political figures would receive such attention over deciding whether to run for political office. Such familiarity has its price, making it harder, but not impossible, for Jackson to benefit in a presidential primary campaign from the kind of momentum Jimmy Carter enjoyed in 1976 after Iowa and New Hampshire, and Gary Hart in 1984 after New Hampshire.

Jackson's strong support among black voters, who make up one-fifth of all Democratic primary voters, gives him a strong political foundation on which to build. Even though the reality of a Rainbow Coalition has remained elusive, the addition of support from liberal and highly educated whites makes Jackson an even stronger figure in Democratic nomination politics. Whether Jackson can gain the nomination in some future campaign is open to question, whether he will exert a major influence in Democratic nomination politics is not.

12

The Decline in College Entry Among African Americans: Findings in Search of Explanations

Robert M. Hauser

The papers are filled with news about the problems of African American students in attending college, the not-at-all vestigial manifestations of racism on U.S. college campuses, increasingly visible evidence that African American and other minority students will not tolerate anything less than first-class university citizenship, and a variety of proposals to attract more African American students to college and to improve the chances of their success and enjoyment of college life.[1] The purpose of this chapter is to outline trends in schooling, especially trends in college entry and

Support for this research was provided by grants from the Spencer Foundation, the National Institute on Aging, the Graduate School of the University of Wisconsin–Madison, and the Kenneth D. Brody Foundation, and by grants for core support of population research from the National Institute of Child Health and Human Development (HD-5876) and from the William and Flora Hewlett Foundation to the Center for Demography and Ecology at the University of Wisconsin–Madison. This work began as an effort to provide background information on trends in schooling for the Panel on Education of the Committee on the Status of Black Americans, National Academy of Sciences–National Research Council. Some of the work has appeared in Jaynes and Williams 1989, esp. ch. 7, and in Hauser and Anderson 1991. Kenneth A. Shaw and Thomas G. Mortenson prompted my curiosity about trends in post–high school aspirations of black and white seniors, and Lawrence Bobo, Michael Hout, Robert Mare, and Paul Siegel provided other helpful suggestions. I thank Yu Xie, Kee Cheol Ryoo, and Jon Herron for research assistance. The opinions expressed herein are those of the author.

[1] In counterpoint to these signs of concern about college-going opportunities, there are also increasing signals of frustration and despair about black educational performance, some of it harking back to the "great IQ debate" of the 1970s and hinting at genetic sources of black-white differences in academic ability (Herrnstein 1990a and 1990b; Hauser, Jaynes, and Williams 1990). Although academic performance certainly affects college entry, the best available data support the view that black academic performance improved during the period of declining black college entry (Hauser and Anderson 1991).

completion among African American and white youth, and to evaluate several of the hypotheses that have been offered to explain the divergence of African American and white college chances since the mid 1970s.

Early in 1985, the Harvard sociologist Nathan Glazer handed me an article from the *New York Times* reporting the release of a statement from an advocacy group, the Children's Defense Fund (1985). It claimed that the chances of African Americans attending college were declining, and that the decline ought to be addressed at the level of national policy. My first reconnaissance of the report suggested that its statistics were defective (Hauser 1986). Fairly firm in two beliefs, I went on to construct my own trend estimates: first, the advocacy group's dismay with the college support policies of the Reagan administration was well founded; second, its portrayal of declining African American college chances was exaggerated and had little basis in fact. I was wrong about the second part.

African American chances for college entry peaked around 1977, when they approached those among whites. Black college entry declined through the early 1980s, while white college entry grew to unprecedented levels. The college–going chances of African Americans recovered after the mid 1980s, but they now lag far behind those of whites.

If the amount of misinformation in circulation is any guide, there does now appear to be a lot of public concern about African American college attendance. Here are a few of my favorite items: the *Wisconsin State Journal*, among other papers, has attributed the fall of African American college attendance largely to a decline in attendance by black men. In our analyses, and in other analyses carried out by Reynolds Farley at the University of Michigan, there is ample evidence of gender equality; young African American men and women have shared the decline in college chances.[2] On the other hand, it is possible to go too far in describing the problem. On the MacNeil-Lehrer Newshour, an African American judge gave an impassioned address in which he declared that there are as many black men of college age in prison as attending colleges. That is utter nonsense.[3] It is a striking statistic, and so perverse in its stereotypic implications that I could imagine its leading to a cabinet resignation had it come instead,

---

[2] It is easy to reach misleading conclusions about this issue if one examines black or white men and women in isolation (Koretz 1990). The main trends are that women's college chances have improved relative to those of men, regardless of race, while African American college chances have declined relative to those of whites, regardless of gender. If one only compares African American men and women, men's chances appear to be getting worse. If one compares black and white men and women, it becomes possible to see how African American women have shared declining college chances with African American men, as well as sharing rising college chances with white women (Hauser 1993).

[3] One story about the origin of this statistic is that it devolved from a valid statement, that there were as many black men in prisons as in college dormitories.

say, from our secretary of education. There are three to five times as many young African American men in colleges as in prisons, which is not, of course to say that the preponderance of college-going is as high as I might like it to be.

In 1980, there were 335,000 black men between 18 and 24 years old enrolled in colleges and universities (U.S. Bureau of the Census 1984a, table 260). In that same year, there were 44,900 black men aged 18 to 24 in prisons and 25,600 in local jails or workhouses (U.S. Bureau of the Census 1984b, table 14). Thus there were almost five black men aged 18 to 24 years old in college for each one imprisoned in 1980. It is difficult to obtain more recent estimates of imprisoned black men aged 18 to 24, which confirms my suspicion that the claim is pure speculation. The numbers of jail and prison inmates are not reported regularly by age, race, and sex in publications of the Bureau of Justice Statistics, and, except in the census, populations of jail and (state and federal) prison inmates are obtained from different sources. There were 80,671 black male jail inmates in 1983, the most recent year for which data from the census of jails are available (U.S. Bureau of the Census 1987a, table 303), and of these, 31,955 were aged 18 to 24 (U.S. Bureau of Justice Statistics n.d.). At the end of 1983 there were 191,020 black males in state and federal prisons (U.S. Bureau of Justice Statistics 1986). The population in prisons is older than that in jails; for example, 44.4 percent of black men in jails were aged 18 to 24 in 1980, but 35.8 percent of black men in prisons were aged 18 to 24 in 1980. If the relationship between age and type of imprisonment were the same in 1983 as in 1980, I estimate there would have been 60,000 black males aged 18 to 24 in prisons in 1983. Thus, a rough estimate is that there were 92,000 black men aged 18 to 24 in jails or prisons in 1983. According to the October Current Population Survey, 331,000 black men aged 18 to 24 were enrolled in college in 1983, and another 172,000 were enrolled in school below the college level (U.S. Bureau of the Census 1984c, table 6).

Another, similarly striking statistic, constructed by Marc Mauer (1990), compares the number of young (20- to 29-year-old) black men "under the control of the criminal justice system,"[4] which he estimated to be 610,000 in 1989, with the number of black men of all ages enrolled in college, 436,000 in 1986 (Center for Education Statistics 1988, table 1). Here, too, the reader is supposed to be impressed by how much larger the former figure is than the latter. News reports declaring "1 in 4 young black men sentenced" (e.g., *Wisconsin State Journal*, February 27, 1990) failed to mention that the sentencing estimate followed the enrollment

---

[4] This is defined as the total number of persons in state and federal prisons and jails, plus those on probation and parole (Mauer 1990).

estimate by three years in a period when the "criminal" population was growing rapidly. Moreover, the "1989" estimate was obtained by extrapolating counts using growth rates from earlier in the decade. The estimates, described as conservative by their author, were apparently constructed in ignorance of the disparity between estimates of black enrollment by the National Center for Education Statistics (NCES) from institutional sources and by the U.S. Bureau of the Census from household surveys[5]— the Census Bureau's estimate of black male college enrollment at all ages in 1986 is 580,000 (U.S. Bureau of the Census 1990, table A4); that is, it is 144,000 higher than the estimate used by Mauer. Mauer is scarcely "conservative" in his willingness to include college enrollment at all ages in his comparison: among African Americans, as among whites, a substantial share of college enrollment occurs at ages 18 and 19. Moreover, his estimate of the prevalence of contact with the criminal justice system excludes about 225,000 African American men aged 20 to 29 who were in military service (U.S. Bureau of the Census 1987b, tables 1 and 3), while his estimate of exposure to higher education excludes about 500,000 civilian black men aged 20 to 29 who were not currently enrolled, but had completed at least one year of college (U.S. Bureau of the Census 1988, table 1).

One of the reasons for this sort of misinformation is the failure of our statistical system to monitor the transition from youth to adulthood. Our society is spending a great deal more on surveys to find out who may or may not get elected to Congress and the presidency and how large our production of farm products will be than it spends to find out what happens to our youth after high school and how it happens. To take one of the worst examples that I know of, our National Center for Education Statistics last measured the effect of social background and academic achievement on college entry in 1984, following up a sample of the high school graduation class of 1982. Its next planned measurement of the same kind will not take place until 1994, and the new survey will not be quite comparable to the previous one.

After youths leave secondary school, they typically enter—or try to

---

[5] The Current Population Survey (CPS), the monthly labor force survey of the U.S. Bureau of the Census, carries out a special supplement on school enrollment of persons aged 3 to 34 years old each October. The CPS is a well-designed national household survey; its major weakness as source of postsecondary educational statistics is the relatively small number of individuals of college age who are included in any one year and the consequent sampling variability of enrollment estimates. The NCES is the National Center for Education Statistics, whose estimates of college enrollment are based on a federal-state cooperative program of reports by institutions. The NCES has a history of inaccurate and untimely reporting, largely owing to inadequate staff and budget (Levine 1986), and there are major, unresolved discrepancies between CPS and NCES estimates of enrollment trends during the 1970s and 1980s (Koretz 1990).

enter—the labor market, or they continue school in colleges or other institutions, or they enter military service, or they take up housekeeping. Increasingly, individuals participate in more than one of these activities, for example, combining work with schooling. The part of our statistical system run by the Bureau of the Census ignores almost all people in military service in its routine surveys, so we learn nothing about them except yearly estimates of their total number by age, color, and sex. It is a long-standing tradition that the Department of Education, in its longitudinal surveys of student populations, pays inadequate attention to labor market outcomes, while the Department of Labor, in its surveys of youth, gives inadequate attention to schooling processes. The effect of this fragmentation of responsibility is that once youths leave high school, our statistical system treats them almost as if they had dropped off the face of the earth. It comes as no small wonder that much of the public discussion of college attendance takes place in a factual vacuum.

Below, I describe some of the historical background of racial differences in schooling since 1940, and especially since 1960, at all levels of the educational system. Then I return to recent trends in African American college entry and several of its possible causes.

Trends in Educational Attainment of African Americans and Whites

African American educational attainments have grown and moved toward convergence with white attainments over the past 50 years, but these gains are not complete, and neither were they inevitable. They have been won by the constant striving and struggle of the African American community under highly variable conditions of discrimination by or support from the white community. Figure 12.1 shows the median years of schooling completed for those aged 25 to 29, using the 1940 to 1980 censuses. This age range is especially useful for comparisons of schooling between African Americans and whites and across time because secondary schooling is usually completed before the age of 25, and by that age most men have completed military service. In short, I assume that most 25- to 29-year-olds have completed the transition from youth to adulthood, and the succession of cohorts of young adults gradually transforms the educational attainment distribution in the population as a whole.

The median years of schooling for young African Americans has risen sharply and the gap between African Americans and whites has narrowed considerably. For example, in 1940 the median schooling of young African American men was 6.5 years, whereas that for young white men was 10.5 years, leaving a gap of 4 years. The gap between black and white

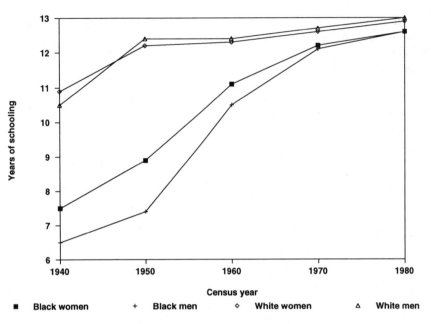

Fig. 12.1. Median years of schooling: population 25 to 29, 1940–1980.

women was 3.4 years (7.5 versus 10.9) in 1940. By 1980, the overall gap in median years of schooling had declined to less than half a year (12.6 for African Americans versus 13.0 for whites). As the educational attainments of African Americans and whites have grown, they have become so concentrated at several transition points in the schooling process, especially at high school graduation, that it is better to examine changes in the share of the population that has complete major schooling transitions.

Figure 12.2 shows the percentage of persons aged 25 to 29 years old with an elementary school education or less, a level of schooling that was traditionally identified with functional literacy, but is probably less than that required for normal adult functioning today. More than 70 percent of young African American adults had completed no more than elementary schooling in 1940, while fewer than 40 percent of whites had an elementary education or less. The share of adult Americans with this minimal level of schooling declined markedly by 1980. Although there were still relatively more African Americans than whites with eight or fewer years of schooling, fewer than 7 percent of African Americans were so handicapped.

Reflecting the historic deprivation of African Americans in the South, as well as regional traditions that also affected whites, there have long been differentials in schooling between the South and other regions. However, with a few important exceptions, regional differences and trends are now far less significant than black–white differences and trends.

Figure 12.3 shows the growth in high school completion among young adults since 1940. For all practical purposes, high school completion rules access to white-collar jobs; while many high school graduates hold blue-collar jobs, very few people without a high school diploma hold white-collar jobs. This display is almost a mirror image of the trend in elementary schooling. As recently as 1940, among African Americans only 11 percent of men and 14 percent of women had completed high school, but white completion rates were already at or near 40 percent. By 1980, high school completion had become almost universal among white men and women; more than 87 percent of white adults reported that they had completed twelve years of school. There was very rapid growth in high school completion in the African American population: by 1980, 76 percent of women and 74 percent of men had completed 12 years of school. Still, about one quarter of young African American adults do not graduate from high school.

Figure 12.4 shows the growth in college completion among young adults since 1940. In this upper part of the schooling distribution, which

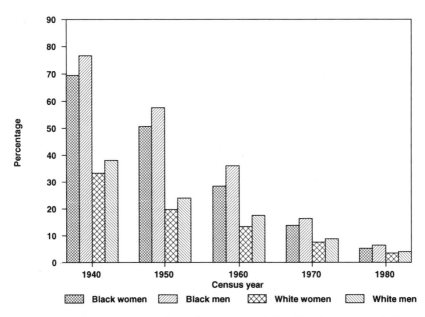

Fig. 12.2. Percentage with eight or fewer years of schooling: persons aged 25 to 29, 1940–1980.

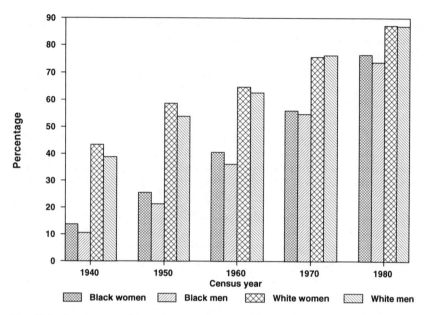

Fig. 12.3. Percentage with twelve or more years of schooling: persons aged 25 to 29, 1940–1980.

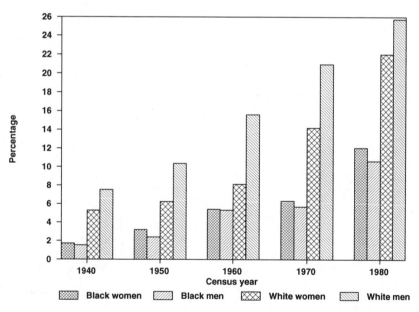

Fig. 12.4. Percentage with sixteen or more years of schooling: persons aged 25 to 29, 1940–1980.

conditions access to professional and managerial jobs and to other positions of leadership in society, African Americans lagged far behind whites
in 1940, and rapid growth has not closed the gap. In 1940 fewer than 2 percent of African American men or women had completed sixteen years of
schooling. By 1960, more than 5 percent of African Americans had completed college, but growth was slow between 1960 and 1970. The most
rapid period of growth in college completion among African Americans
was between 1970 and 1980, when 12 percent of young women and 11
percent of young men had completed four years of college. Throughout
this period, college completion has remained far more common among
whites than among African Americans. As recently as 1970, the share of
college graduates among African Americans was similar to that among
whites in 1940. The chances of a white youth completing college remain
about twice those of an African American youth.

Early Childhood Education

Educational attainments have grown in the African American population as schooling has increased both at younger and older ages; both
processes continue. Figure 12.5 illustrates the diffusion of schooling across
ages by displaying age-specific school enrollment rates in the cohorts of
African American men who were five years old in 1930, in 1950, and
in 1970. The first of these cohorts reached maturity just after the end of
World War II, while the last is just completing its entry into adulthood—
it is the first of the Sesame Street generations. In the oldest cohort, the age
pattern of enrollment is both lower and more peaked than in the younger
cohorts. In the cohort aged five in 1930, enrollment rates exceeded 90 percent only between the ages of ten and twelve, but in the cohort aged five
in 1970, the rates were greater than 90 percent from ages seven to fourteen
and greater than 95 percent from ages nine to twelve. Figure 12.6 shows
the ratios of black to white enrollment rates in the same three cohorts; the
differentials in enrollment follow much the same pattern as the enrollment
rates among African Americans. Enrollment was less probable at every
age among African Americans than among whites in these cohorts, but
black enrollment rates approached those of whites in a wider range of ages
in each successive cohort.

The growth in formal schooling at younger ages still continues as
nursery school, Head Start, and kindergarten have completed their diffusion throughout the nation. Although the effects of participation in early
schooling on academic achievement are not always impressive, the correlation of early school entry with later school-leaving across cohorts does
point to continuing growth in educational attainment unless the historic

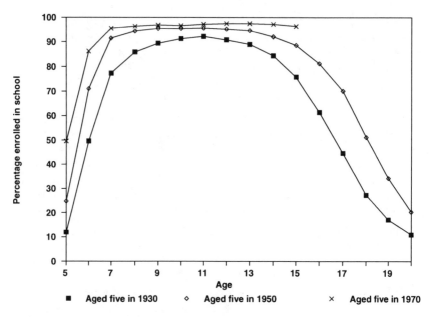

Fig. 12.5. Age-specific school enrollment rates: black males aged five, 1930–1970.

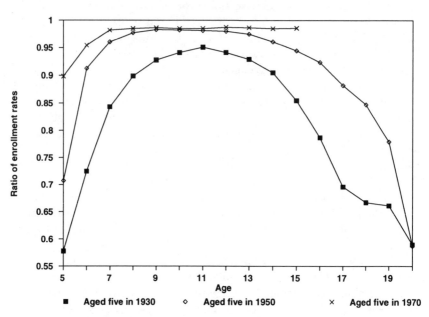

Fig. 12.6. Ratios of black to white age-specific school enrollment rates: males aged five, 1930–1970.

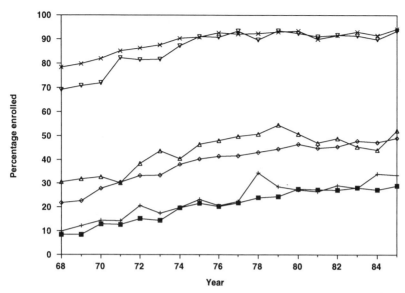

Fig. 12.7. School enrollment at ages three to five: black and white children, 1968–1985.

pattern is broken.[6] Moreover, political support for Head Start has been built through local community engagement in the program, its relatively low cost, and its coincidental function of providing child care. Figure 12.7 shows age-specific school enrollment rates of cohorts of black and white children at ages three, four, and five, from 1968 to 1985. During this period, for the first time, rates of participation in early schooling have not only grown dramatically among black and white children, but they often have been greater among African Americans. The growth in schooling is most impressive at the youngest ages: among African American children, between 1968 and 1985 participation grew from 69 percent to 93 percent at age five, from 30 percent to 52 percent at age four, and from 10 percent to 34 percent at age three. The sensitivity of participation in early schooling to general social conditions and public policy is suggested both by the overall increase in participation since the late 1960s and by the leveling off of growth in the late 1970s; there may even have been a decline in school participation of three- and four-year-olds after 1978.

[6] Curiously, the Congressional Budget Office (1987) failed to consider earlier school entry as a factor in increased black educational achievements in cohorts born after the early 1960's.

High School Dropout

Just as early childhood education is the current locus of interest in the diffusion of schooling to younger ages, high school completion and college entry are of primary interest at older ages. It is far more difficult to measure and interpret trends in schooling at older than at younger ages, partly because age and grade in school are not so tightly linked, and partly because it is far more difficult to sample relevant populations by the later teen years. This is the reason I have relied upon reports of schooling at ages 25 to 29 as my main source of information about high school completion.

It is difficult to reconcile estimates of 75 percent of African Americans and 87 percent of whites completing high school by ages 25 to 29 with common reports of high school dropout rates approaching or even exceeding 50 percent. Such differences may occur for many reasons. First, no doubt there is real variation in dropout rates from place to place. Second, there is little standardization of concepts or methods for the measurement of high school dropout or even of high school completion. Although high residential mobility is characteristic of low-income, central city populations, school and administrative records are often unable to distinguish school dropout from moves between schools or school districts. Also, by ages 25 to 29 reports of high school completion may refer to certification by examination or the completion of other forms of high school equivalence. About 450,000 people each year earn high school equivalence by completing the GED (General Educational Development Test), and about 60 percent of these individuals are less than 24 years old (GED Testing Service 1986). African Americans are overrepresented among those taking the GED; the American Council on Education reports that 18 percent of GED test-takers in a 1980 sample were African American (Malizio and Whitney 1981). If African Americans are represented in this proportion among those taking and passing the GED at younger ages, then more than 40,000 young African American adults could be completing high school in this way each year. Third, some members of relevant populations just do not appear in social surveys. By age eighteen, substantial numbers of young people with high school diplomas have entered military service and are far less likely to be covered in the Current Population Survey, which is our most standardized source of dropout measurements. Furthermore, after age sixteen, there are very serious, and perhaps growing problems of covering the African American population, especially that of African American men.

The best national series on high school dropout rates has been con-

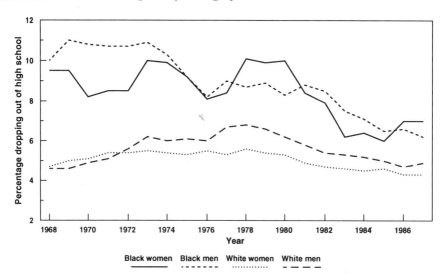

Fig. 12.8. Yearly dropout rate from grades 10 to 12: persons aged 14 to 24, 1968–1987. Three-year averages from October CPS as reported by Kominski 1989 and Frase 1989.

structed by Robert Kominski (1990) of the U.S. Bureau of the Census.[7] Based on data from the October Current Population Survey (CPS), they show the percentage of individuals aged 14–24 who were enrolled in grades 10–12 a year earlier, who had not completed the 12th grade, and were not currently enrolled in school. These series, as extended to 1987 by NCES, are shown in Figure 12.8 for black and white men and women. Among African American men, these annual dropout rates declined from more than 10 percent in 1968 to 1973 to just over 6 percent in the late 1980s. Among African American women, there was no consistent pattern of decline until 1980, but dropout rates declined further and faster than those of men through 1985. Among whites, there was a gradual increase in dropout rates from the late 1960s through the late 1970s, especially among men, but rates declined to less than 5 percent through the late 1980s. The peak level of dropout among whites—just under 7 percent among men in the late 1970s—was barely higher than the smallest dropout rates observed for African Americans in the mid 1980s.

[7] These series were initially developed by Kominski in U.S. Bureau of the Census (1987c), and they have been adopted and extended to cover the years 1968 to 1987 by the National Center for Education Statistics (Frase 1989).

Recent Trends in School Completion

Recent schooling trends appear with some time lag in rates of high school completion (Fig. 12.9) and college graduation (Fig. 12.10) among 25- to 29-year-olds. For blacks and whites alike, there are no stable sex differences in rates of high school completion. From the mid 1960s to the late 1970s, high school completion grew from just over 70 percent to just under 90 percent among whites, and it has since leveled off. Among young African American adults aged 25 to 29, high school completion has grown dramatically and almost continuously, from about 50 percent in 1965 to about 80 percent in the early 1980s. Still, among young adults, high school graduation rates of whites exceed those of African Americans by about 10 percentage points, which is to say that African Americans are about twice as likely as whites not to complete high school.

Among African Americans, rates of college graduation are again quite similar for men and women: These grew from about 6 percent in the mid to late 1960s to about 12 percent in the mid 1970s, and they have since leveled off. At the far right-hand side of Figure 12.10, we may begin to see a decline in college graduation among African Americans that follows from the declines in college entry of the late 1970s. Among whites, men were far more likely to have graduated from college than women as re-

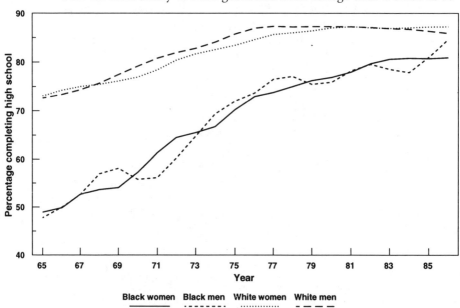

Fig. 12.9. High school completion rates: persons aged 25 to 29, 1965–1986.

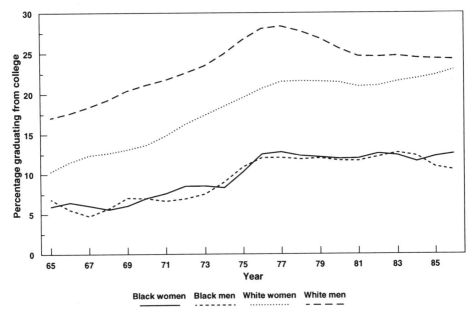

Fig. 12.10. College graduation rates: persons aged 25 to 29, 1965–1986.

cently as the mid 1960s, and graduation rates grew in parallel through the mid 1970s to a plateau where 21 percent of young adult women and 28 percent of young adult men completed four or more years of college. For white men, however, peak college graduation rates of the late 1970s appear to have been a delayed effect of the Vietnam conflict, and their chances of graduation have gradually declined toward those of white women. Among young adults in the 1980s, whites were about twice as likely as African Americans to have graduated from college.

The Decline in African American College Entry

It is difficult to measure the turnaround in college chances of African Americans. The lack of regular, large-scale, longitudinal surveys of high school graduates keeps us from learning about changes in the rate and timing of college entry and completion as they occur, and it keeps us from offering much more than educated guesses about sources of change. It takes more than a decade, while 18-year-olds reach ages 25 to 29 and CPS data are collected and processed, before we can measure the completion of college. Thus, it is only in the last year or two of the series in Figure 12.10 that we could observe the decline in African American college chances that

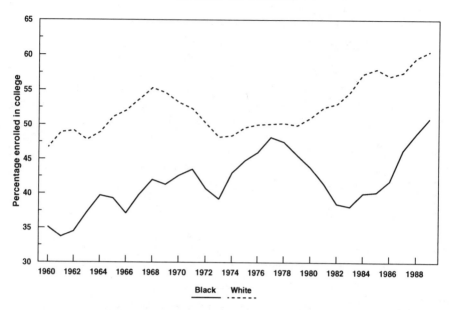

Fig. 12.11. College enrollment rates among recent high school graduates, 1960–1989. Data are three-year moving averages.

began in the late 1970s. In the following discussion, I rely most heavily on reports of current college enrollment among recent high school graduates, as reported in October Current Population Surveys. These data are limited in content; they are retrospective, not prospective; and the number of cases in each year is very small.[8] Thus the October CPS series are more useful in characterizing long-term trends than year-to-year fluctuations in college entry. The findings reported here pertain to college entry in the first year after high school graduation, but similar trends and differentials occur if the series are revised to cover the first two years after high school graduation.

Figure 12.11 shows the trend in this series of measurements of college entry by African Americans and whites.[9] The chances of college entry among African Americans grew from around 35 percent in the early 1960s to 50 percent in 1977. Between 1977 and 1982 to 1986, black college entry chances fell sharply to 40 percent or less—little more than in the early

[8] There are about 180 recent African American high school graduates in each October Current Population Survey, and there are about ten times as many majority graduates.

[9] The data for 1960 to 1967 and for 1986 to 1989 were obtained from Mortenson 1990a; before 1968 these data refer to nonwhites, rather than blacks alone. The data for 1968 to 1985 are my tabulations from October Current Population Surveys. The data shown in Figure 12.11 are three-year moving averages and thus do not correspond precisely to percentages reported in the text.

1960s—and they subsequently recovered to the level of the mid 1970s. However, the recovery left the college chances of African Americans about as far behind those of whites as they were in the 1960s. Just when the college chances of blacks began to fall, those of whites began a steep climb, from around 50 percent in the mid 1970s to 60 percent in the late 1980s. In 1984, when the differential was greatest, the odds that an African American high school graduate would enter the first year of college within a year were less than half the corresponding odds for a white high school graduate.

What is responsible for the seesaw pattern of college chances among African Americans? Why did college chances decline after the mid 1970s? Why did they rise again in the late 1980s? And what accounts for the disparate trends among blacks and whites? These are not easy questions to answer. To explain the trends, we have to find characteristics or circumstances of the African American population that affect the chances of college entry, that have changed over time in correspondence with the aggregate trends among African Americans, and that have not followed the same trend among whites as among African Americans.[10] We know almost nothing about the recent recovery, even though it began soon after the decline was first detected (Hauser 1993).[11] In the remainder of this chapter, I focus on the period from the late 1960s to the early 1980s, covering the rise and fall of black college chances, but not the recovery of the late 1980s. Even for the former period, relevant data are sadly lacking, and—rather than offering positive explanations of the trend—the argument proceeds mainly by ruling out some of the proposed explanations.

Before going further, we ought to ask whether the decline is real. The most frequently used indicator of college-going chances is the percentage enrolled among 18- to 24-year-old high school graduates (see, e.g., Wilson and Carter 1989, table 1). In this series, also based on the October CPS, African American enrollment peaked at 33.4 percent in 1976 and bottomed out at 26.1 percent in 1985. While it confirms the adverse trend, it also has serious flaws. Because the indicator covers a broad age group, it is subject to less sampling variability than the rate of enrollment among recent high school graduates. By the same token, it is less sensitive to true, year-to-year changes in enrollment chances. Worse yet, it confounds differences in chances of college entry with differences in rates of completion and in the pace of schooling (Hauser 1986). For example, the 18- to 24-year-old age group includes many individuals who have completed

---

[10] It is thus not sufficient merely to review the array of variables that are known to be associated with differences in schooling between whites and African Americans (compare Merisotis 1990).

[11] This is yet another indication of our poor ability to monitor educational trends.

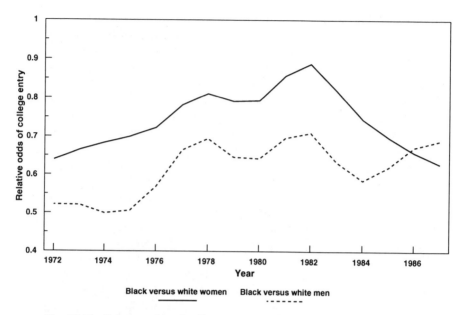

Fig. 12.12. Relative odds of college entry: black versus white high school graduates aged 21 to 24, 1972–1987. Data are three-year moving averages.

college and are no longer enrolled, and part-time attendance increases the
enrollment rate because a student must enroll for more years to earn a
degree.

However, it is possible to confirm the trends in college entry that have
been observed in the October CPS data with an independently derived
series from the March CPS (Fig. 12.12). The March CPS does not ascer-
tain school enrollment in the same way as the October CPS, but it does
ask for the highest grade in school attended and whether that grade was
completed. To track chances of college entry, I look at the chances that a
high school graduate has attended grade 13 or higher by the time he or she
has reached ages 21 to 24.[12] Figure 12.12 shows the odds that an African
American high school graduate will enter college relative to the odds that a
white high school graduate will enter college. The trend lines are roughly
parallel for women and men, with women at an advantage in all but the
most recent years. They show an increase in the college-entry chances of
African Americans relative to whites from cohorts reaching ages 21 to 24

[12] Although there is a lag in this series relative to the year in which most cohorts complete high school, the lag is much shorter than that required to monitor the completion of
college. Presumably, most high school graduates who will ever enter college have done so
by the time they are 21 years old.

in the early 1970s through the early 1980s, followed by a sharp decline. At their peak, the chances of African American women were almost 90 percent of those of white women, and the chances of African American men were about 70 percent of those of white men. By the middle 1980s, the college entry chances of African American high school graduates who had reached ages 21 to 24 were 60 to 70 percent of those of whites.

Explaining the Decline

One might think that the peak of college entry in the 1970s was abnormally high, given the other social and economic conditions of African Americans. Perhaps it was a temporary product of an unusual level of public support and enthusiasm, which may even have drawn an unusual number of college entrants who were unlikely to earn a degree (Humphreys 1988). I do not think this is the case. It is difficult to imagine that the "normal" level of continuation from high school to college among African Americans in the middle 1980s should have been lower than that in the 1960s, given only what we know about the succession of cohorts in the parental generation. That is, given that the social and economic conditions of African Americans improved from the 1940s through the early 1970s—I deliberately except the period of stagnation and loss since 1973—we would expect more African American youth today to complete high school and attend college than in the late 1960s. I believe that the problem is not to explain the peak attendance of the mid 1970s, but the subsequent decline.

Of course, the selectivity of high school graduation itself deserves to be considered as a possible source of decline in college entry. Rates of high school completion did increase among African Americans during the 1970s and 1980s. As the selectivity of high school graduation declines, one might argue, continuation to college should decline. Yet selectivity seems an unlikely source of declining college entry; there is no historic evidence for white cohorts that would suggest a negative correlation between rates of high school completion and rates of continuation to college. On the contrary, among whites, growth in college attendance has been driven by a combination of increased rates of high school completion and stable or slightly increasing rates of continuation to college. Moreover, academic performance among African American high school students improved steadily, both before and during the period of declining college chances (Congressional Budget Office 1986, ch. 4; Jaynes and Williams 1989: 348–54; Humphreys 1988; Mullis and Jenkins 1990: 13–17).

If we look back at Figure 12.9 and consider the fact that most high school graduates finished the 12th grade about ten years before they reached ages 25 to 29, we can see that the most rapid growth in high school graduation among African Americans appears to have taken place well before the decline in the chances of college entry. That is, high school graduation cannot have grown fast enough in recent cohorts of African American youth for selectivity to have played a major, negative part in reducing college entry.

More Explanations

The causes of the decline in college enrollment among African Americans are not easily pinpointed. Several other explanations have been offered. Solomon Arbeiter, of the College Board, considered four accounts of this trend: (1) shortcomings of the available data; (2) shifts in the economic status of African Americans relative to that of other groups; (3) the changing structure of financial aid; and (4) shifts in the outcomes of competition between schools, businesses, and the military for college-age African American youth (Arbeiter 1986). A fifth possibility, advanced in a recent report to the Department of Education (Chaikind n.d.), asserts that differences in black–white college attendance rates result from differences in academic achievement.

Is It Full-time and Four-Year?

The published census data that are used in most reports on African American college attendance do not distinguish between part-time and full-time college attendance. These data also do not differentiate between enrollment in two- and four-year institutions. As a result of these limitations in the data, it is possible that much of the observed decline is attributable to those attending on a part-time basis, or at two-year institutions. If this were the case, then the overall trend would overstate the decline in African American enrollment at four-year institutions. Arbeiter (1986: 5) rejects this as an explanation, noting that (1) the largest decline in total African American enrollment, comparing data for 1980 and 1982, occurred at four-year institutions, whereas there was an increase in African American enrollment at two-year institutions; (2) there has been an absolute decline, comparing figures for 1976 and 1982, in full-time African American enrollment at both four- and two-year institutions; and (3) there has been a decline of 9.1 percent from 1980 to 1985 in the number of African Americans taking the Scholastic Aptitude Test, suggesting a decline in the number of African Americans aspiring to college degrees. However, there is no evidence of decline in college aspirations among African American high school seniors (Hauser and Anderson 1991). Also,

I have looked at enrollment in four-year colleges as a percentage of all college enrollment, and the data suggest that nonenrollment at four-year colleges is central to the decline in African American college enrollment.

Do Changes in Family Income Explain the Trend?

The lower incomes of African American families explain part of the black-white gap in college entry, and during the 1970s African American high school graduates were more likely to enter college than white graduates with the same family income. However, the college-entry chances of African Americans have fallen so far since 1980 that family income can no longer account for the black-white difference.

These trends affect both African American men and women, and they affect most income groups in the African American population. That is, the rise and decline of African Americans' chances for college entry, absolutely and relative to those of whites, have essentially nothing to do with changes in family income or with changes in the college-going chances of men and women. Only the very highest income families in the African American population experienced any improvement in college-going chances after 1980, and even this group lost ground relative to whites.

In Figure 12.13, the college-going chances of African Americans and whites are compared with and without controls for family income, sex, re-

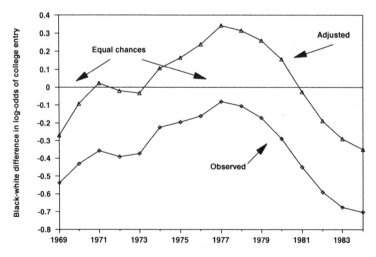

Fig. 12.13. Black-white differences in college entry: observed and adjusted for family income, sex, region, and metropolitan location, 1969–1984. Data are three-year moving averages.

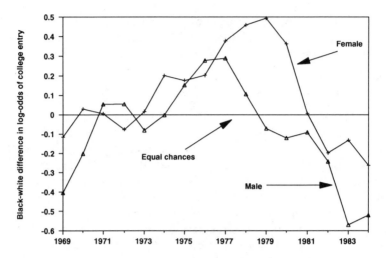

Fig. 12.14. Black-white differences in college entry among men and women: observed and adjusted for family income, region, and metropolitan location, 1969–1984. Data are three-year moving averages.

gion, and metropolitan location.[13] The lower trend line shows a three-year moving average of the natural log of the ratio of the odds of college entry among African Americans to the odds of college entry among whites. This measure has a natural point of equality, shown near the top of the graph, where the logarithm of the odds ratio is zero. That is, at this point, the odds of college entry among African Americans, as given by the ratio of entrants to nonentrants, are equal to the odds of college entry among whites. There was a long swing from the late 1960s to the middle 1980s during which the college-going chances of African American high school graduates first moved toward those of whites and then diverged, perhaps to a point more distant than in the late 1960s: in 1984, the odds that an African American high school graduate would enter the first year of college within a year were less than half the corresponding odds for a white high school graduate.

The upper trend line in Figure 12.13, denoted "adjusted" in the legend, is a comparable measure of difference in the chances of college entry, but it is based upon a statistical model in which the effects of sex, region, metropolitan status, and family income have been controlled. That is, the upper trend line controls differences between African Americans and whites and changes in the sex composition, geographic location, and economic standing of African Americans and whites. Two features of the diagram stand

13 For more detailed analyses, see Hauser 1987a.

out. First, the two lines are virtually parallel throughout the period from 1969 to 1984. Thus, the observed trend in black–white differences in college entry is in no way a consequence of changes across cohorts in sex composition, geographic location, or economic standing. Specifically, changes in African American family incomes do not explain the reversal in college chances. Second, the adjusted trend line always lies above the observed line. That is, once I take account of the differing social composition of the African American and white populations (on the variables included in the model), the differences in chances of college entry are more nearly centered around the zero point of equal chances. In the observed data, the chances for college entry of African Americans barely reach the point of equality in the period around 1977; in the adjusted series, the chances for college entry among African Americans were as good or better than those among whites almost continuously from 1971 to 1981. As shown in Figure 12.14, the trends are similar for men and for women. By 1982, the decline of the Carter and early Reagan eras had brought the chances of African Americans below those of economically and socially comparable whites.

Academic Achievement and College Attendance

It is sometimes suggested that declines in African American academic achievement could account for declines in college entry. Two reports, conducted for the Department of Education and released in 1987, attempted to study the impact of selected determinants of African American college attendance, specifically achievement levels and family income (Chaikind n.d.; Meyers 1987). They contend that a principle determinant of African American college attendance is achievement-test performance, which is true, and that this somehow explains the trend, which is not true.

The achievement factor is left out of my analysis. Does that matter? Yes and no. It matters because I have probably understated the improvement in African American college chances relative to those of whites, when other social factors are controlled. Thus, it may well be that the adjusted college-going chances of African Americans were even greater than those of whites and exceeded them for a longer period than is suggested by the displays in Figures 12.13 and 12.14. But the omission of academic achievement probably does not matter when it comes to explaining the trend in college chances. Both of the reports to the Department of Education are based on cross-sectional studies, not on cross-time comparisons. Neither report directly relates actual changes in levels of achievement or in family background to changes in college attendance from one cohort to another. Yet by implication these reports offer an account of change over time in African American college attendance rates that emphasizes black-white differences in achievement and that was repeatedly used by the Department of Education in an effort to explain away the observed decline.[14]

Although African American students continue to perform less well on tests than white students, the available evidence about changes in levels of academic achievement among African American high school students in the 1970s and 1980s shows that their achievement levels were on the increase, absolutely and relative to those of whites, during the period of declining college entry (Applebee et al. 1990; Humphreys 1988; Jaynes and Williams 1989; Linn 1988; Mullis and Jenkins 1990). The best available data come from the National Assessment of Educational Progress (NAEP)— not from commercial achievement tests, in which everyone is above average!—but the finding does not depend upon a single test or population (Congressional Budget Office 1986: xvii). For example, in the NAEP test of reading proficiency, the mean performance of seventeen-year-old African Americans rose from 240.1 in 1975 to 242.5 in 1980 and 264.2 in 1984 (Mullis and Jenkins 1990: 65); the increase from 1975 to 1984 is more than half a standard deviation.[15] During the same period, the white mean was virtually unchanged at about 295. Thus, in spite of the concurrent decline in high school dropout, about 40 percent of the differential in black and white reading achievement at age seventeen disappeared between 1975 and 1984. It is not at all plausible that changes in academic achievement among African Americans explain either the trend in African American college enrollment or the difference in trend between blacks and whites.

Aspirations and Plans

There are good reasons to think that periodic measurements of youths' plans and aspirations provide useful and valid clues about their social and economic futures. For many years, William H. Sewell and others have worked to develop and test a social psychological model of the formation and effects of late adolescent aspirations and expectations (Sewell 1971; Sewell and Hauser 1972; Hauser 1973; Sewell and Hauser 1975; Sewell, Hauser, and Wolf 1980; Hauser, Tsai, and Sewell 1983). Briefly, this model postulates that socioeconomic background and ability affect aspirations

[14] "U.S. Report Adds Fuel to Heated Debate over College Attendance by Blacks," *Chronicle of Higher Education*, April 29, 1987; "Further Decline in Minority Enrollment is Feared," *New York Times*, January 20, 1988.

[15] These trend findings are highly reliable, for the standard errors of the reading proficiency scores are 2 points or less in each year. Also, the upward trend actually began before 1975 and continued after 1984. Black reading achievement was lower in 1971 than in 1975 and higher in 1988 than in 1984.

for schooling and careers by way of their realization in school performance and in social support from significant others. Consequently, much
of the influence of these prior variables on post–high school education,
occupational success, and earnings is mediated by plans and aspirations,
which account for much of the variation in post-school success. For example, when variables are corrected for errors of measurement, the social
psychological model accounts for 68.6 percent of the variance in post–high
school educational attainment in a large cohort of Wisconsin high school
graduates (Hauser, Tsai, and Sewell 1983: 31).[16] If data on adolescent aspirations or plans have not been much used in studies of trends in schooling,
it is primarily because we have lacked comparable periodic measurements
of them.

Monitoring the Future

Fortunately, we do have one major survey resource, the series of *Monitoring the Future* (MTF) surveys (Bachman, Johnson, and O'Malley 1980),
which has measured the post–high school plans and aspirations of high
school seniors using exactly the same questions each year since 1975.[17]
These surveys ask about plans and desires to attend several types of schools
and to enter military service; unfortunately, they do not ask any questions
about immediate post–high school labor market entry. The MTF surveys, conducted by the Survey Research Center of the Institute for Social
Research at the University of Michigan, are based upon a nationally representative sample of some 15,000 to 19,000 high school seniors each year
in approximately 125 public and private high schools in the conterminous
United States. The sampling design is rather inefficient for cross-sectional
analyses, but more powerful for trend comparisons.

Another explanation that has been offered for the decline in African
American college entry is change in the educational goals of African
American youth. The idea is that African American youth would prefer to attend vocational or technical schools, or two-year colleges, rather
than four-year colleges or universities. This claim has no basis in fact. The

[16] Of course, the Wisconsin studies are by no means unique in documenting the importance of aspirations and expectations in post-school experience. Although several critics
have doubted the validity of this model among African Americans, there is solid support for
it (Gottfredson 1981; Wolfle 1985).

[17] Although the MTF surveys began in 1975, there were too many missing data on these
items in the 1975 survey, and they have not been used in the present report. The MTF survey
has been conducted under the auspices of the National Institute on Drug Abuse; it is the
source of most of our national data on teenage drug use. Although it is potentially a major
source of data on college attendance—because it incorporates a selective follow-up design—
it has never been exploited by the National Center for Education Statistics as a potential
source of data on college entry.

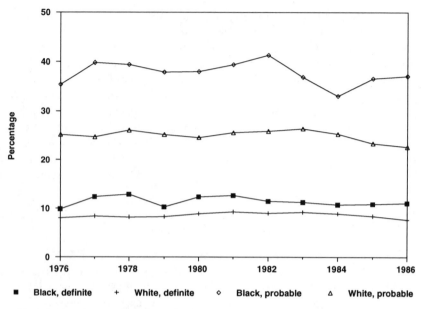

Fig. 12.15. Plans to attend a technical or vocational school: black and white high school seniors, 1976–1986.

MTF surveys show that there has been little or no change in the plans or aspirations of high school seniors to attend technical or vocational schools (Fig. 12.15) or to complete a two-year college program (Fig. 12.16); if anything, the data show that the interest of African American seniors in these two types of post–high school education has declined since 1982.[18] At the same time, the aspiration to complete four years of college has grown almost as much among African American as among white seniors (Fig. 12.17); however, after 1984 there may be a new tendency for the collegiate aspirations of African Americans to lag behind those of whites.

As a further test and elaboration of these findings, Hauser and Anderson (1991) looked at time series of college plans and aspirations by sex, controlling social background—region, urban location, intact family, mother's education, and father's education—using MTF data for approximately 138,000 seniors from 1976 to 1986. Their findings about college plans are reported in Figures 12.18 and 12.19.[19]

Figure 12.18 shows observed and adjusted trends in the college plans of

[18] For additional details, see Hauser 1987b.

[19] The dependent variable is the percentage of high school seniors with probable or definite plans to attend college. Hauser and Anderson 1991 found similar results in their analysis of trends in college aspirations.

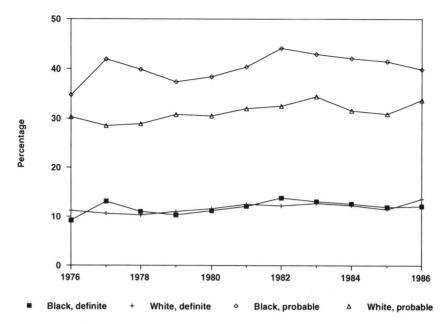

Fig. 12.16. Plans to complete a two-year college program: black and white high school seniors, 1976–1986.

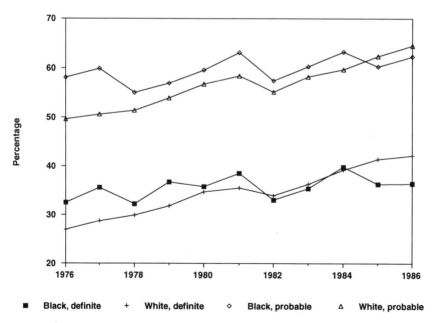

Fig. 12.17. Plans to complete a four-year college program: black and white high school seniors, 1976–1986.

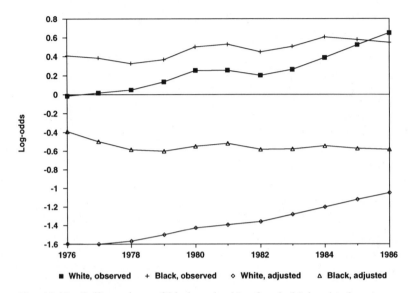

Fig. 12.18. College plans of black and white female high school seniors, 1976–1986. Adjusted series control region, urban residence, family structure, and parents' education.

African American and white women. The upper two lines are the observed trends, while the lower two trend lines have been adjusted for region, urban location, family structure, and parents' education. The intercepts of the adjusted trend lines have been chosen arbitrarily, so there is nothing informative about the relative location of the observed and adjusted lines. The important matters are the trends and black–white differences in the trends. As we have already seen, the observed trend in college plans is upward for black and white women. The adjusted trend is also upward throughout the decade for white women, while for African American women, there may be a decline from 1976 to 1978, followed by a plateau for the remainder of the decade. Evidently, the trend in white women's plans is strong, regardless of social background, while the trend for African American women is explained by favorable changes in social background, primarily, increasing levels of parental schooling.

Figure 12.19 shows a parallel analysis of college plans among African American and white men, and the findings are similar to those among women. There are similar trends toward growth of college plans in the aggregate among black and white men. When social background is controlled, the trend remains favorable among whites, but there is a suggestion of decline among African Americans.

Although the sources of trends in college plans are evidently different among black and white high school seniors, there was growth from 1976 to 1986 in the plans and aspirations of all four groups: African American and white, male and female. Among whites, plans grew regardless of social background, as specified by regional and urban location, parental schooling, and family structure; among African Americans, the trends were driven by favorable changes in background. All the same, nothing in the data would suggest that changes in plans could account for the turnaround in the college-going chances of African Americans.

Military Service

It has also been proposed that changes in recruitment into military service may help to explain the decline in African American college entry relative to that of whites. Plans and aspirations to enter military service after high school graduation have increased among African American high school seniors of both sexes (Fig. 12.20). The percentage of African American male seniors with definite or probable plans to enter the Armed Forces rose from 36.7 percent in 1977 to 50.0 percent in 1985. Plans to enter military service have grown slightly among white male seniors, from 16.6 percent in 1977 to 21.3 percent in 1985.

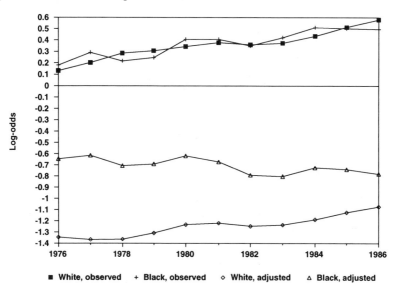

Fig. 12.19. College plans of black and white male high school seniors, 1976–1986. Adjusted series control region, urban residence, family structure, and parents' education.

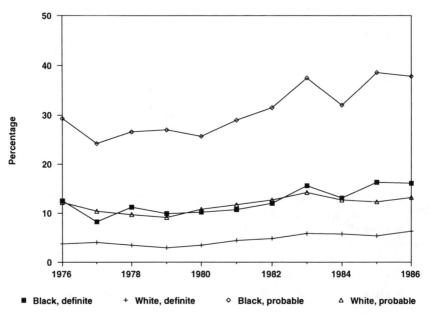

Fig. 12.20. Plans to enter the armed forces: black and white high school seniors, 1976–1986.

These trends in plans to enter the military leave many questions unanswered. To what degree does military service compete for African American seniors who would otherwise enter college, rather than choosing other forms of schooling or entry into the labor market after high school? Do African American seniors choose military service because of the aggressive marketing of schooling entitlements that can be earned within the Armed Forces or for other reasons? Are black youth who enter military service successful in earning and using their potential schooling entitlements?[20] One other factor is that the Armed Forces, more than the schools or any other institution of American life, have become an arena in which African Americans and whites, men and women, can work and live together under conditions of substantial equality. As a matter of public policy, it is an open question whether military service should be made increasingly attractive relative to college entry for students with the academic potential to attend and graduate from college.

Despite these questions, the available evidence does not support the argument that increased military recruitment contributed to the decline

[20] Holly Hexter and Elaine El-Khawas (1988: 21–27) report high initial use of entitlements under the new GI Bill, but they report no data separately for African Americans.

in black college entry. The Armed Forces are increasingly successful in attracting African American recruits who have completed high school and in rejecting recruits who have dropped out. The share of black male military recruits with high school diplomas increased from 52.0 percent in 1971 to 61.8 percent in 1976 and 91.6 percent by 1982. This would appear to be consistent with the diversion of potential black male college entrants to military service. At the same time, during the period from 1976 to 1982, the number of black men joining the military declined from 67,500 to 57,450, and the number of high school graduates among these grew only from 41,700 to 52,650 (Hexter and El-Khawas 1988: 5). Overall, the share of recent black male high school graduates who joined the Armed Forces declined continuously from 21 percent in 1979 to 14 percent in 1986 (ibid.: 36).[21] That is, the chances that black male high school graduates joined the military service declined at the same time that their chances of college entry were declining. There is little evidence that competition for black men between colleges and the military service contributed to the decline in black college entry.[22]

What About Financial Aid?

From 1980–81 to 1985–86, the total federal, state, and college "package" of financial aid declined 3 percent after controlling changes in the consumer price index, but the real financial situation became worse than that because the costs of attending a state college or university rose about 17 percent faster than the general cost of living (College Board 1986). From 1975–76 to 1985–86, the percentage of all financial aid that took the form of outright grants declined from 80 percent to 46 percent, while the percentage of financial aid in the form of loans increased from 17 percent to 50 percent. This has probably hurt African Americans college-going chances more than those of whites.

At equal levels of current family income, African American youth are less economically secure than whites because African American families are more vulnerable than white families to unemployment; at equal levels of current family income, African American youth are less wealthy than whites because African American families typically have accumulated far less in economic assets than white families. Furthermore, and perhaps more important, African American youth more often than white youth

---

[21] These statistics are based on the recent high school graduates used previously in my analyses (Hauser 1987a and 1987b), augmented by independent estimates of new military recruitment.

[22] There is also little evidence of such competition for white men, but the percentages of white men joining the military service and entering college increased at the same time that both percentages declined among black men.

lack other social resources in the home, school, and community that support and encourage high achievement and college attendance.

Numerous studies of the social, economic, motivational, and academic factors that lead students to aspire to and to attend college show that family income per se is by no means a leading cause of those decisions (Sewell, Hauser, and Wolf 1980). High academic achievement is a major factor in college-going. Social and economic characteristics of the family other than income—the presence of both parents, their level of schooling and occupation, and their level of encouragement and support—are far more important than family income. Social support from teachers and friends are also important, and all of these factors affect college-going in large degree through the ambition or determination of the student to succeed. At any income level, African American students have fewer resources and encouragements to succeed.

Willingness to Borrow

As one recent report indicates, "Minority students are less likely to borrow than white students; fewer than one-third of low-income minority aid recipients secure a GSL [guaranteed student loan], compared with more than two-fifths of low-income white aid recipients" (Miller and Hexter 1985). Thomas Mortenson (1989a, 1989b, 1990b, 1990c) has carried out the most extensive studies to date of the influence on low-income students of the changing structure of higher education finance. He concludes:

The enrollment objective of student financial aid is to remove financial barriers to higher educational opportunity for those who can demonstrate need for assistance to pay college attendance costs. Between 1966 and the late 1970s, when grant assistance was greatly expanded, the participation of individuals from lower income groups also greatly increased. Between 1980 and the present, when loans have become the dominant form of federal student financial aid, between 40 and 50 percent of the participation gains made by students from the bottom quartile of the family income distribution between the mid 1960s and the mid 1970s have been lost. . . . Loans have characteristics that differ from grants: they add risk and financing costs to the higher educational investment decision, and the addition of these costs reduces the net benefits of college attendance for those who use student loans. The more loans are used to finance college, the greater the reduction in net benefits of college attendance. . . . People from low family income background are—and always have been—less willing to borrow money to finance educational expenses than are people from higher family income levels. (Mortenson 1990b: i–ii)

Why are African American students less willing than white students to borrow funds to support their college attendance? In a purely economic analysis, a student's willingness to borrow will be affected by the economic return to his or her investment. A person would be willing to deposit more money in a bank account that pays $100 per year for 40 years than in one that pays $90 per year for 40 years. And surely a person will invest more money to obtain a guaranteed $100 per year than to obtain a possible $100 per year. Given the history of economic discrimination against African Americans in this country and the perception of fewer good jobs, less chance of promotion from within, and less likelihood of being retained in times of recession, a rational African American student will not expect the same economic rewards with the same degree of certainty as a white student who makes the same investment of time and money in college education. If the expected rewards are less, then the amount of money that a rational student will borrow to invest should also be less. Historically, college-educated African Americans have suffered a greater disparity in earnings relative to those of whites than have African Americans with lower levels of schooling. This traditional pattern was reversed in the 1970s, but the earnings of college-educated African Americans have since declined relative to those of college-educated whites (Smith and Welch 1987).

There is also a secondary, psychological factor affecting willingness to borrow. As shown in Figure 12.21, African American students are over-

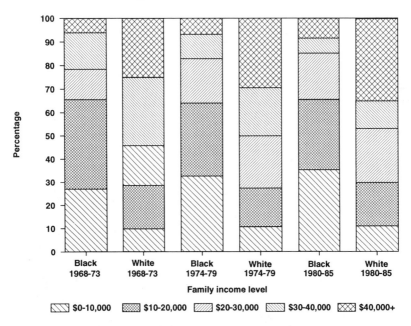

Fig. 12.21. Family income of black and white high school graduates.

whelmingly from very low-income families. This diagram very likely understates the disparate economic resources of African American and white students because it refers to total family income, not to per capita family income. During the period from 1968–73 to 1980–85, the percentage of recent African American high school graduates with family incomes below $10,000 per year (in 1985 dollars) increased sharply, from 27 percent to 35 percent; the percentage of African American graduates with family incomes greater than $40,000 per year also increased from 6.1 percent to 8.5 percent. Among white graduates, the percentage of families with incomes below $10,000 grew from 9 to 10 percent, but the percentage of families with incomes over $40,000 grew from 25 percent to 35 percent. That is, the income distributions for families of African American and white students are almost mirror images: 35 percent above $40,000 for whites and below $10,000 for African Americans, 10 percent below $10,000 for whites and above $40,000 for African Americans. A typical $10–12,000 debt will appear much larger to an African American student—where it will often be larger than his or her annual family income—than to a white student.

Conclusion

Let me close by summarizing what I think we know and do not know about the trend in African American college entry. First, counter to the long growth swing from the 1940s to the mid 1970s, college entry declined among African American high school graduates from the mid 1970s to the mid 1980s. We should keep in mind that the decline does not have the same implications for all institutions. I have talked about broad national trends, and what holds nationally need not follow precisely in Madison or Berkeley, at Harvard, in the large urban universities, or in the traditional African American colleges. Part of the college recruitment activity that we now witness reflects a seemingly benign, but sometimes harmful, competition among institutions for African American students, as well as an effort to increase the number of opportunities to attend college.

Second, the peak college attendance of the mid 1970s was not abnormally high, at least not in the context of the encouraging public policies of that period, and neither did increased high school graduation produce lower rates of college entry.

Third, we cannot blame the decline either on African American youth or on their families. It is not explained by changes in family income or in academic achievement, by an increased interest in technical, vocational, or two-year colleges, or by a decreasing interest in completing a four-year college program.

Fourth, we cannot blame the decline on competition from the military. The share of black high school graduates entering military service declined at the same time that the share entering college declined.

As best I can read the present evidence (which is, of course, far from complete), the major factor driving down African American college attendance was its decreasingly attractive terms of support, both financial and social. Not only was the societal package of aid for college attendance smaller relative to need, but it has increasingly been targeted to the needs and preferences of middle-income families. Given overall trends in college costs, I do not want to minimize the needs of white and middle-income families for assistance in financing college. They, too, have suffered increased real costs and stagnant real incomes for the past decade and a half. Nonetheless, the needs of African American youth are different, and the mix of aid types and its marketing—if you will pardon that term—should be different for them.

The lesson here is that what goes down may come up, if we look hard enough at what changed along the way. One of the most significant characteristics of the African American population is its vulnerability to general social and economic conditions and to changes in public policy.

If change in financial support for college-going is the strongest single explanation of the decline in black college entry, then it may account for the recovery as well, and it may be useful in future efforts to gain racial equality. The terms of support have not changed greatly during the recent years in which black college entry appears to have recovered. In the total aid package, the mix of grants, loans, and work-study programs remained virtually unchanged from 1983–84 to 1988–89: 48 or 49 percent in grants and in loans and 3 to 4 percent in work-study programs. At the same time, reversing the slide of the early 1980's, the total package of federal, state, and institutional aid has grown. Between 1983–84 and 1988–89, total aid expenditures grew 23.5 percent in real dollars, while the costs of attending public four-year and two-year colleges increased by 9.7 percent and 10.7 percent (College Board 1989). During the same period, college enrollment of 18- to 24-year-olds increased by only 4 percent (U.S. Bureau of the Census 1990).

This evidence, like that relating college costs and finances to the decline in black college entry, is indirect and speculative. We have almost no direct information about the effects of college funding on college entry in any year and even less about its role in changing rates of college entry. We know a great deal about how much money has been given or loaned to college students, but almost nothing about who did not enter college for lack of funds, or who did obtain grants or loans but would have attended college without them. Changing relationships between the costs of college and the availability of financial resources may be the most likely explanation for recent trends in black college entry, but they remain no more than a likely story. We are unlikely to do better in improving access to college than we do in improving the measurement, explanation, and monitoring of college access.

African American youth are an increasingly large share of all American youth. We once could talk as if African Americans were about 10 percent or a bit more than 10 percent of Americans. That is no longer the case, and it will be far from the case in the foreseeable future. In 1969, African American births made up 15 percent of all black or white births in the United States; in 1984, African American births made up 18 percent of all black or white births. We already know, then, how diverse the high school class of 2002 will be; it will not become easier for us then than it is now to meet the challenge of preparing all of our youth for life in the twenty-first century.

Bibliography

Abelson, R. P. 1959. "Modes of Resolution of Belief Dilemmas." *Journal of Conflict Resolution* 3: 343–52.

Adams, James, and William Dressler. 1988. "Perceptions of Injustice in a Black Community." *Human Relations* 41, no. 10: 753–67.

Adorno, T. W., E. Frenkel-Brunswik, D. J. Levinson, and R. N. Sanford. 1950. *The Authoritarian Personality*. New York: Harper.

Allport, Gordon W. 1954. *The Nature of Prejudice*. Cambridge, Mass.: Addison-Wesley.

Altmeyer, Bob. 1988. *Enemies of Freedom: Understanding Right-Wing Authoritarianism*. San Francisco: Jossey-Bass.

Amir, Y. 1969. "Contact Hypothesis in Ethnic Relations." *Psychological Bulletin* 71: 319–42.

———. 1976. "The Role of Intergroup Contact in Change of Prejudice and Ethnic Relations." In *Towards the Elimination of Racism*, ed. Phyllis A. Katz. New York: Pergamon Press.

Ansolabehere, Stephen, and Gary King. 1990. "Measuring the Consequences of Delegate Selection Rules in Presidential Nominations." *Journal of Politics* 52: 609–21.

Apostle, Richard A., Charles Y. Glock, Thomas Piazza, and M. Suelze. 1983. *The Anatomy of Racial Attitudes*. Berkeley: Univ. of California Press.

Applebee, Arthur N., Judith A. Langer, Ina V. S. Mullis, and Lynn B. Jenkins. 1990. "The Writing Report Card, 1984–1988: Findings from the Nation's Report Card." In *National Assessment of Educational Progress*. Princeton, N.J.: Educational Testing Service.

Arbeiter, Solomon. 1986. "Minority Enrollment in Higher Education Institutions: A Chronological View." In *Research and Development Update*. New York: College Board.

Arkin, S. 1980. "Discrimination and Arbitrariness in Capital Punishment: An Analysis of Post-Furnam Murder Cases in Dade County, Florida, 1973–1976." *Stanford Law Review* 33: 75–101.

Arocha, Zita. 1986. "Disappointment for Suburbanites." *Washington Post*, November 23.

Ashmore, Richard D., and Frances K. Del Boca. 1981. "Conceptual Approaches to

Stereotypes and Stereotyping." In *Cognitive Processes in Stereotyping and Intergroup Behavior*, ed. David L. Hamilton. Hillsdale, N.J.: Lawrence Erlbaum.

Bachman, Jerald, Lloyd D. Johnson, and Patrick O'Malley. 1976, 1986. *Monitoring the Future*. Ann Arbor: Institute for Social Research, Univ. of Michigan.

———. 1980. *Questionnaire Responses from the Nation's High School Seniors, 1978*. Ann Arbor: Institute for Social Research, Univ. of Michigan.

Bahr, H. M., and B. A. Chadwick. 1974. "Conservatism, Racial Intolerance and Attitudes Toward Racial Assimilation Among Whites and American Indians." *Journal of Social Psychology* 94: 45–56.

Banks, James. 1984. "Black Youths in Predominantly White Suburbs." *Journal of Negro Education* 53, no. 1: 3–17.

Banks, William. 1984. "Afro-American Scholars in the University." *American Behavioral Scientist* 27: 325–38.

Banks, W. S. M. 1950. "The Rank Order of Sensitivity to Discriminations of Negroes in Columbus, Ohio." *American Sociological Review* 15, no. 4: 529–34.

Barnett, A. 1985. "Some Distribution Patterns for the Georgia Death Sentence." *University of California Davis Law Review* 18: 1327–74.

Bartels, Larry M. 1988. *Presidential Primaries and the Dynamics of Public Choice*. Princeton, N.J.: Princeton Univ. Press.

Bartels, Larry M., and C. Anthony Broh. 1989. "Review: The 1988 Presidential Primaries." *Public Opinion Quarterly* 53: 563–89.

Baucom, D. H., P. K. Besch, and S. Callahan. 1985. "Relation Between Testosterone Concentration, Sex Role Identity, and Personality Among Females." *Journal of Personality and Social Psychology* 48: 1218–26.

Beckham, Barry. 1980. "From Campus to Corporation." *Black Enterprise*, February, pp. 57–60.

Bell, Derrick. 1985. "Civil Rights in 2004: Where Will We Be?" Working paper # CR-2. College Park, Md.: Center for Philosophy and Public Policy, University of Maryland.

Bensing, R. C., and O. Schroeder, Jr. 1960. *Homicide in an Urban Community*. Springfield, Ill.: Thomas.

Berthoff, Rowland. 1979. "Independence and Attachment, Virtue and Interest: From Republic Citizen to Free Enterprise, 1987–1937." In *Uprooted Americans: Essays to Honor Oscar Handlin*, ed. Richard Bushman et al. Boston: Little, Brown.

Bettelheim, B., and M. Janowitz. 1949. "Ethnic Tolerance: A Function of Social and Personal Control." *American Journal of Sociology* 55: 137–45.

Bienen, L., N. Alan, D. W. Denno, P. D. Allison, and D. L. Mills. 1988. "The Reimposition of Capital Punishment in New Jersey: The Role of Prosecutorial Discretion." *Rutgers Law Review* (Fall).

Billeaux, David. 1988. "Explaining the Impact of Racial Make-up on Government Employee Organization Effectiveness." Paper presented at the annual meeting of the American Political Science Association. Washington D.C.

Billig, M., and Henri Tajfel. 1973. "Social Categorization and Similarity in Intergroup Behavior." *European Journal of Social Psychology* 55: 27–52.

Blau, Peter, and Otis Dudley Duncan. 1967. *The American Occupational Structure*. New York: Wiley.

Blau, Francine, and John Graham. 1989. "Black/White Differences in Wealth and Asset Composition." Working paper # 2898. Cambridge, Mass.: National Bureau of Economic Research.

Bleier, R. 1984. *Science and Gender: A Critique of Biology and Its Theories on Women.* New York: Pergamon Press.

Bobo, Lawrence. 1983. "Whites' Opposition to Busing: Symbolic Racism or Realistic Group Conflict?" *Journal of Personality and Social Psychology* 45: 1196–1210.

———. 1988. "Group Conflict, Prejudice, and the Paradox of Contemporary Racial Attitudes." In *Eliminating Racism: Profiles in Controversy*, ed. P. A. Katz and D. A. Taylor. New York: Plenum Press.

———. 1989. "Worlds Apart: Blacks, Whites, and Explanations of Racial Inequality." Paper presented at the meetings of the Midwest Political Science Association, Chicago.

Bogardus, E. S. 1925. "Measuring Social Distance." *Journal of Applied Sociology* 9: 299–308.

Bollen, Kenneth A. 1989. *Structural Equations with Latent Variables.* New York: Wiley.

Bosworth, Kris. 1989. *Study of Turnover in Racial/Ethnic Minorities in Wisconsin State Government.* Madison: Center for Health Systems Research and Analysis, Univ. of Wisconsin.

Bowers, J. B., and G. L. Pierce. 1980. "Arbitrariness and Discrimination under Post-Furman Capital Statutes." *Crime and Delinquency* 26: 563–635.

Bowers, W. 1983. "The Pervasiveness of Arbitrariness and Discrimination Under Post-Furnam Capital Statutes." *Journal of Criminal Law and Criminology* 74: 1067–1100.

Bowman, Phillip, Alida Quick, and Shirley Hatchett. N.d. [c. 1983]. "Social Psychological Status of the Black Population." Univ. of Michigan. MS.

Bradbury, Katherine, Karl Case, and Constance Dunham. 1989. "Geographic Patterns of Mortgage Lending in Boston, 1982–1987." *New England Economic Review*, September/October, pp. 3–30.

Bradford, J. M., and D. Bourget. 1987. "Sexually Aggressive Men. First Gerald J. Sarwer-Foner Clinical Symposium: Current Trends in Psychiatry." *Psychiatric Journal of the University of Ottawa* 12: 169–75.

Braithwaite, Ronald. 1981. "Interpersonal Relations Between Black Males and Black Females." In *Black Men*, ed. Lawrence E. Gary. Beverly Hills, Calif.: Sage Publications.

Brashler, William. 1978. "Black Middle Class: Making It." *New York Times Magazine*, December 3, p. 140.

Brewer, Marilyn B. 1979. "In-group Bias in the Minimal Intergroup Situation: A Cognitive-Motivational Analysis." *Psychological Bulletin* 86: 307–24.

Brewer, Marilyn B., and M. Silver. 1978. "Ingroup Bias as a Function of Task Characteristics." *European Journal of Social Psychology* 8: 393–400.

Brigham, John C. 1971. "Ethnic Stereotypes." *Psychological Bulletin* 76: 15–33.

Brigham, J. C., J. J. Woodmanese, and Stuart W. Cook. 1976. "Dimensions of Verbal Racial Attitudes: Interracial Marriage and Approaches to Racial Equality." *Journal of Social Issues* 32: 9–21.

Brimmer, Andrew. 1987. "Income and Wealth." *Ebony* 42, no. 10: 48.

Brink, William, and Louis Harris. 1966. *Black and White.* New York: Simon & Schuster.

Britt, Donna. 1990. "They've Never Felt the Prejudice We Feel." *Washington Post*, January 28, pp. F1, F6.

Broh, C. Anthony. 1987. *A Horse of a Different Color: Television's Treatment of Jesse Jackson's 1984 Presidential Campaign.* Washington, D.C.: Joint Center for Political Studies.

Brown, Michael, and Steven Erie. 1981. "Blacks and the Legacy of the Great Society." *Public Policy* 29, no. 3: 299–330.

Brown, R. J. 1978. "Divided We Fall: An Analysis of Relations Between Sections of a Factory Work-Force." In *Differentiation Between Social Groups: Studies in the Social Psychology of Discrimination*. London: Academic Press.

Brown, Roger W. 1986. *Social Psychology*. 2d ed. New York: Free Press.

Burstein, Paul. 1979. "Public Opinion, Demonstrations, and the Passage of Anti-Discrimination Legislation." *Public Opinion Quarterly* 79: 157–72.

Cain, Bruce E., I. A. Lewis, and Douglas Rivers. 1989. "Strategy and Choice in the 1988 Presidential Primaries." *Electoral Studies* 8: 23–48.

Campbell, Angus. 1971. *White Attitudes Toward Black People*. Ann Arbor: Institute for Social Research, Univ. of Michigan.

Campbell, Bebe. 1984. "To Be Black, Gifted, and Alone." *Savvy*, December, pp. 67–74.

Campbell, D. T. 1956. "Enhancement of Contrast as Composite Habit." *Journal of Abnormal Psychology and Social Psychology* 53: 350–55.

——— . 1967. "Stereotypes and the Perception of Group Differences." *American Psychologist* 22: 817–29.

Carmines, Edward G., and Richard A. Champagne, Jr. 1990. "The Changing Content of American Racial Attitudes: A Fifty Year Portrait." In *Research in Micropolitics*, vol. 3, ed. Samuel Long. Greenwood, Conn.: JAI Press.

Carmines, Edward G., and James A. Stimson. 1982. "Racial Issues and the Structure of Mass Belief Systems." *Journal of Politics* 44: 2–20.

——— . 1989. *Issue Evolution: Race and the Transformation of American Politics*. Princeton, N.J.: Princeton Univ. Press.

Casas, J. Manuel, Joseph G. Ponterotto, and Michael Sweeney. 1987. "Stereotyping the Stereotyper: A Mexican American Perspective." *Journal of Cross-Cultural Psychology* 18: 45–57.

Cauthen, Nelson R., Ira E. Robinson, and Herbert H. Krauss. 1971. "Stereotypes: A Review of the Literature." *Journal of Social Psychology* 84: 103–25.

Cavanagh, Thomas E., and Lorn S. Foster. 1984. "Jesse Jackson's Campaign: The Primaries and Caucuses." In *Election '84, Report #2*. Washington, D.C.: Joint Center for Political Studies.

Cazenove, Noel. 1983. "Black Male–Black Female Relationships." *Family Relations* 32 (July): 341–50.

Center for Education Statistics. 1988. *Trends in Minority Enrollment in Higher Education, Fall 1976–Fall 1986*. U.S. Department of Education, Survey Report, *CS 88-201*. Washington, D.C.: Government Printing Office.

Center for Political Studies. 1986. *American National Election Study, 1986*. Ann Arbor: Institute for Social Research, Univ. of Michigan.

Center for Public and Urban Research, Georgia State University. 1981. "Selected Responses to a Survey Conducted in the Five-County Metro Area in July–August, 1981." Mimeo.

Centers, R. 1949. *The Psychology of Social Classes: A Study of Class Consciousness*. Princeton, N.J.: Princeton Univ. Press.

Chaikind, Stephen. N.d. *College Enrollment Patterns of Black and White Students*. Washington, D.C.: Decision Resources Corporation.

Children's Defense Fund. 1985. *Black and White Children in America: Key Facts*. Washington, D.C.: Children's Defense Fund.

Christiansen, K., and R. Knussmann. 1987a. "Sex Hormones and Cognitive Functioning in Men." *Neuropsychobiology* 18: 27–36.

———. 1987b. "Androgen Levels and Components of Aggressive Behavior in Men." *Hormones and Behavior* 21: 170–80.

Christie, R., and M. Jahoda. 1954. *Studies in the Scope and Method of "The Authoritarian Personality."* Glencoe, Ill.: Free Press.

Christie, R. C., and F. Geis. 1971. *Studies in Machiavellianism.* New York: Academic Press.

Clark, K. B., and M. P. Clark. 1947. "Racial Identification and Preferences in Negro Children." In *Readings in Social Psychology*, ed. T. Newcomb and E. L. Hartley. New York: Holt.

Clarke, John, ed. 1969. *Malcolm X: The Man and His Times.* Toronto: Collier Books.

Clarke, R. B., and D. T. Campbell. 1955. "A Demonstration of Bias in Estimates of Negro Ability." *Journal of Abnormal Psychology and Social Psychology* 51: 585–88.

Cohen, J., and P. Cohen. 1983. *Applied Multiple Regression/Correlation Analysis for the Behavioral Sciences.* Hillsdale, N.J.: Lawrence Erlbaum.

Cole, Leonard. 1976. *Blacks in Power: A Comparative Study of Black and White Elected Officials.* Princeton, N.J.: Princeton Univ. Press.

College Board. 1986. *Trends in Student Aid, 1980–1986.* Washington, D.C.: College Board.

———. 1989. *Trends in Student Aid, 1980–1989.* Washington, D.C.: College Board.

Collins, Sharon. 1989. "The Marginalization of Black Executives." *Social Problems* 36, no. 4: 317–31.

Congressional Budget Office. 1986. *Trends in Educational Achievement.* Washington, D.C.: Government Printing Office.

———. 1987. *Educational Achievement: Explanations and Implications of Recent Trends.* Washington, D.C.: Government Printing Office.

Converse, P. E. 1964. "The Nature of Belief Systems in Mass Publics." In *Ideology and Discontent*, ed. D. E. Apter. New York: Free Press.

Cook, Stuart W. 1985. "Experimenting on Social Issues: The Case of School Desegregation." *American Psychologist* 51: 452–60.

Corbett, Michael. 1982. *Political Tolerance in America: Freedom and Equality in Public Attitudes.* New York: Longman.

Cox, O. C. 1948. *Caste, Class, and Race: A Study in Social Dynamics.* New York: Doubleday.

Crocker, J., and I. Schwartz. 1985. "Prejudice and In-group Favoritism in a Minimal Intergroup Situation: Effects of Self-Esteem." *Personality and Social Psychology Bulletin* 11: 379–86.

Crocker, J., L. L. Thompson, K. M. McGraw, and C. Ingerman. 1987. "Downward Comparison, Prejudice and Evaluations of Others: Effects of Self-Esteem and Threat." *Journal of Personality and Social Psychology* 52: 907–16.

Crosby, Faye. 1980. "Recent Unobtrusive Studies of Black and White Discrimination and Prejudice." *Psychological Bulletin* 87, no. 3: 546–63.

Cruse, Harold. 1967. *The Crisis of the Negro Intellectual.* New York: Morrow.

———. 1987. *Plural but Equal: Blacks and Minorities in America's Plural Society.* New York: Morrow.

Dabbs, J. M., and R. Morris. 1990. "Testosterone, Social Class, and Antisocial Behavior in a Sample of 4,462 Men." *Psychological Science* 1: 209–11.

Dahl, R. A. 1971. *Polyarchy: Participation and Opposition.* New Haven, Conn.: Yale Univ. Press.

Dator, J. A. 1969. "Measuring Attitudes Across Cultures: A Factor Analysis of the Replies of Japanese Judges to Eysenck's Inventory of Conservative-Progressive Ideology." In *Comparative Judicial Behavior: Cross-cultural Studies of Political Decision-making in the East and West*, ed. G. Schubert and D. J. Danelski. New York: Oxford Univ. Press.

Davis, A., B. B. Gardner, and M. R. Gardner. 1941. *Deep South: A Social Anthropological Study of Caste and Class*. Chicago: Univ. of Chicago Press.

Davis, George, and Glegg Watson. 1985. *Black Life in Corporate America: Swimming in the Mainstream*. Garden City, N.Y.: Doubleday, Anchor Books.

Davis, J. A. 1975. "Communism, Conformity, Cohorts and Categories: American Tolerance in 1954 and 1972–73." *American Journal of Sociology* 81 (November): 491–513.

Davis, James A., and Tom W. Smith. 1989. *General Social Surveys, 1972–1989: Cumulative Codebook*. Chicago: National Opinion Research Center, Univ. of Chicago.

Davis, K. 1941. "Intermarriage in Caste Systems." *American Anthropologist* 43: 376–95.

Dawson, Michael. 1986. "Race and Class in the Formation of Afro-American Political Attitudes: 1972–1983." Ph.D. diss., Harvard University.

Dearden, J. 1974. "Sex-linked Differences of Political Behavior: An Investigation of Their Possible Innate Origins." *Social Science Information* 13: 19–45.

Dent, R. R. 1983. "Endocrine Correlates of Aggression" (Paper presented at the 6th annual meeting of the Canadian Neuro-Psychopharmacology, Saskatoon, Canada), *Progress in Neuro-Psychopharmacology and Biological Psychiatry* 7: 525–28.

Denton, Herbert, and Barry Sussman. 1981. " 'Crossover Generation' of Blacks Express Most Distrust of Whites." *Washington Post*, March 25, pp. A1, A2.

Dollard, J. 1937. *Caste and Class in a Southern Town*. New Haven, Conn.: Yale Univ. Press.

Dollard, J., L. W. Doob, N. E. Miller, O. H. Mowerer, and R. R. Sears. 1939. *Frustration and Aggression*. New Haven, Conn.: Yale Univ. Press.

Domhoff, G. W. 1967. *Who Rules America?* Englewood Cliffs, N.J.: Prentice-Hall.

Dovidio, John F., and Samuel L. Gaertner. 1986. "Prejudice, Discrimination, and Racism: Historical Trends and Contemporary Approaches." In *Prejudice, Discrimination, and Racism*, ed. John F. Dovidio and Samuel L. Gaertner. San Diego, Calif.: Academic Press.

Drake, St. Clair, and H. Cayton. 1945. *Black Metropolis: A Study of Negro Life in a Northern City*. New York: Harcourt, Brace.

Du Bois, W. E. B. [1903] 1986. *The Souls of Black Folk*. In *Writings*, ed. Nathan Huggins. New York: Library of America.

Dumas, Rhetaugh. 1980. "Dilemmas of Black Females in Leadership." In *The Black Woman*, ed. La Frances Rodgers-Rose. Beverly Hills, Calif.: Sage Publications.

Duncan, Otis D. 1969. "Inheritance of Poverty or Inheritance of Race?" In *On Understanding Poverty: Perspectives from the Social Sciences*, ed. Daniel P. Moynihan. New York: Basic Books.

Dworkin, Anthony G., and Douglas L. Eckberg. 1986. "Consciousness and Reality: The Chicano Movement and Chicano/Anglo Mutual Stereotypy." *International Journal of Sociology and Social Policy* 6: 61–74.

Eckstein, H. 1980. "Theoretical Approaches to Explaining Collective Political Violence." In *Handbook of Political Violence*, ed. T. R. Gurr. New York: Free Press.

Ehrenkranz, J., E. Bliss, and M. H. Sheard. 1974. "Plasma Testosterone: Correlation with Aggressive Behavior and Social Dominance in Man." *Psychosomatic-Medicine* 36: 469–75.

Eibl-Eibesfeldt, I. 1989. *Human Ethology*. New York: Aldine de Gruyter.

Eichelberger, Brenda. 1977. "Voices on Black Feminism." *Quest* 3, no. 4: 16–28.

Ekehammar, B., and J. Sidanius. 1982. "Sex Differences in Socio-Political Ideology: A Replication and Extension." *British Journal of Social Psychology* 21: 249–57.

Ekehammar, B., J. Sidanius, and E. Nilsson. 1989. "Social Attitudes and Social Status: A Multivariate and Multinational Analysis." *Personality and Individual Differences* 10: 203–8.

Ekland-Olson, S. 1988. "Structured Discretion, Racial Bias and the Death Penalty: The First Decade after Furnam in Texas." *Social Science Quarterly* 69: 853–73.

Elias, M. 1981. "Serum Cortisol, Testosterone, and Testosterone-binding Globulin Responses to Competitive Fighting in Human Males." *Aggressive Behavior* 7: 215–24.

Ellison, Christopher, and David Gay. 1990. "Religion, Religious Commitment, and Life Satisfaction Among Black Americans." *Sociological Quarterly* 31, no. 1: 123–47.

Erie, Steven. 1980. "Public Policy and Black Economic Polarization." *Policy Analysis* 6, no. 3: 305–17.

Eysenck, H. J. 1951. "Primary Social Attitudes as Related to Social Class and Political Party." *British Journal of Sociology* 2: 198–209.

———. 1953. *The Structure of Human Personality*. London: Methuen.

———. 1971. "Social Attitudes and Social Class." *British Journal of Social and Clinical Psychology* 10: 210–12.

———. 1975. "The Structure of Social Attitudes." *Journal of Social and Clinical Psychology* 14: 323–31.

———. 1976. "The Structure of Social Attitudes." *Psychological Reports* 39: 463–66.

Eysenck, H. J., and T. T. Coulter. 1972. "The Personality and Attitudes of Working Class British Communists and Fascists." *Journal of Social Psychology* 87: 59–73.

Eysenck, H. J., and G. D. Wilson. 1978. *The Psychological Basis of Ideology*. Lancaster, England: MTP Press.

Fairchild, Halford H., and Joy Asamen Cozens. 1981. "Chicano, Hispanic, or Mexican American: What's in a Name." *Hispanic Journal of Behavioral Sciences* 3: 191–98.

Farley, Reynolds, and Walter Allen. 1987. *The Color Line and the Quality of Life in America*. New York: Russell Sage Foundation.

Farrell, R. A., and V. L. Swifert. 1978. "Legal Disposition of Inter-group and Intra-group Homicides." *Sociological Quarterly* 19: 565–76.

Feldman, Stanley. 1983. "Economic Individualism and American Public Opinion." *American Politics Quarterly* 11: 3–29.

Fernandez, John. 1981. *Racism and Sexism in the Corporation*. Lexington, Mass.: Lexington Books.

Firebaugh, Glenn, and Kenneth E. Davis. 1988. "Trends in Antiblack Prejudice, 1972–1984: Region and Cohort Effects." *American Journal of Sociology* 94: 251–72.

Foley, L. 1987. "Florida After the Furnam Decisions: The Effect of Extralegal Factors on the Processing of Capital Offense Cases." *Behavioral Sciences and the Law* 5: 457–65.

Foley, L., and R. Powell. 1982. "The Discretion of Prosecutors, Judges and Juries in Capital Cases." *Criminal Justice Review* 7: 16–22.

Foner, Eric. 1970. *Free Soil, Free Labor, Free Men: The Ideology of the Republican Party Before the Civil War*. New York: Oxford University Press.

Fordham, Signithia, and John Ogbu. 1986. "Black Students' School Success." *Urban Review* 18, no. 3: 1–31.

Frase, Mary J. 1989. *Dropout Rates in the United States: 1988. Analysis Report*, NCES 89-609. National Center for Education Statistics. Washington, D.C.: Government Printing Office.

Frazier, Franklin. 1957. *Black Bourgeoisie*. Glencoe, Ill.: Free Press.

Frederickson, G. M. 1981. *White Supremacy: A Comparative Study in American and South African History*. Middletown, Conn.: Wesleyan Univ. Press.

Frenkel-Brunswik, E. 1948. "A Study of Prejudice in Children." *Human Relations* 1: 295–306.

Freud, Sigmund. 1959a. *Inhibitions, Symptoms and Anxiety*. New York: Norton.

———. 1959b. *Group Psychology and the Analysis of the Ego*. 1922. New York: Norton.

Gaines-Carter, Patrice. 1984. "Remembering Times Before Black was Beautiful." *Washington Post*, February 19, c1, c5.

———. 1985. "Is My 'Post-Integration' Daughter Black Enough?" *Washington Post*, February 24, p. c1, c4.

GAO [General Accounting Office]. 1990. "Death Penalty Sentencing: Research Indicates Pattern of Racial Disparities." In *United States General Accounting Office. Report to Senate and House Committees on the Judiciary*.

Garfinkel, H. 1949. "Research Note on Inter- Intra-racial Homicides." *Social Forces* 27: 370–81.

GED [General Educational Development] Testing Service. 1986. "The 1986 GED Statistical Report." Washington, D.C.: American Council on Education.

Geer, John G. 1988. "Assessing the Representativeness of Electorates in Presidential Primaries." *American Journal of Political Science* 32: 929–45.

Genovese, Eugene. 1972. *Roll, Jordan, Roll: The World the Slaves Made*. New York: Pantheon Books.

Giddings, Paula. 1984. *When and Where I Enter: The Impact of Black Women on Race and Sex in America*. New York: Morrow.

Gilbert, G. M. 1951. "Stereotype Persistence and Change Among College Students." *Journal of Abnormal and Social Psychology* 46: 245–54.

Gilliam, Dorothy. 1990. "A Different Denial." *Washington Post*, January 29, D3.

Gilliam, Franklin, and Kenny Whitby. 1989. "Race, Class, and Attitudes Toward Social Welfare Spending." *Social Science Quarterly* 70, no. 1: 88–100.

Gilligan, Carol. 1982. *In a Different Voice: Psychological Theory and Women's Development*. Cambridge, Mass.: Harvard University Press.

Gimbutas, M. A. 1989. *The Language of the Goddess: Unearthing the Hidden Symbols of Western Civilization*. New York: Harper & Row.

Glock, Charles Y., Robert Wuthnow, Jane Allyn Piliavin, and Metta Spencer. 1975. *Adolescent Prejudice*. New York: Harper & Row.

Goodenough, F. K., and J. E. Anderson. 1931. *Experimental Child Study*. New York: Appleton-Century.

Gorsuch, Richard L., and D. Aleshire. 1974. "Christian Faith and Ethnic Prejudice: A Review and Interpretation of Research." *Journal for the Scientific Study of Religion* 13: 281–307.

Gottfredson, Denise C. 1981. "Black-White Differences in the Educational Attainment Process: What Have We Learned." *American Sociological Review* 46 (August): 542–57.

Gough, Harrison G. 1951. "Studies in Social Intolerance: II: A Personality Scale for Anti-Semitism." *Journal of Social Psychology* 33: 247–55.

———. 1987. *The California Psychological Inventory Administrator's Guide*. Palo Alto, Calif.: Consulting Psychologists Press.

Gough, Harrison G., and A. B. Heilbrun, Jr. 1983. *The Adjective Check List Manual*. Palo Alto, Calif.: Consulting Psychologists Press.

Gough, Harrison G., and R. Lazzari. 1974. "A 15-item Form of the F Scale and a Cross-cultural Application." *Journal of Psychology* 88: 39–46.

Gould, K. M. 1946. *They Got the Blame: The Story of Scapegoats in History*. New York: Association Press.

Green, E. 1964. "Inter- and Intra-racial Crime Relative to Sentencing." *Journal of Criminal Law, Criminology and Police Science* 55: 348–58.

———. 1970. "Race, Social Class and Criminal Arrest." *American Sociological Review* 35: 476–90.

Gross, S., and R. Mauro. 1984. "Patterns of Death: Analysis of Racial Disparities in Capital Sentencing and Homicide Victimization." *Stanford Law Review*.

Guichard, Charles P., and Margaret A. Connally. 1977. "Ethnic Group Stereotypes: A New Look at an Old Problem." *Journal of Negro Education* 46: 344–56.

Gurin, Patricia, Shirley Hatchett, and James Jackson. 1989. *Hope and Independence: Blacks' Response to Electoral Party Politics*. New York: Russell Sage Foundation.

Gutman, Herbert. 1976. *The Black Family in Slavery and Freedom, 1750–1925*. New York: Random House, Vintage Books.

Hadley, Charles D., and Harold W. Stanley. 1989. "Super Tuesday 1988: Regional Results, National Implications." *Publius: The Journal of Federalism* 19: 19–37.

Hagen, John, and Celesta Albonetti. 1982. "Race, Class, and the Perception of Criminal Injustice in America." *American Journal of Sociology* 88, no. 2: 329–55.

Hagen, Michael G. 1989. "Voter Turnout in Primary Elections." In *The Iowa Caucus and the Presidential Nominating Process*, ed. Peverill Squire. Boulder, Colo.: Westview Press.

Hakmiller, K. L. 1966. "Threat as a Determinant of Downward Comparison." *Journal of Experimental Social Psychology* 2: 32–39.

Hampson, E., and D. Kimura. 1988. "Reciprocal Effects of Hormonal Fluctuations on Human Motor Perceptual-Spatial Skills." *Behavioral Neuroscience* 102: 456–59.

Hampson, S. E., Oliver P. John, and L. R. Goldberg. 1986. "Category Breadth and Hierarchical Structure in Personality: Studies in Asymmetries in Judgments of Trait Implications." *Journal of Personality and Social Psychology* 51: 37–54.

Harding, J., B. Kutner, H. Proshansky, and I. Chein. 1954. "Prejudice and Ethnic Relations." In *Handbook of Social Psychology*, ed. Gardner Lindzey 2: 1021–61. Cambridge, Mass.: Addison-Wesley.

Hare, Nathan. 1965. *Black Anglo-Saxons*. New York: Marzani Munsell.

Harris, D. B., Harrison G. Gough, and W. E. Martin. 1950. "Children's Ethnic Attitudes: II. Relationship to Parental Beliefs Concerning Child Training." *Child Development* 21: 169–81.

Harris, Fredrick, and Linda Williams. 1986. "JCPS/Gallup Poll Reflects Changing Views on Political Issues. *Focus* (newsletter of the Joint Center for Political and Economic Studies, Washington, D.C.) 14, no. 10.

Hartley, E. L. 1946. *Problems in Prejudice*. New York: King's Crown Press.

Hartz, Louis. 1955. *The Liberal Tradition in America: An Interpretation of American Political Thought Since the Revolution*. New York: Harcourt, Brace.

————. 1964. *The Founding of New Societies: Studies in the History of the United States, Latin America, South Africa, Canada, and Australia.* New York: Harcourt, Brace & World.

Hauser, Robert M. 1973. "Disaggregating a Social-Psychological Model of Educational Attainment." In *Structural Equation Models in the Social Sciences,* ed. A. S. Goldberger and O. D. Duncan. New York: Seminar Press.

————. 1986. "Notes on the Distribution of Schooling in the Black Population." Working paper no. 86-8. Madison: Center for Demography and Ecology, Univ. of Wisconsin.

————. 1987a. "College Entry Among Black High School Graduates: Family Income Does Not Explain the Decline." Working paper no. 87-19. Madison: Center for Demography and Ecology, Univ. of Wisconsin.

————. 1987b. "Post–High School Plans of Black High School Graduates: What Has Changed Since the Mid-1970s?" Working paper no. 87-26. Madison: Center for Demography and Ecology, Univ. of Wisconsin.

————. 1990. "Changes in Occupational Status Among U.S. Men from the 1970s to the 1980s." Madison: University of Wisconsin, Center for Demography and Ecology.

————. 1992. "Trends in College Entry Among Blacks, Hispanics, and Whites." In *The Economics of Higher Education,* ed. Charles Clotfelter and Michael Rothschild. National Bureau of Economic Research. Chicago, Ill.: Univ. of Chicago Press.

Hauser, Robert M., and Douglas K. Anderson. 1991. "Post–High School Plans and Aspirations of Black and White High School Seniors, 1976–1986." *Sociology of Education* 64 (October): 263–77.

Hauser, Robert M., Gerald D. Jaynes, and Robin M. Williams, Jr. 1990. "Explaining Black-White Differences." *The Public Interest* 99 (Spring).

Hauser, Robert M., Shu-Ling Tsai, and William H. Sewell. 1983. "A Model of Stratification with the Response Error in Social Psychological Variables." *Sociology of Education* 56: 20–46.

Hemmons, Willa Mae. 1980. "The Women's Liberation Movement: Understanding Black Women's Attitudes." In *The Black Woman,* ed. La Frances Rodgers-Rose. Beverly Hills, Calif.: Sage Publications.

Herbert, Adam. 1974. "The Minority Administrator." *Public Administration Review* 34, no. 6: 556–63.

Herrnstein, R. J. 1990a. "On Responsible Scholarship: A Rejoinder." *The Public Interest* 99 (Spring): 120–27.

————. 1990b. "Still an American Dilemma." *The Public Interest* 98 (Winter): 3–17.

Hexter, Holly, and Elaine El-Khawas. 1988. *Joining Forces: The Military's Impact on College Enrollments.* Washington, D.C.: American Council on Education.

Hinkle, S., and R. Brown. 1990. "Intergroup Comparisons and Social Identity: Some Links and Lacunae." In *Advances in Social Identity Theory,* ed. D. Abrams and M. Hogg.

Hirschman, Albert. 1982. *Shifting Involvements: Private Interest and Public Action.* Princeton, N.J.: Princeton Univ. Press.

Hochschild, Jennifer L. 1981. *What's Fair? American Beliefs About Distributive Justice.* Cambridge, Mass.: Harvard Univ. Press.

Hochschild, Jennifer L., and Monica Herk. 1990. "'Yes, but . .': Principles and Caveats in American Racial Attitudes." In *Nomos: Majorities and Minorities,* ed. John Chapman and Alan Wertheimer. New York: New York Univ. Press.

Holt, James. 1975. "The New Deal and the American Anti-statist Tradition." In

The New Deal, ed. John Braeman, Robert H. Bremmer, and David Brody. Columbus: Ohio State Univ. Press.

Hopkins, Anne. 1980. "Perceptions of Employment Discrimination in the Public Sector." *Public Administration Review* 40, no. 2: 131–37.

Horowitz, E. L. 1936. "The Development of Attitudes Toward the Negro." *Archives of Psychology* 194.

Hout, Michael. 1984. "Occupational Mobility of Black Men: 1962 to 1973." *American Sociological Review* 49 (June): 308–22.

Howard, J. W., and Myron Rothbart. 1980. "Social Categorization and Memory for In-group and Out-group Behavior." *Journal of Personality and Social Psychology* 38: 301–10.

Howard, Jeff, and Ray Hammond. 1985. "Rumors of Inferiority." *The New Republic*, Sept. 9, pp. 17–21.

Howard, Lawrence, and Joyce Roberson. 1975. "The Black Administrator in the Public Bureaucracy." *Journal of Afro-American Issues* 3, no. 2: 219–35.

Hughes, Everett. 1945. "Dilemmas and Contradictions of Status." *American Journal of Sociology* 50: 353–57.

Humphreys, Lloyd G. 1988. "Trends in Levels of Academic Achievement of Blacks and Other Minorities." *Intelligence* 12: 231–60.

Hylton, Richard. 1989. "Minority Firms Feel the Pinch." *New York Times*, April 16, p. F4.

Ifill, Gwen, and David Maraniss. 1986. "In Atlanta, Struggling with Success." *Washington Post*, January 20, pp. A1, A10.

Inter University Consortium for Political and Social Research. 1986a. American National Election Survey. Ann Arbor, Mich.

———. 1986b. *1981 ABC News Washington Post Survey*. Ann Arbor, Mich.

Jackman, Mary R. 1978. "General and Applied Tolerance: Does Education Increase Commitment to Racial Integration?" *American Journal of Political Science* 22: 302–24.

———. 1981. "Education and Policy Commitment to Racial Integration." *American Journal of Political Science* 25, no. 2: 256-69.

Jackman, Mary R., and Mary Scheuer Senter. 1983. "Different, Therefore Unequal: Beliefs About Trait Differences Between Groups of Unequal Status." *Research in Social Stratification and Mobility* 2: 309–35.

Jackman, Mary R., and Michael J. Muha. 1984. "Education and Intergroup Attitudes: Moral Enlightenment, Superficial Democratic Commitment, or Ideological Refinement." *American Sociological Review* 49: 751–69.

Jackman, Mary R., and Robert Jackman. 1983. *Class Awareness in the United States*. Berkeley: Univ. of California Press.

Jackson, James, Linda Chatters, and Harold Neighbors. 1986. "The Subjective Life of Quality Black Americans." In *Research on the Quality of Life*, ed. Frank M. Andrews. Ann Arbor: Institute for Survey Research, Univ. of Michigan.

Jackson, Jesse L. 1987. *Straight from the Heart*. Edited by Roger D. Hatch and Frank E. Watkins. Philadelphia: Fortress Press.

Jaynes, Gerald David, and Robin M. Williams, Jr., eds. 1989. *A Common Destiny: Blacks and American Society*. Washington, D.C.: National Academy Press.

Jeffcoate, W., N. B. Lincoln, C. Selby, and M. Herbert. 1986. "Correlations Between Anxiety and Serum Prolactin in Humans." *Journal of Psychosomatic Research* 30: 217–22.

Jennings, M. Kent, and Richard G. Niemi. 1981. *Generations and Politics: A Panel*

Study of Young Adults and Their Parents. Princeton, N.J.: Princeton Univ. Press.

John, Oliver P. 1990. "Still Stable After All These Years: Ethnic Stereotypes in the Rothbart & John Longitudinal Study." In *Paper prepared for delivery at the Conference on Prejudice, Politics and Race in America Today, Berkeley, March 22–24.*

Johnson, G. B. 1941. "The Negro and Crime." *Annals of the American Academy of Political Social Science* 271: 93–104.

Jones, Edward. 1973. "What It's Like to be a Black Manager." *Harvard Business Review* 51, no. 4: 108–16.

———. 1986. "Black Managers: The Dream Deferred." *Harvard Business Review* 64 (May/June): 84–93.

Jones, James M. 1972. *Prejudice and Racism.* Reading, Mass.: Addison-Wesley.

Jöreskog, Karl G., and Dag Sörbom. 1986. *LISREL: Analysis of Linear Structural Relationships by the Method of Maximum Likelihood.* Version 6. Upsala, N.J.: Univ. of Upsala.

———. 1989a. *LISREL 7: A Guide to the Program and Applications.* 2d ed. Chicago: SPSS.

———. 1989b. *PRELIS: A Program for Multivariate Data Screening and Data Summarization.* 2d ed. Mooresville, Ind.: Scientific Software.

Kanter, Rosabeth Moss. 1977. *Men and Women of the Corporation.* New York: Basic Books.

Karlins, Marvin M., Thomas L. Coffman, and Gary Walters. 1969. "On the Fading of Social Stereotypes: Studies in Three Generations of College Students." *Journal of Personality and Social Psychology* 13: 1–16.

Katz, D. 1960. "The Functional Approach to the Study of Attitudes." *Public Opinion Quarterly* 24: 163–204.

Katz, D., and K. W. Braly. 1933. "Racial Stereotypes of 100 College Students." *Journal of Abnormal and Social Psychology* 28: 280–90.

———. 1935. "Racial Prejudice and Racial Stereotypes." *Journal of Abnormal and Social Psychology* 30: 175–93.

Keil, T., and G. Vito. 1989. "Race Homicide Severity, and Application of the Death Penalty: A Consideration of the Barnett Scale." *Criminology* 27: 511–35.

Kelly, D. D. 1985. "Sexual Differentiation of the Nervous System." In *Principles of Neural Science,* ed. E. R. Kandel and J. H. Schwartz. 2d ed. New York: Elsevier.

Kemp, Evan. 1990. Statement of chairman, Equal Employment Opportunity Commission before the National Research Council Commission on Behavioral and Social Science and Education, Washington, D.C., March 15.

Kennedy, Paul. 1987. *The Rise and Fall of the Great Powers: Economic Change and Military Conflict from 1500 to 2000.* New York: Random House.

Kerlinger, F. N. 1972. "The Structure and Content of Social Attitude Referents: A Preliminary Study." *Educational and Psychological Measurement* 32: 613–30.

Kimura, D. 1983. "Sex Differences in Cerebral Organization for Speech and Praxis." *Canadian Journal of Psychology* 37: 19–35.

———. 1987. "Are Men's and Women's Brains Really Different?" *Canadian Psychology* 28: 133–47.

Kinder, Donald R. 1986. "The Continuing American Dilemma: White Resistance to Racial Change 40 Years After Myrdal." *Journal of Social Issues* 42, no. 2: 151–71.

Kinder, Donald R., and David O. Sears. 1981. "Prejudice and Politics: Symbolic Racism Versus Racial Threats to the Good Life." *Journal of Personality and Social Psychology* 40, no. 3: 414–31.

Kinder, Donald R., T. Mendelberg, M. C. Dawson, L. M. Sanders, S. J. Rosenstone, J. Sargent, and C. Cohen. 1989. "Race and the 1988 American Presidential Elections." Paper prepared for the annual meeting of the American Political Science Association, Atlanta.

King, Martin Luther, Jr. 1967. *Where Do We Go from Here: Chaos or Community?* Boston: Beacon Press.

Kleck, G. 1981. "Racial Discrimination in Criminal Sentencing: A Critical Evaluation of the Evidence with Additional Evidence on the Death Penalty." *American Sociological Review* 46: 783–805.

Klein, G. S., H. L. Barr, and D. L. Wolitzky. 1967. "Personality." *Annual Review of Psychology* 18: 467–560.

Klein, S. 1989. "Relationship of Offender and Victim Race to Death Penalty Sentences in California." RAND Corp. MS.

Klemm, M. F. 1986. "The Determinants of Capital Sentencing in Louisiana, 1975–1984." Ph.D. diss., Univ. of New Orleans.

Klose, Kevin. 1984. "A Tormented Black Rising Star, Dead by Her Own Hand." *Washington Post.* August 5, c1, c2.

Kluegel, James R. 1978. "The Causes and Costs of Racial Exclusion from Job Authority." *American Sociological Review* 43 (June): 285–301.

———. 1985. "If There Isn't a Problem, You Don't Need a Solution: The Bases of Contemporary Affirmative Action Attitudes." *American Behavioral Scientist* 28, no. 6: 761–84.

———. 1990. "Trends in Whites' Explanations of the Gap in Black-White Socioeconomic Status, 1977–1989." *American Sociological Review* 55: 512–25.

Kluegel, James R., and Elliot R. Smith. 1986. *Beliefs About Inequality: Americans' Views of What Is and What Ought to Be.* Hawthorne, N.Y.: Aldine de Gruyter.

Kominski, Robert. 1990. "Estimating the National High School Dropout Rate." *Demography* 2 (May): 303–11.

Koretz, Daniel. 1990. *Trends in the Postsecondary Enrollment of Minorities.* Santa Monica, Calif.: RAND Corp.

Kosova, Weston. 1990. "Savage Gus." *New Republic*, January 29, p. 26.

Krueger, J., Myron Rothbart, and N. and Sriram. 1988. "Category Learning and Change: Differences in Sensitivity to Information that Enhances or Reduces Intercategory Distinctions." *Journal of Personality and Social Psychology* 56: 866–75.

Kuklinski, James H., and T. Wayne Parent. 1981. "Race and Big Government: Contamination in Measuring Racial Attitudes." *Political Methodology* 7: 131–59.

Lakatos, Imre. 1970. "Falsification and the Methodology of Scientific Research Programmes." In *Criticism and the Growth of Knowledge*, ed. Imre Lakatos. New York: Cambridge Univ. Press.

Landry, Bart. 1987. *The New Black Middle Class.* Berkeley: Univ. of California Press.

LaPiere, R. T. 1934. "Attitudes Versus Actions." *Social Forces* 13: 230–37.

Latimer, Leah. 1986. "Will Integration Hurt My Black Son's Education." *Washington Post*, April 20, c1, c4.

Leggon, Cheryl. 1980. "Black Female Professionals." In *The Black Woman*, ed. La Frances Rodgers-Rose. Beverly Hills, Calif.: Sage Publications.

Lemyre, L., and P. M. Smith. 1985. "Intergroup Discrimination and Self-esteem in the Minimal Group Paradigm." *Journal of Personality and Social Psychology* 49: 660–70.

Leventhal, A. M. 1966. "An Anxiety Scale for the CPI." *Journal of Clinical Psychology* 15: 479–80.

Levine, Daniel B., ed. 1986. *Creating a Center for Education Statistics: A Time for Action*. Washington, D.C.: National Academy Press.

Levinson, D. J., and R. N. Sanford. 1944. "A Scale for the Measurement of Anti-Semitism." *Journal of Psychology* 17: 339–70.

Levy, Frank. 1987. *Dollars and Dreams: The Changing American Income Distribution*. New York: Russell Sage Foundation.

Lewis, I. A., and William Schneider. 1983. "Black Voting, Bloc Voting, and the Democrats." *Public Opinion* 6, no. 5: 12–15, 59.

Lewis, P., H. Mannle, and H. Vetter. 1979. "A Post-Furnam Profile of Florida's Condemned—A Question of Discrimination in Terms of Race of the Victim and a Comment on Spenkelink v. Wainwright." *Stetson Law Review* 9: 1–45.

Lichter, Linda. 1985. "Who Speaks for Black America?" *Public Opinion* 8, no. 4: 41–44, 58.

Lichter, Linda, and Robert Lichter. N.d. [c. 1989]. "Howard Beach Youth: A Study of Racial and Ethnic Attitudes." Washington, D.C.: Center for Media and Public Affairs.

Linn, Robert L. 1988. "State-by-State Comparisons of Achievement: Suggestions for Enhancing Validity." *Educational Researcher* 17 (April): 6–9.

Lippmann, Walter. 1922. *Public Opinion*. New York: Harcourt, Brace.

Lipset, Seymour Martin. 1959. "Democracy and Working-class Authoritarianism." *American Sociological Review* 24: 428–501.

———. 1987. "Blacks and Jews: How Much Bias?" *Public Opinion* 10 (July/August): 4–5, 57–58.

Lipset, Seymour Martin, and W. Schneider. 1978. "The Bakke Case: How Would It Be Decided at the Bar of Public Opinion?" *Public Opinion*, March/April, pp. 38–44.

Litwack, Leon F. 1961. *North of Slavery: The Negro in the Free States, 1790–1860*. Chicago: Univ. of Chicago Press.

Locke, John. 1947. "A Letter Concerning Toleration." In *John Locke on Politics and Education*. New York: Walter J. Black.

———. 1960. *Two Treatises of Government*, ed. Peter Laslett. London: Cambridge Univ. Press.

———. 1980. *Second Treatise of Government*. Edited by C. B. McPherson. 1690. Indianapolis: Hackett Publishing Co.

Logan, Harold. 1986. "Blacks Helping Blacks." *Washington Post*, November 23, p. D5.

Louis Harris and Associates. 1978. *A Study of Attitudes Toward Racial and Religious Minorities and Toward Women*. New York: Louis Harris and Associates.

———. 1989. *The Unfinished Agenda on Race in America*, vol. 2. New York: Louis Harris and Associates.

Loury, Glenn. 1986. "Why Should We Care About Group Inequality?" Kennedy School of Government, Harvard Univ. MS.

Lugones, Maria, and Elizabeth Spelman. 1983. "Have We Got a Theory for You!" *Women's Studies International Forum* 6, no. 6: 573–81.

McClain, Leanita. 1986. *A Foot in Each World: Essays and Articles*. Edited by Clarence Page. Evanston, Ill.: Northwestern Univ. Press.

McClosky, Herbert, and John Zaller. 1984. *The American Ethos: Public Attitudes Toward Capitalism and Democracy*. Cambridge, Mass.: Harvard Univ. Press.

McConahay, John B. 1986. "Modern Racism, Ambivalence and the Modern Racism Scale." In *Prejudice, Discrimination, and Racism*, ed. John F. Dovidio and

Samuel L. Gaertner, pp. 91–125. Orlando, Fla.: Academic Press.

McConahay, John B., and Joseph C. Hough, Jr. 1976. "Symbolic Racism." *Journal of Social Issues* 32: 23–45.

McFadden, Robert. 1988. "Public's Differences over the Brawley Case." *New York Times*, October 29, pp. 1, 32–33.

McPherson, J. M. 1988. *Battle Cry of Freedom: The Civil War Era*. New York: Oxford Univ. Press.

Malebranche, David. 1989. "No Labels, Please." *The Vigil* 1, no. 1: 8.

Malizio, Andrew G., and Douglas R. Whitney. 1981. "Who Takes the GED Tests? A National Survey of Spring 1980 Examinees." Washington, D.C.: American Council on Education.

Mangione, Jerre. 1942. *Mount Allegro*. New York: Harper & Row.

Marable, Manning. 1982. "Reaganism, Racism, and Reaction." *Black Scholar* 13 (Fall): 2–15.

Margolis, Michael, and Khondaker Hague. 1981. "Applied Tolerance or Fear of Government? An Alternative Interpretation of Jackman's Findings." *American Journal of Political Science* 25: 241–55.

Marin, Gerardo. 1984. "Stereotyping Hispanics: The Differential Effect of Research Method, Label, and Degree of Contact." *International Journal of Intercultural Relations* 8: 17–27.

Martin, Elmer, and Joanne M. Martin. 1978. *The Black Extended Family*. Chicago: Univ. of Chicago Press.

Martire, Gregory, and Ruth Clark. 1982. *Anti-Semitism in the United States: A Study of American Prejudice in the 1980s*. New York: Praeger.

Marx, Gary T. 1967. *Protest and Prejudice: A Study of Belief in the Black Community*. New York: Harper & Row.

Mauer, Marc. 1990. "Young Black Men and the Criminal Justice System: A Growing National Problem." Washington, D.C.: The Sentencing Project.

Mazur, A., and T. A. Lamb. 1980. "Testosterone, Status, and Mood in Human Males." *Hormones and Behavior* 14: 236–46.

Mercer, G. W., and E. Cairns. 1981. "Conservatism and Its Relationship to General and Specific Ethnocentrism in Northern Ireland." *British Journal of Social Psychology* 20: 13–16.

Merisotis, Jamie. 1990. "Factors Affecting Minority Participation in Higher Education: A Research Synthesis." Washington, D.C.: Advisory Committee on Student Financial Assistance.

Merriman, W. Richard, and Edward G. Carmines. 1988. "The Limits of Liberal Tolerance: The Case of Racial Policies." *Polity* 20: 518–26.

Merriman, W. Richard, and T. Wayne Parent. 1983. "Sources of Citizen of Attitudes Toward Government Race Policy." *Polity* 16.

Meyers, David E. 1987. "Changes in Achievement Levels and Attendance in Postsecondary Schools: A Technical Note." Washington, D.C.: Decision Resources Corporation.

Michels, R. 1962. *Political Parties: A Sociological Study of the Oligarchical Tendencies of Modern Democracy*. 1911. New York: Free Press.

Miller, S., and Holly Hexter. 1985. "How Low-Income Families Pay for College." Washington, D.C.: American Council on Education.

Milloy, Courtland. 1990. "Bearing the Burden of Being the Black Mayor of the White Man's Plantation." *Washington Post*, January 21, p. A16.

Mills, C. Wright. 1956. *The Power Elite*. New York: Oxford University Press.

Minerbrook, Scott. 1990. "Gender-Line Anxieties." *Emerge*, January, pp. 32–36.

Mitchell, Constance. 1988. "Leveraged Leap: Some Blacks Plunge into the Mainstream in Creating a Business." *Wall Street Journal*, May 11, pp. 1, 16.

Mitchell, Jacquelyn. 1983. "Visible, Vulnerable, and Viable: Emerging Perspectives of a Minority Professor." In *Teaching Minority Students*, ed. James Cones III, John Noonan, and Denise Jamba. San Francisco: Jossey-Bass.

Mitchell, Jacquelyn. 1982. "Reflections of a Black Social Scientist." *Harvard Educational Review* 52, no. 1: 27–44.

Moreland-Young, Curtina. 1989. "A view from the Bottom: A Descriptive Analysis of the Jackson Platform Efforts." In *Jesse Jackson's 1984 Presidential Campaign: Challenge and Change in American Politics*, ed. Lucius J. Barker and Ronald W. Walters. Urbana: Univ. of Illinois Press.

Morganthaler, Eric. 1988. "Tough Business: Black Entrepreneurs Face Huge Hurdles in Place Like Miami." *Wall Street Journal*, May 17, pp. 1, 20.

Morin, Richard. 1990. "57 Percent of Poll Respondents Say the Mayor Should Resign." *Washington Post*, January 21, p. A17.

Morris, Lorenzo, and Linda F. Williams. 1989. "The Coalition at the End of the Rainbow: The 1984 Jackson Campaign." In *Jesse Jackson's 1984 Presidential Campaign: Challenge and Change in American Politics*, ed. Lucius J. Barker and Ronald W. Walters. Urbana: Univ. of Illinois Press.

Morrison, Joan, and Charlotte Zabusky. 1980. *American Mosaic: The Immigrant Experience in the Words of Those Who Lived It*. New York: Meridian, New American Library.

Mortenson, Thomas G. 1989a. "Family Income, Children, and Student Financial Aid." *ACT Student Financial Aid Research Report Series* 89-1. Iowa City: American College Testing Program.

———. 1989b. "Missing College Attendance Costs: Opportunity, Financing, and Risk." *ACT Student Financial Aid Research Report Series* 89-3. Iowa City: American College Testing Program.

———. 1990a. "College Entrance Rates for Recent High School Graduates." *ACT Financial Aid Research Briefs* 5. Iowa City: American College Testing Program.

———. 1990b. "The Impact of Increased Loan Utilization Among Low Family Income Students." *ACT Financial Aid Research Report Series* 90-1. Iowa City: American College Testing Program.

———. 1990c. "The Reallocation of Financial Aid from Poor to Middle Income and Affluent Students: 1978 to 1990." *ACT Student Financial Aid Research Report Series* 90-2. Iowa City: American College Testing Program.

Mosca, Gaetano. 1939. *The Ruling Class: Elements of Political Science*. 1895. Translated from the Italian by Hannah D. Kahn. New York: McGraw-Hill.

Mosley, Myrtis. 1980. "Black Women Administrators in Higher Education." *Journal of Black Studies* 10, no. 3: 295–310.

Mullins, L. S., and R. E. Kopelman. 1988. "Toward an Assessment of the Construct Validity of Four Measures of Narcissism." *Journal of Personality Assessment* 52: 610–25.

Mullis, Ina V. S., and Lynn B. Jenkins. 1990. *The Reading Report Card, 1971–1988: Trends from the Nation's Report Card*. Princeton, N.J.: Educational Testing Service.

Murphy, E. 1984. "The Application of the Death Penalty in Cook County." *Illinois Bar Journal*.

Muthén, Bengt. 1984. "A General Structural Equation Model with Dichotomous

Ordered Categorical, and Continuous Latent Variable Indicators." *Psychometrika* 49: 115–32.

Muzzio, Doug. 1989. "Jesse Jackson: Did He Have a Chance?" In *The '88 Vote*, ed. Carolyn Smith. New York: Capital Cities/ABC.

Myrdal, Gunnar. 1944, 1964. *An American Dilemma: The Negro Problem and Modern Democracy*. New York: Harper & Row.

Nakell, B., and K. Hardy. 1987. *The Arbitrariness of the Death Penalty*. Philadelphia: Temple Univ. Press.

National Opinion Research Center. 1990. *General Social Survey 1972–1990; Cumulative Codebook*. Chicago: Univ. of Chicago.

New York Times/CBS News Poll Post-Election Survey, press release, November 1988. New York City.

Newcomb, T. M. 1947. "Autistic Hostility and Social Reality." *Human Relations* 1: 69–86.

Niemi, Richard G., John Mueller, and Tom W. Smith. 1989. *Trends in Public Opinion: A Compendium of Survey Data*. Westport, Conn.: Greenwood Press.

Nilsson, E., B. Ekehammar, and J. Sidanius. 1987. "Education and Ideology: Basic Aspects of Education Related to Adolescents' Sociopolitical Attitudes." *Political Psychology* 8: 395–411.

Novak, Michael. 1972. *The Rise of the Unmeltable Ethnics: Politics and Culture in the Seventies*. New York: Macmillan.

Oliver, Melvin, and Thomas Shapiro. 1989. "Race and Wealth." *Review of Black Political Economy* 17, no. 4: 5–25.

Olweus, D., A. Mattsson, D. Schalling, and H. Low. 1988. "Circulating Testosterone Levels and Aggression in Adolescent Males: A Causal Analysis." *Psychosomatic Medicine* 50: 261–72.

Oreskes, Michael. 1990. "Bush and G.O.P. High in Black Approval." *New York Times*, April 13, p. 12.

Page, Clarence. 1986. Introduction to Leanita McClain, *A Foot in Each World: Essays and Articles*, ed. Clarence Page. Evanston, Ill.: Northwestern Univ. Press.

Palmer, Stacy. 1983. "In the 'Fishbowl': When Blacks Work at Predominantly White Colleges." *Chronicle of Higher Education*, September 14, pp. 19–21.

Parent, T. Wayne. 1984. "Individual explanations for Structural Problems: Blacks and Economic Redistribution Policy." Paper presented at the annual meeting of the Midwest Political Science Association. Chicago.

Parent, T. Wayne, and Paul Stekler. 1985. "The Political Implications of Economic Stratification in the Black Community." *Western Political Quarterly* 38, no. 4: 521–38.

Parent, T. Wayne, Calvin C. Jillson, and Ronald E. Weber. 1987. "Voting Outcomes in the 1984 Democratic Party Primaries and Caucuses." *American Political Science Review* 81: 67–84.

Parenti, M. 1986. *Inventing Reality: The Politics of the Mass Media*. New York: St. Martin's Press.

Pareto, Vilfredo. 1901. *The Rise and Fall of the Elites*. New York: Arno.

———. 1935. *The Mind and Society*. 1916. Translated from the Italian by A. Bongiorno and A. Livingston. New York: Harcourt & Brace.

Park, Bernadette, and Myron Rothbart. 1982. "Perception of Out-group Homogeneity and Levels of Social Categorization: Memory for the Subordinate Attributes of In-group and Out-group Members." *Journal of Personality and Social Psychology* 42: 1051–68.

Park, R. E. 1924. "The Concept of Social Distance." *Journal of Applied Sociology* 8: 339–44.

Paternoster, R. 1983. "Race of Victim and Location of Crime: The Decision to Seek the Death Penalty in South Carolina." *Journal of Criminal Law and Criminology* 74: 754–85.

Paternoster, R., and A. M. Kazyaka. 1988. "The Administration of the Death Penalty in South Carolina: Experiences over the First Few Years." *South Carolina Law Review* 39: 245–414.

Patterson, Orlando. 1973. "The Moral Crisis of Black America." *The Public Interest* 23 (Summer): 43–69.

Peabody, D. 1968. "Group Judgments in the Philippines: Evaluative and Descriptive Aspects." *Journal of Personality and Social Psychology* 10: 290–300.

———. 1984. "Personality Dimensions Through Trait Inferences." *Journal of Personality and Social Psychology* 46: 384–403.

Pettigrew, Thomas F. 1979. "The Ultimate Attribution Error: Extending Allport's Cognitive Analysis of Prejudice." *Personality and Social Psychology Bulletin* 5: 461–76.

———. 1982. "Prejudice." In *Dimensions of Ethnicity*, ed. Stephan Thernstrom, Ann Orlov, and Oscar Handlin. Cambridge, Mass.: Belknap Press.

———. 1985. "New Black-White Patterns: How to Best Conceptualize Them?" *Annual Review of Sociology* 11: 329–46.

Pettigrew, Thomas, and Joanne Martin. 1987. "Shaping the Organizational Context of Black American Inclusion." *Journal of Social Issues* 43, no. 1: 41–78.

Plissner, Martin, and Warren Mitofsky. 1988. "The Changing Jackson Voter." *Public Opinion* 8, no. 4: 56–57.

Pohlman, E. W. 1951. "Evidence of Disparity Between the Hindu Practice of Caste and the Ideal Type." *American Sociological Review* 16: 375–79.

Powell, G. E., and R. A. Stewart. 1978. "The Relationship of Age, Sex and Personality of Social Attitudes in Children Aged 8–15 Years." *British Journal of Social Psychology* 17: 307–17.

Pratto, Felicia, Jim Sidanius, and L. M. Stallworth. 1993. "Sexual Selection and the Sexual and Ethnic Basis of Social Hierarchy." In *Social Stratification and Socioeconomic Inequality: A Comparative Biosocial Analysis*, ed. L. Ellis. New York: Praeger.

Preston, Michael. 1989. "The 1984 Presidential Primary Campaign: Who Voted for Jesse Jackson and Why." In *Jesse Jackson's 1984 Presidential Campaign: Challenge and Change in American Politics*, ed. Lucius J. Barker and Ronald W. Walters. Urbana: Univ. of Illinois Press.

Putnam, R. D. 1976. *The Comparative Study of Political Elites.* Englewood Cliffs, N.J.: Prentice-Hall.

Quinley, Harold E., and Charles Y. Glock. 1979. *Anti-Semitism in America.* New York: Free Press.

Radelet, M. 1981. "Racial Characteristics and the Imposition of the Death Penalty." *American Sociological Review* 46: 918–27.

Radelet, M., and G. Pierce. 1985. "Race and Prosecutorial Discretion in Homicide Cases." *Law and Society Review* 19: 587–621.

Radelet, M., and M. Vandiver. 1983. "The Florida Supreme Court and Death Penalty Appeals." *Journal of Criminal Law and Criminology* 74: 913–26.

Ranney, Austin. 1972. "Turnout and Representation in Presidential Primary Elections." *American Political Science Review* 66: 21–37.

Raspberry, William. 1990. "Black Creativity, Black Solutions." *Washington Post*, March 10, p. A25.

Ray, J. J. 1984. "Half of All Racists Are Left-Wing." *Political Psychology* 5: 227–36.

———. 1990. "Authoritarian Behavior and Political Orientation: A Comment on Rigby." *Journal of Personality Assessment* 54: 419–22.

Reed, Adolph L., Jr. 1986. *The Jesse Jackson Phenomenon: The Crisis of Purpose in Afro-American Politics*. New Haven, Conn.: Yale Univ. Press.

———. 1987. "A Critique of Neo-Progressivism in Theorizing About Local Development Policy." In *The Politics of Urban Development*, ed. Clarence Stone and Haywood Sanders. Lawrence: Univ. Press of Kansas.

Rejeski, W. J., M. Gagne, P. E. Parker, and D. R. Koritnik. 1989. "Acute Stress Reactivity from Contested Dominance in Dominant and Submissive Males." *Behavioral Medicine* 15: 118–24.

Reskin, Barbara, and Patricia Roos. 1990. *Job Queues, Gender Queues: Explaining Women's Inroads into Male Occupations*. Philadelphia: Temple Univ. Press.

Reynolds, V., V. Falger, and I. Vine. 1987. *The Sociobiology of Ethnocentrism: Evolutionary Dimensions of Xenophobia, Discrimination, Racism and Nationalism*. Beckenham, Kent: Croom Helm.

Riedel, M. 1976. "Discrimination in the Imposition of the Death Penalty: A Comparison of the Characteristics of Offenders Sentenced Pre-Furnam and Post-Furnam." *Temple Law Quarterly* 49: 261–87.

Rieder, Jonathan. 1985. *Canarsie: The Jews and Italians of Brooklyn Against Liberalism*. Cambridge, Mass.: Harvard Univ. Press.

Riley, Norman. 1986. "Attitudes of the New Black Middle-Class." *The Crisis* 93, no. 10: 14–18, 31–32.

Rivera, Edward. 1982. *Family Installments: Memories of Growing up Hispanic*. New York: Morrow.

Rodriguez, Richard. 1982. *Hunger of Memory: The Education of Richard Rodriguez*. Boston: Godine.

Rokeach, Milton. 1960. *The Open and Closed Mind: Investigations into the Nature of Belief Systems and Personality Systems*. New York: Basic Books.

———. 1973. *The Nature of Human Values: Individual and Social*. New York: Free Press.

———. 1979. "The Two-Value Model of Political Ideology and British Politics." In *Understanding Human Values: Individual and Social*, ed. M. Rokeach. New York: Free Press.

Rosenberg, M. 1965. *Society and the Adolescent Self-image*. Princeton, N.J.: Princeton Univ. Press.

Rosenberg, M., and R. G. Simmons. 1972. "Black and White Self-esteem Among Children and Adults." *American Journal of Sociology* 84: 53–77.

Rothbart, Myron, and P. Birrell. 1977. "Attitude and the Perception of Facts." *Journal of Research in Personality* 11: 209–15.

Rothbart, Myron, M. Evans, and S. Fulero. 1979. "Recall for Confirming Events: Memory Processes and the Maintenance of Social Stereotypes." *Journal of Experimental and Social Psychology* 15: 343–55.

Rothbart, Myron, and Oliver P. John. 1985. "Social Categories and Behavioral Episodes: A Cognitive Analysis of the Effects of Intergroup Contact." *Journal of Social Issues* 41: 81–104.

Rothbart, Myron, and S. Lewis. 1988. "Inferring Category Attributes from Exemplar Attributes: Geometric Shapes and Social Categories." *Journal of Personality and Social Psychology* 55: 861–72.

Rothbart, Myron, and B. Park. 1986. "On the Confirmability and Disconfirmability of Trait Concepts." *Journal of Personality and Social Psychology* 50: 131–42.

Rothbart, Myron, and M. Taylor. 1992. "Category Labels and Social Reality: Do We View Social Categories as Natural Kinds?" In *Language and Social Cognition*, eds. G. Semin and K. Fiedler.

Ryan, William. 1976. *Blaming the Victim*. 1971. New York: Random House Vintage Books.

Sachdev, I., and R. W. Bourhis. 1985. "Social Categorization and Power Differentials in Group Relations." *European Journal of Social Psychology* 15: 415–34.

———. 1987. "Status Differentials and Intergroup Behavior." *European Journal of Social Psychology* 17: 277–93.

Sagar, H. A., and J. W. Schofield. 1980. "Racial and Behavioral Cues in Black and White Children's Perceptions of Ambiguously Aggressive Acts." *Journal of Personality and Social Psychology* 39: 590–98.

Salvador, A., V. Simon, F. Suay, and L. Llorens. 1987. "Testosterone and Cortisol Responses to Competitive Fighting in Human Males: A Pilot Study." *Aggressive Behavior* 13: 9–13.

Sandler, Bernice. 1986. *The Campus Climate Revisited: Chilly for Women Faculty, Administrators, and Graduate Students*. Washington, D.C.: Association of American Colleges.

Scaramella, T. J., and W. A. Brown. 1978. "Serum Testosterone and Aggressiveness in Hockey Players." *Psychometric Medicine* 40: 262–65.

Scheibe, K. 1970. *Beliefs and Attitudes*. New York: Holt, Rinehart & Winston.

Schulman, S., and W. Darity, Jr. 1989. *The Question of Discrimination: Racial Inequality in the United States Labor Market*. Middletown, Conn.: Wesleyan Univ. Press.

Schuman, Howard, and John Harding. 1963. "Sympathetic Identification with the Underdog." *Public Opinion Quarterly* 27: 230–41.

Schuman, Howard, and Shirley Hatchett. 1974. *Black Racial Attitudes: Trends and Complexities*. Ann Arbor: Institute for Social Research, Univ. of Michigan.

Schuman, Howard, Charlotte Steeh, and Lawrence Bobo. 1985. *Racial Attitudes in America: Trends and Interpretations*. Cambridge, Mass.: Harvard University Press.

Schwartz, Mildred. 1967. *Trends in White Attitudes Towards Negroes*. Chicago: National Opinion Research Center, Univ. of Chicago.

Sears, David O. 1988. "Symbolic Racism." In *Eliminating Racism: Profiles in Controversy*, ed. Phyllis A. Katz and Dalmas A. Taylor. New York: Plenum Press.

Sears, David O., and Donald R. Kinder. 1970. "The Good Life, 'White Racism,' and the Los Angeles Voter." Paper delivered at the annual meeting of the Western Psychological Association, Los Angeles.

———. 1971. "Racial Tensions and Voting Behavior in Los Angeles." In *Los Angeles: Viability and Prospects for Metropolitan Leadership*, ed. W. Z. Hirsch. New York: Praeger.

Sears, David O., Jack Citrin, and Rick Kosterman. 1987. "Jesse Jackson and the Southern White Electorate." In *Blacks in Southern Politics*, ed. Laurence W. Moreland, Robert P. Steed, and Tod A. Baker. New York: Praeger.

Sears, David O., Carl P. Hensler, and Leslie K. Speer. 1979. "Whites' Opposition to 'Busing': Self-Interest or Symbolic Politics?" *American Political Science Review* 73: 369–84.

Seltzer, Richard, and Robert Smith. 1985. "Race and Ideology." *Phylon* 46, no. 2: 98–105.

Selznick, Gertrude, and Stephen Steinberg. 1969. *The Tenacity of Prejudice: Anti-Semitism in Contemporary America*. New York: Harper & Row.

Sewell, William H. 1971. "Inequality of Opportunity for Higher Education." *American Sociological Review* 36 (October): 793–809.

Sewell, William H., and Robert M. Hauser. 1975. *Education, Occupation, and Earnings: Achievement in the Early Career*. New York: Academic Press.

———. 1972. "Causes and Consequences of Higher Education: Models of the Status Attainment Process." *American Journal of Agricultural Economics* 54 (December): 851–61.

Sewell, William H., Robert M. Hauser, and Wendy C. Wolf. 1980. "Sex, Schooling and Occupational Status." *American Journal of Sociology* 86 (November): 551–83.

Sherif, M. 1967. *Group Conflict and Cooperation*. London: Routledge & Kegan Paul.

Sherif, M., O. J. Harvey, B. J. White, W. R. Hood, and C. W. Sherif. 1988. *The Robbers' Cave Experiment: Intergroup Conflict and Cooperation*. 1961. Middletown, Conn.: Wesleyan Univ. Press.

Sidanius, Jim. 1976. *Further Tests of a Swedish Scale of Conservatism*. Reports from the Department of Psychology, (no. 467). Stockholm: Univ. of Stockholm.

———. 1984. "Political Interest, Political Information Search and Ideological Homogeneity as a Function of Socio-political Ideology: A Tale of Three Theories." *Human Relations* 37: 811–28.

———. 1989. "Symbolic Racism and Social Dominance Theory: A Comparative Application to the Case of American Race Relations." Paper delivered at the annual meetings of the Society for Experimental Social Psychology, Los Angeles.

Sidanius, Jim, E. Brewer, E. Banks, and B. Ekehammar. 1987. "Ideological Constraint, Political Interest and Gender: A Swedish-American Comparison." *European Journal of Political Research* 15: 471–92.

Sidanius, Jim, E. Devereux, and Felicia Pratto. 1992. "A Comparison of Symbolic Racism Theory and Social Dominance Theory as Explanations for Racial Policy Attitudes." *Journal of Social Psychology* 131: 377–95.

Sidanius, Jim, and B. Ekehammar. 1976. "Cognitive Functioning and Sociopolitico Ideology: A Multidimensional and Individualized Analysis." *Scandinavian Journal of Psychology* 17: 205–16.

———. 1979. "Political Socialization: A Multivariate Analysis of Swedish Political Attitude and Preference Data." *European Journal of Social Psychology* 9: 265–79.

———. 1980. "Sex-related Differences in Socio-political Ideology." *Scandinavian Journal of Psychology* 21: 17–26.

———. 1983. "Sex, Political Party Preference and Higher-Order Dimensions of Socio-political Ideology." *Journal of Social Psychology* 115: 233–39.

Sidanius, Jim, B. Ekehammar, and J. Ross. 1979. "Comparisons of Socio-political attitudes between two democratic societies."

Sidanius, Jim, and Felicia Pratto. 1990. "Performance Evaluation and Attribute Heterogeneity: A Study of Real Groups in Real Situations." University of California, Los Angeles. MS.

———. In press. "Racism and Support of Free-market Capitalism: A Cross-cultural Study of the Theoretical Structure." *Political Psychology*.

Sidanius, Jim, Felicia Pratto, and R. Govender. 1990. "Social Dominance, Social

Attitudes and Legitimizing Myths: An Application to the American Dilemma."
Under review

Sidanius, Jim, Felicia Pratto, M. Martin, and L. M. Stallworth. 1991. "Consensual
Racism and Career Track: Some Implications of Social Dominance Theory."
Political Psychology 12: 691–720.

Sidanius, Jim, Felicia Pratto, and M. Mitchell. 1992. "Group Identity, Social
Dominance Orientation, and Intergroup Discrimination: Some Implications of
Social Dominance Theory." University of California, Los Angeles. MS.

Sigelman, Lee, and Susan Welch. 1991. *Black Americans' Views of Racial Inequality:
The Dream Deferred*. New York: Cambridge Univ. Press.

Simmons, Ozzie G. 1961. "The Mutual Images and Expectations of Anglo Americans and Mexican Americans." *Daedalus* 90: 286–99.

Simmons, R. G., L. Brown, D. M. Bush, and D. A. Blyth. 1978. "Self-esteem
and Achievement of Black and White Adolescents." *Social Problems* 26: 86–96.

Simon, Kate. 1982. *Bronx Primitive: Portraits in a Childhood*. New York: Viking.

———. 1986. *A Wider World: Portraits in an Adolescence*. New York: Harper & Row.

Skevington, S. 1981. "Intergroup Relations and Nursing." *European Journal of Social
Psychology* 11: 43–59.

Smedley, Joseph W., and James A. Bayton. 1978. "Evaluative Race-Class Stereotypes by Race and Perceived Class of Subjects." *Journal of Personality and Social
Psychology* 36: 530–35.

Smith, A. Wade. 1985. "Social Class and Racial Cleavages on Major Social Indicators." *Research in Race and Ethnic Relations* 4: 33–65. Greenwich, Conn.: JAI Press.

Smith, Carolyn, ed. 1985. *The '84 Vote*. New York: ABC.

———. 1989. *The '88 Vote*. New York: Capital Cities / ABC.

Smith, D. M. 1987. "Patterns of Discrimination in Assessments of the Death
Penalty: The Case of Louisiana." *Journal of Criminal Justice* 15: 279–86.

Smith, Earl. 1989. "A Comparative Study of Occupational Stress Among Black
and White U.S. College and University Faculty." Paper presented at the annual
meeting of the American Sociological Association.

Smith, James P., and Finis R. Welch. 1987. *Black Economic Progress after Myrdal*. Santa
Monica, Calif.: RAND Corp.

Smith, Robert. 1990. "Recent Elections and Black Politics." *PS* 23, no. 2: 160–62.

Smith, T. W., and P. B. Sheatsley. 1984. "American Attitudes Toward Race Relations." *Public Opinion* 7: 14–16.

Sniderman, Paul M. 1975. *Personality and Democratic Politics*. Berkeley: Univ. of
California Press.

Sniderman, Paul M., and Michael Gray Hagen. 1985. *Race and Inequality: A Study
in American Values*. Chatham, N.J.: Chatham House.

Sniderman, Paul M., and Philip E. Tetlock. 1986a. "Symbolic Racism: Problems
of Motive Attribution in Political Analysis." *Journal of Social Issues* 42, no. 2:
129–50.

———. 1986b. "Reflections on American Racism." *Journal of Social Issues* 42, no. 2:
173–87.

Sniderman, Paul M., Philip E. Tetlock, J. M. Glaser, D. P. Green, and Michael
Hout. 1989. "Principled Tolerance and the American Mass Public." *British Journal of Political Science* 19: 25–46.

Sniderman, Paul M., Richard A. Brody, and James H. Kuklinski. 1984. "Policy
Reasoning and Political Values: Problem of Racial Equality." *American Journal
of Political Science*.

Sniderman, Paul M., Richard A. Brody, and Philip E. Tetlock, eds. 1991. *Reasoning and Choice*. New York: Cambridge Univ. Press.

Sniderman, Paul M., Thomas Piazza, Ada Finifter, and Philip E. Tetlock. 1989. "Black Tolerance." Paper delivered at the annual meeting of the Midwest Political Science Association, Chicago.

Sniderman, Paul M., Thomas Piazza, Philip E. Tetlock, and A. Kendrick. 1991. "The New Racism." *American Journal of Political Science* 35, no. 2: 423–47.

Sokoloff, Natalie. 1989. "Are Professionals Becoming Desegregated?" Paper presented at the annual meeting of the American Sociological Association. San Francisco.

St. George, Arthur, and Patrick McNamara. 1984. "Religion, Race and Psychological Well-being." *23*.

Stacey, B. G., and R. T. Green. 1971. "Working-class Conservatism: A Review and an Empirical Study." *British Journal of Social and Clinical Psychology* 10: 10–26.

Stanley, Harold W., and Richard G. Niemi. 1988. *Vital Statistics on American Politics*. Washington, D.C.: Congressional Quarterly.

———. 1990. *Vital Statistics on American Politics*. 2d ed. Washington, D.C.: Congressional Quarterly.

Steele, Shelby. 1990. *The Content of Our Character*. New York: St. Martin's Press.

Stone, Clarence. 1989. *Regime Politics*. Lawrence: Univ. Press of Kansas.

Stouffer, Samuel. 1955. *Communism, Conformity and Civil Liberties*. New York: Doubleday.

Stricker, Lawrence. 1982. "Dimensions of Social Stratification for Whites and Blacks." *Multivariate Behavioral Research* 17: 139–67.

Sullivan, John L., James Piereson, and George E. Marcus. 1982. *Political Tolerance and American Democracy*. Chicago: Univ. of Chicago Press.

Susman, E. J., G. G. Inoff, E. D. Nottelmann, and D. Loriaux. 1987. "Hormones, Emotional Dispositions, and Aggressive Attributes in Young Adolescents." *Child Development* 58: 1114–34.

Swift, Jonathan. 1935. *Gulliver's Travels*. 1726. New York: Oxford Univ. Press.

Swigert, V. L., and R. A. Farrell. 1976. *Murder, Inequality, and the Law: Differential Treatment in the Legal Process*. Lexington, Mass.: D. C. Heath.

Tajfel, Henri. 1970. "Experiments in Intergroup Discrimination." *Scientific American* 233: 96–102.

———. 1978. *Differentiation Between Social Groups: Studies in the Social Psychology of Intergroup Relations*. London: Academic Press.

———. 1982a. *Social Identity and Intergroup Relations*. Cambridge: Cambridge University Press.

———. 1982b. "The Social Psychology of Intergroup Relations." *Annual Review of Psychology* 1: 149–78.

Tajfel, Henri, and J. C. Turner. 1986. "The Social Identity Theory of Intergroup Behavior." In *Psychology of Intergroup Relations*, ed. S. Worchel and W. G. Austin. Chicago: Nelson-Hall.

Tate, Katherine, Ronald Brown, Shirley Hatchett, and James Jackson. 1988. *The 1984 National Black Election Study Sourcebook*. Ann Arbor: Institute for Social Research, Univ. of Michigan.

Taylor, Donald M., and Fathali M. Moghaddam. 1987. *Theories of Intergroup Relations: International Social Psychological Perspectives*. New York: Praeger.

Taylor, M. C., and E. J. Walsh. 1979. "Explanations of Black Self-esteem: Some Empirical Tests." *Social Psychology Quarterly* 42: 242–53.

Taylor, S. E., and M. Lobel. 1990. "Social Comparison Under Threat: Downward Evaluation and Upward Contacts." *Psychological Review*. In press.

Terkel, Studs. 1980. *American Dreams*. New York: Pantheon Books.

Thompson, Daniel. 1986. *A Black Elite: A Profile of Graduates of UNCF Colleges*. Westport, Ct.: Greenwood Press.

Treiman, D. J. 1977. *Occupational Prestige in Comparative Perspective*. New York: Academic Press.

Trescott, Jacqueline. 1985. "So Close and Yet so Far." *Washington Post*, January 6, H1ff.

Triandis, Harry C., Judith Lisansky, Bernadette Setiadi, Bei-Hung Chang, Gerardo Marin, and Hector Belancourt. 1982. "Stereotyping Among Hispanics and Anglos: The Uniformity, Intensity, Direction, and Quality of Auto- and Heterostereotypes." *Journal of Cross-Cultural Psychology* 13: 409–26.

Troeltsch, Ernst. 1960. *The Social Teaching of the Christian Churches*, vol. 2. Trans. by Olive Wyon. New York: Harper.

Tursky, B., M. Lodge, M. S. Foley, R. Reeder, and H. Foley. 1976. "Evaluation of Cognitive Components of Political Issues by Use of Classical Conditioning." *Journal of Personality and Social Psychology* 34: 865–73.

U.S. Bureau of Justice Statistics. 1986. "State and Federal Prisoners, 1925–85." *Bulletin*, October.

U.S. Bureau of Justice Statistics. "Unpublished Data." Correction Unit Division.

U.S. Bureau of the Census. 1984a. *Detailed Population Characteristics. 1980 Census of Population*. Vol. 1, *Characteristics of the population*, pt. 1, ch. D. United States summary. Washington, D.C.: Government Printing Office.

——. 1984b. *1980 Census of Population*. Vol. 2, *Persons in Institutions and Other Group Quarters. Subject Reports*. Washington, D.C.: Government Printing Office.

——. 1984c. *School Enrollment—Social and Economic Characteristics of Students*. October 1983. Advance Report. Current Population Reports, series P-20, no. 394. Washington, D.C.: Government Printing Office.

——. 1986. *Household Wealth and Asset Ownership: 1984*. Household Economic Studies Series P-70. 7. Washington, D.C.: Government Printing Office.

——. 1987a. *Statistical Abstract of the United States, 1987*. Washington, D.C.: Government Printing Office.

——. 1987b. *Estimates of the Population of the United States, by Age, Sex, and Race: 1980 to 1986. Population Estimates and Projections*. Current Population Reports, series P-25, no. 1000. Washington, D.C.: Government Printing Office.

——. 1987c. *School Enrollment—Social and Economic Characteristics of Students: October 1983. Population Characteristics*. Current Population Reports, series P-20, no. 443. Washington, D.C.: Government Printing Office.

——. 1988. *School Enrollment—Social and Economic Characteristics of Students: October 1986. Population Characteristics*. Current Population Reports, series P-20, no. 429. Washington, D.C.: Government Printing Office.

——. 1989a. *Money Income of Households, Families, and Persons in the United States, 1987*. Current Population Reports, series P-60, no. 162. Washington, D.C.: Government Printing Office.

——. 1989b. *Voting and Registration in the Election of November 1988*. Current Population Reports, series P-20, no. 440. Washington, D.C.: Government Printing Office.

——. 1990. *School Enrollment—Social and Economic Characteristics of Students: Octo-

ber 1988 and 1987. Population Characteristics. Current Population Reports, series P-20, no. 443. Washington, D.C.: Government Printing Office.

———. 1991a. *Statistical Abstract of the United States 1991.* Washington, D.C.: Government Printing Office.

———. 1991b. *Money Income of Households, Families, and Persons in the United States, 1990.* Current Population Reports, series P-60, no. 174. Washington, D.C.: Government Printing Office.

U.S. Department of Education. 1991. *The Condition of Education, 1991,* vol. 2: *Postsecondary Education.* Washington, D.C.: Government Printing Office.

U.S. Department of Labor. 1991. *A Report on the Glass Ceiling Initiative.* Washington, D.C.: Department of Labor.

van den Berghe, P. L. 1978a. "Race and Ethnicity: A Sociobiological Perspective." *Ethnic and Racial Studies* 1: 401–11.

———. 1978b. *Man in Society: A Biosocial View.* New York: Elsevier North Holland.

van Knippenberg, A., and H. van Oers. 1984. "Social Identity and Equity Concerns in Intergroup Perceptions." *British Journal of Social Psychology* 23: 351–61.

Vanneman, Reeve, and Lynn Weber Cannon. 1987. *The American Perception of Class.* Philadelphia: Temple Univ. Press.

Vito, G., and T. Keil. 1988. "Capital Sentencing in Kentucky: An Analysis of the Factors Influencing Decision Making in the Post-Gregg Period." *Journal of Criminal Law & Criminology* 79: 483–508.

Ward, D. 1985. "Generations and the Expression of Symbolic Racism." *Political Psychology* 6: 1–18.

Wartzman, Rick. 1988. "St. Louis Blues: A Blighted Inner City Bespeaks the Sad State of Black Commerce." *Wall Street Journal,* May 10, pp. 1, 16.

Weber, Max. 1958. *The Protestant Ethic and the Spirit of Capitalism.* New York: Scribner.

Weigel, R. H., and P. W. Howes. 1985. "Conceptions of Racial Prejudice: Symbolic Racism Reconsidered." *Journal of Social Issues* 41, no. 3: 117–38.

Welch, Susan, and Lee Sigelman. 1989. "How Black Americans View Racial Discrimination." Paper given at the meetings of the Midwest Political Science Association, Chicago.

Welch, Susan, and Lorn Foster. 1987. "Class and Conservatism in the Black Community." *American Politics Quarterly* 15, no. 4: 445–70.

Welch, Susan, and Michael Combs. 1985. "Intra-racial Differences in Attitudes of Blacks." *Phylon* 46, no. 2: 91–97.

Wellman, David T. 1977. *Portraits of White Racism.* Cambridge: Cambridge Univ. Press.

Westcott, Diane. 1982. "Blacks in the 1970's: Did They Scale the Job Ladder." *Monthly Labor Review* 105, no. 6: 29–38.

Westie, Frank, and David Howard. 1954. "Social Status Differentials and the Race Attitudes of Negroes." *American Sociological Review* 19, no. 5: 584–91.

Wheaton, Blair, Bengt Muthén, Duane Alwin, and Gene Summers. 1977. "Assessing Reliability and Stability in Panel Models." In *Sociological Methodology, 1977,* ed. David Heise. San Francisco: Jossey-Bass.

Wilkins, Roger. 1989. "Middle-class Blacks Must Start Revolution for Less Fortunate." *Atlanta Constitution and Journal,* November 12.

Williams, Juan. 1989. "Alex Williams and the Crossover Strategy." *Washington Post Magazine,* February 12, pp. 18ff.

Willie, C. V. 1979. *Caste and Race Controversy*. Bayside, N.Y.: General Hall.

Wills, Garry. 1979. *Nixon Agonistes: The Crisis of the Self-Made Man*. New York: New American Library.

Wills, T. A. 1981. "Downward Comparison Principles in Social Psychology." *Psychological Bulletin* 90: 245–71.

———. 1987. "Downward Comparison as a Coping Mechanism." In *Coping with Negative Life Events: Clinical and Social Psychological Perspectives*, ed. C. R. Snyder and C. Ford. New York: Plenum Press.

Wilson, G. D. 1973a. "The Concept of Conservatism." In *The Psychology of Conservatism*, ed. G. D. Wilson. New York: Academic Press.

———. 1973b. "The Factor Structure of the C-scale." In *The Psychology of Conservatism*, ed. G. D. Wilson. New York: Academic Press.

Wilson, G. D., and C. Bagley. 1973. "Religion, Racialism and Conservatism." In *The Psychology of Conservatism*, ed. G. D. Wilson. New York: Academic Press.

Wilson, G. D., and H. S. Lee. 1974. "Social Attitude Patterns in Korea." *Journal of Social Psychology* 94: 27–30.

Wilson, Reginald, and Deborah Carter, J. 1989. "Eighth Annual Status Report: Minorities in Higher Education." Washington, D.C.: American Council on Education.

Wilson, William J. 1978. *The Declining Significance of Race*. Chicago: Univ. of Chicago Press.

Wink, Paul, and Harrison G. Gough. 1990. "New Narcissism Scales for the California Psychological Inventory and the MMPI." *Journal of Personality Assessment* 54: 446–62.

Wolfle, Lee M. 1985. "Postsecondary Educational Attainment Among Whites and Blacks." *American Educational Research Journal* 22 (Winter): 501–25.

Wuthnow, Robert. 1982. "Anti-Semitism and Stereotyping." In *In the Eye of the Beholder: Contemporary Issues in Stereotyping*, ed. Arthur G. Miller. New York: Praeger.

Zawadski, B. 1948. "Limitations of the Scapegoat Theory of Prejudice." *Journal of Abnormal and Social Psychology* 43: 127–41.

Zeisel, H. 1981. "Race Bias in the Administration of the Death Penalty: The Florida Experience." *95*.

Zipp, John. 1989. "Did Jesse Jackson Cause a White Backlash Against Democrats? A Look at the 1984 Presidential Election." In *Jesse Jackson's 1984 Presidential Campaign: Challenge and Change in American Politics*, ed. Lucius J. Barker and Ronald W. Walters. Urbana: Univ. of Illinois Press.

Zweigenhaft, Richard, and G. William Domhoff. 1991. *Blacks in the White Establishment?* New Haven: Yale Univ. Press.

Index

In this index an "f" after a number indicates a separate reference on the next page, and an "ff" indicates separate references on the next two pages. A continuous discussion over two or more pages is indicated by a span of page numbers, e.g., "57–59." "Passim" is used for a cluster of references in close but not consecutive sequence.

Library of Congress Cataloging-in-Publication Data

Prejudice, politics, and the American dilemma / edited by Paul M.
   Sniderman, Philip E. Tetlock, and Edward G. Carmines.
      p. cm.
   Includes bibliographical references and index.
   ISBN 0-8047-2132-7 (cl.) : ISBN 0-8047-2482-2 (pb.)
    1. United States—Race relations.   2. Race discrimination—
Political aspects—United States.   3. Afro-Americans—Politics
and government.   I. Sniderman, Paul M.   II. Tetlock, Phillip.
III. Carmines, Edward G.
E185.615.P75   1993
305.8′00973—dc20   93-22210
                                                     CIP